TEXT AND CONTEXT IN THE HISTORY, LITERATURE AND RELIGION OF ORISSA

STUDIES IN ORISSAN SOCIETY, CULTURE AND HISTORY

Editors: HERMANN KULKE and BURKHARD SCHNEPEL

Vol. 1: Jagannath Revisited: Studying Society, Religion and the State in Orissa, edited by Hermann Kulke and Burkhard Schnepel

Vol. 2: The Jungle Kings: Ethnohistorical Aspects of Politics and Ritual in Orissa, by Burkhard Schnepel

Vol. 3: Text and Context in the History, Literature and Religion of Orissa, edited by Angelika Malinar, Johannes Beltz and Heiko Frese

Text and Context in the History, Literature and Religion of Orissa

Edited by

ANGELIKA MALINAR
JOHANNES BELTZ
HEIKO FRESE

MANOHAR
2004

First published 2004

ISBN 81-7304-566-6

Published by
Ajay Kumar Jain for
Manohar Publishers & Distributors
4753/23 Ansari Road, Daryaganj
New Delhi 110 002

Printed at
Lordson Publishers Pvt Ltd
Delhi 110 007

Contents

Acknowledgements

On behalf of the Orissa Research Programme we wish to extend our sincere thanks to the Government, research institutions and scholars in India, especially in Orissa, who generously welcomed and supported our academic endeavours. With our work we hope to repay at least a little of what this country has given to us. We would also like to acknowledge the valuable contributions made at the Salzau Conference 2000 by Bishnu Mohapatra, Malay Mishra, Prasanna Kumar Nayak and Martin Brandtner.

Many colleagues and friends helped with the preparation of this volume and to whom we owe many thanks. We would like to express our special gratitude to B.N. Varma of Manohar Publishers, and to N. Dentzien, J. Heinke, N. Aulike, T. Schwabedissen, W. Ulbrich and S. Möller from Kiel for their painstaking technical and administrative work and their cheerful acquiescence to all our requests. Without their support this edition would not have been possible.

Last but not the least we wish to thank the German Research Council (DFG) for their generous financial support.

Introduction

The call for an interdisciplinary approach that spread throughout the humanities in the last quarter of the twentieth century has now become a well-known topic on the academic agenda, one that guides many research projects and has resulted in a search for new perspectives and methods. While this call was welcomed as a chance to broaden frameworks for discussion, it also complicated matters since scholars were not only asked to deal with the notions, tools and controversies of their own disciplines, but also to explain their particular perspective to colleagues in other fields. This necessitated, but also encouraged, self-reflection and sharpened the awareness of the cultural and historical contexts that influence the individual disciplines. It is not just coincidence that in recent decades this self-reflection has invited fundamental methodological discussion in which the exchange of concepts became a major issue. Moreover, there is an increasing interest in the history of the disciplines. This holds especially true in the case of disciplines that are now regarded as having been connected to the project of Western colonialism and whose terminology is now being critically studied as part of this specific political and economic power structure. Yet, the complexity of the situation and the necessity to explain one's own approach to 'others' is a challenge not only on a theoretical, but also on a social level. Interdisciplinary work implies an attempt to 'socialize' knowledge that is quite separate from moving in the circles of one's own people and dealing exclusively with intra-disciplinary issues. It demands from scholars that they take an interest in the individuality of their colleagues in other disciplines, as well as an enduring tolerance of fundamental methodological and conceptual differences, which might remain even after years of dialogue and debate. Thus if ivory towers could be replaced by an ensemble of garden plots with transparent fences and unlocked gates, mutual visits might become easier. The interplay of differences and similarities is an integral part of the chorus of disciplines that are now often subsumed under the heading of the 'cultural sciences' (Kulturwissenschaften). Although this interplay may sometimes be felt to be a burden and even a disadvantage, especially when faced with the 'hard facts' of the natural sciences, it in fact enriches and nourishes the discourse within this field.

The present volume is embedded in the context of the interdisciplinary exchange that is part of the 'Orissa Research Programme' (ORP) on *Various Identities: Socio-Cultural Profiles of Orissa in Historical and Regional Perspectives*. This Programme was approved in 1999 by the German Research Council (DFG) with participating scholars from the Universities of Berlin, Frankfurt, Heidelberg, Kiel and Tübingen. The Programme was explicitly designed as the follow-up to an earlier, similarly interdisciplinary project conducted from 1970-1975 (known as the Orissa Research Project). This first project was pioneering in that it was faced with the tasks of an interdisciplinary agenda as indicated above. It resulted in an in-depth study of the cult of the state deity Jagannātha in Puri.[1] The new project was started with the intention of complementing and enhancing this work not by dealing with the 'central' institutions of Orissa, but by focussing on traditions and regions on its peripheries and margins such as local kingdoms, tribal societies, decentralized religious communities, traditions of Oriya literature, etc.[2] Another aspect of the project was to explore theoretical issues that (1) were related to the aims and scope of research (e.g. notions of 'centrality', 'regional identity' etc.); and (2) arose out of the different methods and notions that guide research in those disciplines that are participating in the project (e.g. the notion of 'text'). Annual conferences that form a part of the project provide a forum for discussing these issues and thus putting the interdisciplinary approach into practice. The first conference, on 'Text and Context: In Orissa (and beyond)', which took place in May 2000, was thematically planned by Axel Michaels and Burkhard Schnepel, who subsequently decided to transfer the task of publishing the papers to the present editors. The present volume

[1] Cf. A. Eschmann, H. Kulke, G.C. Tripathi (eds.) 1978.

[2] A first initiative for the new project that resulted in its concrete planning was a conference in Heidelberg in 1997. Cf. the proceedings in Kulke and Schnepel (eds.) 2002.

is the first of a series of conference volumes, which mirror the work of the Orissa Research Programme.

In taking up the issue of text and context, the members of the ORP and the guest and keynote speakers at the conference opened up a very central and controversial field for discussion. The notions of 'text' and 'context' moved philologists, historians, literary specialists, anthropologists, cultural scientists and the only architect who participated in the conference in quite different ways. In each case this happened against the background of education and often years of research in the discipline; in many cases with an awareness of the difficulties implied by these notions with regard to their connotations and actual content; sometimes also with certain preconceptions about what the 'Other' does when dealing with text and context or both. Discussions among these scholars resulted in clarifications, corrections and self-reflection, which shifted certain boundaries while demarcating others. The papers collected in this volume reflect these different dimensions of the discussion. They also mirror the understanding of, and the actual dealing with, 'texts' and 'contexts' in respect of South Asian and especially Orissan studies. Before turning to the individual contributions, some remarks on the notions of 'text' and 'context' will serve to recall some larger frames of academic discussion.

II

The juxtaposition of 'text' and 'context' in connection with research methods and ideas is itself to be understood as a result of developments in several disciplines since the 1950s. It points to a dialogue between 'text-oriented' disciplines (e.g. philology, literary studies, history, philosophy) and those dealing with 'extra-textual' (e.g. social) contexts (e.g. anthropology, sociology). Milton Singer pleaded for such a dialogue within South Asian Studies as early as 1961. In his own studies,[3] Singer has demonstrated the usefulness of combining the study of 'texts' with regard to their use in actual perfomative 'contexts'. The emphasis on 'context' was also

[3] Cf. Singer 1961 and, for example, Singer 1966.

accompanied by a renewed impetus of self-reflection within the different disciplines. In the case of South Asian Studies, this was also sustained by a critical analysis of the connection between colonial rule and constructions of the culture of the colonized 'Other'. One of the results of this process can be seen in the expansion and redefinition of the notion of 'text'. For the first time in the long history of European traditions of rhetoric, grammar, hermeneutics and the philosophy of language, the notion of 'text' became the dominant category for the elements and structured formation of language. In this way, the notion of 'text' also entered the field of social and cultural sciences.

A brief reminder of this history will serve to delineate the implications of present uses of the term more precisely. As is well known, 'text' and 'context' are both derived from the Latin *textus* and *contextus*; both words transport the basic meaning of 'weaving' and its result, the *textus* with its characteristic *textura*. This connection with craftsmanship is also retained in later, more theoretical reflections on the terms. However, neither word played a major role in the important works of antiquity on language and rhetoric, nor were they used in theoretical reflections. Rather, the term *oratio* (speech) was used when it came to reflecting on the mechanisms that allowed meaning to be created in daily speech as well as in intentionally composed (public) speech. In this connection, the term *contextus* was used when dealing with the correctness of the semantic and syntactic interconnections of the elements of language.[4]

In contrast to *oratio*, until the eighteenth century, the word *textus* was mainly used for the material and materialized side of 'speech'. Rather than being a concept, it was a name for these very materializations: texts were the written and sometimes also illuminated codices; in ecclesiastical contexts, they were the *sacra scriptura* that appeared in folios or book-form and were therefore venerated in the course of the liturgy. This specialized usage of the word 'text' restricted its meaning to what had been written down, codified and transmitted. By the eighteenth century, 'textual

[4] Cf. Knobloch 1990, 71-2; Stierle 1974.

criticism' and 'philology' emerged as an independent and 'rational' science.[5] Philology developed its own methods and theories regarding problems of editing, constituting texts and reconstructing the exact wording on the basis of already extant texts or manuscripts. Another aspect of this development was that traditional ways of interpretation were replaced by the notion that meaning is dependent on 'understanding'. Thus, interpretation became a more individualized affair between an academic interpreter and the text as the actual and only reliable location of meaning. Correspondingly, 'context' was regarded primarily as something 'intra-textual' and referred to the interconnection of the parts of the text. In this sense, 'context' was used as a means of clarifying difficult or corrupt passages. Correspondingly, meaning was regarded as a product of grammatical correctness and as dependent *inter alia* on the rationality, truthfulness and the cognitive content (*der geistige Inhalt*) that were 'textualized' by the author. With Schleiermacher's *Hermeneutik* this notion of interpretation was again modified by drawing attention to the 'dialogical' structure of interpretation. The process of 'understanding' was regarded as a fundamental mode of communication between the author and the reader, the speaker and the listener.[6] The methodological repertoire of 'Hermeneutics' would allow one to transform this dialogue into a scientific interpretation. However, the preconditions of understanding can never be fully disclosed or explained, and therefore understanding implies that one has to deal with the well-known 'hermeneutical circle'. Because this 'circle' is part of the process of understanding, interpretation has to be regarded as an open-ended process.[7] The notion of 'understanding' became an important issue in nineteenth-century philosophical debates, whose basic positions entered the theoretical discussion, and continue to nourish them even today.

With the emergence of historicism in the nineteenth century and the growing awareness of the remoteness of the past of literary

---

[5] Cf. Hentschke; Muhlack 1972.

[6] Cf. Frank 1977.

[7] Cf. Schleiermacher 1977, 76.

remains, texts were seen as expressions of cognitive contents belonging to specific historical circumstances. With the realization of an extant 'cultural diversity',[8] it became obvious that texts were embedded in referential frames of meaning of the respective culture. Now, therefore, texts also had to be related to history and culture. In this connection, 'context' also became the term for such 'extra-textual' frames of reference. True to the historical perspective on texts, these frames should primarily be the 'original' ones, i.e. those contemporary with the text. This context of setting, or what was also called *Sitz im Leben,*[9] had to be reconstructed by collecting data from the text that could be related to data taken from other sources. The sources that could be used in reconstructing the original setting comprised archaeological remains, coins, seals, iconographic data etc., as well as other texts. However, this interplay of 'text' and 'context' also worked the other way round: texts were also treated as historical documents that would provide information on the very context of which they were part - in other words, they would be taken as sources for their own contextualization. Therefore, it was a major task to gain access and even to save cultural knowledge by making its 'texts' accessible, that is, by having manuscripts edited and translated. This 'hermeneutic circle' turned out to be productive and resulted in reconstructions of cultural contexts in which the interdependence between text and context has been demonstrated time and again.

The project of historical contextualization can thus be seen as an endeavour to authenticate remains and memories from the past and to provide them with historical and material reality. This project of reconstructing history came to be questioned when historians fell under the influence of theories circulating in literary studies that dealt with the preconditions of the production of textual meaning and thus with the basic structures of 'narration'.[10] These structures would also apply to historical accounts and historiography, and thus

---

[8] For a case study see Pagden 1995.

[9] This term was coined by the theologian H. Gunkel in the context of the *Literarkritik* that was developed within Biblical theology.

[10] Cf. Veeser, 1989; Conrad and Kessel 1994.

they tended to blur the strict separation between 'fact' and 'fiction'. The insight that traditions are also invented and historical events become history through their very narration, even if they are 'objectively' reported, is by now almost taken for granted. Nonetheless, the material side continues to exist and inscriptions are still inscriptions, even though they might be used in different contexts and for different ends. Therefore historical reconstructions, and with them history as a independent discipline, continue to exist. What has been gained, however, is an increasing awareness of the use not only of historical facts, but also of academic historiography as a possible source for the 'invention of tradition' or even as being at its service.[11] Not only are philology, art history, literary studies etc. now dealing with the 'history of reception', but also historical science is taking into account the history of the reception of history (-writing). In this connection, the concept of collective and cultural memory (comprising *Gedächtnis* and *Erinnerung*) gained acceptance through the works of Connerton and Assmann[12] as the overarching category not only in reconstructing 'factual history', but also in dealing with the ways in which history and collective memory are created in those cultural contexts that do not primarily use western types of historiography. For some time now, studies of 'historical consciousness' in South Asia have been relativizing the thesis of an 'absence of history' even in early India.[13] Recently the concept of 'cultural memory' has opened up new perspectives, especially in dealing with regional and local traditions of historiography and remembrance.[14]

The notions of 'text' and 'context' were again perceived from a different perspective and thus enriched with new dimensions of meaning when the texts and contexts of contemporary societies and cultures became the focus of research within the new discipline of

---

[11] This has been shown, for example, by Chatterjee 1992 for Indian historiography in the colonial context.

[12] Cf. Connerton 1989; Assmann 1999.

[13] Cf., for example, Thapar 2000; Falk 2002.

[14] Cf. the fundamental study of practices of memory in regional and local contexts of western Indian 'little kingdoms' by Basu 2003.

anthropology or ethnology. As a new genre of texts, 'ethnography' came into being, which stimulated discussions on processes of understanding, dialogue and translation that also promoted research in the neighbouring disciplines. In this connection texts were no longer primarily assessed in their written form; rather 'speech' was again regarded as an at least equally relevant media of meaning. Seen from the perspective of their actual situatedness in a specific context of social interaction, texts were just instances of the use of language among a number of things that became objects of study in the field of linguistic pragmatics. It is symptomatic of the affinity between anthropology and linguistics that Malinowski, one of the founding figures of anthropology, is also regarded as an initiator of pragmatics and of discourse and conversation-analysis.[15] Malinowski is arguing for a broader definition of 'context' that includes not only the specific situation of speech, but also the 'context of cultural reality'. He claims that the use of language must be analysed with regard to the context of the socio-cultural situation in which it is used.[16] This shift in focus also implied a distance from 'text-focussed' disciplines that did not take the interactional or performative dimension of texts into account. In turning to the actual social context of speech, the text-related practices of communities, who base their collective identity on oral traditions and not on books, also came into view. This resulted in a renewed interest in 'oral texts' and so-called 'folk-traditions', which were collected and analysed in their own right. This became a task not only for 'folklorist', but one that has increasingly attracted philologists too in the field of South Asian Studies.[17]

However, the focus on context had still another aspect. The scope of objects observed and recorded widened, as it now included 'action', i.e. rituals, dance, healing etc. A larger theoretical frame for analysing these different objects was created within semiotics, in which a variety of objects were treated as 'signs' that transported or evoked a readable 'signified content'. It did not take long for signs

---

[15] Goodwin and Duranti1992, 14ff.; Dilley 1999, 24-6.

[16] Cf. Malinowski 1923.

[17] Cf. for example Coburn 1992; Brückner 1995.

to be treated as texts, and any cultural product or event could be read like a text. That this shift again transformed the scientific agenda could be seen when projects of 'text-analogous' (Ricoeur) readings of cultural contexts or events became, with Geertz, 'interpretive anthropology'. The method and aim of this approach has often been summarized in the catchphrase 'culture as text'. The task of the ethnographer is to 'read' observable social actions that include institutionalized as well as habitual forms of behaviour. Culture was regarded as an 'acted document' that is embodied, spoken and written by many actors. It is, however, read by the ethnographer who then re-produces, recreates and writes the text of the culture that he or she has studied. This approach incited discussions about the authority and position of the ethnographer as the author of this text. The discussion of what has been labelled 'the crisis of ethnographic representation'[18] mirrors the problems that are implied in this convergence of 'text' and 'context' under the guideline of 'textualisation'.

The structuralist approach is also connected with this expansion of the notion of 'context' by putting a renewed emphasis on the way, in which the elements constitute a 'text' through the very logic of their interconnection. A text is a meaningful 'whole' through its texture, that is through its being a product of the interweaving (*con-texere*) of its elements. At the same time, the texture is operative too as the arrangement of the elements follows a certain logical structure that combines them with one another. Although this combination resulted in the emergence of a 'whole' this was not conceived as a substance or an essence. Due to the persistence of the structures of its arrangement, it was nevertheless seen as resisting the tides of history and thus certain forms of 'external' contextualization. This resistance could be observed in the functioning of the logical structure that would succeed again and again in binding the elements together and closing the boundaries necessary for its existence. The endeavour to show that societies as wholes are constituted by, and constitutive of, certain structures or systematic arrangements of their organizational elements (as for

[18] Cf. Berg; Fuchs (eds.) 1993.

example kinship, rituals, concepts) became a commitment of this line of research. As can be often observed in the history of science, it was not that long before attempts were made to resist this focus on 'logic' and the persistence of 'wholes'. This resulted in fields of research, sometime collectively and not always correctly labelled as 'post-modern', that point to the very context-dependence and individuality implied in dealing with cultural values and texts that were regarded as having been neglected in structuralist studies. Also, the focus of interest is directed at the participants of the situation, the interactional and inter-subjective character of a social performance. Here, the dimension of the interdependence between author and recipient again comes into play, in shifting the focus from the side of production to that of reception. It was stressed that the intersubjective frame of reception plays a major role in what is then regarded as and agreed upon as 'meaning'. Research also showed to what extent individual speech invokes and recreates general cultural patterns and conventions. What is actually accepted as a text depends to a large extent on the recipients, i.e. the audience, a sponsor etc., and on what is actually demanded within a frequently already culturally codified situation. In this connection, major contributions have also been made by scholars who deal with the artistic side of text and textual performance. Within South Asian studies, the work of Blackburn can be regarded as paradigmatic here.[19] Indicative of this increased interest in the diverse contexts and media of textual performance is its expansion into the study of the creation and re-creation of 'classical texts' in modern mass media.[20]

This brief survey of certain strands of academic discourse on text and context might provide some background against which the essays collected in this volume may be read. One important frame of reference that encompasses the divergent notions of 'text' and 'context' is the academic discourse itself and the fact that it has become a major player in the production of 'culture(s')'. As was to be expected, not only does the notion of 'context' imply different

---

[19] Cf., for example, Blackburn 1988.

[20] Cf. for example Lutgendorf 1990, Malinar 1995.

things in each discipline, so too does the notion of 'text'. Moreover, the different disciplines also actually deal with different texts. Editing texts, struggling to establish a correct or meaningful wording, are tasks that cannot be fulfilled by dealing with the actual context of speaking, and *vice versa*. Historians, philologists, and anthropologists all deal with contexts, be they intra-, inter-, or extra-textual, whenever they are trying to make sense of the objects of their study. These contexts are sometimes similar (mostly when 'texts' are referred to the contexts of a situation or a text), but more often they differ in their material and phenomenal dimensions (e.g. what is emerges as a text in the course of a ritual). This situation, however, makes both texts and contexts open to contesting interpretations: a diversity of subjects both invites and necessitates different approaches and concepts in research. The definitions and implications of the two terms vary in different disciplines and have to be kept in mind if dialogue and exchange is to be meaningful.

III

Although the contributions to this volume take up the problem of text and context individually some of them can be grouped together either because they share a common disciplinary affiliation, or because they are concerned with similar texts and contexts. The papers also mirror a common interest in texts and traditions at the periphery or even the margins of dominant centres and cults in Orissa. Thus we come across chronicles of 'little kingdoms', 'subaltern' or 'non-centralized' religious groups, goddesses 'in-between' several traditions and textual performance in the urban context of a district town, as well as texts and contexts that help to explore the important issue of modern Oriya identity.

The first and last two essays address larger theoretical issues connected with the notions of text and context and may be read as flanking the other contributions in this regard. Dietrich Harth addresses the fundamental notion or thesis of the 'readability of cultures' in the context of major theoretical debates on the application of hermeneutics in literary studies and anthropology. He also points out the difficulties involved in the task of translation, a problem that most of the essays in this volume are confronted with. The theoretical problems that are implied in the 'analogy between written text and social action', which is postulated in the 'culture-as-text' approach are outlined, something which may serve as a basis for further interdisciplinary discussions. This holds especially true for one of Harth's conclusions: 'theories are, if they resist the temptation of dogmatic closure, ambiguous themselves, a quality they share with their objects.' Axel Michaels deals with similar theoretical problems in his reflections on the possible or desirable consequences of the 'cultural turn' in the social sciences for Indology. Being traditionally a philological discipline that employs methods of textual and literary criticism and explores texts as possible sources for the reconstruction of Indian cultural history, Indology should now open itself up to a wider range of contexts by, for example accepting fieldwork as a legitimate method of dealing with textual production and reception. This does not mean that philology should be abolished, but rather that its scope should be widened by preparing more critical editions and translations of 'oral texts'. Georg Pfeffer's essay moves the theoretical issues closer to Orissa and the tasks of the ORP in dealing with the implications of the concept of the 'tribe' in anthropology. He argues that 'tribal society' cannot be adequately conceptualized by resorting to postmodern terminology. Rather, tribal societies resist established structures on several levels: their concepts are different not only from the neighbouring Hindu caste system, but also from the values that dominate modern western society. The latter include the agendas of the different disciplines: tribal society has not been acknowledged as an entity with a value system of its own either by physical anthropologists, who dominate the discipline in India, or by intellectuals (historians, sociologists etc.), who otherwise display a commitment to 'subaltern' discourse. Pfeffer concludes that the study of tribal societies in Orissa shows the limitations of postmodern notions of 'negotiation' and 'agency', since one is dealing with people who, against all the odds, live and act in the context of 'existing understandings of their cultural order'.

In dealing with texts and contexts that belong to the regional traditions and the different communities of Orissa probings into their history imply specific interplays between texts and contexts. This is demonstrated in the essays of those members of the ORP who are primarily concerned with historical sources. Hermann Kulke deals with the theme of the 'invention of tradition' as an incentive for historiographical writing in India. He shows how historical contexts result in the production of texts that provide Ranpur with a history. As a case study he analyses a recently compiled chronicle of the Ranpur kingdom that points to a power struggle as its extra-textual context of 'historical reality'. Kulke proposes to distinguish between three different levels in which the kingdom and the kings of Ranpur are provided with a past: (1) mythological level, which serves to insert Ranpur into a pan-Indian context; (2) legends that assert the position of Ranpur in the arena of regional powers; and (3) historical accounts that relate events that happened to the immediate local environment. The interweaving of these different levels, which relate to very different cultural and historical contexts constitutes the text of the chronicle. The fruitfulness of interdisciplinary exchange is demonstrated in the paper by Niels Gutschow, which deals with the same text as Kulke, but relates it to a different material context, namely the architectural structure of the town of Ranpur. It is shown how the chronicle reports, comments on and interprets the creation of urban space as a major dimension of kingship. The stages in the process and thus different parts of the chronicle are visually 'translated' into graphics of the maps that Gutschow has created.

The question of the relationship between texts and history is not necessarily addressed by turning to chronicles, records or narratives only - it might also be unfolded by dealing with symbols, monuments or 'titles'. This is demonstrated by Georg Berkemer in his discussion of the use of the title 'Gajapati', which functions as a cipher for the claims of different Orissan rulers for hegemony and thus an imperial status for their kingdoms. Berkemer applies the notion of 'narrative abbreviature' in order to show how one word might evoke and transport a whole traditional and thus highly contextualized discourse that is only understandable if the reader or audience is familiar with it. This familiarity indicates, in this case, that the signs and texts of history are related in this case to the repositories of 'collective memory'. Heiko Frese addresses the problems involved in making historical and literal sense of the accounts transmitted in Nepali and Oriya Chronicles. He outlines the differences between and annals and historical narratives with regard to the Oriya chronicles and relates them to the theoretical debates of the 'New Historicism'. Working with the chronicles shows that their 'amorphous' traits cannot emerge if one keeps to the concept of a unitary history or of a single historical reality, but only when one confronts the interplay of contexts mirrored in such 'marginal' forms as the 'little Oriya chronicles'.

In shifting to the field of religion and literature, the interplay between texts and contexts is not only bound to contexts of history, but also to fields of experience and performance. Johannes Beltz examines the relationship between a religious poem and its use in ritual contexts of healing. The author of the poem is Bhīma Bhoi, one of the founding figures of Mahima Dharma, a religious tradition strongly rooted in Orissa that also helped build up traditions of 'Oriya-ness'. Beltz points to the different interpretations that are given to Bhima Bhoi and his text when they are invoked in political and academic contexts. Angelika Malinar deals with a text that is intrinsically bound to enactment and performance: a *mantra*. Being a genre of its own, a *mantra* depends on recitation or the meditative practices of memorization in order to unfold its meaning. Malinar analyses a specific form of the institutionalisation of this textual practice in a monastery belonging to the Caitanya tradition in Bhubaneswar. In dealing with the context of the genre, its spiritual affiliation and the spatial setting she shows that, as a context, textual performance serves to unfold the powers ascribed to the text. The use of both a text and a story in the context of the worship of the goddess Mangala is explored by Beatrix Hauser. She shows how women create 'performative texts' while conducting rituals for 'their' goddess. Not only are texts used in a performance, but a performance itself might serve as a 'performative text' in another situation. In taking up the issue of female agency, Hauser shows on the one hand how the text in its wording and as a 'whole' is primarily regarded as an object of recitation, while on the other hand certain elements of the story's plot are extracted by the women directly as instructions that are regarded as helpful in coping with the troubles of daily life. Burkhard Schnepel considers other instances of contextualization with regard to one particular narrative. He shows how the story varies in its written, vocal and theatrical forms, as well as which rhetorical and performative strategies are employed in each case. Special attention is given to the performance of the text in a tradition of popular theatre in Orissa, the Danda Nata. He argues that texts have a performative quality and, conversely, that performances also explore the textual qualities of what is staged. Cornelia Mallebrein focuses in her essay on the goddess Patkhanda. She shows how this deity, originally worshipped by the Mutkia Kondh, has remained linked to the collective memory of this tribe in being embedded in the Hindu forms of goddess worship. In her analysis of the oral texts of tribal and Brahmin priests as well as the local *zamindar*, Mallebrein demonstrates the different social and historical contexts that are associated with the goddess. These texts therefore allow the history of the 'Hinduization' of the Goddess to be traces. This history is commemorated in the annual Patkhanda festival.

While these previous essays all take up aspects of specific Orissan traditions, another group of essays deals with texts and contexts that are explicitly connected with the quest for an Oriya identity and thus testify to a consciousness about the region as a 'whole'. Indicative of the problems implied in this quest is the title of Kishor K. Basa's article, 'Imagining Orissa'. Basa deals with those elements that contributed to, and were even reinvented for, the creation of an Oriya identity, apart from the dominant reference to the Jagannatha cult. Archaeological sites, dance traditions, inscriptions etc. have all been used and transmitted by government institutions such as the department of tourism, politicians and academic publications in order to fabricate a referential framework for 'Oriya-ness'. Gaganendra Nath Dash shows how important medieval texts have been reinterpreted in the context of the modern quest for an Oriya tradition. In his analysis of the medieval debates on the appropriateness of the ritual usage of the highly erotic text of the Gitagovinda within the Jagannatha temple, Dash shows that modern reinterpretations may result in a reduction of the complexity of the medieval context. In both historical settings competing interests were at work, which incited the production of texts aimed at legitimizing the different positions. Dash argues that the medieval texts that were produced to support a certain position were used by modern historians as 'traditional' and thus authentic sources to claim that Jayadeva, the author of the Gitagovinda, was an Oriya and not a Bengali. Subhakanta Behera shows how an Oriya identity based on the Jagannatha cult has been articulated in Oriya texts from the fifteenth to seventeenth centuries, and how they were re-invented in the twentieth century by discussing the interpretation of Jagannatha as an incarnation of the Buddha. This interpretation was propagated by a group of five Oriya poets called the Pancasakha. This was against a competing theological tradition within the Caitanya tradition, which regarded Jagannatha as an incarnation of Krishna. What had been a theological controversy has, by the twentieth century, been recast as a regional tension between 'Bengali' and 'Oriya' forms of Vaishnavism. Behera points out a comparable trend in reinterpreting the legend of the origin of Jagannatha transmitted in the Deulatola with regard to its reworking in a twentieth-century play. The importance of the relationship to Bengal and Bengalis in the creation of Oriya literature and identity is also a major argument in the essay by Barbara Lotz. She not only analyses the literary structure and narrative devices of the autobiographies of three important political leaders of Orissa, but also elaborates on the historical contexts that are evoked in the texts. Most important here are the establishment of the western educational system and new forms of mass communication, for example journals. Seen against the background of the well-established connection between texts and authors in western discourses, Lotz's essays intrigues us by showing how the three authors cope with, and even struggle against, the position and notion of the 'author'.

Rather then proposing general conclusions about texts and contexts in Orissa, the essays clearly demonstrate the wide spectrum of questions that can be addressed to a rich corpus of texts, traditions, performances and concepts. It is to be hoped that this collection of essays will be received as a fruitful contribution to the study of the Orissa and will serve to introduced the scope of Orissan studies to the larger public.

The Editors

References

Assmann, J. 1999. *Das Kulturelle Gedächtnis: Formen und Wandlungen Kulturellen Gedächtnisses*, München: Beck.

Basu, H. 2003. *Von Barden und Königen. Ethnologische Studien zum Gedächtnis und zur Göttin in Kacch*. New York, Bern: Lang.

Berg, E.; Fuchs, M. (eds.). 1993. *Kultur, Soziale Praxis, Text. Die Krise der Ethnographischen Interpretation*, Frankfurt: Suhrkamp.

Blackburn, S. H. 1988. *Singing of Birth and Death: Texts in Performance*, Philadelphia: University of Pennsylvania Press.

Brückner, H. 1995. *Fürstliche Feste. Texte und Rituale der Tulu-Volksreligion an der Westküste Südindiens*, Wiesbaden: Harrassowitz.

Chatterjee, P. 1992. 'History and the Nationalization of Hinduism', in *Social Research* 59, 111-49.

Coburn, T. 1992. *Encountering the Goddess: A Translation of the Devi-Mahatmya and a Study of its Interpretation*, Delhi: Sri Satguru Publications.

Connerton, P. 1989. *How Society Remembers*, Cambridge: Cambridge University Press.

Conrad, C. and M. Kessel (eds.). 1994. *Geschichte Sschreiben in der Postmoderne. Beiträge zu einer Aktuellen Diskussion*, Stuttgart: Reclam.

Dilley, R. 1999. 'Introduction: The Problem of Context', in Dilley, R. (ed.). *The Problem of Context*. New York, Oxford: Berghahn, 1-49.

Eschmann, A. ; H. Kulke and G.C. Tripathi (eds.). 1978. *The Cult of Jagannath and the Regional Tradition of Orissa*. New Delhi: Manohar.

Falk, H. 2002. *Frühe Zeitrechnung in Indien, in Falk, H. (Hrsg.). In: Vom Herrscher zur Dynastie. Zum Wesen Kontinuierlicher Zeitrechnung in Antike und Gegenwart*. Bremen: Hempken, 77-105.

Frank. M. 1977. 'Einleitung', in Schleiermacher, 7-67.

Geertz, C. 1973. 'Thick Description: Toward an Interpretive Theory of Culture' in *The Interpretation of Cultures. Selected Essays by C. Geertz*. New York: Basic Books, 3-30.

Goodwin, C. and A. Duranti. 1992. 'Rethinking Context: An Introduction', in Duranti, A. and C. Goodwin (eds.), *Rethinking Context. Language as an Interactive Phenomenon*, Cambridge: Cambridge University Press, 1-42.

Hentschke, A.; U. Muhlack. 1972. *Einführung in die Geschichte der klassischen Philologie*, Darmstadt: Wissenschaftliche Buchgesellschaft.

Knobloch, C. 1990. 'Zum Status und zur Geschichte des Textbegriffs. Eine Skizze', in *Zeitschrift für Literaturwissenschaft und Linguistik* 77, 66-87.

Kulke, H. and B. Schepel (eds.). 2002. *Jagannatha Revisited: Studying Society, Religion and the State in Orissa*, Delhi, Heidelberg: Manohar.

Lutgendorf, P. 1990. 'Ramayan: The Video', in *The Drama Review* 34, 2, 127-76.

Malinar, A. 1995. 'The Bhagavadgītā in the Mahābhārata TV Serial: Domestic Drama and Dharmic Solutions', in V. Dalmia; H. v. Stietencron (eds.), *Representing Hinduism. The Construction of Religious Traditions and National Identity*, New Delhi: Sage, 442-67.

Malinowski, B. 1923. *The Problem of Meaning in Primitive Languages, in The Meaning of Meaning*; Ogden, C. K.; Richards, I.A. (eds.). New York: Kegan Paul, 451-510.

Pagden, A. 1995. 'The Effacement of Difference: Colonialism and the Origins of Nationalism in Diderot and Herder' in G. Prakash (ed.), *After Colonialism. Imperial Histories and Postcolonial Displacements*, Princeton: Princeton University Press, 129-52.

Schleiermacher, F. D. E. (1977). *Hermeneutik und Kritik. Mit einem Anhang Sprachphilosophischer Texte Schleiermachers. Herausgegeben und eingeleitet von M. Frank*, Frankfurt: Suhrkamp.

Singer , M. 1966. 'The Rādhā-Krishna Bhajanas of Madras City', in M. Singer (ed.), *Krishna: Myths, Rites, and Attitudes*, Chicago, London: University of Chicago Press, 90-138.

Singer, M. 1961. 'Text and Context in the Study of Contemporary Hinduism' in *Adyar Library Bulletin* 25, 274-303

Stierle, K. 1974. 'Zur Begriffsgeschichte von Kontext', in *Archiv für Begriffsgeschichte* 18, 144-49.

Thapar, R. 2000. *History and Beyond*, New Delhi, Oxford: Oxford University Press.

Veeser, H.A. (ed.) 1989. *The New Historicism.* New York: Routledge.

1

Are Cultures Readable? Reconsidering Some Questions of Method

Dietrich Harth

In der Phänomenologie handelt es sich immer um die Möglichkeit, d.h. den Sinn, nicht um Wahrheit und Falschheit.

LUDWIG WITTGENSTEIN

To *read* the world as if it were a book written by a numinous Author is a venerable convention reaching far back to the days of cosmo-theological myths of creation. To *read* culture as if it were a text composed and written by society and its particular collective agents and to look analytically at the world of man-made symbolic orders is a rather new attitude.[1] There seems to be a need for permanently debating the key concepts involved in the business of analysing and reading cultures as texts, while the obvious attraction of this metaphor appears to be connected to those inter- and transcultural exchanges which in the long run seem to produce a very mobile and at the same time global texture of different cultural styles and patterns. The following pages, a modest contribution to the ongoing debate, do not pretend to offer some new rules or procedures of culture analysis. They just try to reflect from different angles some of the essential features of the above mentioned key concepts. Reflections, however, do not supply solutions and are not authorized to omit neither contradictions nor doubts.

---

[1] As to the world-as-book tradition cf. Blumenberg 1996. There are of course numerous publications pondering the methodological questions brought up by the culture-as-text model. I only mention the writings of Clifford Geertz, Crapanzano's critical commentaries and a collection of essays in German, edited by Neumann and Weigel (2000), which is an attempt to promote the interdisciplinary dialogue between literary research and interpretive anthropology.

So, reconsidering some questions of method is not like designing a systematic blueprint for the use of comprehensive theory-building. My aim is to show that notions like *text* and *context* belong to a set of interpretive categories, and that to favour *readability* as a criterion of cultural hermeneutics is more promising than to cling to the linguistic or structuralist notion of a formal textuality. And my argument is that cultural processes and their ascribed meaningfulness (*Sinn und Bedeutung*) should not be subsumed under the objectivity defined by nomological-functionalist theories, nor are they an unconditional prey of those who believe in the absurd. The sense and meaning of cultural processes, writing and reading included, do not cease to be objects for negotiations, what we very well know and agree with when experiencing actions and artefacts as appearances gleaming with a puzzling significance.

Legibility, Readability, Divination

My paper is an instance of the question raised in its title. This coincidence is neither accidental nor does it on first sight seem to be of great importance. The trivial fact is: I read a text, which had to be written down in order to give it under particular circumstances a voice with the expectation of being not only perceived but also understood. There is, by the way, a peculiar semantic link in English between 'understanding' and 'reading' which allows us to ask a person who is expected to have difficulties in understanding a verbal utterance or a non-verbal gesture 'Do you read me?' So when I read a text to an audience the activity on the audience's behalf is not only listening but it encompasses reading as well, the reading of a reading in the sense of interpreting an individual speech. In other words, language use gives us our first clue that cultures may be readable, because this assumption insinuates that the structure of cultural practice is analogous to the structure of language use.

But reading is more than mimicing a legible structure or misinterpreting an intentional utterance. It is, as Jean-Paul Sartre reminds us, not the poor reproduction of a 'given' meaning but an *act of guided creation*[2]: the reader producing, during the process of tracking the composed texture of writing, his or her interpretation in the feeble shape of what could be called a 'virtual' text, while he or she is reflecting this experience in order to work it out in the manner of a well-articulated interpretation.

It is of some importance to mark at this point the difference between the concepts of *legibility* and *readability*. To make my paper legible meant to acquire and to practice at least a bit of the linguistic competence that an English native speaker has bred in the bone. Legibility, therefore, stands for the technical mastery of using, in speaking and writing, a specific language system provided a proper training in grammar, rhetoric, (logical) discourse and (literary) style. In a rather wide sense the concept includes those features of sign-practice that are the very objects of semiotics. Trivially all cultural phenomena are sign-produced and have to be considered, so to say, as *legible* structures by birth. That means all 'legible structures' have to be seen as textualized or – *sit venia verbo* – textualizable phenomena, whence we conclude that *legibility* is nothing else but a necessary formal component to the concept of text.

Yet, the notion of 'text' does not mean here the formal linkage of language signs or transphrastic elements. As a hermeneutic category the term rather defines the coherency of situationally embedded speech acts. The thus indicated communicative situation consists of two correlative patterns: the pattern of communication, and the pattern of action, determined by place and time, and in addition, by the intentions of the participants. The phenomenological description of an event like this cannot comprehend these components all at once. It has to differentiate analytically, in order to be able to ascribe to the event as a whole – for example a family celebration, a ritual initiation or the mise en scène of political power – sense and meaning.

If a culture is seen as a 'complex whole' (W. Griswold) the same holds true for a written text which through analytical reading will unfold step by step its specific parts: rhythmic, semiotic,

[2] Sartre 1948, 15.

compositional and semantic patterns or segments. There is a great deal of difficulty in using a similar method in analytically reading the 'complex whole' of a culture apart from the fact that culture, seen for instance as a performance, defies the formality of distinct demarcation lines. But this does not affect its legibility as long as we are aware that textualizing any cultural event or process is nothing else but a mode of perceiving the universe of cultures as a mobile connectionist network of dissonant signs. This sort of symbolism has a very old tradition and must not be misunderstood as the property of an academically inclined mind.

The notion of *divination* discloses the essential meaning of approaching the cultural universe with the attitude of someone reading a book. Legibility, as we have seen, is a necessary condition of this approach because it includes the key to the architecture and formal connectivity of that universe of rules and symbols which is behind each individual utterance. *Readability*, however, refers to that what theorists of interpretation call the 'sense' (*Sinn*) of that 'complex whole' considered here as a cultural universe. Sense is not the same as the meaning of a particular sign, be it lexical or occasional; it is, so to say, the general or possible 'meaning' ascribed to an utterance, a particular speech act, a communicative event the form of which can be described as a genre-specific configuration of textual patterns. To 'read' (interpret) the sense not only of a complex whole but also of an individual utterance, therefore, is a question not of a simple discovery procedure like decoding a secret writing but affords the above mentioned Sartrean creativity because of the incommensurability of all symbolically mediated actions. *Sinn*, phenomenologically explored, means – to quote Wittgenstein[3] – potentiality, not necessity. Certainty here is futile. Guessings, conjectures, hypotheses are the only means by which we can actively approximate that sense of an utterance (verbal or non-verbal) to which we want to respond.[4]

---

[3] Wittgenstein 1967, 63.

[4] For a systematic discussion of the hermeneutical implications cf. Frank 1980, 13-34, and Kurz 1977.

Sometimes the interpretation of non-written signs, practised for instance in shamanistic rituals, is not in accord with our ordinary experience of reading and our will to freely constitute the sense of an action or text. In that case all is different, because the sign-'reading' of the shaman is carried out with the aim to understand and thereby to *subdue* the involved persons and recalcitrant material objects to a magically effective power. The comparison shows that reading in the sense of interpreting does not necessarily exert any power over its object, may it be a written text or a significant action. The modes and methods of reading/understanding therefore entail a reflexive distance between the reader (*interpres*) and the object (*interpretandum*), be it a book or an action, a distance that also tells something about the difference between *understanding* (*Verstehen*) and *coming to an understanding* (*Verständigung*). To come to an understanding presupposes always at least an initial communication, which goes beyond one-sided information about the emotions, beliefs and desires of the other. The psychoanalyst or anthropologist who wants to understand the other person, therefore, first has to arrange a situation of dialogue by communicating with the 'client' or 'native' about the most prolific moments for both, the I and the 'Other'. But it is in his most detached moments, in the calm and isolated situation of retrospectively contemplating his experiences, that the analyst tries to describe the confrontation, to deeply understand the sense and the meaning (*Sinn und Bedeutung*) of the collected data and stories, to argue with his colleagues common opinions and finally to compose his own written interpretations; a process which very well demonstrates the labyrinthine ways of approximating by method and divination the *sense* (*Sinn*) of a legible 'complex whole'.

What I call 'method and divination' in this context cannot be defined in a formal way nor is it a unique or substantive procedure. It rather is an attitude of deliberate, but reliable explicitness encompassing criticisability insofar as it is essential to the justification of the interpretative findings.

Translation

I will leave this statement at this point, for the sake of further elaboration, without any comment, and return again to the dialectical interplay between the title and the content of my own writing. Obviously there is a muddle of languages behind my own writing and style of expression, my mode of thinking being moulded by German, my writing and its syntactic organization for heteronomous reasons being obliged to follow the rules and norms of a foreign language which I do not use in every day life and very seldom in academic communications.[5] If – to freely paraphrase a famous sentence by Ludwig Wittgenstein – the boundaries of my language are the boundaries of my culture, I, while composing and writing an English essay, awkwardly sit on the threshold between two languages and definitely between two different systems of meaning. Whether this then means to sit between two different symbolic orders or in the middle of cultural difference I do not yet know. Anyway, 'sitting on the threshold' may sound a bit too shamanistic, but perhaps just this place outside commonplace attitudes may help to find a way into that cognitive state of affairs Todorov once called the *'exotopie, qui produit la connaissance nouvelle'*.[6]

There is a very common basic term used to describe the communicative negotiations (*Sprachspiele*) between two different languages and world views; I refer to the notion of *translation*. Translation means crossing borders. Yet, I do not want to confine this meaning to crossing the borders or boundaries between two or even more different languages. There is also translation, in the strict sense of the metaphor 'trans-latio', between different modes of thought, and between the social varieties of speech within one and the same linguistic community, and even between different states of power in the old-fashioned sense of '*translatio imperii*'. And, of course, in the case of a scholar reading aloud his own, linguistically

[5] I, therefore, had to rely on the friendly help and critical comments of William Sax, to whom I want to say a most cordial thanks.

[6] Todorov 1982, 14.

masked thoughts in front of an attentive but more or less anonymous and culturally mixed audience, I presume, a lot of translating has to be enacted. Not to mention the fact, that – as we know from Malinoswki's shift from the 'context of words' to the 'context of situation' and finally to the 'context of culture' – translating is dependent upon more than one move of contextualization.[7]

So my not at all hazardous point is that translation in a broad sense can be regarded as a constitutive part of all communicative events, be it reading, listening, talking or bringing out the meaning of an action, a performance, an event, etc., by interpretation – especially when there is a need to give this interpretation the shape of a printed page or of a symbolic action.[8] The concept of 'cultural translation', some decades ago introduced by British social anthropologists into academic discourse, may have paved the path for what in contemporary discourse is called 'textualisation of cultures'.[9] When we look closely at the metaphorical meaning of the term itself, we can see that it refers to the dialectic process or mutual interaction which evolves in all speech acts: the Latin *translatio* has the meaning to carry something from one side to the other. And that is what for instance I myself have to do when I try to express my German-moulded thoughts and feelings through the medium of a foreign language. But that is, of course, also the very task of the ethnographer's work in the field, who carries all his cultural preconceptions into a world of habits and beliefs that are not his own, only to find out, when returning home, that his private habits have been, so to speak, translated by the experience outside and that he should be – as Nigel Barley put it – 'simply uncritically grateful to be a Westerner, living in a culture that seems suddenly very precious and vulnerable.'[10] When working out this paper I

[7] Malinowski 1935, 17ff.

[8] It is obvious that the comparison of different translations of one and the same original text can show a great diversity of perceptions and discriminate interpretations. Cf. for instance the multifarious translations and stage-realizations of Shakespeare's dramatic writings in India, Sisir Kumar Das 2001.

[9] Asad 1986.

[10] Barley 1983, 190.

twice had a very similar dream: travelling in a place beyond my ordinary worldly experience – sure, there were some shapes of strange buildings and some more or less ghostly streets – I was very anxious to find a fixed point of orientation, some sort of an indicator that would tell me what kind of order the dream-world could offer to the intruder. And as far as I remembered when I woke up, one of the signs was a bunch of green apples which I considered to be a rather ambiguous indication: either a set of suggestions for getting closer to knowledge, or a reflection of myself in the attitude of a greenhorn – in any case, it certainly was the epiphany of a cultural and at the same time textual archetype if one recalls the story of the apple tree told in the Bible. And so the dream, understood as a context, unconsciously accompanying the pleasures of daytime thinking, gave proof to that '*Eigensinn*' which is part of our second nature and cannot even be uprooted by the most sophisticated methods of self-criticism or self-denial in the course of strengthening one's own empathy for the otherness of the other.

If we go a bit further we might conclude that translation is a way of mediating between identity and alterity. Translation is indeed a mode of transition and the only response to the need for intercultural communication.[11] If I want to spell out what is called cultural identity I would perhaps use all my wit to proselytize for an abundant heritage of German traditions. Changing from German to English, however, forces on me the attitude of a traveller, who, while he is marching in-between two languages, at each turn is afraid of being taken by surprise.

My suggestions about translation as a constitutive part of communicative interaction so far have been very general and it is time to remember that in English (I am told by my dictionary) there exists a common linguistic reference which under particular circumstances can be considered synonymous with 'translation', i.e. 'interpretation', the trade-mark of Interpretive Anthropology. The interpreter in both senses, as a translator of spoken and written language as well as an interpreter and analyst of social life and cultural symbols, without doubt is in the position of a go-between,

[11] Cf. Meschonnic 1999, 73.

he himself being the incarnation of trans-latio. The condition of the translator as well as of the interpreter is the condition of the 'marginal man', who stays on the verge of two different linguistic systems or cultural patterns. For this and other reasons, which I will discuss later, it seems reasonable to conceptualize interpreting and translating as two aspects of one and the same operation, the operation we are used to call culture analysis, the analyst being constantly in the state of the 'marginal man'. If this is true we already at this point can see a strong contiguity between the activities of interpreting, translating and reading, comprising what Clifford Geertz calls 'anthropological understanding'.[12]

The questions of reading and translation, of interpretation and understanding traditionally belong to the core of the discipline of philology where theories of interpretation and literary hermeneutics have found their most complete elaboration. But long ago the philological questions overthrew the narrow framework of the more traditionally carved out problems of genre evolution and historical grammar. Marginality, however, has survived and may be considered the prerequisite of that distancing attitude called reflection which intrinsically marks the operation called interpretation in philology as well as in ethnography, history or the social sciences.

Texts and translations are assumed rather as means and media of cultural production and transnational communication. The theory of translation, therefore, is not confined to linguistic operations but pays attention to political implications as well and has extended its scope to the general topics of cultural transfer including a keen awareness of the untranslatability of that which makes cultures reciprocally different.[13] The staging of a written drama, the ritual dancing of an orally transmitted myth, the painting of a scene out of a holy scripture all translate, i.e. quote and interpret, particular aspects of the 'given' text, while obliterating by this very operation other specific aspects of the same phenomenon. And in each case the elements of the translated are changed, or better enhanced by

[12] Geertz 1977.

[13] Spivak 1992.; Dingwaney 1995.

hitherto undiscovered meanings, because to translate does not mean to carry an unchangeable content from one code to another code but has to be understood as the opening of a debate about different views of one and the same topic.

This awkward proximity between translation and interpretation is observed with suspicion especially in the discourse of postcolonial criticism. To translate means here anyway more than a simple transfer from one language into another language. It seems as though Wittgenstein's identification of the boundaries of a language with the boundaries of a world belongs to the unquestioned assumptions of this approach. Because the suspicion aims at that type of appropriation through translation which, without hesitation, assimilates everything that cannot be understood to one's own linguistic and cultural habit and style. But, I think there is no sound reason to exaggerate this suspicion, as some do, seeing in translation a sort of cultural 'violence'.[14]

There is, of course, no simple rule to avoid adulteration. Translations call for criticism, because they obviously and necessarily work with various kinds of rhetorical dislocation and condensation and consequently produce 'another' text which never should be mistaken as the mere reproduction of the 'original' in the guise of another language. My point is, if the alien cultural practice *seen as a text* (a texture of actions and utterances) becomes the 'object' of cultural analysis, translation is a necessary strategy. And the conclusion I would finally like to draw from the above considerations culminates in the assertion that – to speak with Peirce and Eco – the phenomenon called 'text' (something mute and absent) has to be seen not as a petrified structure but as a 'dynamic object' the changing appearances of which unfold in a never ending series of translations, criticisms and interpretations.[15]

---

[14] Cf. Dingwaney/Maier 1995, and Bachmann-Medick 1996.

[15] Eco 1990, 335: 'L'Oggetto Testuale è sotto gli occhi del suo interprete, il testo stesso diventa l'Oggetto Dinamico [...]. Quando interpretiamo un testo parliamo di qualcosa che preesiste alla nostra interpretazione e i destinatari del nostro atto interpretativo dovrebbero concordare, in qualche misura, sul rapporto tra la nostra interpretazione e l'oggetto che l'ha determinata.'

It is true: this openness of the act of interpretation is often suspected of arbitrariness. The answer, however, could be that the process of reading protects the interpretation against an uncontrolled any-ness, if the reader takes the text at the same time as an object constructed by reading and as a yardstick (parameter) of his reading experience seriously. An adjustment, which is at the basis also of Sartre's idea of reading as an act of 'guided creation'. To sum up: reading in the sense of a creative process cannot be separated from the acts of translation and interpretation which the reader accomplishes while recognizing and at the same time transforming the textual patterns and their unexpected content. Reading is never a pure or linear apprehension of something given, nor is it the simple repetition of an intentional meaning. It rather is an imaginative and constructive process of building a virtual text with a new meaning by amalgamating two worlds: the world of the book and the world of the reader.[16]

Text and Context

All this affects the textualization of cultures and the different levels of anthropological or cross-cultural understanding, not to mention the outcome we are used to accepting as statements of proofed knowledge. But it is worthwhile to keep in mind that this should not be considered a weakness of ethnological and cultural understanding. To see it like that usually goes together with a well-known 'fallacy of misplaced concreteness'[17] which suggests that – given the right tools for scientific observation – the semantics of social and cultural practices can be foreseen and decoded like the path of a mechanical tracker.

What was said above about the text also applies to the context, which is no less a text in the sense of an understandable phenomenon constituted by reading; in other words: an object *and* a

---

[16] To quote from Alberto Manguel's *A History of Reading* (1996), reading is the 'apotheosis' of writing. For a more prosaic discussion of the creative construction of meaning in the practice of reading cf. Wittrock 1981.

[17] Alfred Schütz 1973, 4.

condition of interpretation. Perhaps it is useful to discriminate, in a very broad sense, between the two types of *internal* and *external* context. The concept of the *internal context* might then refer to the relations between the (structural or semantic) elements constituting a dialogue, a narrative, a speech, a poem, an essay, etc., while the concept of the *external context* might aim at a diffuse potential of other texts that could be of use in widening the scope of understanding the focal text within a floating space of intertextual conditions, traditional symbols, linguistic systems, morphological frames, genre conventions and/or subjective preconceptions. And, of course, one could again distinguish two more subcategories: the external contexts the analyst makes use of, and the process of contextualization as a socially situated practice within the cultural segments the anthropologist has chosen as his objects of research.[18]

The prefix 'con-' marks the relational character of all contexts, and is a reminder not to forget the relationism which principally belongs to the text as such, e.g. its relations to a particular language, to an authorial agency and to the reader's and interpreter's imagination. In addition, the prefix 'con-' suggests that a qualitative difference has to be taken notice of here. The decision to regard as con-text what in a different situation would be seen as the focal text, often is a question of deliberation: what the interpreter calls 'context' usually will be selected out of a limitless variety of other 'texts' in order to explain the first specified 'text', or in other words, to give the focal text a meaning with the help of indications dug up on the site of the con-texts. Neither text nor context are 'given' phenomena, they are selected and validated by the interpreter. Their relation, which often appears to be self-evident is dependent not only upon the personal encyclopaedia of the reader but also upon the scope of his research interests and conceptual frames.[19] And, we should not forget, the first context of research is research itself: 'the interpretation changes the text, the changed text

---

[18] Hobart 1986.

[19] 'Encyclopaedia' comprising the reader's world knowledge and professional competence: Eco 1990, 145-50 and 1992, 68.

calls forth a new interpretation, and so on and so forth.'[20] In terms of hermeneutics, therefore, the notion of context signifies nothing else but the interpreter's practice to 'create connections' and to develop a heightened sense for the inclusive and at the same time exclusive effects of his contextualizations.

> But it is also clear that ... context is not 'given'. What is not given cannot be called upon or applied; it must first be created. Furthermore, there is nothing inherent in context that makes it a corrective for misunderstanding. A text 'reduced to writing' may give us the illusion of an inside and an outside, of a part and a whole, or of lower and higher levels of understanding. In reality, in acts that produce ethnographic knowledge, creations of context are of the same kind.[21]

One cannot escape context; not even the postmodern interpreter, because one of the contexts guiding his playful conjectures presents itself as a (deconstructionist) theory of decontextualized reading.[22]

When using the terms 'text' and 'context' not as interpretive categories but as instruments useful to depict the interwoven structure of a verbal utterance, the analyst may construct something like a textual space. This multi-dimensional space is seen as consisting of words, sentences, paragraphs, intervals, chapters, books, genres, literatures, etc. And each of these units appears enclosed by the next higher and more complex one so that the complete textual space seems to be constructed like a hierarchy of infinite text-levels, not to mention the connections of these with the diachronic dimension of text-building and context-determination. This is, of course, a rather artificial construction which nevertheless may serve to make visible the essential context-dependence of all language-use, oral or written.

---

20 Gruenwald 1995, 79.

21 Fabian, in Dilley 1999, 97-8.

22 There is no way out, as Taussig (1993, 237-8) hopes, but the critical reflection of one's own preconceptions.

Another meaning of 'context', however, emerges when the interwoven complex of speech and action is seen in connection with the extra-linguistic, i.e. with the so-called 'situational data'. Yet, when speaking of 'data' I certainly want to avoid the idea of objectively given bare facts. The 'data' the historian collects and uses in his retrospective constructions of a past situation are to a maximum degree written documents, the significance of his archaeological and pictorial findings more or less depending on these written contexts. And even the ethnographer who under particular circumstances acts as a 'participant observer' in the cultural practices of a foreign world collects his 'data' by singling them out of the spatio-temporal flow of events under the premise of a preconceived research opinion and corresponding theoretical bias. In short, as George Herbert Mead put it, 'data' are abstractions. To perceive an action as a so-and-so action affords on the observer's side a notion of what type of action could be discriminated from other types. So the constituents of what an action, an agent and agency are, have to be more refined than the action, the agent and the agency themselves. What's more, situational context-data belong to that sort of evidence which is attainable only through the selective and at the same time constructive approach of the observer to what he – seen from his subsequent endeavour of putting his interpretations into a readable form – has witnessed in the past present of the particular event under investigation.

In short, contexts must never be seen as determinants of interpretation. Of course, internal contexts guide the interpretative moves of the reader and give his assumptions about the latent sense of the chosen text the necessary support. To 'create' that sense, and in the end to objectify it, can only succeed when the interpreter/reader precedingly has used exactly the same text as a source of information. This information forms the contextual knowledge he needs to articulate that (un)intended and hidden sense of the text he is eager to (re)construct. Therefore, to see one and the same semantic system either as text or as context is a question of the interpreter's practice and is not dependant upon a queer set of features forming a chimerical thing in itself. I conclude: the concepts of text as well as of context – be it internal or external –

are *interpretive categories* and hence can only be elucidated in connection with those terms which belong to the theory of reading and understanding.[23]

Text-building in Culture Analysis

The reflected interplay between text and context does not belong to the common sense experience of everyday life. But it has to do with the attitude of the interpreter constituting a world of *readable* signs and sign-linkages. And it is true, the criterion of readability is not an academic invention, it belongs to a heritage of divination that reaches back as far as the habit of tracking down the game's footprints.

When we seriously ask if there is a method or if there are methods in *reading* cultures, we have to admit that this does make sense only when we accept that there are analogies, if not affinities, between the fabric of writing and the fabric of socio-cultural phenomena beyond writing, and this is a question of text-building under the premise of theoretical and methodological decisions. Before I discuss the criterion of readability, which is at the heart of our problem, I would like to quote and subsequently comment upon a passage from Clifford Geertz's essay *Blurred Genres: The Refiguration of Social Thought*:

> When we speak our utterances fly by as events like any other behaviour; unless what we say is inscribed in writing (or some other established recording process), it is as evanescent as what we do. If it is so inscribed, it of course passes, like Dorian Gray's youth, anyway; but at least its meaning – the said, not the saying – to a degree and for a while remains. This too is not different for action in general: its meaning can persist in a way its actuality cannot. The great virtue of the extension of the notion of text beyond things written on paper or carved into stone is that it trains attention on precisely this

[23] As to a relevant theory furthering the interpretive methods in the social sciences cf. Habermas I, 152-203.

> phenomenon: on how the inscription of action is brought about, what its vehicles are and how they work, and on what the fixation of meaning from the flow of events – history from what happened, thought from thinking, culture from behaviour – implies for sociological interpretation. To see social institutions, social customs, social changes as in some sense 'readable' is to alter our whole sense of what such interpretation is and shift it toward modes of thought rather more familiar to the translator, the exegete, or the iconographer than to the test giver, the factor analyst, or the pollster.[24]

The argument we find in this quotation can be considered one of the cornerstones of so-called Interpretive Anthropology: Interpreting social life 'is like trying to read (in the sense of *construct a reading of*) a manuscript', and culture can be seen as a process of 'text-building'.[25] The notion of text offering the interpreter the opportunity of reading social life as a complex, but decipherable – to use Geertz's wellknown metaphor – 'web of significance'; to study cultures as a system of meaning is positioned against the earlier behaviourist, functionalist or formal structuralistic approaches. Interpretive or, as it is sometimes called, symbolic anthropology, therefore focuses

- on the production of meanings,
- on negotiations of meaning,
- on competing discourses,
- on hegemonic and counter-hegemonic developments, and
- on ritualized ways of embodying the semantics of social commitments.

This attention of the cultural analyst and interpreter on construing, negotiating and changing meaning in order to permanently reorganize the universe of discourse of specific groups or societies

---

[24] Geertz 1993, 31.

[25] Geertz 1973, 10, and 1993, 32.

gave a push to academic self-critique that I would like to subsume under the title of meta-ethnography. The 'meta' meaning, that all the features that are to be studied as constituents of the cultural world chosen as the particular object of research must, turning from the observed to the observer, be questioned on the side of the interpreter so that the meaning of *his* terms and concepts, the competitive attitude of *his* writing and the structural, narrative or stylistic organization of *his* discourse are equally important as the objectifying of the semantics of the target culture. The very notion of *hermeneutics* (theory of reading and understanding), often used to characterize the major methodical interest of Interpretive Anthropology, is quite in accord with this tendency to illuminate and eventually to control the presumptions, the academic pre-conditions and pre-understandings, which shape the methods, and at the same time guide the choice of perspectives in research. These presumptions are, by the way, not seldom the first and unrecognized contexts of research.

Nota bene: Hermeneutics must not be misunderstood as a set of tools fit to decipher a 'given' meaning. It rather indicates an *epistemology of understanding* – and at the same time of reading as well as of translation –, which does not focus on a *given* object of research and knowledge but reflects *how* knowledge and research find and define their objects. This stance implies what quite often in theoretical or methodological discourse is called a fallacy: the circularity of interpretative operations. When – to give two fitting examples – culture is studied in analogy to a literary text, this is done with the aim of representing the results again in the form of a corresponding text, the subject of which, however, has switched from the actor to the author (i.e. the literal meaning of ethno-*graphy*); and to study cultural practices with the plan for a book in mind is nothing else but another confirmation of the perspectivism innate in all cognitive moves. Second example: When the ethnographer speaks of 'reading a culture', he presumes that his written conjectures about this very culture will eventually find resonance in a reading public. Here we touch the question, on what grounds the authority of the ethnographic author should be legitimized? Marcus and Cushman in their useful and informative paper *Ethnographies as Texts* have discussed this topic.[26] Their proposal is to validate the authority of the ethnographer by thoroughly scrutinizing the following constructive tasks:

- establishing a narrative presence,
- envisioning a textual organization,
- pre-encoding the presentation of data, and
- anticipating the expectations of an imagined reader.

The fourth point, which is my own addition, in my eyes is of prominent importance because it makes use of the classic rhetorical device that the author has to reflect the potential expectations of the ideal reader, whom he wants to address.[27] There is, trivially, a big difference depending on whether one wants to convince – and striving to convince someone is a virtue of those who have dug up some relevant knowledge – a Western expert, a lay, or an indigenous reader. The other constructive tasks of text-building are not at all independent from that, as could be easily proven by showing to which measure the authority of a scholarly written text depends upon a set of communicative standards safeguarded by the academic institution.

But let us go back to the question as to what it may mean to 'read' a culture. Certainly, the idea of reading a 'culture' in its entirety is nonsense, especially since the term gives expression to a precarious and contingent process of creative practices and changing lifestyle attitudes. So 'culture' here must be reduced to some specific observable traits and traces, which the reader/interpreter considers representative of the social life of a group or community. I maintain that all cultural activities and phenomena are *readable* even if there is – as in ritual[28] – no certainty about an involved intentionality.

---

[26] Marcus and Cushman 1982, 39.

[27] About the 'ideal reader' as a constituent element of the narrative text cf. Eco 1979.

[28] 'Clearly rituals are not really objects, but an object-like existence is given to them by the fact that they are ontologically constituted beyond individual intentions.' Humphrey/Laidlaw 1994, 267.

Circularity in Interpretation

The circularity of the interpretative operation (*hermeneutischer Zirkel*) calls to mind that all methodically guided interpretations construe the totality, or better, the dissonant unity of their objects on the basis of those preconceptions extracted from the results of a most thorough analysis devoted to the details of exactly the same objects.[29] This makes evident that the phenomena we call 'objects' of research, even if they do share the characteristics of those things which are materially well definable, are to a maximum degree phenomena in the literal sense of the Greek '*phainesthai*', a verb which is at the root of the terms 'phenomenon', 'phenomenology' and 'fantasy'. In some cases there might be a keen interest of the interpreter in the imaginative and in the imprints of imagined lifeworlds (secular myths, utopian communities, etc.) on the social or cultural reality he has chosen as his research field (imagination being the Latin-rooted synonym of the Greek word '*phantasia*'), but there is always the need to make use of one's own imagination in order to produce a certain conjectural, i.e. interpretative hypothesis at all. Yet, the use of imagination during the course of creatively 'reading' a specific cultural practice as text must not inhibit that self-analytical reflection which gives the interpreter the right to consider his own approaches in anthropological understanding a rational choice. Imagination plays, as Max Weber has pointed out, a decisive part in the process of understanding the semantics of any human action, since – as I would like to repeat – understanding (reading) the other is a process of 'guided creation'. And in a very pointed form one could prolong this observation beyond the act of understanding to all actions taking part in building and transforming symbolic orders in general, including the ethnographer's 'work of

---

[29] Cf. Eco's description of the circle in Eco 1992, 64: 'Thus, more than a parameter to use in order to validate the interpretation, the text is an object that the interpretation builds up in the course of the circular effort of validating itself on the basis of what it makes up as its result.'

imagination', if we are ready to concede the truth of Pierre Bourdieu's sentence that 'all social functions are social fictions'.[30] It certainly is not enough to accept the circularity of the interpretative operation. To avoid uncontrolled misinterpretations which only lead to misunderstandings and erroneous conjectures one has to be aware of the dangers that lurk behind the unscrupulous application of determining classificatory schemes to the social and cultural units one has chosen to 'read' and study without asking why and for what reason. The 'Inclusivism' – to quote an example[31] – seen by some interpreters as a basic and peculiar feature of the Indian mentality in fact is a historical response to that inclusivism of the colonial powers that could be seen from the point of view of the colonized as a violent form of exclusivism (from power, sovereignty, etc.).

The example shows that an overall acceptance, which could very well rely on Indian sources, can easily entangle the interpreter in an elusive circle. It furthermore shows that the definitions and classifications the researcher believes to be neutral analytical instruments form part of the same culture which he wants to explore with the help of these same instruments. So he is in danger of falling prey to a self-deception similar to that of the scholar of religion who mistakes the ideology of religious fanaticism as an expression of a genuine and deep-rooted belief. Another example we could discuss here at length is the rather odd, but politically popular idea of applying a holistic, but at the same time exclusive, notion of national culture to those transitional and culturally fragmented societies, which under postcolonial and/or postcommunistic conditions are in a state of transition and turmoil.

The term circularity reminds us of the hermeneutic circle, and circularity, seen from a general and perhaps rather abstract point of view, may indeed characterize the specific logic of methodical interpretation, because this logic proclaims that it is imperative to get as far as possible inside the world one endeavours to understand. This includes all the burdens one has to endure by learning the

[30] Bourdieu 1985, 76. Cf. also Greenblatt 1988, 17.

[31] Cf. Vivekananda, 1989, 251f.; Gottlob 2000, 99.

foreign idioms of the text-worlds (even if they are written in our mother tongue) and, of course, of those unfamiliar languages which are the media of writing and interacting in alien cultures. If this learning process is not misapprehended as a means to only amend research strategies, it inevitably will change the categories and habitual patterns of thought the interpreter considers his property. That does not at all mean assimilation into otherness. It is sufficient to look at one's own property with the eyes of the other, a change of viewpoint or of perspective (Blickwinkel) the result of which could be the concession that the hitherto familiar-seeming terms of culture and its dominating concepts of interpretation are not central but peripheral and, therefore, open for negotiation. If this happens – I am speaking about the attitudes of the anthropologist – it will be possible to overcome the force of his or her academic upbringings and it will consequently be possible for him or for her to use the process of cultural translation in order to check and transform the outworn tracks of conceptualizing.[32] To get away with the 'asymmetric ignorance' between researcher and the researched, it could then be useful to follow Dipesh Chakrabarty's proposal and imagine a world-history 'that does not yet exist', e.g. a history of Europe as one of the minor, i.e. provincial cultures.[33]

One of the classical doctrines of interpretation reads: not to subdue the interpretandum to preconceptualized notions and terms but to be falsified by the stubbornness of the alien text-world. So, circularity in interpretation eventually turns out to be a special case of the circulation of meaning and at the same time gives proof of the idea that meaning in text can never be nailed down but is always open for permanent negotiation. While the version of scholar A is criticized by scholar B, the dialogical principle that according to Michail Bakhtin should regulate all historical and anthropological understanding emerges as a principle that promotes discussions between representatives of different versions of understanding.[34] This, in the eyes of many scholars, guarantees the openness of

---

[32] Asad 1986.

[33] Chakrabarty 1992, 20; Gottlob 2000, 107f.

[34] Friedrich 1993.

interpretation and is at the same time a strong case against the illusion of a 'fixed meaning' (Geertz). And what is more, it calls into question the claim that the interpreter should be able to reconstruct in a full sense what he imagines to be the 'social logic' of a 'given' text.[35]

The rupture between the written document and the world of cultural and social experience to which it belongs cannot be denied. A written text can never be considered the sheer exponent of a social or cultural system because it has its own *immanent logic*. And to read a cultural practice as text seems to plunge into a rather deep pit of illogic if the reader expects a logic the immanence of which belongs to his perception and not to the perceived. A reading, which uses the concept of text as a means to look at the interconnected phenomena of actions and utterances as if they were in the unswerving state of a functionally organized and rigidly structured system, squanders the possibility of understanding it as a ferment for sociocultural change. But *readability* as well as *textuality* are teaching something else. They refer not only to a processual structure of perception but also include all features of a dynamic system of changing meanings.

Circularity, for instance, is a component of textuality, because it is the enticement of the text as a world of potential meaning that draws the reader into that business of interpretation which, as the prefix 'inter' signals, happens as the circular communication between reader and text proceeds. The specific text or document does not 'fix' meaning, it is nothing else but a source of potential meaning, which the reader who acts in the role of an interpreter uses according to his or her own intentions. And if his or her intention it is to reconstruct the 'social logic' of that period to which the particular text refers, it is not a question of looking for some ominous structure 'behind' the text, because the concept of 'social logic' *in re* is a need for contextualizations that far exceed the limits of only one single text. The information one gathers by collecting and reading the other texts, which in the light of the text in focus are

[35] As claimed by Spiegel 19

to be considered con-texts, can help construct a *hypothetical* meaning. Contexts are discovered by the interpreter, they are not part of the field encountered.

Textualizing Cultures, and a Note on the History of Interpretation

Hypothetical meanings are not to be mistaken as the unshakeable expression of an objective state of affairs. They are constituted with the help of the interpreter's imagination and creative wit to collect and to combine a set of con-texts that fits into his or her project of anthropologically understanding the utterances and actions forming an essential part of the culture system. It is, of course, most important to be conscious of the difference between the interpretation of a text and the interpretation of a culture system. The text to be analysed may form part of the culture in question, yet this should warn the interpreter against taking it as a representation of the whole; despite the unfortunate habit of reading particular, especially the canonized texts metonymically as *pars pro toto*.

To 'read' a culture is not the same as reading a drama, a novel or a history book. It is a highly imaginative task, to a certain degree comparable to the scholastic programme of contemplating the Book of Nature in order to get in contact with the wisdom of the Unspeakable. There is an important truth in the attitude of paying respect to the Unspeakable even if it bears the name of an author, whose individual features could easily be identified. The 'text' of culture and the Book of Nature are neither reducible to the ideas and intentions of one well-known author, nor do they consist of a universe of alphabetical signs the comprehension of which does not afford any kind of exegesis including divination. And yet, the metaphors of 'Book' and 'text' suggest that both components – authorial intentions and some sort of sign-material – have to be taken for granted, because otherwise the rhetoric of 'reading' would make no sense.

Before discussing some more aspects of reading, translation and textuality let me continue with a short recollection of the nineteenth century history of hermeneutics and language philosophy, to which we owe – notwithstanding all changes of paradigmata or perspectives which have happened since then – some of the most important insights into the fundamental principles of a methodically trained reading and understanding. The key concept of *text* emerges under the guise of figurative speech in Wilhelm von Humboldt's philosophy of language as well as in Wilhelm Dilthey's writings on the philosophy of science. Both use the term *texture* ('*Gewebe*'), which is in close relationship to Clifford Geertz' *web*, in order to circumscribe the complexity of cultural phenomena. Humboldt's metaphor *symbolic texture* ('*symbolisches Gewebe*') describes not only the system of language but also world history ('*Sprache und Weltgeschichte*').[36] And both discern the logical impossibility of analysing this web from outside: interpreter and historian are both entangled in the same web they want to disentangle. The differences of natural languages do not alter this situation since to investigate the world system embodied in another language or in the histories that have become strange again in any case presupposes understanding. But understanding is translation, i.e. the above mentioned crossing of boundaries between different languages, different modes of thinking, different ways of life and different cultural habits. So the difference between us and them has not to be seen as a divide never to be bridged. The common ground of mutual understanding Humboldt is searching in what he calls the 'work of mind' ('*Arbeit des Geistes*'), this being a paraphrase of all linguistic facts and of language in general.

Dilthey on the other hand is concentrating on an anthropological universal, i.e. the common psychological disposition of empathy which provides every human being the possibility of understanding each other. Neither Dilthey nor Humboldt has misinterpreted the methodically trained hermeneutic understanding as a means to level the differences between individuals, groups, societies and cultures. On the contrary, Humboldt's dialectic mode of thought induced him to mark 'difference' as a version of not-understanding which turns up in all communicative interactions. In his treatise *Ueber die*

---

[36] Humboldt 1963, 396 and 403. About Dilthey cf. Harth 1998, 58ff.

Verschiedenheit des menschlichen Sprachbaues und ihren Einfluß auf die geistige Entwicklung des Menschengeschlechts (1830-1835) we read: 'Alles Verstehen ist ... immer zugleich ein Nicht-Verstehen, alle Uebereinstimmung in Gedanken und Gefühlen zugleich ein Auseinandergehen.' (... *all understanding is always at the same time a not-understanding, all concurrence in thought and feeling at the same time divergence.*)[37] With this argument Humboldt enforces what can be considered the first principle of the hermeneutic condition: the acceptance of an alterity, which can approximately be bridged but never be blotted out by interpretation. To ponder, theorize and philosophize about understanding (*Verstehen*) expresses the simple truth that understanding is neither given nor a matter of fact. On the contrary, the reason to strive for understanding is difference, i.e. the impossibility of complete accord.

The frequent use of the metaphor '*Gewebe*' (*texture* or *web*) from Humboldt to Geertz indicates, so to speak, a systemic composure of the heterogeneous facts of socio-cultural life. Ominous ideological trends in the theory of culture and society often enough have claimed this composure to be of biological, ethnic or racial origin. The notion or image of 'web' is, as the quotation from Geertz has shown, an equivalent of text, if we keep the Latin original in mind. It is time now to find out why the interpreter of cultures prefers the text analogy to other possible and current comparisons or models like drama or game. I will try to prepare an answer by scrutinizing a small selection of text-theories and have for that reason consulted Jurij Lotman's structuralist position, Harald Weinrich's linguistic proposals, Umberto Eco's theory of semiosis and Paul Ricœur's important and influential philosophical reflections concerning the notion of text and the definition of textuality; the latter being a notion which comprises all traits that make a text a text. For the sake of brevity I will combine the major arguments without again mentioning the authors' names.

[37] Humboldt 1963, 439. Engl. transl. in Humboldt 1988, 63.

Text Models and Applications

The so-called *cultural turn* in ethnology and social sciences is a parting from positivistic and scientific thinking. Under positivistic signs the power of the interpreter, including the field worker as well as the historian, over its objects – the critics of this paradigm assure us – was left unquestioned. Even the structuralists, who had nevertheless developed a consciousness of the decisive power of concepts and methods over the analyst's mind, retained within their taxonomic fetishism something of an inheritance from objectivist model-building. On the other hand, questioning the nature and scope of structures promoted contacts between the theory of culture and language theory, and gave the semantic perspective an important breakthrough. The contexts of theory-building have changed: hard theories of the nomological type no longer prevail; soft theories of language research and literary hermeneutics have conquered the field and have given weight to those questions concerned with the use and effect of symbols in social and cultural practice.

The spreading of the metaphors of reading and (con)textualizing throughout cultural studies at first seems to lead in another direction. The decision of the anthropologist of culture, the sociologist or historian for the text model first of all limits the possibilities and the freedom of the interpreter. However, the interpreter is relatively free to adopt this course. One's choice to regard the world philosophically, historically, religiously or poetically, can be justified neither by induction nor by deduction. It is a choice between divergent paradigms, or – differently said – a selection from a multitude of possible viewpoints, which may elucidate different aspects of the world. So the question is, why look at a world of cultures as if these were spelled out like written texts? If there is nothing other than what the poststructuralists tell us, a world made up of a multitude and diversity of texts, then there is not much hope for a free choice between divergent paradigms.

Yet, many reasons could be found to defend the universalism of the text model. First of all, there is the simple fact that writing and reading are the elementary prerequisites for a reflected and knowledge-oriented view of world and man. Second, there is the widely accepted conviction – pace Plato – that no medium is better suited to manufacture quantitative and qualitative orders of being than writing. Third, the text metaphor connected with the idea of organization points out that texts do not partition themselves mutually, but are all potentially linked, which reflects the widespread use of the context term. 'Everything is interrelated': this saying of the Indian storyteller, who prolongs the life of the tradition by orally distributing the traditionally handed down written mythologies,[38] matches the poststructuralist view that there is nothing beyond that semiotic connectivity which is at the heart of all textual operations and is therefore the basic principle of textuality itself. Fourth, and finally, a powerful and culturally widespread tradition suggests that all humans capable of reading and writing look at nature and the universe as a book written by a supreme being, not to speak of the evocative role of the book as a matrix of 'reading' the human condition.[39]

Let us regard first the theoretical and methodical implications connected with the text model. To understand a religious celebration, a political ritual, or the play of the folk theatre as texts inevitably excludes the points of view of those persons who are involved as activists and/or participants. This is because the term 'text', like every other theoretically-founded descriptive term, does not belong to the 'facts' (*Tat-Sachen*) but rather to the perspective of the researcher, who regards and describes these circumstances. We could, therefore, say that at a very general methodical level, 'text' operates as a *heuristic* model. When applied, the model subordinates the specific cultural practice (celebration, ritual, play, etc.) to a formal structure which suspends the experienced performance of this practice by specific generalizations and abstractions. The structure of any written text conveying sense and meaning (*Sinn und Bedeutung*) has to be in accordance not only with orthography and grammatical rules (syntax and semantics) but

---

[38] Narayan 1994, 4.

[39] For example the special role of the self-book metaphor; cf. Jager 2000.

also with certain conventions of formality (genre, composition), communication and publishing practices (para-texts).

Against this background, the term 'text-structure' appears as a summary of the collectively shared formal and semantic regularities and conventions belonging to the writing culture of a community. The 'social logic' of the texts, which the historical or ethnographical interpreter wishes to reconstruct, could therefore perhaps be considered a function of the structure of those texts produced within the boundaries of a particular group and its cultural habits, and not as an outward phenomenon.

But the restriction reads: As each written text is to be understood as a part of a whole writing culture which might be described historically and regionally, equally each cultural action (e.g. celebration, play or ritual) which the interpreter with the help of the text model would like to 'read', i.e. to understand, is one part of the religious, political, aesthetic, etc., culture maintained by the community, the communal culture as a whole being itself a complex whole of different cultural activities; hence arises the problem of selection and evaluation. In literary criticism, selection and evaluation have already occurred: the interpreter usually adheres to a given canon or sets up an anti-canon, before he himself opens the literary account in order to read and analyse. To set up, however, a canon of the cultural practices of a community does not make much sense. Each group, each social player has his own way of life and his own life-style. What is common to all is nothing other than the *imaginaire social*, a vague and permanently contested image of shared values, ideals, identities and symbols. If we want to understand this world of signs and beliefs with the help of the text model we once more have to ask in which sense the notion of text has to be transformed (translated) in order to fulfil the task of a useful optical instrument.

First, the trivial: the indispensable elements of all written texts are the characters and the rules governing the organization of the characters into words, sentences, paragraphs, chapters or similar formal patterns. The code – be it a lexical code, a code of grammar, of style or of genre – usually does not turn up in the text itself, and yet it seems a precondition for its legibility, namely, for intentionally structuring and reading the text. By some theorists the code, which is nothing else but a synonym for our term 'legibility', is seen as a normative set of general rules not only guiding the organization of writing and composing but also as an instruction for properly reading the text; reading in this case used to designate an act of decoding (there are many ways of reading). In this respect the concept of code is neatly connected to the construction of meaning, be this the work of the author or that of the reader. But it lacks the creative aspects of that constitution of *Sinn* (sense) described above as an act of divination and interpretation. The meanings, however, of words, sentences, paragraphs, etc., *within* the text are not only dependent upon the specific codes coming from *outside*. All the existing elements of a particular text have their own specific meanings which are the result of a so-called context-determination. Therefore, on the level of text-semantics, we have to distinguish at least between two interconnected types of meaning:

1. CODE-MEANING – dependent on consciously or unconsciously realized rules of speech and writing which with respect to the legibility of the item affords lexical and grammatical competences.
2. TEXT-MEANING as a result of the determination of code-meaning by the surrounding context. To understand this meaning is not only a question of decoding, since it also affords what is called the hermeneutic competence to experience communication, because all texts – written or oral – can be considered communicative acts the intention of which gives the spoken or written text its effective individual shape. Hermeneutic competence is nothing other than the rational capability to produce and to read the procedural and ever changing textures of linguistically mediated interactions.

Before we decide to convey these interconnected types of meaning to the realm of sociocultural understanding we have to consider the particularities of the written text. The first duty of historical and, to a certain degree, of ethnohistorical research is to study the written records and not the process of an action the interpreter attended himself as an eyewitness.

The concept of text in fact is a handicraft metaphor, it evokes the image of a weaver (textor) sitting at the loom producing a tissue or carpet by moving the shuttle to and fro. The metaphorical use of the concept is old and widespread. It keeps the allusion to creative doing, which does not alone satisfy a basic need because the patterns, which the weaver inserts into the fabric, do not support the material value or the user's pragmatic expectations of his commodity. So there is a surplus we should not forget when transferring the concept onto other than handicraft products. The transfer, to make a first point, makes sure that the object alluded to as a text has to be considered as something made, created, produced, or to put it another way, a materially perceivable thing that refers to a maker (*author*), to a set of rules for production (*poetics*) and to a person or group who is in want of the product (*consumer*). A written or spoken text may approximately fit this model, since there is an author, a set of codes and a recipient or addressee (individual or collective).

To repeat this in a more elaborate way: The indispensable features of a text are: (1) a stock of discriminate symbols (*sign system*), (2) a person uttering and composing the text (*author*), (3) a set of rules for text-building (*code*) and (4) a recipient sharing at least a part of the rules used for text-building (*reader*). The possible rules are not confined to a singular code-register. On the contrary, text-building normally makes use – even in one and the same genre – of a heterogeneous variety of different codes, since there are:

- genre (strategies of composition),
- rhetoric (strategies of persuasion),
- logic (strategies of argument),
- style (strategies of aesthetic amplification).

To apply this structure to a cultural system does not at all seem appropriate, especially since it is pretty obvious that text-weaving and its particular products are small particles in the whole mosaic of culture. If one considers culture a process of symbolic action carried out by a group or society or any other collective unit it seems to lack intentionality. So it is without a well defined subject acclaimed to have the authority and authorial meaning of a written utterance, and it lacks, so to speak, the patterns which can be identified in the written text by applying the above mentioned methods for reading a code-guided action.

Of course, applying the text model as a methodical analogy to the 'reading' of a culture system does not afford complete congruency, and yet, the choice of the model should be backed by a rich consonance in order to provide reliable conditions for a promising outcome. To read cultures as semiotic systems of signs and symbols first was proposed by the School of Tartu (Lotman 1990). Practically all cultural and social phenomena – ritual, language, art, gestures and so forth – are semiotic, i.e. in our sense *readable* phenomena. But there was a limit as to what could be regarded as a text, since the cultural semiotics of the Tartu school kept to substantial features that would decide if a cultural unit is worth interpreting, the criterion of semantic content being the only criterion that would help to distinguish between a cultural text and a non-text. Textuality in this view is not restricted to formality, but depends upon the interpreter's competence to judge and, finally, leaves him the choice whether to put aside what he takes to be nothing else but a routine, or to make it the target of his analysis. To make textuality a question of semiotic competence is a concession to the arbitrariness of textualism and text theory. And, indeed, there are many different and contradictory theories, models and paradigms, but none of them can be induced on the basis of a sound empirical proof; even in linguistics the variety of concepts matches nothing else but a wide range of different theoretical designs open for permanent change.[40]

Therefore, the following conclusion seems imperative: The language of the written text is mute until it comes into being through the act of reading. Each text as such is dead, mummified, virtual, or to quote once more W. v. Humboldt: Language 'hat nirgends, auch in der Schrift nicht, eine bleibende Stätte, ihr

[40] Cf. Gülich/Raible 1977.

gleichsam todter Theil muß immer im Denken aufs neue erzeugt werden' (438). When reading as an institutionalized craft has to be a *methodical operation*, the aim of which is to understand the meaning and to produce the sense of a particular text, it is right and proper to call it interpretation. But we must not forget that the result of this operation – the identity of a particular text – has always to be produced anew and is prey to constant discussion and re-evaluation, the identity being dependant upon the ever floating gap (difference) between the focalized and the ignored. Exactly this precarious dynamic and contingency nurture the text's virtual life, and so one could very well argue that the criterion of textuality is beyond a strict methodological stipulation.

From a point of view of precision we could argue that the characteristic feature of textuality is directly dependent upon the procedures of a trained formal analysis because the figurative criterion of weaving has its root in the rational criterion of connectivity. 'Connectivity' suggests that interwoven constellation of parts and whole, or, in other words, unity in variety (*Einheit in der Mannigfaltigkeit*) which automatically seems to accompany all our thinking about a complex universe of signs. At this point, according to my opinion, the analogy between written text and social action must be even more carefully examined:

1. Social actions manifest themselves in several media, texts in the only medium of linguistic signs and/or written characters.
2. The observation of social actions belongs to the very situation in which the action to be observed unfolds, while texts are read independently of the situation of their production.
3. Each written text has its own legibility which must not be misunderstood as a referential token of the surrounding world. Paul Ricœur's '*occultation du monde circonstanciel*'[41] paraphrases very well the fact that a written text can be seen and experienced as an autonomous world (*une quasi-monde*).[42]

---

[41] Ricœur 1970, 185.

[42] Ibid.

4. A written text is, to a certain degree, its own interpreter since the textures of actions, images, arguments, speeches, etc. – the peculiar and individual properties of one and the same text – are the outcome of an internal energy the source of which can be traced by reading it, in a decontextualized context, as an expression of the *intentio operis.*
5. From this follows: To methodically interpret a text means to detect and at the same time constitute the internal meaning of the particular text universe and, therefore, has to be distinguished from using the text as an argument, as an index of the author's personal experiences or as a document of historical and/or social events.

The distinction, suggested above, between interpretation and use of a text makes it possible to draw a methodological line between contextual and intertextual readings on the one hand and versions of interpretation on the other hand. Interpretation has as its task investigating the meaning of the particular text-world, and is for that reason obliged to methodically open a path into the text-internal system of self-interpretation. Only when this is done it may be reasonable to use the reading thus achieved in order to employ the particular text as a link to those questions which are at the heart of contextualist and/or intertextualist interests.

The fact, however, that a written text usually is read independently of its first emergence does not exclude the quest for intentionality. Eco insists on three forms of intentionality, which might become effective in each text interpretation:

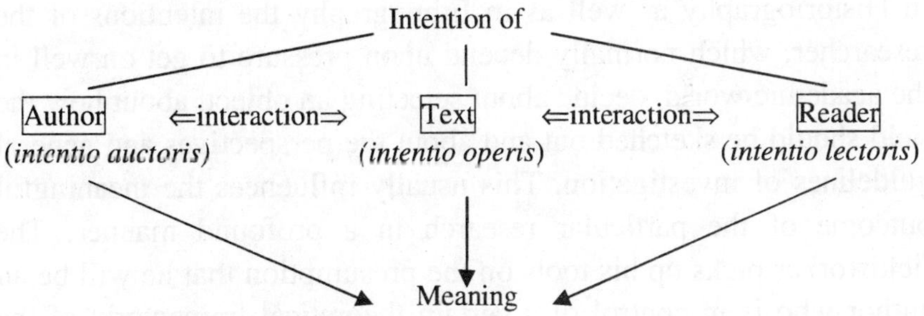

The arrows indicate that between the author, the text and the ideal reader, imagined by the author himself, there is an interrelation which in a radical sense differs from the communicative interrelations apparent in situations of social interaction.

But if one wants to transfer the model of intentionalist interpretation to the analysis and interpretation of social actions then some crucial modifications must be made: in place of the author's intention (*intentio auctoris*) are to be set the intentions of the actors (*intentiones actorum*), in place of the *intentio operis* the unconscious and unforeseen *intentiones actionis* and, finally, in place of the *intentio lectoris* the intentions of the observer and analyst. This transfer or translation of the model of text-interpretation into the field of cultural analysis might open the eyes for different types of intention effective in social action. And it could remind us that there is a gap between even the most thoroughly thought out intention and the concrete action, the actions often enough causing effects that were not intended, the reason being the heteronomy of the conditions of acting.

Once again we encounter an obvious incompatibility between the interpretations of texts and that of cultures with the help of the text model. The *intentio auctoris* in writing necessarily includes the hope to find and even to instruct a reading subject, while in social action the intention of the actors to count with the attention of a possible observer and interpreter has to be considered a disturbing fact for both sides.

Academic Constraints and Theory-building

In Historiography as well as in Ethnography the intentions of the researcher, which normally depend upon pressure to get on well in the academic world, decide about selecting an object, about how the field should be sketched out and about the perspectives and general guidelines of investigation. This usually influences the meaningful outcome of the particular research in a profound manner. The fieldworker picks up his tools on the presumption that he will be an author who is in control of a certain theoretical framework, of the collected data, of the faculty to convincingly represent what he 'read' in the field and, last but not least, control of himself as a member of a different (academic) culture. Reading social actions as textual configurations implies – as I have tried to point out above – theoretical interest not only in the general assumptions of socio-anthropological epistemology, but implies interest also in those questions that refer to the rhetoric, i.e. the representational text-building of anthropological knowledge. Accordingly the authority of the author has to be seen as a problematic source of evidence. And both attitudes are effective as intentional factors already in the earliest phase of organizing and preparing the course of fieldwork and/or of historical investigation. There is, of course, nothing wrong with that because the correlation between means and ends is a rational choice we are used to carrying out not only in scientific research but also in every day life.

One of the very old methodological questions in anthropology refers to the application of the terminologies, textualities included, developed in academic departments of Western cultures to cultures of non-Western origin. One often hears the claim that to use Western concepts in order to describe and interpret non-Western phenomena encourages a clash of cultures rather than facilitating mutual understanding. If this really were the case, all academic disciplines striving for better understanding – we call them humanities – would just be public nuisances. I believe that behind this argument lurks a politically, if not morally tainted fallacy. Controversies about the adequacy and justification of concepts and theoretical presumptions are nowhere as passionate as in the academic disciplines concerned with interpreting and comprehending linguistic and sociocultural phenomena. In these disciplines theory-building is a very versatile affair. And this is one of the reasons why those theories, in comparison with scientific hardware, are called soft theories and theories of limited range – limited in time and in scope, permanently open for objection and subsequent changes.

The fact is that theory-building in the humanities – including cultural studies and social anthropology – is an immanent aspect of communication and text-building within the confines of the specific discipline, that is, within the confines of a very particular cultural segment, i.e. academia. They, therefore, must not be misunderstood as doctrinal and fixed in their meaning. On the contrary: these theories are, if they resist the temptation of dogmatic closure, ambiguous themselves, a quality they share with their objects which may facilitate the restructuring of the systematic preconditions during the course of research.[43] And what is more, those key concepts with metaphorical or figurative traits may inspire the creative imagination of the researcher to go further in the invention of new research conceptions and strategies than a tightly defined operational imperative would allow.

These rather abstract remarks should not obscure the dependence of cultural research and corresponding theory-building on cultural change in general or on the changes in ordinary language-use. Cultures perceived as readable become portable cultures and this mirrors the fact that cultures in our times – and today there is no culture which is not in touch with modernity – are losing their centres and show more and more the features of migrant and interlacing performative patterns.

---

[43] cf. Mommsen 1979.

References

Asad, T. 1986. 'The Concept of Cultural Translation in British Social Anthropology', in Clifford and Marcus, 141-64.

Bachmann-Medick, D. (ed.) 1996. *Übersetzung als Repräsentation fremder Kulturen*, Berlin.

Bal, M. 1999. *The Practice of Cultural Analysis. Exposing Interdisciplinary Interpretation*, Stanford: Stanford University Press.

Barfield, T. (ed.) 1998. *The Dictionary of Anthropology*, Oxford: Blackwell.

Barley, N. 1983. *The Innocent Anthropologist: Notes from a Mud Hut*, London: Penguin.

Berg, E. and M. Fuchs (eds.). 1993. *Kultur, Soziale Praxis, Text. Die Krise der Ethnographischen Repräsentation*, Frankfurt a. M.: Suhrkamp.

Blumenberg, H. 1996. *Die Lesbarkeit der Welt*, Frankfurt a. M.: Suhrkamp.

Chakrabarty, D. 1992. 'Post-Coloniality and the Artifice of History: Who Speaks for the Indian Pasts?', in *Representations* 37, 1-26.

Clifford, J. and G.E. Marcus (eds.). 1986. *Writing Culture. The Poetics and Politics of Ethnography*, Berkeley: University of California Press.

Colebrook, C. 1997. *New Literary Histories: New Historicism and Contemporary Criticism*, Manchester and New York: Manchester University Press.

Crapanzano, V. 1992. *Hermes' Dilemma and Hamlet's Desire. On the Epistemology of Interpretation*, Cambridge: Harvard University Press.

Das, S.K. 2001. *Indian Ode to the West Wind: Studies in Literary Encounters*, Delhi: Pencraft International.

Dilley, R. (ed.). 1999. *The Problem of Context*, New York and Oxford: Berghahn.

Dingwaney, A. 1995. 'Translating "Third World" Cultures', in A. Dingwaney and C. Maier (eds.), *Between Languages and Cultures: Translation and Cross-Cultural Texts*, Pittsburgh, London: University of Pittsburgh Press, 3-15.

Eco, U. 1979. *Lector in fibula*, Mailand: Bompiani.

Eco, U. 1990. *I limiti dell'interpretazione*, Mailand: Bompiani.

Eco, U. 1992. *Interpretation and Overinterpretation*, ed. S. Collini, Cambridge: Cambridge University Press.

Fabian, J. 1999. 'Ethnographic Misunderstanding and the Perils of Context', in Dilley, 84-104.

Frank, M. 1980. *Das Sagbare und das Unsagbare. Studien zur neuesten französischen Hermeneutik und Texttheorie*, Frankfurt a. M.: Suhrkamp.

Frank, M. 1988. *Die Grenzen der Verständigung. Ein Geistergespräch zwischen Lyotard und Habermas*, Frankfurt a. M.: Suhrkamp.

Friedrich, J. 1993. *Der Gehalt der Sprachform. Paradigmen von Bachtin bis Vygotskij*, Berlin.

Geertz, C. 1973. *The Interpretation of Cultures*, New York: Basic Books.

Geertz, C. 1977. *'From the Native's Point of View*: On the Nature of Anthropological Understanding', in J.L. Dolgin et al. (eds.), *Symbolic Anthropology. A Reader in the Study of Symbols and Meanings*, New York: Columbia University Press, 480-92.

Geertz, C. 1988. *Works and Lives: The Anthropologist as Author*, Stanford: Stanford University.

Geertz, C. 1993. *Local Knowledge: Further Essays in Interpretive Anthropology*, London: Fontana.

Gottlob, M. 2000. 'Inklusionen und Exklusionen in der Begegnung zwischen Indien und Europa', in R. Kloepfer and B. Dücker (eds.), *Kritik und Geschichte der Intoleranz*, Heidelberg: Synchron, 93-110.

Greenblatt, S. 1988. *Marvelous Possessions*, Oxford: Clarendon Press.

Grigely, J. 1995. *Textualterity: Art, Theory, and Textual Criticism*, Ann Arbor: The University of Michigan Press.

Griswold, W. 1994. *Cultures and Societies in a Changing World*, Thousands Oaks, CA.

Gruenwald, I. 1995. 'The *Scripture-Effect*: An Essay on the Sociology of the Interpretative-Reading of *Texts*' in J. Assmann and B. Gladigow (eds.), *Text und Kommentar (Archäologie der literarischen Kommunikation IV)*, München: Fink, 75-91.

Gülich, E. and W. Raible. 1977. *Linguistische Textmodelle: Grundlagen und Möglichkeiten*, München: Fink.

Habermas, J. 1981. *Theorie des Kommunikativen Handelns I: Handlungsrationalität und Gesellschaftliche Rationalisierung*, Frankfurt a. M.: Suhrkamp.

Harth, D. 1998. *Das Gedächtnis der Kulturwissenschaften*, Dresden/München: Dresden University Press.

Hobart, M. 1986. 'Context, Meaning and Power' in M. Hobart and R.H. Taylor (eds.), *Context, Meaning and Power in Southeast Asia*, Ithaca, NY: Cornell University Press, 7-19.

Humboldt, W. v. 1963. *Werke inFfünf Bänden*, ed. A. Flitner and K. Giel, Vol. III: *Schriften zur Sprachphilosophie*, Darmstadt: Wissenschaftliche Buchgesellschaft.

Humboldt, W. v. 1988. *On Language: the Ddiversity of Human Language-structure and its Influence on the Mental Development of Mankind*, transl. by P. Heath, Cambridge: Cambridge University Press.

Humphrey, C. and J. Laidlaw. 1994. *The Archetypal Actions of Ritual: A Theory of Rritual Illustrated by the Jain Rite of Worship*, Oxford: Clarendon Press.

Jager, E. 2000. *The Book of the Heart*, Chicago: University of Chicago Press.

Kondylis, P. 1999. *Das Politische und der Mensch. Grundzüge der Sozialontologie I: Soziale Beziehung, Verstehen, Rationalität*, Berlin: Akademie Verlag.

Kurz, G. 1977. 'Hermeneutische Aspekte der Textlinguistik', in *Archiv für das Studium der Nneueren Sprachen und Literaturen*, vol. 214, 262-80.

Lotman, J.M. 1972. *Die Struktur Literarischer Texte*, München: Fink.

Lotman, J.M. 1990. *Universe of Mind. A Semiotic Theory of Culture*, London/New York: Taurs.

Malinowksi, B. 1935. *Coral Gardens and their Magic: a Study of the Methods of Tilling the Soil and of Agricultural Rites in the Trobriand Islands*, London: Allen and Unwin.

Manguel, A. 1996. *A History of Reading*, New York: Viking.

Marcus, G.E. and D. Cushman 1982. 'Ethnographies as Texts', *Annual Review of Anthropology* 11, 25-69.

Meschonnic, H. 1999. *Poétique du Traduire*, Lagrasse: Verdier.

Mommsen, W.J. 1979. 'Die Mehrdeutigkeit von Theorien in der Geschichtswissenschaft', in *Theorie und Erzählung in der Geschichte*, ed. J. Kocka and Th. Nipperdey, München: dtv, 334-70.

Narayan, R.K. 1994. *Gods, Demons and Others*, London: Minerva.

Neumann, G. and S. Weigel (eds.) 2000. *Lesbarkeit der Kultur. Literaturwissenschaft zwischen Kulturtechnik und Ethnographie*, München: Fink.

Plessner, H. 1985. *Gesammelte Schriften*, Vol. VII, Frankfurt a. M.: Suhrkamp.

Probst, P. 1992. 'Die Macht der Schrift. Zum Ethnologischen Diskurs über eine Populäre Denkfigur', *Anthropos* 87, 167-82.

Rappaport, R.A. 1999. *Ritual and Religion in the Making of Humanity*, Cambridge: Cambridge University Press.

Reckwitz, A. 1999. 'Praxis – Autopoiesis – Text. Drei Versionen des *Cultural Turn* in der Sozialtheorie', in A. Reckwitz and H. Sievert (eds.), *Interpretation, Konstruktion, Kultur. Ein Paradigmenwechsel in den Sozialwissenschaften*, Opladen: Westdeutscher Verlag, 19-49.

Ricœur, P. 1970. 'Qu'est-ce qu'un texte? Expliquer et comprendre', in *Hermeneutik und Dialektik II: Sprache und Logik. Theorie der Auslegung und Probleme der Einzelwissenschaften*, ed. R. Bubner, K. Cramer, R. Wiehl, Tübingen: Mohr, 181-200.

Sartre, J.-P. 1948. *Situations II*, Paris: Gallimard.

Smagorinsky, P. and C. O'Donnell-Allen 1998. 'Reading as Mediated and Mediating Action: Composing Meaning for Literature through Multimedia Interpretive Texts', in *Reading Research Quarterly* 33, 198-226.

Spiegel, G. 1990. 'History, Historicism, and the Social Logic of the Text in the Middle Ages', in *Speculum* 65, 59-86:

Spivak, G.C. 1992. 'The Politics of Translation', in M. Barrett and A. Phillips (eds.), *Destabilizing Theory: Contemporary Feminist Debates*, Stanford, Calif.: Stanford University Press, 177-200.

Stierle, K. 1974. 'Zur Begriffsgeschichte von Kontext', in *Archiv für Begriffsgeschichte* 18, 144-9.

Taussig, M. 1993. *Mimesis and Alterity: A Particular History of the Senses*, New York/London: Routledge.

Todorov, T. 1982. 'Comprendre une culture: du dehors / du dedans', in *Extréme-Orient – Extréme-Occident* 1, 9-15.

Vivekananda, S. 1989. *The Complete Works.* Vol. III (Mayavati Memorial Edition), Calcutta.

Weinrich, H. 1976. *Sprache in Texten*, Stuttgart: Klett.

Witte, S. 1992. 'Context, Text, Intertext: Toward a Constructivist Semiotic of Writing', in *Written Communication* 9, 237-308.

Wittgenstein, L. 1967. Schriften, vol. 3, Frankfurt a. M.: Suhrkamp.

Wittrock, M.C. 1981. 'Reading Comprehension', in *Neuropsychological and Cognitive Processes in Reading*, Oxford: Oxford University Press.

2

The Making of a Local Chronicle: The *Raṇapur Rājavaṃśa Itihāsa*

Hermann Kulke

Until 1971, when Indira Gandhi finally abolished the royal privileges of India's *rājās*, there were probably few ruling houses in the world who could have claimed an older dynastic tradition than the small 'Feudatory State' of Ranpur in central Orissa. Even the date of accession to the throne of Japan's first emperor – which according to Japan's imperial chronicle *Nihon shoki* took place in 660 BC – sounds rather modest in comparison with Ranpur. The Chronicle *Raṇapur Rājavaṃśa Itihāsa* traces the origin of the dynasty back to the year 56 of the Kali Age, or 3045 BC, and the foundation of Ranpur to the year 1374 of the Kali Age, or 1727 BC. The main concern of this paper, however, is not Ranpur's fantastic age but its 'invented tradition'.[1] In it Ranpur's ambiguous relations with the dominant Khurda dynasty as well as the role of its chronicle and historiography as a major means of competition with Khurda are described. Thus, it is a contribution to ethno-history as introduced in south India by N. Dirks' seminal works[2] which have influenced more recent studies on Orissa by B. Schnepel, G. Berkemer and G.N. Dash.[3]

I

Ranpur belongs to the roughly two dozen 'fort-born' (*gaḍajāta*, English *Garhjat*) chieftaincies or feudatory states which peopled the map of the hilly hinterland of coastal Orissa until their merger with independent India in 1948/9. The tribal chiefdoms in this area are as

[1] Hobsbawn and Ranger 1983.

[2] Dirks 1982, 1987.

[3] Schnepel 1993, 1995; G. Berkemer 1997; G.N. Dash 1998.

old as the known history of Orissa. Already in the third century BC Aśoka referred in his inscriptions to the forest tribes (*āṭavi*) in his empire and to unconquered border (people) beyond the conquered coastal region of Orissa.[4] These forest tribes are mentioned again in an inscription near Ranpur of AD 600 which refers to 'eighteen forest states' (*aṣṭādaśa-āṭavī-rājya*) and praises *Maṇināga-Bhaṭṭaraka*, later to become known as *Maṇināgeśvarī*, the famous tutelary deity of Ranpur.[5] Again in 885 AD, a local ruler of this area is mentioned as the 'Lord of the eighteen Gondamas', a title which obviously referred to eighteen tribal Gond chieftaincies.[6] During this time Ranpur seems to have come under the rule of the Bhañja kings of *Khiñjalimaṇḍala* centred around Baudh. They too were of tribal, most likely of Gond origin, and worshipped the wooden pillar deity Stambheśvarī, but they also constructed marvellous Hindu temples, like the twin temples of Gandharadi.[7]

Almost next to nothing is known of the history of these tribal chieftaincies during the period of the early medieval regional kingdom of Orissa under the Somavaṃśīs and Gaṅgas in the tenth to fifteenth centuries. But in all likelihood they continued to exist, as they reappeared all of a sudden under the imperial Gajapatis of the Sūryavaṃśa in the late fifteenth century. The kings of this dynasty seem to have tried to form a kind of *cordon sanitaire* around the coastal core area of their far-flung empire through integration of the 'fort born' tribal chiefdoms in the hilly hinterland. The inscriptions of the Gajapatis refer to them as 'forest countries' (*māladeśa*), 'feudal lords' (*sāmanta* or *rājā*) and *gaḍajāta-rājā*.[8] Their relationship with their imperial masters, however, was not free of tension. Kapilendra, the founder of the Sūryavaṃśa, explicitly warned them that any violation of his royal orders was

---

[4] Rock Edict XIII and second Dhauli Separate Rock Edict, Hultzsch 1969, 67 and 98.

[5] Sircar 1949/50, 331.

[6] Sahu 1956, vol. II, 353.

[7] Tripathy, S. 1974, 67, Donaldson 1985-7, vol. I, 217.

[8] Tripathy, K.B. 1962.

tantamount to a rebellion (*droha*) against Lord Jagannātha.[9] The great 'heroic' kings of this dynasty, in particular its second ruler Puruṣottama Deva, played an important role in the legendary accounts of Orissa's local dynastic chronicles. As will be shown later, Ranpur's chronicle was no exception to this rule.

II

After the destruction of the Gajapati kingdom and the Jagannātha cult at Puri by the Afghan Sultanate of Bengal in AD 1568, the local chief of Khurda, Rāmachandra, succeeded in establishing a local princedom and in restoring the Jagannātha cult at Puri in 1590. Two years later, after the final conquest of Orissa by the Mughals, Rāmachandra was acknowledged by Akbar and his famous Rājput general Mānsingh as local successor to the Gajapatis and was invested with nearly two dozen small chieftaincies and principalities in the hinterland of Mughal territory or Mughalbandi in coastal Orissa.

The dominant ritual position of the Khurda *rājās* among the tributary chiefs of Orissa was based on their renewal and control of the Jagannātha cult at Puri. In the mid-seventeenth century a Mughal governor of Orissa reported to his imperial master Aurangzeb that 'all the other zamindars of the country worship him [the Rājā of Khurda] like a god and disobedience of his orders they regard as a great sin'.[10] Their political position, however, was continuously threatened by the Mughal governors of Orissa, who invaded Khurda and Puri several times in their attempt to annex Khurda and control Puri's lucrative pilgrimage economy. Until 1751, when the Mughals and their Nawabs of Bengal were ousted from Orissa by the Marathas, Jagannātha and his earthly deputies, the Gajapatis of Khurda, had to take refuge in various places in south Orissa about a dozen times.[11] Under the Hindu Marathas, Khurda's position became even more precarious. In order to subvert

---

[9] Ibid., 272.

[10] Muraqat-i-Hassan, quoted in Sarkar 1916, 340.

[11] Kulke 1984a.

Khurda's dominant role among the *rājās* of central Orissa, the Marathas brought most of them under the control of their governors at Cuttack. They even tried to appropriate the ritual role of Khurda's *rājās* in the Jagannātha cult through the performance of the famous 'sweeping ceremony' (*cherā pahañrā*), that is the sweeping of Jagannātha's chariot during *ratha yātrā*, the most important royal prerogative of the Khurda kings.[12]

In their desperate struggle to retain their dominant position and control over Puri and its Jagannātha cult, the *rājās* of Khurda initiated a policy of ritually integrating their feudatory chiefs into the Jagannātha cult of Puri. Whereas the former 'imperial' Gajapatis had monopolized the cult of their 'state deity' and threatened disloyal chiefs with his divine wrath, the Khurda Rājās tried to win their support by sharing their own ritual rights in the Jagannātha cult with them. On their visits to Puri, Orissan chiefs were granted special ritual privileges in the cult of Puri by 'royal letters' (*chāmu ciṭāu*).[13] For instance, one of the most respected services to Jagannātha was the *cāmara sebā*, the waving of a fly whisk made from the tail of a yak. According to their status, distinguished visitors were allowed to perform this service in front of Jagannātha with a *cāmara* with a gold or silver handle or a handle wrapped in cotton. The exact place in the sanctum sanctorum where this service was performed was another indicator of the status of the visitor. The higher the status, the nearer to Jagannātha one was allowed to stand. The hierarchy of status-ascribing rituals and privileges was established and maintained by these royal letters and became Khurda's most important means of ritual power in the eighteenth century. We are in the lucky position that out of about 150 such 'royal letters' for about forty princely families of eastern India, 13 letters were issued in favour of Ranpur.[14]

But Khurda's position was not only threatened by the governors of the imperial Mughals or the Marathas. The feudatory

---

[12] Ray 1960; K.N. Mahapatra 1969; Kulke 1979.

[13] Kulke, 1992.

[14] The edition of these *chāmu ciṭāus* is being prepared by G.N. Dash, S.K. Panda and H. Kulke.

chiefs and *rājās* of central Orissa also represented a grave danger to Khurda's dominant position and its claim to Gajapati status. Particularly during the breakdown of the Mughal authority in the early eighteenth century and the establishment of Hindu rule under the Marathas in the second half of the century, Khurda's feudatories strove for greater autonomy. In a few cases this struggle led temporarily to open rebellion as happened in the case of Ranpur. More subtle means of ritual competition and contestation seem to have been of even greater significance. A frequently occurring method was to copy the Puri model through town-planning and in particular by constructing Jagannātha temples in the 'capitals' of the Garhjat states.[15] During the eighteenth century Jagannātha temples and Puri-like car-festivals seem to have been established in several feudatory states in central Orissa as a kind of declaration of 'ritual independence' from Khurda. Another major means of competition was participation in, and in some cases even the appropriation of, Khurda's and Puri's sacred past through historiography in the shape of local chronicles, to which we now turn our attention.

III

India's late medieval dynastic chronicles usually comprise three distinct though strongly interrelated sections which may be termed mythological, legendary and historical. The *mythological* part mainly consists of well-known accounts from the Purāṇas and epics, particularly the *Mahābhārata*, and thus represents a localized blueprint of the *assumed pan-Indian* tradition. The second or *legendary* section contains nearly exclusively the legendary traditions of *regional* heroes and gods and their *constructed* relation with the respective localities of the chronicle. As already mentioned, Orissa's late medieval chronicles link their dynastic traditions particularly with the legendary deeds of the great Gajapati kings of the Sūryavaṃśa in the late fifteenth century, e.g. Puruṣottama Deva's famous Kāñcī Kāberī campaign in south India. It is this legendary section where 'historical reconstruction' of the

[15] Kulke 1980.

past is most evident and where the present necessities guide the search for the past. But parts of it also contain a faint allusion to, even knowledge of,[16] the historical events of the region. The third or *historical* section of the chronicle narrates *local* events, quite often with a great deal of historicity. It usually covers the history of several generations before the date of its composition and is based mainly on oral traditions of the *remembered* past. But usually the authors of these chronicles also had access to contemporary written sources, like the documents of their own princely courts, literary material like earlier dynastic genealogies, and the famous Oriya poems of the sixteenth to eighteenth centuries, like the *Deuḷa Tolā* with its strong emphasis on the tribal tradition of Jagannātha.[17] As will be shown by the example of the chronicle of Ranpur, the three sections typical of India's medieval local chronicles reflect three distinct though interrelated perceptions of the past which may be described as follows: (i) the mythological section, reflecting an *assumed* pan-Indian past, (ii). the legendary section, propagating a localized *constructed* regional past, and (iii) the historical section, presenting the *remembered* local past.

These chronicles also depict two seemingly contradictory 'funnel-like' perceptions of space and time. Their sacred space has a pan-Indian dimension in the mythological section, which is reduced to a regional level in the legendary accounts, and finally ends up in the local context of the historical narrative accounts. As regard to the perception of the sacred past, the funnel appears to be reversed as we find a scheme which Romila Thapar calls a 'telescoping process'.[18] Whereas contemporary events are narrated in great detail, earlier sections are drastically pruned. The more distant the events the shorter the narrations, until only the 'bare bones of names' of the genealogy are left over in the hoary past of the 'time-funnel'. But the telescoping process also allows for a focusing on particular events of the distant past and their detailed

[16] This is a slightly modified quotation from G. Siegel 1975, 316: 'The search for the past was guided by present necessities'.

[17] Geib 1975; Dash 1998.

[18] Thapar 1978, 280f.

narration. The seemingly contradictorily structured perceptions of time and space are interlinked or even reconciled by narrative accounts which are interspersed throughout the tedious genealogical lists of the chronicles. Most important among these are stories about the foundation of the local 'dynasty' and its 'capital', the step-by-step extension of its sacred space and events which led to the establishment of ritual-political relations with the great regional dynasty. This peculiar rhythm of genealogical lists and short accounts is a typical stylistic device in these chronicles.

IV

The *Raṇapur Rājavaṃśa Itihāsa* was compiled in the year 1962 from a variety of sources by Damodar Singh Deo of the Ranpur Raj family.[19] In the detailed foreword we are told that a chronicle had been written down continuously up to the mid-nineteenth century on palm leaves which still existed in Damodar's childhood. The work was continued right up to the 'merger' of Ranpur in 1948 by a total of five successive authors. We are thus well-informed about the authorship of the different chapters dealing with Ranpur's history under British rule since the early nineteenth century. But we have no information about the date of the earlier palm leaf chronicle and, in particular, the beginning of its compilation. However, as the detailed narration of its historical section does not extend beyond the early eighteenth century, and as it is known that a more or less reliable recollection of the past usually covers only two or three generations, we may assume that 'historical writing' in Ranpur

---

[19] A handwritten copy of the *Raṇapura Rājavaṃśa Itihāsa* (*RRI*) still exists in the family of the late Damodar Singh Deo at Ranpur. It contains 91 pages covering Ranpur's history up to 1971 and two additional pages on the coronation of Dilip Chandra Srichandana in 1982. In 1974 A. Das translated the chronicle up to 1971 for the former Orissa Research Project. Prof. G.N. Dash is at present preparing a new translation for a monograph on Ranpur to be published together with N. Gutschow and H. Kulke. In 1974 Lingaraj Sarangi of Ranpur prepared the *Śrī Raṇapur Durga Śrī Śrī Śrī Rājavaṃśānukramaṇi* (*RRA*) for the ORP, a free rendering of the *RRI* with only few minor additions. The present paper is based on the *RRI*.

began not much earlier than the late eighteenth century. This assumption is confirmed by the fact that only since 1775 Ranpur's chronicle refers to the regnal (*aṅka*) years of the Khurda *rājās* although historical events in Orissa had been dated according to these *aṅkas* as a kind of Oriya era since the reign of Rāmachandra I in the late sixteenth century. If we accept the late eighteenth century and the early decades of the nineteenth century as the hypothetical time bracket of the date of Ranpur's early palm leaf chronicle, a look at the political situation in central Orissa during these decades may offer us a clue to its understanding and the causes of its compilation.

As already mentioned, the last decades of the eighteenth century witnessed the dismemberment of Khurda and the gradual appropriation of its ritual privileges in the Jagannātha cult of Puri by the Marathas, a situation which in turn was used by the feudatory states of central Orissa to strengthen their own autonomy.[20] In 1804, i.e. a year after their conquest of Orissa, the British finally ousted the Khurda dynasty from its ancestral homeland. But already five years later the 'Christian' East India Company had to reinstate the Khurda *rājā* as superintendent of the Jagannātha temple at Puri, as it was unable to tackle the administration of eastern India's greatest religious institution. Having become 'kings without a kingdom' in the literal sense of the word, the Khurda *rājās* struggled desperately – now as 'Rājās of Puri' – to regain their dominant position among the feudatory chiefs of Orissa, who had meanwhile been acknowledged as subordinate allies of the East India Company. Whereas formerly the *rājās* of Khurda had tried to strengthen their alliance with their feudatory chiefs through a policy of 'ritual sharing', Mukunda Deva, the then Rājā of Khurda/Puri, revised this policy and prevented princely visitors from exercising their inherited ritual rights in the Jagannātha temple.[21] Moreover, during these years the East India Company began to enquire about the history and traditions of their newly acquired Indian allies and to produce their first 'colonial histories' which strengthened and

[20] Ray 1960; Kulke 1992.

[21] Kulke 1974; Mukherjee 2000.

even 'awakened' their interest in their own history. The famous Mackenzie Collection, with its hundreds of local *vaṃśāvali* chronicles collected mainly in south India and sporadically also in south Orissa, was the most spectacular result of this great 'orientalist endeavour'.[22] In 1821, most likely under Mackenzie's influence, the final Sanskritized version of the Puri chronicle, the *Kaṭakarājavaṃśāvali*, was written.[23] In the same year A. Stirling wrote his famous 'Minute' on the land system in Orissa and its history and subsequently produced the first 'history' of Orissa, based solely on Puri's Sanskrit chronicle and other traditional accounts.[24] The policy of the Marathas and of the East India Company towards Khurda and the beginning of colonial historical writing in Orissa may have encouraged feudatory chiefs of central Orissa to validate their own autonomy and identity vis-à-vis Khurda/Puri and their own princely neighbours through the construction of their own dynastic histories.

V

But writing local history did not exhaust itself in competing with a weakened but still superior regional authority. Of equal if not greater importance was the integration of local traditions into the reconstructed sacred past. The indigenous tradition of Ranpur centres around two goddesses, Maṇināgeśvarī and Khilā Muṇḍā. Maṇināgeśvarī, whose predecessor finds a mention in an inscription of AD 600, belongs to the eight great mother goddesses of Orissa. The iconography of her idol, a uniconic flat round stone (*chatā pathara*) worshipped in a small temple on top of Maninaga Hill, proves her tribal origin. As the tutelary and most powerful deity of Ranpur her origin myth forms the centrepiece of the mythological section of the chronicle of Ranpur. It begins with Niṣāda, the elder brother of Pṛthu, the ideal mythological Hindu king of the Bhāgavata Purāṇa. But as Niṣāda was small, dark-faced and with a

[22] Dirks 1993.

[23] Tripathi and Kulke 1987.

[24] Stirling 1821 and 1822; Kulke 1987.

flat nose, the Brahmans sent him into the jungle. In the year 56 of the Kali Age (= 3045 BC) Hṛṣīkeśa, his fourty-sixth descendant and another epic hero, came to the Ekāmra forest (Bhubaneswar) and began to worship the *dārubrahma*, the wooden god Jagannātha. Nineteen generations later, when the two brothers Biśvabāsu and Biśvabāsaba were worshipping the wooden deity, the great King Indradyumna – who, according to Ranpur's chronicle, belonged to the epic Pāṇḍava dynasty – came in search of Viṣṇu. He discovered the *dārubrahma* and took it to Puri, where he began the construction of the first temple.[25] As Biśvabāsu was very grieved about the loss of his deity, the god appeared to him in a dream. He directed his brother Biśvabāsaba to take the flat, round stone, his original pedestal, to Ranpur and to worship it on Maninaga Hill. Biśvabāsaba acted accordingly and founded Ranpur at the foot of Maninaga Hill in the Kali Age year 1374 (1727 BC). Biśvabāsu remained at Puri and became the mythical ancestor of the present-day tribal Daitapati priests of Puri.[26]

The account thus traces the origin of the Ranpur dynasty and its tutelary deity back to a time when Jagannātha was not yet residing at Puri. It is significant that Ranpur's purely tribal origin is neither disavowed nor embellished. Niṣāda, the mythical forefather of Biśvabāsaba, stands paradigmatically for all those Indian tribes which remain outside the realm of orthodox Brahmanism. In Oriya tradition Biśvabāsu (and thus indirectly also his brother Biśvabāsaba) personifies the ideal leader of the Saora (*Śabara*) tribe. And, as we know from various traditions of Puri, as his original devotee Biśvabāsu was nearest to Jagannātha.[27]

The other important goddess of Ranpur is *Khilā Muṇḍā*. She too is a tribal deity and representative of a typical subsidiary tutelary deity of a princely state.[28] At her place of origin, in a jungle that still exists about 20 km south-east of Ranpur, she resided in a termite hill until recently, when a temple was constructed. Once a

---

[25] Geib 1975.

[26] Dash 1998.

[27] Geib 1975; Dash 1998.

[28] Kulke 1984b.

year, during Durgā Pūjā, she is brought on a long bamboo stick to the palace of Ranpur, where she is worshipped by the royal family and its rājaguru. Whereas the story of the powerful Maṇināgeśvarī has been included in the mythological section of the chronicle of Ranpur, Khilā Muṇḍā plays an equally important role in the historical section, which deals with Ranpur's history during the Khurda period (1592-1803).

Her inclusion into the 'Ranpur pantheon' occurred in the early eighteenth century. From the collection of 'Royal Letters' we know that, during 1695-1703, Rājā Banamāli of Ranpur received three *chāmu ciṭāus* from Maharaja Divyasiṃha of Khurda (1689-1715), who granted him the special privilege of performing the *chūrī khaṇḍa sebā* in the Jagannātha temple at Puri. During this ritual he had 'to hold the two weapons, the dagger (*chūrī*) and the sword (*khaṇḍa*) and to proceed in front of the Lord [Jagannātha] when he goes for hunting'.[29] Despite apparently excellent relations, the Ranpur chronicle tells us that for unknown reasons Banamāli rebelled against the *rājā* of Khurda, killed his son and was himself beheaded. For the following eighteen years Ranpur was under the control of Khurda. Nārāṇa, Banamāli's uncle, took refuge in the southern jungles of Ranpur and worshipped Khiḷā Muṇḍā. One day the goddess appeared to him in the form of a monkey. When Nārāṇa saw the monkey jumping from one tree to another, only to return to the first tree before reaching its goal, he understood it as an auspicious sign from the goddess. He took his sword, began to reconquer Ranpur with the help of the local tribe and, after defeating the troops of Khurda, became the new *rājā* of Ranpur. Since then Khiḷā Muṇḍā, her priest, and a group of her local tribal devotees have been invited to the palace in Ranpur during Durgā Pūjā. As a subsidiary tutelary deity she forms a direct link between the dynasty and the local tribal population.

The legendary section of the chronicle contains another most interesting account of Ranpur's indigenous roots. Jagannātha, the

---

[29] *Chāmu ciṭāu* of the 11 aṅka of Divyasimha Deva of Khurda, *Jagannātha Sthalavṛttāntam*, Government Oriental Manuscript Library, Madras (ORP translation by S.N. Rajaguru, 142).

eighty-seventh Rājā of Ranpur, had no issue. After worshipping the deity Bananidhi Deva in a neighbouring village Śiva came to him in a dream and told him to preserve ashes of cow dung (*vibhūti*), out of which a son would be born. He kept the ashes in a bowl (*tumbā*) for ten months until two sons emerged from it. The significance of this account becomes clearer when we look at the story of Nidhi, the grandfather of Ranpur's childless *rājā*. We are told that Nidhi refused to pay respect and tribute to the Bhañja king of neighbouring Baudh, who imprisoned him and annexed Ranpur. Several years later Nidhi's son approached Puruṣottama Deva, the great Gajapati King of Puri and, according to the second RRA-version of Ranpur's chronicle (see note 18), even accompanied him in his famous Kāñchī Kāberī campaign to south India. With the help of the Gajapati, he defeated Baudh and became *rājā* of Ranpur after his father's death.

These narrations of Ranpur's struggle against, and separation from, Baudh and the establishment of an independent 'kingdom' and especially the story of its two princelings born from ashes seem to contain Ranpur's actual foundation myth and, most likely, a clue to its historical context. Although we have no further corroborative evidence, we can assume that until the fifteenth century Ranpur, like the neighbouring feudatory states of Nayagarh and Daspallah, had been part of the powerful Bhañja kingdom of Baudh. The story of Ranpur's princelings recalls the much older origin myth of the Bhañjas, whose family name is derived from the tradition that their ancestor was born from a 'broken' (*bhaṅga/bhañja*) egg. Since the ninth century they had been praised in their inscriptions as the 'egg-born dynasty' (*aṇḍaja-vaṃśa*).[30] Like Daspallah, Ranpur seems to have gained its status as a *garhjat* 'state' only under the Sūryavaṃśī Gajapatis, perhaps even with their active support, when they surrounded their coastal core area with a semicircle of dependent princely states.

---

[30] For example, Raṇabhañja's inscription of the year 9, in S. Tripathy 1974, 67.

VI

The compiler of the Ranpur chronicle inserted this foundation myth right into the centre of its legendary section. It is preceded by Ranpur's early legendary 'history', which consists of an endless genealogical list of altogether 83 kings. It is interrupted by short references to historical kings, for instance to Yayāti Keśarī and Choḍagaṅga, the legendary and historical founders of Puri's first Jagannātha temple, and to Narasiṃha, the historical founder of the Konarak temple. The hopelessly wrong dates of these kings, e.g. Choḍagaṅga is dated to the first millennium BC instead of *c.* 1100 AD, prove that this portion of the chronicle was 'constructed' on the basis of oral traditions without any knowledge of Puri's Mādaḷā Pāñji temple chronicle or its nearly correct dates of Choḍagaṅga and Narasiṃha.

The second part of the legendary section begins immediately after the story of the princelings being born from ashes. It links Ranpur's sacred past and its historical identity directly with the imperial Gajapatis and Jagannātha, the 'state deity' (*rāṣṭradevatā*) of Orissa. The great Gajapati Puruṣottama Deva liberated Ranpur from Baudh, and the *rājā* of Ranpur participated in his glorious Kāñchī Kāberī campaign, the great symbol and literary topos of Oriya kingship.[31] Even more important events were reported in the chronicle during the reign of Puruṣottama's son Pratāparudra. Uddhava, the then Rājā of Ranpur, used to pay regular visits to Puri during its twelve annual festivals. But on one occasion he was detained on his way to Puri by a flood. Having missed the festival by one day, he prostrated himself in the temple before Jagannātha and fasted for seven days. Jagannātha thereupon came to the Gajapati Pratāparudra in a dream and told him to honour the *rājā* of Ranpur with a sacred sari from the temple treasury and to hand 'His' holy Mādhava image over to him, in order to enable him to perform the twelve festivals in his own capital. After returning to Ranpur Uddhava initiated these festivals and constructed a palace and the first temples to Jagannātha and to Maṇināgeśvarī. He thus

---

[31] Dash 1978, 1979; Mohapatra 1996.

followed the 'Puri model' of the imperial Gajapatis,[32] without, however, neglecting his powerful tutelary goddess on top of Maninaga Hill. The legendary section continues its narration of Uddhava's successors and their enlargement and embellishment of Ranpur's sacred space during the rule of the imperial Gajapatis. We are even informed that Mukunda Deva, the last imperial Gajapati, 'was glad to give his daughter in marriage to [the Ranpur Rājā] Padmanābha Narendra' who received various royal insignia as dowry. The section ends with Kālapāhār's invasion of Ranpur in AD 1568[33] without, however, mentioning any desecration or even destruction of its temples.

VII

The subsequent historical section deals with the history of Ranpur during the Khurda period. It is remarkable that the chronicle is almost entirely silent about Ranpur's history before the well-known story of Banamāli's rebellion against Khurda in the early eighteenth century and his final victory with the help of its new 'subsidiary' tutelary goddess Khiḷā Muṇḍā. The only events worth mentioning before Banamāli were the granting of the title *Saptagaḍa* ('seven forts') *Behera* by the Khurda *rājā* to Giridhara of Ranpur, and his victory over neighbouring Banpur.

Hence, the real historical narration begins only with Giridhara's son and successor Banamāli Narendra. He introduced a unique tradition in Orissa: 'He prepared a stone image of his father and placed it in front of the deity Maṇināga. Since then the *rājās* of this family continued this custom of preparing stone images after the death of the *rājās*.'[34] These images depict the *rājās* on their elephants and are still kept today in the Talamaṇināgeśvarī temple at the foot of Maninaga Hill near the place of the old palace. The chronicle continues that Banamāli 'developed the town, the main road and its street', constructed two temples and a tank in Ranpur,

[32] Cf. N. Gutschow, this volume.

[33] Cf. G.N. Dash, this volume.

[34] *RRI*, 26.

and dedicated two images to the Jagannātha temple at Puri. As already mentioned, Banamāli received three 'royal letters' from Maharaja Divyasiṃha of Khurda (1689-1715), but for unknown reasons, he rebelled against Khurda and was beheaded. Only after eighteen years was his successor Nāraṇa able to end Khurda's occupation of Ranpur with the help of the tribal deity Khiḷā Muṇḍā.

The ambivalent relationship between the 'little kings' of Ranpur and the superior maharajas of Khurda[35] became most evident under Nāraṇa's second successor Rāmachandra Nārendra. He renewed the attacks against Khurda when his namesake on the throne of Khurda, Rāmachandra II, fought a desperate struggle against Taqī Khān, the Mughal *subahdār* at Cuttack. However, in 1734, two years before Rāmachandra of Khurda was overthrown by Taqī Khān, he issued three 'royal letters' in favour of Rāmachandra of Ranpur, granting him special privileges during his visits of the Jagannātha temple at Puri.

During these dramatic years, when Khurda even lost its Gajapati kingship to the neighbouring princely state of Patia for a time, Rāmachandra of Ranpur began a series of conspicuous activities, which are described in detail in the chronicle.[36] He assigned special revenues for the *amṛta maṇohi* offering to Jagannātha at Puri and established the Brahman *śāsana* village Rāmachandrapur, both the prerogatives of the Khurda Gajapatis. In competition with the privilege of the Khurda *rājās* to have an additional palace near the Jagannātha temple at Puri, Rāmachandra of Ranpur gave up his palace at the foot of Maninaga Hill and constructed a new one near Ranpur's Jagannātha temple. He also replaced the Dadhibābana or 'Single Deity' of Jagannātha in this temple with the Jagannātha trinity, constructed three chariots, and performed Ranpur's first car festival. Rāmachandra of Ranpur thus copied the 'Puri model' and he even seems to have competed with Khurda's Gajapati kingship. At least, this is the message which the author of the Ranpur chronicle obviously tried to convey to his audience. It is even likely that he projected the great 'historical'

[35] For a similar situation in Jaipur/Koraput cf. Schnepel 1993.

[36] RRI, p. 32.

deeds of Rāmachandra of Ranpur on to Uddhava, Ranpur's great hero in the legendary section of the chronicle, in order to validate Ranpur's claim of a close association with the great Gajapatis.

We do not need to continue the detailed story of Ranpur's history in the late eighteenth century up to the British conquest of Orissa in 1803. Suffice it to mention again that since Rāmachandra's successor Nārasiṃha several events in Ranpur's history are dated by the regnal or *aṅka* years of the ruling *rājās* of Khurda, to my mind a clear indication for the beginning of historical writing in Ranpur during these decades.

VIII

Recalling our working hypothesis about a late eighteenth century origin for Ranpur's first palm-leaf chronicle, we may now try to come to some tentative conclusions about its 'making' and context. In its endeavour to create its own historical and spatial identity, the Ranpur chronicle seems to have followed a double strategy. A major aim was competition with, and even the contestation of, the authority of Khurda. But of equal importance was the integration of various local traditions into the dramatically enlarged construct of Ranpur's sacred past. The Ranpur chronicle succeeded in a unique way in intertwining these two historiographical strategies.

The dominant position of the Khurda *rājās* as Jagannātha's 'first servants' (*ādya sebaka*) was contested by the Ranpur chronicle through its own invented tradition. Of particular importance in this context is the direct descent of the Ranpur dynasty from Biśvabāsaba, who was, together with his famous brother Biśvabāsu, Jagannātha's first devotee. Moreover, the image of Maṇināgeśvarī, Ranpur's powerful tutelary deity, was declared to be Jagannātha's sacred pedestal before his appropriation and removal to Puri by Indradyumna. Furthermore, although Rāmachandra of Khurda may have been rightly praised as 'Second Indradyumna' by Puri's temple chronicle for his renewal of the cult at Puri after its desecration by Kālapāhār, Ranpur's temple and cult of Jagannātha needed no solemn renewal. According to the Ranpur chronicle, and in contrast to Puri, Ranpur and its cult had remained unmolested by Kālapāhār. Although the chronicle explicitly mentions Kālapāhār's invasion of Ranpur, it is completely silent about any desecration of its temples by this proverbial iconoclast. The Ranpur cult was thus established by the order of Jagannātha and with the support of the imperial Gajapati kings long before the Puri cult had to be renewed by Rāmachandra of Khurda. Moreover, Jagannātha had even ordered that his most sacred Mādhava image should be worshipped at Ranpur, an image which, according to various traditional Oriya accounts,[37] was the predecessor of Puri's wooden image of Jagannātha. Without stating it explicitly in its chronicle, Ranpur seems to have tried to assert that it possesses the only Jagannātha temple in Orissa with an uninterrupted tradition, established under the imperial Gajapatis and unspoiled by the iconoclast Kālapāhār.

The achievements of the chronicle with respect to Ranpur's indigenous tribal roots and their 'genealogical historization' are equally impressive. Through the construction of a genealogical descent of Biśvabāsaba, the founder ancestor of Ranpur, from Niṣāda, the mythological ancestor of India's tribes, the Ranpur chronicle succeeded in combining regional Oriya and the pan-Indian tribal origin myths and in localizing them in Ranpur's sacred past. Moreover, by identifying the aniconic *mūrti* of Ranpur's powerful tutelary goddess, Maṇināgeśvarī, as Jagannātha's original pedestal, Ranpur linked its sacred past with Jagannātha's Śabara tradition and acknowledged Maṇināgeśvarī's tribal origin. The myth of the two princelings born from ashes and the acceptance of Khiḷā Muṇḍā as a subsidiary tutelary deity corroborate Ranpur's indigenous tribal roots.

Looking at this 'biography'[38] of the Ranpur chronicle one may get the impression that there are two separate genealogical trajectories and perceptions of the past: a pan-Indian/regional one and a local/tribal one. Late medieval local chronicles like Ranpur's indeed pursued a double strategy of universalization and

---

[37] For example, Dash 1998, 38ff; Geib 1975, 159ff.

[38] Dirks 1993.

localization. Universalization was achieved by linking local traditions with regional and pan-Indian traditions. This quest for universalization was complemented through the persistent localization of mythical actions. The mythological and legendary sections of these chronicles are therefore 'by definition repositories of localized myths and legends', as David Shulman once wrote in connection with local Tamil temple myths.[39] The secret of the popularity and wide circulation of these chronicles and their narrations lies in the blend of their pan-Indian, regional and local 'histories'.

[39] Shulman 1980, 80.

'The Making of Ranpur's Local Chronicle'

		Genera-tions (as mentioned in the chronicle)	**Kali Age** (Christian era added)
Mythological section: 'assumed past' pan-Indian	Ancestor Niṣāda is banished to the jungle	1	-
	Hṛṣīkeśa worships dārubrahma [=*Jagannātha*] at Ekāmra [=*Bhubaneswar*]	47	56 (3045 BC)
	[*Origin myth II:*]	65	1374 (1727 BC)
	Biśvabāsu and Biśvabāsaba worship Jagan-nātha, Indradyumna takes Jagannātha to Puri;		
	Jagannātha orders Biśvabāsaba to worship his sacred pedestal [= *Maṇināgeśvarī*] to Ranpur		
	Epic Pāṇḍavas in Ranpur		
legendary section: 'constructed past' regional	Yayāti Keśarī [*legendary founder of the first Jagannātha temple at Puri*]	[*67*]	
	Choḍagaṅga [*founder of the present Jagannātha temple at Puri*]	[*85*]	
	Chāḷukya *rājā* rewards Ranpur *rājā* Narasiṃha [*founder of the Konarak temple*]		
	Ranpur annexed by Baudh	120	3163 (AD 62)
	[*Origin myth I:*]		
	secession from Baudh		
	princelings born from ashes	150	
	[*Ranpur's emergence under the Imperial Gajapatis of Orissa:*]		
	Participation in Puruṣottama's Kānchī Kāberī		
	Uddhava, Rājā of Ranpur		[late 15th cent. AD]
	Jagannātha orders Pratāparudra to send his holy Mādhava image to Ranpur,		
	beginning of 12 festivals at Ranpur,		
	[*first*] Jagannātha temple and palace at Ranpur,		
	Uddhava receives the title Nārendra		
	Ranpur *rājā* marries Gajapati daughter and receives royal symbols		4601 (AD 1500)

Contnd.

Historical section: 'remembered past' local	Kālapāhār's invasion of Ranpur	162	4680 (AD 1579)
	[*Khurda as Gajapati successor state*]		[AD *1592*]
	Ranpur's *rājā* receives the title Saptagaḍa Behera		
	Rājā Banamāli develops Ranpur town, rebels against Khurda and is beheaded,	167	
	Khiḷā Muṇḍā helps Ranpur to defeat Khurda		[AD *1751/61*]
	[Maratha conquest of Orissa and dismemberment of Khurda]		
	Rāmachandra, *rājā* of Ranpur renewed fights with Khurda, construction of a new palace at Ranpur, images of Jagannātha trinity prepared, car festival introduced at Ranpur,		(AD 1775)
	cyclone in Puri, 49th regnal year of Bīrakeśarī of Khurda, Rāmachandra receives the title Bajradhara		
	Ranpur supports Khurda against the Marathas and is honoured by a 'letter of praise', 12th regnal year of Divyasiṃha of Khurda		(AD 1787)
	Struggle with neighbouring *rājās*		
	[*British conquest of Orissa and defeat of Khurda*]		[*1803/4*]

References

Bakker, H. (ed.). 1992. *The Sacred Centre as the Focus of Political Interest*, Groningen.

Berkemer, G. 1997. 'The Chronicle of a Little Kingdom: Some Reflections on the Tekkali-Tālūka Jamīmdārlā Vaṃśāvalī', in Kölver, 54-96.

Breckenridge, C.A. and P. van der Veer (eds.). 1993. *Orientalism and the Postcolonial Predicament. Perspectives on South Asia*, Philadelphia: University of Pennsylvania Press.

Dash, G.N. 1978. 'Jagannātha and Oriya Nationalism', in Eschmann et al., 359-74.

Dash, G.N. 1979. *Janaśruti Kāñcī Kāberī*, Berhampur.

Dash, G.N. 1998. *Hindus and Tribals – Quest for a Co-existence (Social Dynamics in Modern Orissa)*, New Delhi: Decent Books.

Dirks, N. 1982. 'The Past of a Pāḷaiyakārar: The Ethnohistory of a South Indian Little King', in *Journal of Asian Studies* 41, 655-83.

Dirks, N. 1987. *The Hollow Crown: Ethnohistory of an Indian Kingdom,* Cambridge: Cambridge University Press.

Dirks, N. 1993. 'Colonial Histories and Native Informants: Biography of an Archive', in Breckenridge, 279-313.

Donaldson, T. 1985-7. *Hindu Temple Art*, 3 vols. Leiden: E.J. Brill.

Eschmann, A., H. Kulke, and G.C. Tripathi (eds.). 1978. *The Cult of Jagannath and the Regional Tradition of Orissa*, New Delhi: Manohar.

Geib, R. 1975. *Indradyumna-Legende: Ein Beitrag zur Geschichte des Jagannātha-Kultes*, Wiesbaden: Otto Harrassowitz.

Hobsbawn, E.J. and T. Ranger (eds.). 1983. *The Invention of Tradition*, Cambridge: Cambridge University Press.

Hultzsch, E. 1969. *Inscriptions of Asoka*, Oxford 1925 (repr. New Delhi 1969).

Kimura, M. and Tanabe, A. (eds.) (forthcoming) *The State in India, Past and Present*, Kyoto.

Kölver, B. (ed.). 1997. *Recht, Staat und Gesellschaft im Klassischen Indien (The Law, the State and Administration in Classical India)*, München: Oldenbourg.

Kulke, H. 1974. 'Kings without a Kingdom: The Rajas of Khurda and the Jagannatha Cult', in *South Asia* 4, 60-7.

Kulke, H. 1979. 'Rathas and Rajas: The Car Festival at Puri', in *Art and Archaeological Research Papers (aarp)* 17, 27-34 (repr. Kulke 1993: 66-81).

Kulke, H. 1980. 'Legitimation and Townplanning in the Feudatory States of Central Orissa', in *aarp* 17, 30-40 (repr. in Kulke, H. 1984a. 'Jagannātha under Muslim Rule', in S.R. Sarma (ed.), *Unmana: Souvenir of Akhil Barat Jagannatha Consciousness Conference*, Cuttack (repr. in Kulke 1993, 33-50).

Kulke, H. 1984b. 'Tribal Deities at Princely Courts: The Feudatory Rajas of Central Orissa and their Tutelary Deities (*iṣṭadevatās*)', in S. Mahapatra 1984, 13-24 (repr. in Kulke 1993, 114-37).

Kulke, H. 1987. 'The Chronicles and the Temple Records of the Mādaḷā Pāñji of Puri: A Reassessment of the Evidence', in *Indian Archives* 36, 1-24 (repr. in Kulke 1993, 137-58).

Kulke, H. 1992. 'Kṣetra and Kṣatra: The Cult of Jagannātha and the "Royal Letters" (*chāmu ciṭāus*) of the Rājās of Khurda', in H. Bakker (ed.), 131-42 (repr. in Kulke 1993, 51-65).

Kulke, H. 1993. *Kings and Cults: State Formation and Legitimation in India and Southeast Asia*, New Delhi: Manohar.

Kulke, H. 1993a. 'Reflections on the Sources of the Temple Chronicles of the Mādaḷā Pāñji of Puri', in Kulke 1993, 159-91.

Mahapatra, K.N. 1969. *Khurudhā Itihāsa*, Bhubaneswar: Government of Orissa.

Mahapatra, S. (ed.). 1984. *Folk Ways in Religion: Gods Spirits and Men*, Cuttack: Institute of Oriental and Orissan Studies.

Mohapatra, B. 1996. 'Ways of Belonging: The Kanchi Kaberi Legend and the Construction of Oriya Identity', in *Studies in History* 12, 187-217.

Mukherjee, P. 2000. *Pilgrim Tax and Temple Scandals: A Critical Study of the Important Jagannath Temple Records during British Rule*, ed. by N. Cassel-Gardener, Bangkok: Orchid Press.

Ray, B.C. 1960. *Orissa under the Marathas*, Allahabad: Kitab Mahal.

Rao, V.N., D. Shulman and S. Subrahmanyam. 1992. *Symbols of Substance. Court and State in Nāyaka Period Tamilnadu*, Delhi: Oxford University Press.

Sahu, N.K. (ed.) 1956. *History of Orissa*, 2 vols., Calcutta: Sushil Gupta.

Sarkar, J.N. 1916. 'The History of Orissa in the Seventeenth Century, Reconstructed from Persian Sources', in *Journal of the Bihar and Orissa Research Society* 2, 153-65; 238-49.

Schnepel, B. 1993. *Die Dschungelkönige: Ethnohistorische Aspekte von Politik und Ritual in Orissa*, Stuttgart: Steiner Verlag (English translation New Delhi: Manohar, 2002)

Schnepel, B. 1995. 'Durga and the King: Ethnohistorical Aspects of Politico-Ritual Life in a South Orissan Jungle Kingdom', in *Journal of the Royal Anthropological Institute* 1, 145-66.

Shulman, D. 1980. *Tamil Temple Myths: Sacrifice and Divine Marriage in the South Indian Saiva Tradition*, Princeton: Princeton University Press.

Siegel, G. 1975. 'Political Utility in Medieval Historiography: A Sketch', in *History & Theory* 14, 314-25.

Sircar, D.C. (1949/50). 'Two Plates from Kanas', *Epigraphia India* 28, 328-34.

Stirling, A. 1821. 'Mr. Stirling's Minute on Tenures in Orissa. Dated 10th October 1821', in *Orissa Historical Research Journal* 9, 3/4 (1960), 91-101; 10, 1/2 (1961) App. IV-LXXXIX.

Stirling, A. 1822. 'An Account, Geographical, Statistical and Historical of Orissa Proper or Cuttack', in *Asiatick Researches* 15, 163-338 (published 1825).

Thapar, R. 1978. 'The Tradition of Historical Writing in Early India', in R. Thapar, *Ancient Indian Social History: Some Interpretations*, New Delhi: Orient Longman, 268-93.

Tripathi, G.C. and H. Kulke. 1987. *Kaṭakarājavaṃśāvali: A Traditional History of Orissa with Special Reference to Jagannātha Temple,* Allahabad: Vohra Publishers.

Tripathy, K.B. 1962. *The Evolution of Oriya Language and Script*, Bhubaneswar: Utkal University.

Tripathy, S. 1974. *Inscriptions of Orissa*, vol. IV [Bhanja dynasties], Bhubaneswar: Orissa State Museum.

3

Ranpur Resolved: Spatial Analysis of a Town in Orissa Based on a Chronicle

Niels Gutschow

Introduction

The following analysis or 'reconstruction' of urban space and its religious as well as profane infrastructure is based on a chronicle (*vaṃśāvali*) compiled by Damodar Singh Deo from Ranpur (1906-1994), son of Harihar Singh Deo who was himself adopted by King Benudhara Narendra in 1876 who ruled from AD 1842 to 1899. Harihar Singh Deo had ruled for only two years when Benudhara finally had a son by his third queen in 1878: Krishna Chandra. He took over from his father in 1899 and ruled until 1945.

Damodara must have been motivated by his quasi-royal descent to compile a chronicle with the title *History of the Dynasties of the Ranpur State*[1] in 1962, taking advantage of various documents. He refers to a palm leaf manuscript which reportedly covered the development of the genealogy and events up to *c.* 1830. However, this manuscript was not available while he was compiling his text. The only chronicle available to him and which he could make use of was the one written in verse form by the poet Shridhar Mishra, which also covered the time until Damodar's father was adopted. Damodar's brother, Gopināth Singh Deo (1890-1955), completed the chronicle up to 1939, while Damodar himself added a few events to bring the coverage up to 1962. He also added a couple of footnotes throughout the text trying (not always correctly) to relate the events of Ranpur to the reign of the Gajapati kings, Muslim invaders or Maratha rulers. Damodar's version of the

[1] *Raṇapur Rājavaṃśa Itihāsa.* Cf. Kulke in the present volume.

chronicle, translated in 1974 in the context of the Orissa Research Project, is faithfully quoted throughout this paper. Only a few inconsistencies in spelling and diacritical marks have been edited and personal comments by the translator omitted. A revised translation by Gagan Dash is in process.

In a few instances this essay refers to a second chronicle, which turned out to be more elaborate. This second chronicle was compiled by Liṅgarāj Sarangi, the Rājpurohit of the Ranpur Rājā. In 1974 it was translated under the title *Genealogy of the Royal Family of Ranpur* by A. Das in the context of the Orissa Research Project.

Information related to space culled from the chronicle is translated into a conventional map. This was carried out on the basis of the Settlement Map prepared in 1943/44, probably following the fire that devastated Ranpur in March 1943. The map was prepared on the scale of 1:1250 on four silk sheets. Only three sheets survive in the records room of the *tehsildar's* office which served as the local jail until the late forties. The third sheet was crudely inked on tracing paper a couple of years ago. As a settlement map it only recorded plot boundaries and in rare cases a few individual buildings. Hence a new map on the scale 1:2500 was designed showing actual street alignments and detailed information gathered during a field trip in July 1999.

While Hermann Kulke evaluates the chronicle (see Kulke in the present volume) in the light of the formation of feudatory states in the hinterland of central Orissa, in this essay I screen that document exclusively for information concerning the spatial fabric of Ranpur and the donation and fabrication of religious objects which usually become enshrined in built spaces. Two basic levels can be identified: on one level, spatial interventions (construction of temples) or movements in space (*yātrās,* i.e. processions) tend to be presented by the chronicle as cosmogonic acts or as announcments of a 'new age'. Such acts needed a ritual of renewal or perhaps the transfer of the palace to the centre. On a second level, all notes concerning the building of temples and the installation of rituals are presented with the question whether we are confronted with 'facts' or 'constructs'. In a few cases, as in the case of the construction of the Jagannātha temple, we cannot be absolutely sure, but we think that the chronicle tries to construct an investiture of the king with regalia from Puri in the middle of the sixteenth century at a time when the Gajapatis unexpectedly returned to power before being finally deposed by the Afghan conquest in 1568.

Spatial Interventions: From Creation to Conquest

The chronicle refers to ages (*yuga*) and covers more than five thousand years. Some time after the beginning, in 3045 BC, it mentions one Hṛṣīkeśa (Puruṣottama as consort of Lakṣmī[2]) who worshipped *dārubrahma*, the primordial Wooden God.

After nineteen generations, in 1727 BC, the Wooden God was moved by Indradyumna (it is not mentioned in the chronicle from where) to Puruṣottama, a place which can certainly be identified as Puri. 'God' told the aboriginal Śabara chief Viśvāvasu to send his brother Viśvavāsabha to bring a stone to Ranpur, which would represent Durgā in the form of Maṇināgeśvarī, the Jewel Serpent. Until today Viśvāvasu remains the name of the leaders of Daitas, who carve and create new gods in the context of the Navakalevara ritual[3] and who also figure in the Indradyumna legend. According to the chronicle Viśvāvasabha complied with the order, cleared the forest, and 'became the *rājā* of the area' as the chronicle tells us.

It was certainly important for the myth of the foundation of Ranpur to be closely related to the translocation of the Wooden God from the jungles to Puri. While Viśvāvasu followed the god to the new location, his younger brother was somehow sent away to establish a new territory under the protection of a new goddess. In the present context, the focus is on the definition of the new territory. The chronicles not only describe the quality of place, but seem to refer to the ancient rituals of taking possession of territory.

---

[2] Tripathi 1978b, 42.

[3] Tripathi 1978a, 233.

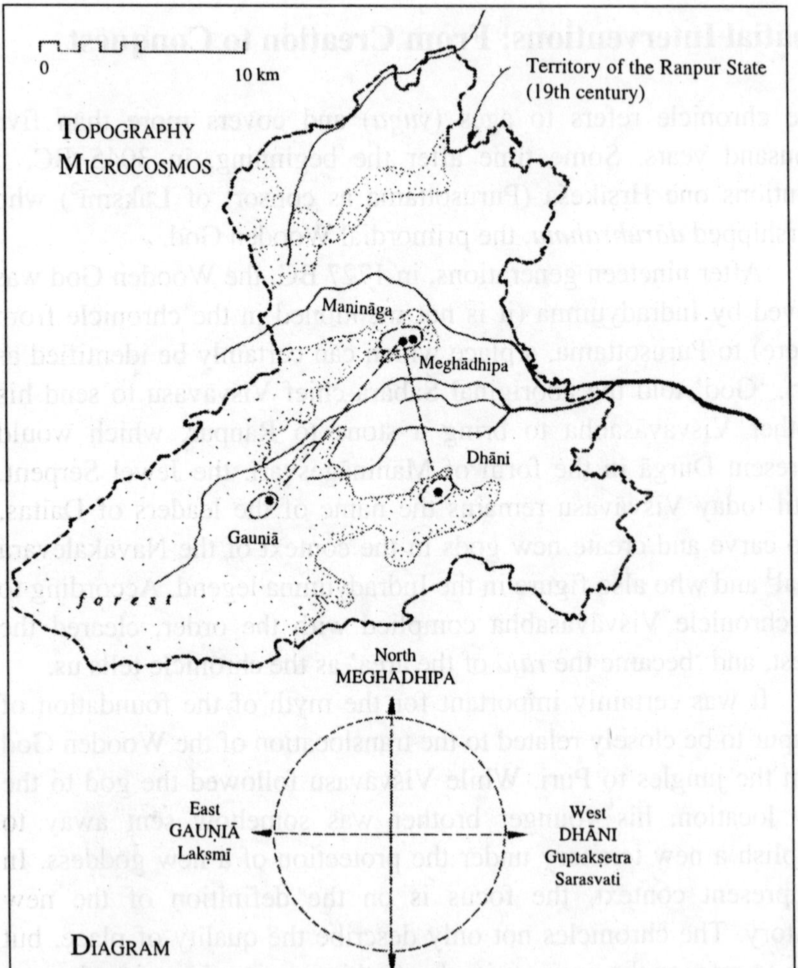

Map 1: Claiming Territory. A Cosmogonic Act

The four directions are defined and therefore tied to goddesses who bestow protection and affluence. The beginning of Ranpur can thus be compared to a cosmogonic act with Viśvāvasabha as the sole actor. Durgā was deliberately placed atop a hill so as to govern the four cardinal directions. Two other promontories and hill tops were identified with Lakṣmī and Sarasvatī. It seems obvious that the two consorts of Viṣṇu have been incorporated into the landscape, while on the main hill a protective goddess, Durgā, is represented. Her seven sisters occupy other important places in Orissa. Ranpur is thus powerfully tied to the larger territory of Utkala. The fourth place is dedicated to an unknown deity who ensures rain and the territory thus probably represents the abode of rain ensuring serpents, the *nāgas*. Nothing is said about a settlement yet.

The chronicle reads as follows:

> A king named Indradyumna of the Pāṇḍava dynasty removed the wooden image [*dārubrahma* from Akambra forest] to Puruṣottama for which Viśvāvasu was very much grieved. Due to sorrow both the brothers slept without food. God could know this and in the dreams He directed the elder brother to send Viśvāvasabha with the flat round stone to Raṇāsurapura and place it on the hillock there. If with a pure heart it is worshipped with various offerings, many works will be done. Both the brothers were instructed accordingly. Then Viśvāvasu resided in Puri. By this time Kali age was advanced by thirteen hundred and seventy-four years. Viśvāvasabha removed the stone with joy and after performing the usual rites, placed it on the summit of the hill. Oh persons with sobriety! That hillock is famed as Maṇināgeśvarī Parvata and the deity is known as Durgā. She is one of the eight goddesses known as Caṇḍī in Bhubaneswar. The summit and the southern portion of the hillock is known as Maṇināgeśvarī and it is well established in the world. On the northern summit of the hill there is a deity known as Meghādhipa. When there is drought, wise men with great enthusiasm approach that deity and offer worship

by holding *saṇkīrtana*. Then there will be profuse rainfall. On the west of the hill it is called Gauṇiā as it is supposed that it had the Gauṇiā of Lakṣmī – a basket to collect the riches of the forest. To the east of the hillock is the hillock named Dhāni. It is written in *Kapila Saṃhitā* that the Pāṇḍavas took rest there with Draupadī. This place is known as the Guptakṣetra where God has his amorous sports. Viśvāvasabha, with this belief was happy to reside there. He cleared the forests, developed the land and became the Rājā of the area.

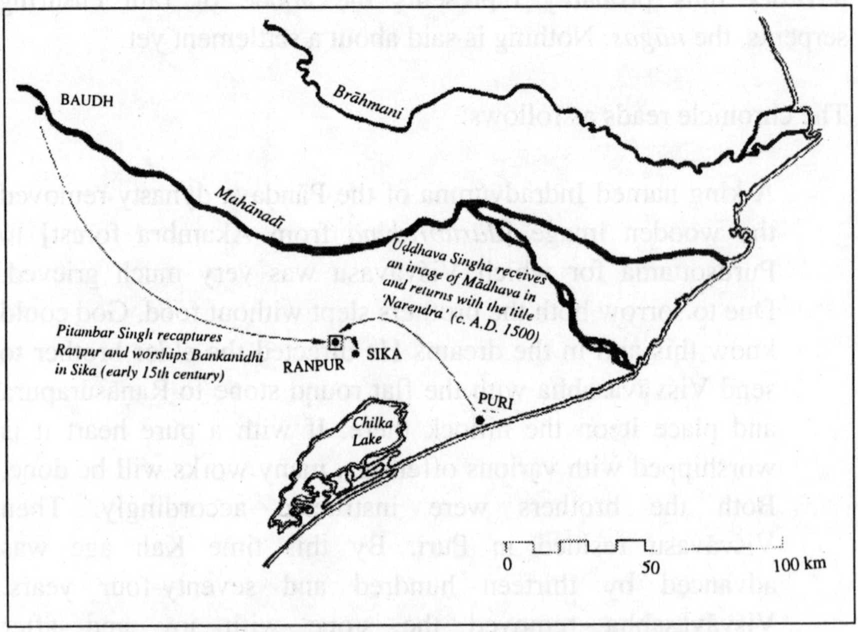

Map 2: Imagined and Constructed Past. Legitimation of Power

After 150 generations, around the middle of the fifteenth century, a king named Pitambar Singh recaptured Ranpur, which had been under the rule of Baudh for quite some time. As his son Jagannātha remained issueless, Śiva appeared and instructed him in such a way that two children were born from ashes. It was Śiva in the form of Bankaniddhi, a deity who is enshrined at Sika, some 8 km east of

Ranpur. The recapture or conquest of Ranpur by Pitambar and the miraculous birth of his two children in the following generation seem to be the two aspects supporting the same cause: the reconfirmation or renewal of Ranpur as a place of kingship. The break in the continuity had to be mended and overcome. For some reason the disassociation of the king with his place must have been so strong that it was believed that only with Śiva's support could the continuity be re-established.

An important event followed three generations later. The great-grandson of one of these two children, Uddhava Singh, went to Puri at the beginning of the sixteenth century in order to seek new or additional legitimation of his power which at that point of time never seemed to be in doubt. Draped in a *sāri* and entrusted with the title Narendra, he returned to Puri with an image of Mādhava, certainly an iconographic representation of Viṣṇu and not the Wooden God.

Though this episode or event has no association with creation, it leads a step further: power needs legitimation and time was ripe to submit to the Gajapati king in Puri not only to receive regalia but also a new god. In earlier events Durgā and Śiva figured prominently. Now the king of Ranpur had to join the mainstream and install Mādhava as the central focus of worship.

The chronicle reads as follows:

> Now, wise men, listen with patience, Niddhi Singh's son felt the absence of his father very much as well as the annexation of the kingdom by Baudh and had been living with a depressed mind. His name was Pitambar Singh. He approached Puruṣottama Deva, fought with the *rājā* of Baudh and recovered the kingdom of Ranpur. Jagannātha was the son of Pitambar Singh. He was issueless. With purity of heart, he fell flat and fasted before the deity of Bankaniddhi Deva in the village Sikua and knowing his desire, Śiva passed this order at midnight of the bright fortnight of the month of Māgha on the fourteenth day: 'Take these pure ashes, keep them carefully and out of them a son will be produced.' He

> kept the ashes in a *tumbā* and worshipped daily. On the completion of ten months on the fourteenth day of the bright fortnight of the month of Kārtika at the 3rd *prahara* two babies were born inside the *tumbā*. They were not born of human beings and so the mother and father reared them carefully.
>
> He [Uddhava Singh, their great-grandson] used to visit Puri to see the twelve festivals.... He paid his respect to God and for seven days fasted with great purity of mind, quietly lay flat before the bar tree. On the dark fortnight of the month of Āśvin on the third day of the lunar month on Thursday when it was the *dvija* star and the occasion was *sovanna*, Lord Jagannātha appeared in a dream before Pratāprudra Deva [the Gajapati ruler at Puri] at dead of night and told him that below a bar tree the *rājā* of Ranpur had been lying prostrated. He should be given *sāri* from the store room and should be escorted to Ranpur. He should be given a Mādhava image which he would carry to Ranpur and there he should perform the twelve festivals.... That day at the 3rd *jāma* of the night, Lakṣmī appeared in the dream and directed him to go to his kingdom, stick to his religion.... As ordered by Lord Jagannātha, from that time observing usual rites all the ceremonies beginning from the bath of Lord Jagannātha are being performed in Ranpur.'

Uddhava Singh not only brought the new god from the centre where the imperial god of Utkala, Jagannātha, resides, but he also built a temple and his queen added a chamber beside the tower, called *mukhāsāla* according to the chronicle. He is said to have performed 'the usual rites for Jagannātha' as well as 'the twelve festivals' – a significant feature in keeping with the norms of the centre.

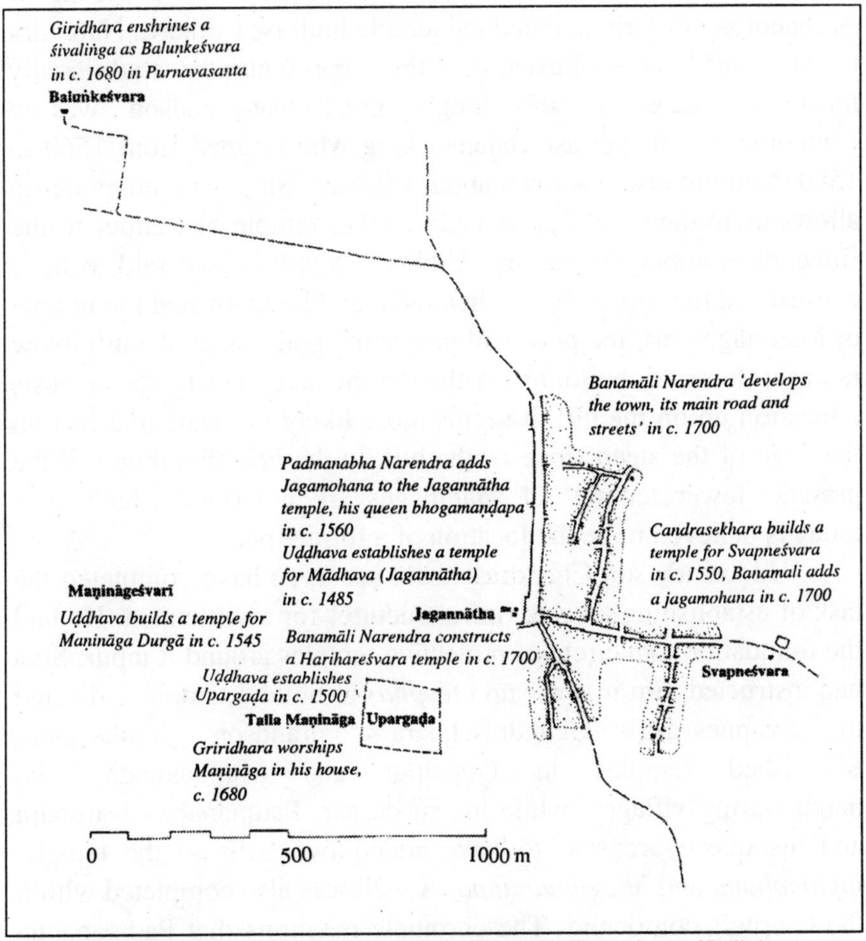

Map 3: From Constructed to Remembered Past. The Emergence of Religious Infrastructure

The chronicle explicitly mentions a temple that the king built. This event is widely accepted by local historians as historical. Although the chronicle mentions *kaliyuga* 4631 (AD 1530) as the date of this achievement, the late Kedarnāth Mahāpatra, Superintendent of Archaeology of Orissa, dated the temple built by Uḍḍhava Narendra to AD 1485.[4] He believes that this represents the traditionally mentioned date, as the king's great-great-grandson was a contemporary of the last Gajapati king who reigned from 1560 to 1580. Nothing else is known about Uddhava Singh and no evidence allows us to date the present or any other temple of Ranpur to the fifteenth or sixteenth century. Uddhava Singh is also said to have constructed the 'upper fort', Upargaḍa, and he renovated the temple of Maṇināgeśvarī, the powerful protecting goddess on the hill. Now it was a 'masonry building'. Although the name Upargaḍa suggests a location up on the hill, it seems more likely to locate that fort on the edge of the steep slope of the hill, in the neighbourhood of the present 'lower temple' of Maṇināgeśvarī, a terrace which until today is believed to be the location of a former palace.

Uḍḍhava's son Chandrasekhara seems to have completed the task of establishing a basic 'infrastructure' for a settlement. He laid the foundation to a circle of protective temples around Ranpur. Śiva had instructed him in a dream (*svapna*) to build a temple dedicated to Svapneśvara. Chandrasekhara's grandson Rāmacandra established temples in Gopalpur and Majhiakanda, two neighbouring villages, while his successor, Padmanābha Narendra and his queen are said to have added two halls to the temple, *jagamohana* and *bhogamaṇḍapa*. A well was also completed within the temple's compound. The chronicle mentions that Padmanābha was a contemporary of the Gajapati ruler Mukunda Deva, who ruled from 1557 to 1568.

Padmanābha was succeeded by his grandson Kunjabihari Narendra. It was Kunjabihari's grandson Giridhara who established supremacy over seven forts to guard the periphery of Ranpur's territory. He also started the worship of Maṇināgeśvarī at his residence and initiated the custom of installing stone images of the

[4] Mahāpatra 1977, 7-9.

rulers which can still be seen within the temple. Giridhara's son Banamāli Narendra not only built temples dedicated to Harihareśvara and Haracaṇḍī, but also added a *jagamohana*-hall to the temple of Svapneśvara. Within the compound of the latter temple he built a Baluṅkeśvara temple and created a water tank called Sāmukhā Pokharī. The chronicle mentions for the first time the development of a town, its streets and lanes during his reign.

After the renewal of the Jagannātha cult in Puri under Rāmacandra of Khurda in 1590, and according to the chronicle it took more than a hundred years for Ranpur to reach an entirely new level of development. At around 1700, the fabric of the settlement is mentioned which at that time could hardly be called 'urban'. In those days only individual buildings were noted as symbols of an otherwise undefined settlement. Banamāli Narendra, of whom it was said that he 'was very efficient in architecture', also 'developed the town, its main roads and streets'. The second chronicle, compiled by Lingaraj Sarangi, who most probably took advantage of the same sources, is more detailed. Maybe the author simply wanted to include a settlement merely as a symbolic establishment. The chronicle says that the king 'established seven streets and 42 small streets'. Obviously, the mere mention of streets was not considered meaningful. A sufficient number was needed to convey the sense of creation and auspiciousness. Besides the numbers 8 or 9 which define a perimeter and its centre, the numbers 7 and 42 as a multiple of 7 refer to the process as they reflect sacred time: a quarter of a month and, in the case of 42, six weeks or three phases of the moon.

The chronicle reads as follows:

> When it was four thousand six hundreds and thirty-one year of *kaliyuga*, the *rājā* constructed a temple and the *rāṇī* its *mukhāsāla* at Rāṇapurgarh. Originally there was a temple of Maṇināgeśvarī Durgā. It was a pleasure for him to erect a masonry building there. Thereafter he died. Oh wise men, now listen, Candrasekhara, the son of Uḍḍhava Narendra became the *rājā*. To the east of the fort of Ranpur there was a

forest and there was a Śiva *liṅga* sprouted from the bottom. Every day over that *liṅga* a cow used to drop milk. People discussed among themselves about this strange incident and at last reported this matter to the *rājā*. In a suspicious mind when the *rājā* had slept, Lord Śiva appeared in a dream and told him that his usual residence is in Kāśī but he has appeared in this forest called Turukāṇi. When the *rājā* woke up from his sleep early in the morning, he saw the carving of a picture like an umbrella, on the top of the *liṅga*. As the deity was discovered as a result of *svapna*, the deity was called Svapneśvara and his worship and offerings of food arrangement was made. The *rājā* engaged sculptors and masons and erected a temple for him. The temple was constructed on the south-east direction from the palace called Upargaḍa which had been constructed by Uḍḍhava Narendra. Padmanābha Narendra [Candrasekhara's great-grandson] constructed *jagamohana* and the *rāṇī bhogamaṇḍapa*. As there was balance of money, to the south a well was dug out. He [Giridhara] erected a temple and enshrined a Śiva *liṅga* in the name of Baluṅkeśvara. He was greatly devoted to Maṇināgeśvarī, worshipped her day and night in his house and pleased her.... He [Banamāli Narendra] developed the town, its main road and the streets. He constructed Harihareśvara temple [and] a portion of the *snānavedī*. He placed the image of a lion there. He constructed the temple of Haracaṇḍī and *jagamohana* in front of the temple of the deity Svapneśvara. He enshrined Baluṅkeśvara deity in the temple towards its north. He caused the digging of a tank and named it Baḍa Sāmukhā.'

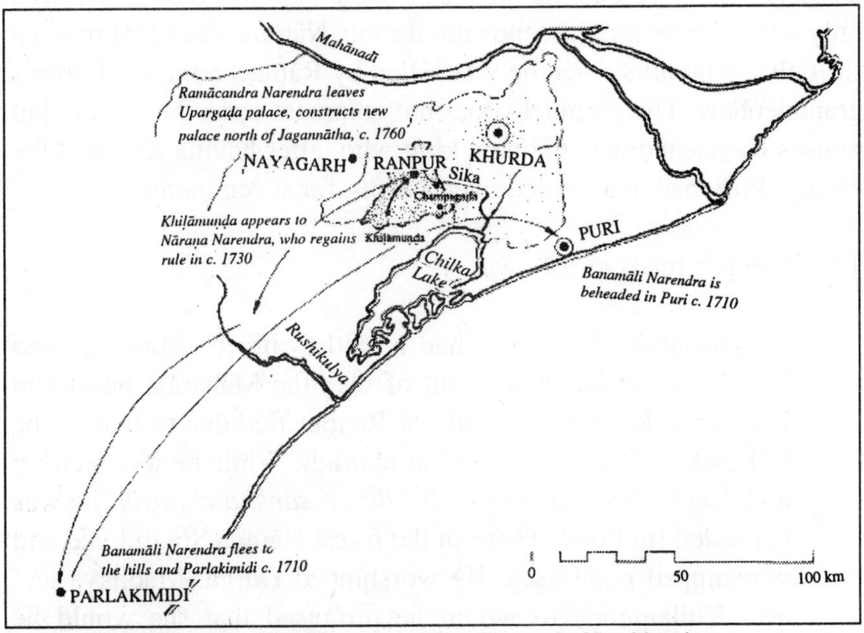

Map 4: Remembered and Re-enacted Past. Renewal of Legitimation

King Banamāli Narendra, who had obviously consolidated the settlement in Ranpur at the beginning of the eighteenth century, killed the Mahārājā of Puri's son in a battle. Ranpur was conquered and levelled, the king fled to Parlakimidi but was finally taken captive and beheaded in Puri. Years of unrest followed until Banamāli's uncle, Nārana Singh, chose a new tutelary goddess, Khiḷā Muṇḍā, and re-captured Ranpur under her protection.

The legendary return of Pitambar Singh to Ranpur in the middle of the fifteenth century already had to be accompanied by an act of creation under the direction of Śiva. It was now the turn of Banamāli Narendra's uncle to be guided in re-establishing his power. Like Viśvāvasu, the legendary founder of the kingdom who once 'cleared the forest' he lived in exile in the forest. There Nārana Singh worshipped Khilā Muṇḍā besides Durgā and Mādhava. A strange incident which occurred was interpreted by him to be an order by the goddess to conquer Ranpur. Since that time, Khilā

Muṇḍā is carried from the forest to Ranpur on the occasion of Daśaharā every year in the form of a bamboo pole which is renewed only when a new king ascends the throne. Nāraṇa's son had reigned for only 18 months when he was killed by Rāmacandra, his father's grandnephew. The chronicle does not comment upon the murder but praises Rāmacandra as the new king who, after having defeated the king of Puri, had again ruled over Ranpur for seven months.

The chronicle reads as follows:

> He [Banamāli Narendra] had a battle with the Mahārājā and killed his son Jenamani. Out of rage the Mahārājā burnt and conquered Ranpur. The *rājā* of Ranpur fled due to fear to the hill areas and later went to Parlakimidi. While he was reciting a *śloka* of prayer ending with '*dhruta śankha chatraḥ'* he was beheaded [in Puri]. There in the forest Nāraṇa Singh lived and worshipped goddesses. He worshipped Durgā, Mādhava and also Khiḷāmuṇḍa to whom he promised that she would be worshipped for 16 days with festivals provided he got back his kingdom. Thereafter rebellion broke out. The *rājā* could not subside it. For 18 years the kingdom was under the control of the Mahārājā. Nāraṇa Narendra, who was living in the forest area, saw one day that goddess Khiḷāmuṇḍa appeared in the form of a monkey and while jumping from one tree to another, did not reach the other tree and returned from half the way and sat on the original tree. He thought that this was something unique and he had never seen this and so this was the proper opportunity to try to get back his kingdom. He got up at once with his sword and proceeded. Seeing him, many people followed him. He cut the bars of the gate and gave the gate the name Jaya Maṅgala gate. The *rājā* left the fort and ran away and Nāraṇa Narendra became the *rājā*. He administered his subjects happily. He brought the image of Durgā from the house of Mahāpatra and worshipped her in the usual festival. Khiḷāmuṇḍa was also worshipped with great pomp. Rāmacandra Singh, son of Rai Singh Chotrai kept himself concealed under the bar tree called Benudhara and

> killed the *rājā* and himself became the *rājā*. As the regular worship of Maṇināgeśvarī throughout the year had been abandoned, there were various troubles in the kingdom and so the *rājā* was depressed. He left Upargaḍa palace. He constructed a new palace on the land of Nāḥlā Sāib to the north of Jagannātha temple. There he lived happily. To the north of the boundary wall of the temple, he got the footprints of Nārāyaṇa deity prepared and placed in a small temple.
>
> Protected by a powerful goddess from the forest, Rāmacandra had successfully overcome the unrest to establish a new continuity. He is said to have constructed a new palace near the temple of Jagannātha. Rāmacandra left the upper fort and built a new palace, thereby obviously seeking proximity and probably also direct access to the temple of Jagannātha. With Rāmacandra the chronicle finally enters the historical phase of the past, as it mentions that a cyclone brought down the blue disc on top of the temple tower in AD 1775.

The chronicle is a bit vague but it must have been Rṟmacandra's son, Sarangadhara, who replaced the deities of the temple by 'large' ones. The old deities were removed to Champāgaḍa, a small village cum fort on the southern periphery of Ranpur's territory. He also performed the car festival, *ratha Yātrā*, with three chariots; this is the first time that the chronicle explicitly mentions 'three' deities. This may indicate the installation of a 'new' Jagannātha perhaps for the first time in the shape of the Wooden God; an event which would probably also have prompted the construction of a new temple. An analysis of the present temple in terms of style seems to suggest such a connection.

Around the middle of the eighteenth century, i.e. between 1730 and 1760, Ranpur seems to have attained a structure which was further consolidated over the next two centuries. Only six kings, with relatively long periods of reign, ruled between 1780 and 1945. The making of deities and the building of temples are

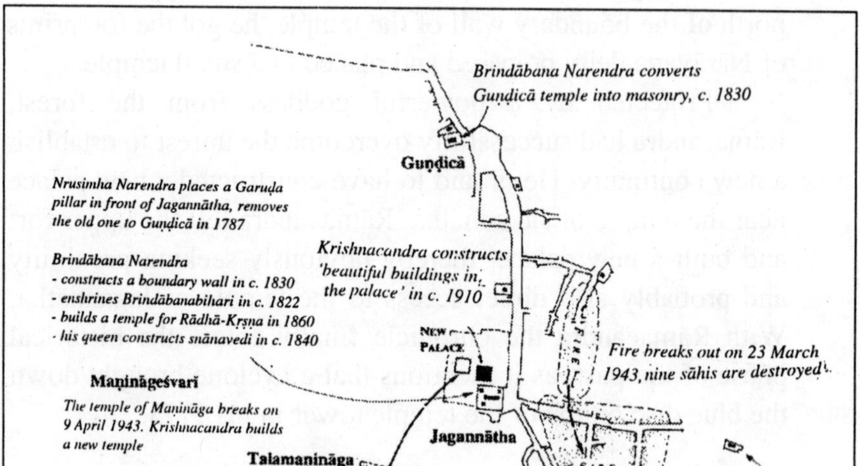
Brindābana Narendra converts
Guṇḍicā temple into masonry, c. 1830
Guṇḍicā
Nrusimha Narendra places a Garuḍa pillar in front of Jagannātha, removes the old one to Guṇḍicā in 1787
Brindābana Narendra
- constructs a boundary wall in c. 1830
- enshrines Brindābanabihari in c. 1822
- builds a temple for Rādhā-Kṛṣna in 1860
- his queen constructs snānavedi in c. 1840
Krishnacandra constructs 'beautiful buildings in the palace' in c. 1910
New Palace
Fire
Fire breaks out on 23 March 1943, nine sāhis are destroyed
Maṇināgeśvari
The temple of Maṇināga breaks on 9 April 1943. Krishnacandra builds a new temple
Jagannātha
Talamaṇināga
Fire
Brindābana Narendra constructs the temple of Talamaṇināga, c. 1830
Old Palace
Ramācandra Narendra leaves the Upargaḍa palace, constructs a new palace north of Jagannātha temple in c. 1740
Benudhara Narendra enshrined Lord Caitanya at a matha in Patarasali in c. 1860
Nrusimha Narendra orders the temples of Maṇināga Svapneśvara, Daṇḍabaluṅkeśvara and Harihareśvara to be plastered in c. 1790
Model Village
Benudhara Narendra joins two tanks to form Sagara in c. 1890
Dewān Śri Ramādeva Ratha constructs a model village in 1943
0
500
1000 m

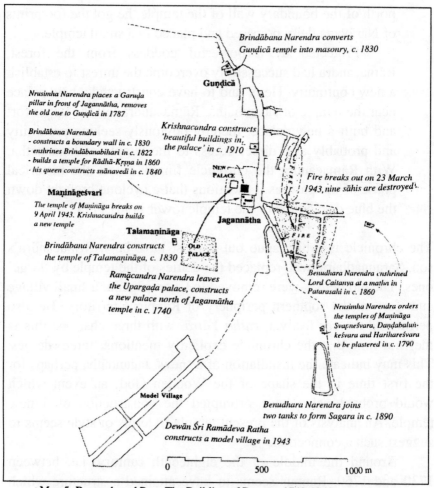

Map 5: Remembered Past. The Building of Ranpur, 1740-1943

recorded in the chronicle, but not a single incident of formative character finds any mention. The king and his imperial god had finally consolidated their roles. What was left for the chronicle was to narrate events the historicity of which has never been in doubt.

As early as 1790, the chronicle records that the walls of *śaiva* temples were plastered with lime, a preferred method of maintenance which was adopted for the temple of Jagannātha only in 1920. Around 1830, a new Guṇḍicā temple replaced an earlier temporary structure and a temple was built for Maṇināgeśvarī as well. Temples dedicated to Brindābanabihari/Kunjabihari and Rādhā-Kṛṣṇa were built within the compound of Jagannātha in *c.* 1822 and 1860 respectively. The chronicle narrates amazing details from the beginning of the nineteenth century that demonstrate the arrival in a well remembered past. For example, it mentions that roof tiles were introduced for the palace in *c.* 1870.

With King Krishnacandra, who ruled from 1899 to 1945, the chronicle recalls, came the establishment of a modern infrastructure from schools to a hospital and a court. Krishnacandra 'travelled in many countries' and 'he constructed beautiful buildings in the palace'. It is not, however, mentioned when at the beginning of the twentieth century was the new palace built so as to reflect Anglo-Indian traditions with entirely new values of interior space and an external demonstration of power.

Needless to say, building activities figure less in the chronicle. Wars with neighbouring Nayagarh (*c.* 1790 and 1830), rebellions (1893) and the murder of the British political agent in 1939 in Ranpur, however, are covered extensively.

The chronicle reads as follows:

> This *rājā* [probably Sarangadhara and not Rāmacandra] was very much devoted to the Vaiṣṇava religion and he prepared the idols of the deities three and half cubit high with four hands and enshrined him in the big temple. He removed the deity who had been there to Champāgaḍa. He prepared three chariots and performed *ratha Yātrā* with pomp and grandeur.

He [king Nrusimha] did the lime plastering of the temple of Maṇināgeśvarī, Svapneśvara, Daṇḍabaluṅkeśvara and Harihareśvara and was happy. He prepared a Gāruḍa pillar and placed it in front of Lord Jagannātha. He removed the old one and placed it in front of the Guṇḍicā house. As the image of Maṇināgeśvarī Durgā had been perforated due to thunderbolt, he had a new image prepared and enshrined it. It was prepared by Trilocana Mahāpatra. He also had the image of Kunjabihari prepared, which was also enshrined. That god was kept carefully in the store room of the *rājā* [in AD 1798]. Then he got the Gaṇeśa image prepared and on its back a stanza in Sanskrit was carved [in AD 1789]. Then he got prepared the images of Śrī Rāma, Sītā and Lakṣmaṇa. The image of Hanumān was prepared of metal and the images of Govinda and Śrī Caitanya out of wood.

He [king Brindabana] converted the Guṇḍicā temple into a masonry one. He constructed the boundary wall of the big temple with bricks. He called sculptors for preparing images and engaged the *parikṣya karaṇa* to keep watch over their works. For Baladeva and Jagannātha he got their hands and feet prepared in silver. He got prepared the conch, the disc, the mace, the plough and various ornaments and enshrined Brindābanabihari deity [in AD 1822] after preparing him. He also prepared the image of the goddess [in AD 1822].

He [king Brajasundara] constructed the temple of Taḷamaṇināga. As the image was broken, he prepared a new image and enshrined it. His queen constructed a *snānavedi*. In the compound of Kunjabihari, he dug a well.

He [king Benudhara] prepared the image of Lord Caitanya and enshrined it in the *maṭha* which he constructed at Patara Sāhi. On the south side of the boundary wall, he constructed a temple and therein enshrined Kṛṣṇa and Rādhā.... As the roof of the palace was burnt, he made it masonry.... Now, please listen a new episode. Gauracandra [Dewan], like a moon appeared. If one recites the good deeds done by him, even one day will be insufficient. He constructed hospitals, post offices, jails, roads, schools,

Dakbungalows, tanks, rest houses, Dolavedi.... Two tanks were joined to assume the name Sagara.... He constructed a masonry temple for Sāna Maṇināgeśvarī.

The *rājā* [Krishnacandra] who was the best of the reputed royal family constructed a bridge over the Banhadhara river and connected with the nine forts of Ranpur. The river Ghargharā is like a waist belt of village Gopalpur. Over it also he constructed a bridge.... The *rājā* was best accomplished in all matters. He observed various festivals and ceremonies which outweighed the beauty of the heavens. The festival *pañcaḍola* was unique in the world. It was celebrated. The *candan* festival which is a panacea for all wordly worries and mishaps, the *jhamu* festival, the *snāna* festival which opens the eyes of the blind were well celebrated. The *ratha Yātrā* was celebrated and large numbers of persons used to be attracted to witness it on the road. How one, who has not seen the *daśaharā* festival will understand the grandeur with which it is celebrated. That day the *rājā* is dressed like a hero and causes fear in the hearts of the enemies. The *rājā* spent a lot for repairing the flight of stairs to the big temple and its kitchen. He constructed the Jhulana temple. His family deity is Maṇināgeśvarī whose vehicle is the lion. He prepared her moving idol for taking it out and celebrating festivals.... He also constructed beautiful buildings in the palace which appeared to be like a necklace of diamonds.... He caused the repair of the big temple by applying lime plaster as the temple was leaking. He kept the lord of the world in a happy condition thinking for the good of the world. On 23 March 1943 in the evening fire broke out from the house of Sauri Sunder's son Abhoy Charan Sahu and gutted the entire Suasia Sāhi. Just on the following day at 10.30 a.m. Haracaṇḍī Sāhi, Patra sāhi, Khatia Sāhi, Beruka Sāhi, Maṅgalacaṇḍī Sāhi, Bodhai Sāhi, Sāmukā Sāhi all burnt to ashes.... According to the plan prepared by Dewan Śrī Rāmadeva Ratha on the land from southern direction of Adabandha village towards

> Lakhapada, a model village was constructed. On 9 April 1943 the upper Maṇināgeśvarī temple broke due to thunderbolt, *rājā* Krishnacandra Singh Deo completely broke it and built a new temple.

From Imagined to Constructed and Remembered Past: Constructs or Facts

An analysis of the built environment as well as of the built structures on the basis of typological and stylistic comparisons offers an opportunity to draw a line between the imagined or constructed past and the remembered past. Such a line is certainly not very noticable and rigid but it can be identified in various contexts.

The shrine of Maṇināgeśvarī Durgā on top of Maṇināgeśvarī Parvat, its transformation into a built structure by Uḍḍhava Narendra in *c.* AD 1530 and the placement of an iconic representation of Maṇināgeśvarī within the palace by Giridhara more than a century later seem to reflect the consolidation of the cult around the *iṣṭadevatā*, the personal deity of the kings of Ranpur. With Giridhara we are transported to the remembered past perhaps for the first time. The errection of memorial stones was also initiated by Giridhara: these are the earliest tangible objects found in Ranpur. The chronicle allows us to follow the plastering of the temple at the end of the eighteenth century and its destruction by lightening in 1943. Even today Maṇināgeśvarī represents the origin and continuity of kingship.

The five protective *śaiva* temples encircling the emerging settlement were not constructed at one go, but in phases. Svapneśvara temple was built in the middle of the sixteenth century by Uḍḍhava's son. Padmanābha Narendra's son established the Candeśvara, the Giridhara Baluṅkeśvara and his son built the Harihareśvara in the centre beside the Jagannātha temple. By the beginning of the eighteenth century that plan must have been complete. The chronicle, however, never assigned protective qualities to the group of five temples; neither did it address the level of the settlement. However, importance is given to the legends that recall divine orders for their construction. We are therefore still moving along the fragile borderline that divides the constructed from the remembered past. The origin is 'constructed', while the present temples seem to have been built only in the eighteenth century if not later.

The chronicle remains vague about the establishment of the Jagannātha temple and the halls subsequently added to it. Contradictory statements even suggest the renovation of the original temple. When Uḍḍhava brought an image of Mādhava from Puri to legitimize his power in *c.* 1530, he is also said to have built 'a temple', to which the queen added a hall. The fact that the chronicle mentions the 'usual rites' and the performance of the 'twelve festivals' should be interpreted as a reference to Jagannātha in whatever form. Some 40 years later, Padmanābha is said to have added another hall and his queen, the daughter of the last Gajapati king, Mukunda Deva, added the third hall. According to the chronicle all this happened in 1579, although it must have happened twenty years earlier. Likewise, the Muslim invasion of Orissa by Kālāpāhār is dated twenty years too late.

Padmanābha, who received Mārkaṇḍeśvara Sāhi, an entire neighbourhood of Puri, as dowry, must have been a powerful ally of the Gajapati king. Such a close link with the centre of the Jagannātha cult could well have resulted in the construction of the first Jagannātha temple. If the present temple was built either by Uḍḍhava in 1530 or by Padmanābha thirty years later, it would certainly be the earliest temple of those capitals of feudatory states which had developed by the beginning of the sixteenth century.

An analysis of the temple, however, does not allow us to confirm this assumption. While Padmanābha's relation to the Gajapati king is supported by historical facts, we must assume that references to the building of temples is resorted to only to give it legitimacy. Until documents concerning the dowry are found, we must assume that the relation between Ranpur and Puri also is constructed. Perhaps some kind of 'original', earlier structure was replaced when Sarangadhara substituted the deities in the second half of the eighteenth century. The fact that the chronicle mentions the height of the new deities explicitly (three and a half cubit = *c.*

140 cm), the only measurement given, goes to suggest that it was only then that the three Wooden Gods were introduced in Ranpur to be enshrined into a new temple. An initial study of the architectural features of the temple tower (*rekha deul*) and the halls (*jagamohana* and *bhogamaṇḍapa*) confirms this assumption. The hall of dance (*naṭamandir*) in between, however, represents a recent addition that might date back to the early twentieth century. It is striking that the chronicle does not mention the construction of this missing link between the two other halls.

Perhaps the earliest occasion on which the construction of the temple could have been undertaken was possibly the 'development' of the town by Banamāli Narendra in the early eighteenth century. The chronicle mentions that a few decades later Rāmacandra built his new palace north of the Jagannātha temple – a clear statement that the temple did exist. A couple of documents dated to the 1730s, *chāmu ciṭāu*, refer to the rights relating to the Jagannātha temple at Puri were granted to Rāmacandra. This is not 'remembered' in Ranpur, but it represents the beginning of a 'documented' past.

Mention of the platform construction for the bathing ceremony (*snānavedī*) by Brajasundara in the 1830s presents another problem. The craftsmanship of the platform suggests an eighteenth rather than a nineteenth century construction. The activity reported for the early nineteenth century could well have been a repair or a renewal of the three seats on top of the platform which is where the three Wooden Gods are placed on the occasion of the bathing ritual performed in July before the chariot starts its journey. Equally precise seems to be the mention of the construction of the lower Maṇināgeśvarī temple and the replacement of a temporary Guṇḍicā structure (the abode to which the Triad travels in the month of Āśāḍha) by a permanent building – two more activities datable to the 1830s. The exquisite carving of the columns of the Guṇḍicā structure demonstrates the difficulties of dating without ample comparative material.

For the time being, the dating of architectural details should be taken to be of a provisional nature, as only extensive studies can lead to a more reliable placement of eighteenth and nineteenth century temples of Jagannātha within an extended chronology.

Despite all this we can say that the Ranpur temples belong to an early phase of temple building in those feudatory Gaḍajāta states that flourished under Khurda supremacy since the early seventeenth century. It was in fact the Pax Britannica that after AD 1803 encouraged the construction of Jagannātha temples. In 11 out of the 17 ex-Feudatory States, Jagannātha temples were built between 1850 and 1930.[5] And beside these temples, several other royal temples were constructed and dedicated to Baladeva, Raghunātha, Gopinātha or Balarāma. With the construction of temples the palaces were also redefined. Originally constructed on hilltops, these residential quarters were built by the *rājās* near the temple in the eighteenth century, and these were in most cases (as also in Ranpur) replaced by palatial buildings in the early twentieth century. These were located in such a way so as to provide direct connection between the compounds of temple and palace.

Context

Damodar's chronicle is preserved by his son Rādhākṛṣṇa, who was adopted by his brother Gopināth and this chronicle has been copied by his nephew Durgācaraṇa, son of his younger brother Brajakishor (1907-67). Both Durgācaraṇa and Rādhākṛṣṇa keep adding notes to the chronicle. Various forms of the chronicle must have circulated in Ranpur for a few generations. The caretakers of the Ranpur temples are aware of the establishment of their respective temple by a certain king, certainly not dividing a constructed from a remembered past. A recent inscription on the Svapneśvara temple tells us that the temple was established by king Candraśekhara and at the Candeśvara temple a long text (see illustration) tells us that it was built by Partha Śrī Candana, the eldest son of King Padmanābha of whom the chronicle says, that 'as he thought ill of his father, he expired soon', in the year 4680 of *kaliyuga* (equal to AD 1579). Such inscriptions make sure that events that are tied to

[5] Kulke 1976, 11.

the established infrastructure of Ranpur were disseminated in the community. The chronicle has in fact not only created an image of the past but also a worldview and both of these survive.

References

Eschmann, Anncharlott, H. Kulke and G. C. Tripathi (eds.). 1978. *The Cult of Jagannath and the Regional Tradition of Orissa*, Delhi: Manohar Publishers.

Kulke, H. 1976. 'Kshatriaization and Social Change. A Study in Orissa Setting', in S. D. Pillai (ed.), *Aspects on Changing India. Studies in honour of Professor G. S. Ghurye*, Bombay: Popular Prakashan, 1-12.

Mahapatra, K. 1977. *The Jagannatha Temples in Eastern India*, Bhubaneswar: Sri Sarada Press.

Tripathi, G. C. 1978a. 'Navakalevara: The Unique Ceremony of the "birth" and "death" of the "Lord of the World", in Anncharlott Eschmann, H. Kulke and G. C. Tripathi (eds.), *The Cult of Jagannath and the Regional Tradition of Orissa*, Delhi: Manohar Publishers, 223-64.

Tripathi, G. C. 1978b. 'On the Concept of Purusottama in the Agamas', in Anncharlott Eschmann, H. Kulke and G. C. Tripathi (eds.), *The Cult of Jagannath and the Regional Tradition of Orissa*, Delhi: Manohar Publishers, 31-60.

4

Jaypur Parlakimedi Vizianagaram: The Southern Gajapatis

Georg Berkemer

I

Some years ago Aleida Assmann wrote an article about the functions of various repositories of knowledge of the past, such as books, libraries, temples and rituals as metaphors for collective processes of *Erinnerung* and *Gedächtnis*.[1] There are of course functional equivalents to others of Aleida Assmann's repositories of knowledge in South Asia. Widespread mythological tales such as the many versions of the *Rāmāyaṇa* and the complex social phenomenon of the temple, for instance, are repositories of multifaceted and contested texts.[2] In the same article,[3] Assmann talks about the temple containing memories of the heroes of the past and its role as a catalyst in the process of reproduction of the collective memory.

In India, the temple, in contrast to the book, is open to all who are willing to partake in the rituals, except for clearly defined exceptions connected with a negative quality, mostly concerning

---

[1] Assmann 1993. While both words are translated into English as 'memory', the first denotes the process of recollection in which something comes back into one's mind, and the second, more statically, means the memory as the repository of anything known.

[2] They are, as David Shulman and Gabrielle Eichinger Ferro-Luzzi have shown, multi-dimensional and polythetic. Their contexts are constructed by various social groups for whom they hold different meanings and memories (Eichinger Ferro-Luzzi 1987 and 1989, Shulman 1980). On the *Rāmāyaṇas* cf. Richman (ed.) 1991, 2000.

[3] Assmann 1993, 14-6. In the same chapter she also writes about the library as an institution for the reproduction of the collective memory. This again does not exist in India in the same way as it does in the West.

impurity. The temple, therefore, is for all except those excluded by definition, whereas the book is for nobody except those included by definition. But the Indian temple is not just a symbol of the universe. It does not contain the whole universe in the way the total book does. It rather represents its centre: the temple is Mount Meru, Kailāśa or Vaikuṇṭha. In its symbolic landscape all the surroundings are laden with meaning: a forest is Vṛndāvana, a tank is the river Gaṅgā.

Thus, Jagannātha is the paradigmatic 'Lord of the Universe'. His temple forms the centre of the world and all its surroundings can be related to this centre, as it is symbolically represented in the *Paṭa Citra* paintings of Puri.[4] But the realm of Jagannātha in these pictures does not extend all the way to the boundaries of the universe, on the contrary, the boundaries of the universe are shrunk to fit the realm of Jagannātha. Pictorial representations as well as myths and the devotees' social actions define a space which is seen through a convex mirror, as it were, in which the centre is enlarged in size and the edges are reduced accordingly.

While dealing with the Khurda rāja of the eighteenth century, Akio Tanabe has shown that in this ritual universe the king can be virtually without power. His role as 'sacrificer legitimizing and authorizing the entitlements in the sacrificial local community' is that of the institution which brings together the realm of the state deity and that of the local, often very inhomogeneous communities.[5]

In this ritual universe, where conflicting claims do not lead to fundamental contradictions, it is quite possible that several kings simultaneously claim to be the ruler of the world, the *cakravatī* or *mahārājādhirāja*, who has conquered all four quarters of the universe. Their rituals are performed in the respective centres of their kingdom, and the lack of border rituals makes their claims contested, but not exclusive statements. These statements are encoded in various 'texts' such as inscriptional *praśasti*s, rituals of

[4] Cf. the *Paṭa Citras*, in which the whole world is depicted from the point of view of the temple. Its sanctum is the centre of the image, surrounded by widening circles of diminishing sanctity (Schmid 2001).

[5] Tanabe 2000, 11.

temple patronage, land grants, political marriages, military campaigns, court literature, etc. These activities produce or reproduce narratives and narrative abbreviatures[6] in the form of myths, *caritams*, oral literature, temple art, symbolic artifacts, royal titles and many other forms of remembering that are functional equivalents to the repositories of knowledge which Aleida Assmann discusses in the context of pre-modern Europe.

The following passages discuss an example of such a narrative abbreviature and repository historical and ritual knowledge, the title of the Gajapati or ruler of Orissa. Gajapati can be seen both as the symbol of highest rank on earth or as one of the various rivalling claims to universal sovereignty, depending on one's point of view. For those within the realm of Jagannātha and the empire of Orissa, it clearly denotes the most exalted state of royalty: from within the realm of the Gajapati, it implies the claim to world rulership. For others looking at it in the context of other claims to imperial rulership, this is a regional title without the legitimatory force of one's own imperial title. And within the context of modern South Asian studies, the holder of that title is just one among other great medieval kings, equal in rank for instance with the *narapati* and the *aśvapati*.[7]

---

[6] The term 'narrative abbreviature' (*Narrative Abbreviatur* in German) has been coined to my knowledge by Jörn Rüsen who used it in discussions on the theoretical issues of historical thinking and the question as to how historical processes and their narrations are related (Rüsen 1982, 1990). I do not think that there exists an explicit definition of the term, but it is clear that its function is to describe that peculiar way of 'telling a story without telling it' which is frequently used to evoke memories of past events when all participants in the communication already know the details. In India, the words 'partition' and '1947' are sure to tap sources of common knowledge in the same way as a formula like '14/18' in Europe as a narrative abbreviature for the history of the First World War. A statue, a song, a flag and other material and immaterial objects can also function as such abbreviatures. Narrative abbreviatures are by themselves repositories of knowledge in their most reduced form.

[7] The title of '*narapati*' (Lord of Men) is traditionally attributed to the Kākaṭīya kings of Warangal, who are also called *gaṇapati*s (lords of the multitudes or troops), and later to the kings of Vijayanagar. The *aśvapati* (Lord of Horses) was the Muslim king of Delhi. In the Mackenzie Collection, the trinity of titles occurs for instance in the Gajapati *Vṛttāṃtamu*, where the king of Voḍḍa is the

II

One subregion of Orissa as a cultural region is the southern part around Mount Mahendra. It is characterized by its bilingual population in the plains who speak Oriya and Telugu, and a large tribal population in the hills of the Eastern Ghats. This region was known as 'Madhyama Kaliṅga' during the Orissan empire and governed by its own viceroy called the *kaliṅgaparīkṣa.* In British times it was the northernmost of the five northern provinces or Northern Circars of the Madras Presidency.

The main corpus of historical material which can be used to discuss the techniques of remembering and legitimation in the various contexts in which the title 'Gajapati' is used in southern Orissa is the Mackenzie Collection. This is unique in the context of Orissan studies, because this southern area belonged to the Madras Presidency of British India, from whose districts Col. Colin Mackenzie assembled a large collection of artefacts, maps and texts.[8] In these texts, the history of the area from the sixteenth to the end of the eighteenth century is often used to explain why the kings of the region claim certain rights and privileges in the texts written and collected in early British times. It can be demonstrated that the rivalling claims in the Mackenzie documents are based on the interrelationship of the dominant regional families of Kaliṅga who tried one after the other to gain the hegemony in the region. There are three of them who used the title 'Gajapati': the Bāhubalendras,

---

Gajapati, the king of Vijayanagara the Narapati and the Sultān of Delhi the Aśvapati. The titles themselves are of course much older. *Aśvapati* already occurs in *Ṛgveda* 8.21.3 as an epithet of Indra, and in the *Mahābharata* (Vana Parvan, Ādi Parvan). The Maukhari dynasty claimed descent from Aśvapati of the *Mahābhārata* and both *narapati* and Gajapati are names of two of the four mythical kings of Jambu-dvīpa. There is also a card game (*krīḍāpātraṃ*) in which the twelve different suits of cards are named after their highest numbers, which are *aśvapati*, *gajapati*, *narapati*, etc. This game is described by Abū al-Fadl ʿAllāmī 1989, 318.

[8] For various aspects of Mackenzie's work pertaining to the north of the Madras Presidency cf. Basu, Joshi, Srinivasachari 1952, Chandrasekharan 1952/58, Cotton, Charpentier, Johnston 1992, Dirks 1993, 1994, Hill 1834/5, Mackenzie 1952, Mahalingam 1972/6, Subrahmanian 1953-7, Wilson 1882.

the Pūsapāṭis and the kings of Parlakimedi. For the fourth family, the kings of Jaypur, who also had a close relationship with the imperial centre of the Orissan empire, no evidence of the use of the title 'Gajapati' itself could be found so far, but they used related symbols of sovereignty.

From 1568, the year of the downfall of the Sūryavaṃśi empire after the death of Teliṅga Mukundadeva, the last imperial ruler of the Orissan empire, members of Mukundadeva's family were the first southern kings who attempted to regain the status of the hegemonial rulers. This family, which S.N. Rajguru calls the 'Cāḷukyas of Mācamāra' or the 'Bāhubalendras' were the dominating regional force at the end of the sixteenth century up to 1604.[9] They trace their descent from the Cōḷa King Kulottuṅga I. Between 1571 and 1604 they tried to instigate the Golkonda Sultāns to conquer Puri and to establish one of them as the patron of Jagannātha. These campaigns had to be abandoned as the Mughal army under the command of Mānasiṃha (Mansingh) marched south from Bengal and occupied the centre of Orissa in 1590. Now any move further to the north would have meant war with the Mughal empire, and it seems that the Golconda Sultān did not dare to risk such a reaction from the central power of the time.[10]

During the next century, this Cāḷukya family lost most of their material resources and had to move from their former *jāgirs* near Anakāpalli to the north where they were granted land by the king of Parlakimedi at the village of Mācamāra. This decline of the Cāḷukyas of Mācamāra caused a power vacuum among the local kings, since there was nobody left with enough material resources to rule under Golconda as the undisputed great king within the traditional power pyramid of Kaliṅga. The other source of traditional power, the patronage over the temple of Puri as a symbol of pan-Orissa sovereignty, was outside their reach as well.

It is significant that the line of the Parlakimedi kings can be traced back to exactly the time when the Bāhublendras had to seek shelter under their overlordship. We can assume that they started to

---

[9] Rajaguru 1972, 100, 130.

[10] Berkemer 1993, 216-29.

use the title Gajapati from that time onwards,[11] but it was not the Parlakimedi king who became the most powerful Hindu ruler of the region in the seventeenth century. Rather it was the kingdom of Jaypur which filled the power gap after the fall of the Bāhubalendras.[12] They controlled the routes through the Eastern Ghats and also most of coastal Kaliṅga in the name of the Golconda Sultāns, whose control over this remote province was never very firm. The kings of Jaypur claimed to be great kings not because they were the descendants of the old imperial kings in the way the Bāhubalendras did, but because of a successful power struggle with the Sūryavaṃśa Gajapatis. In 1479, it is said, Puruṣottama Gajapati came back from his successful campaign against the ruler of Kāñcī. He marched through the jungles of Jaypur, and the king of this jungle kingdom took the opportunity to steal the golden image of his overlord's state deity, the Kanaka Durgā. Thus he came into possession of the legal right to call himself Gajapati.[13]

The Jaypur kings remained in this dominant position until they gradually lost most of their possessions in the plains and also the support of the Golkonda Sultāns to the family of the Pūsapāṭis. This family was granted a military fiefdom in Kaliṅga by the Golkonda Sultān in 1652 and grew gradually more powerful over the next 100 years. By 1760, no one between the Mahandragiri and Rājāmadri, except the Rājā of Parlakimedi, the last remaining of the old southern Gajapatis, could challenge them any more. After the victory over Parlakimedi in the 1760s, the Pūsapāṭis took the imperial title to their names. In 1794 King Pūsapāṭi Vijarāma Rāju II started a war against the British East India Company, mainly over matters of status, and lost his life.[14] This is also the end of the history of the title in the south of the old Orissan empire. From then

[11] S.N. Rajaguru does not use this argument to explain the contradictory claims in his writings that the Parlakimedi Rājās were *both* of Gaṅga and Gajapati origin. If we assume they were traditionally acknowledged as Gaṅgas, the submission of the Bāhubalendras would have made them the 'heirs' of the Gajapati title.

[12] The history of this kingdom has been described in Schnepel 1997.

[13] Schnepel 1997, 141-4.

[14] Dattatreya Sarma 1983, 45-49.

on, even though the title remained as an epithet in the titulature of the Parlakimedi and Pūsapāṭi kings, the rank of the 'true' Gajapati was safe and unchallenged in the possession of the Rājā of Khurda.

III

There are various texts in the Mackenzie Collection which refer to the title 'Gajapati'. It features in those texts together with other symbols of royalty and paramount rulership, such as the statue of the already mentioned state deity (Kanaka Durgā), privileged access to the temple of Jagannātha in Puri, legends of Rajput origin, etc. As the Mackenzie Collection was put together only in the first two decades of the nineteenth century, the title does not denote any actual imperial rulership, as it was originally intended to do. Thus, the title itself in this context is a narrative abbreviature and can be seen as a short form of a repository of knowledge in Aleida Assmann's sense.

Our texts will show that titles have different values in different contexts. Since most of the texts were collected by the former Orissa Project (1971-5), it is not surprising that they refer to past events which took place within the former realm of the imperial Gajapati, out of whose former power pyramid the protagonists of the texts derive their claims to rulership. Since the title is exclusive and of special value only in the context of the Orissan empire, this may be not the only reason why only historical narratives from within the territory of the former empire make up this corpus of legitimatory texts. Legitimation makes sense only if there is a context in which the claims can be understood and interpreted, regardless of the positive or negative answers that it evokes. Those who claim the title always narrate stories from an insider's point of view for other insiders who already know the stories or at least their context and can react with their own narratives accordingly. This type of historical narration for insiders which works by evoking already known events and never refers to contexts may be called endo-historical.[15]

[15] Berkemer 2001.

For outsiders, other contextual levels may be more appropriate and may span over religious festivals and the foundation of temples and villages to diplomacy or the use of brute force. For addressees from outside the imperial power pyramid and its politico-ritualistic structure, such ritual acts and royal titles of other semiotic structures are easier to interpret, e.g. symbols and titles which have been taken away by force from their previous bearers and epithets which reflect military achievements.[16]

As long as the imperial context existed, it was easy to keep the title within the centre of the realm itself. I do not know any text from before the fall of the Orissan empire in 1568 which claims the title 'Gajapati' for anybody except the great king himself. Later, narrations come up in which it is 'taken away' from its previous holder. The following texts from the Mackenzie Collection narrate episodes in which the title plays a role: two short genealogies of the Parlakimedi Rājās,[17] the *Tekkali Zamindar*, the *Bārabāṭi Vīrakṛṣṇadev*, the *Kaifiyat of Gajapati Kings*, the *Langulesvara Itihasa* and the *Gajapati Vṛttāṃtamu*.[18] Besides these, local variations of the *Kāñcī-Kāverī* legend and some inscriptional evidence have to be taken into account. The following paragraphs describe the texts in more detail.

Two Short Genealogies of the Parlakimedi Rājās

Both the *Account of Gajapati Kings of Kimidi* and the *History of the Rulers of Kimidi* are texts that are almost identical one-page statements which relate to the beginning of the royal line of the Khemundi *rājya*s (*c*. 1604). They contain nothing but the names of the first three generations of kings. The texts are important insofar

---

[16]For example, the titles *navakōṭi, Karṇaṭeśvara, Gauḍeśvara* or *Gulbargeśvara* which commemorate victories of the Sūryavaṃśa Gajapatis in Bengal and Andhra, where the title 'Gajapati' is of lesser importance, are found accordingly in the border provinces of the empire (Subrahmanyam 1986).

[17] *Account of Gajapati Kings of Kimidi*; *History of the Rulers of Kimidi*.

[18] This text is not a part of the old Orissa Project Collection, no English translation is available.

as they state matter-of-factly the 'genealogy of the Gajapatis' and mention that Gajapati Jagannāthadeva ruled 'Jagannātha country'.

It is interesting to note that the Parlakimedi records of the Mackenzie Collection start with the time when the Bāhubalendras, the relatives of the last imperial king Mukunda Bāhubalendra of Teliṅgana (r. 1560-8), were on the decline, i.e. from about the beginning of the seventeenth century.

Tekkali Zamindar

This text mentions twice the Mahārāja of Parlakimedi as Gajapati. Right at the beginning he grants the Bommali and Tekkali *taluks* to two brothers, and later the overlord of the Rājā of Tekkali at Parlakimedi is again mentioned as the Gajapati. The context is that of the typical relationship between the great and the little king: marriage, matters of succession and titles.[19] In the latter part of the text, Tekkali gets involved in the war between Parlakimedi and the Pūsapāṭis of Vizianagaram. The Tekkali Rājā took the side of Pūsapāṭi Vijayarāma Rāju (1760-94) against Jagannātha Nārāyaṇa Deva of Parlakimedi (1729-71). From that time on, the text never mentions the title 'Gajapati' again.[20]

Bārabāṭi Vīrakṛṣṇadev

The most complex of the manuscripts mentioned in the Mackenzie Collection is the *Bārabāṭi Vīrakṛṣṇadev*. The text is 'an account of Sri Vīrakṛṣṇadeva Gajapati who was reigning the country of Odradesa (Orissa) from Barabati Kataka and Khurda-Rathipur' (p. 1). While in most cases the Mackenzie Manuscripts tell their histories from the point of view of a single ruling family and narrate their relations with the great king, their neighbours, their temple endowments and agrahāras, as well as their relations with the British, this text looks at the power pyramid from a great king's

---

[19] Tekkali Zamindar, 1, 6, 7, 10, 13.

[20] Ibid., 20.

point of view.[21] The text begins with a history of the Gajapati dynasty. The main figure of the text, King Vīrakṛṣṇadeva Gajapati is the ruler of the fort Bārabāṭi at Cuttack.[22] He lives there with his four sons and two sons-in-law. One major topic of the text are the various claims of his sons and sons-in-law to the imperial title even before Vīrakṛṣṇa's death. All but the youngest and illegitimate son try to get hold of one symbol of rulership either by force, intrigue or theft. In the end, in a scene not dissimilar to the one known from the Mādaḷā Pāñjī where Puruṣottama Gajapati (r. 1465-97) is chosen by Jagannātha as the successor of Kapilendra,[23] it is the youngest son who inherits the throne. All the other male members of the family go to the south of the empire where they become the founders of important southern little kingdoms. The text mentions Jaypur, Parlakimedi and Chinna Kimedi as the kingdoms of the three 'legitimate' sons of Vīrakṛṣṇa, and Poṭnūru and Bhogapuram/Vizianagaram for the sons-in-law. The brothers, descendants of an Oriya king who had 'maintained all the royal paraphernalia which were in vogue in the family of the Gajapati'[24] are the founders of kingdoms in the Oriya speaking part of the south. Their Telugu-speaking in-laws, the descendants of Teliṅga Mukundadeva of the Bāhubalendra family, and Pūsapāṭi Vasavarāja had been given estates already during the lifetime of Vīrakṛṣṇadev. In this way, the text uses the most intimate of all possible metaphors to describe the relations between the southern kingdoms of Parlakimedi, Jaypur and Vizianagaram and the complex pattern of kinship relations. At the same time the text claims the supremacy of the king of Cuttack/Khurda over all of them. Despite various attempts to gain the title and country against the will of Jagannātha and Vīrakṛṣṇadev, the royal insignia stayed with the youngest

---

[21] I have discussed some aspects of this text in more detail elsewhere (Berkemer 1993, 272-84).

[22] His family is also known by the title '*Miryālavāru*' and he is a descendent of an Oriya-rāja to whom the text attributes the title '*Viśvambhara*'. The sons of this Viśvaṃbhara are Viśvambhara (II), Bālakṛṣṇa and Narahari.

[23] *Kaṭakarājavaṃśāvali*, ch. 62.

[24] *Bārabāṭi Vīrakṛṣṇadev*, 7.

'illegitimate' son, the favourite of Jagannātha, at the centre of the realm.

In a final twist the text tells us at the end that 'the Gajapati king was not an intelligent person', so he was not able to hold his capital Katakapuri against the attacking Mussalmans and thus lost his kingdom. By continuing 'but the children of Vasavarājā were very powerful', the text implies that the Pūsapāṭis became the de facto Gajapatis due to their military strength and crafty diplomacy. Vasavarājā starts by murdering his brother-in-law Mukundadeva of Poṭnūru. The rest of the text is devoted to the ascent of the Pūsapāṭis before the time of *Bobbili yuddhamu* (1758).[25]

Kaifiyat of Gajapati Kings

While in the *Bārabāṭi Vīrakṛṣṇadev* the Pūsapāṭi family is clearly the lowest in rank and the meanest in its use of theft and intrigue, the *Kaifiyat of Gajapati Kings* gives us a completely different picture. Contrary to what the title suggests, the text, in fact, is a history of the Pūsapāṭi family. This text is curiously subtitled 'An account of the Gajapatis of Odra country: After the third stage'.[26] The text begins with a 'diplomatic' affair outside of the traditional realm of the Gajapati. Herein the Rājā of Peddāpuram, Vatsarāi Rāyaparāja and Pūsapāṭi Vijayarāma Rāju I of Vizianagaram (r. 1717-58) both wish to be given the title of '*jagatpati*' (Lord of the World) from the Nizam of Hyderabad (here referred to as the 'Nawab of Golkundā'). After some negotiations, the Peddapuram ruler wins the said title while the Pūsapāṭi has to be content with the lesser title of Gajapati. On hearing this, Vijayarāma Rāju applies for a revision, but the Nizam's 'order was unalterable and no rectification was possible, as that was as stable as a stone inscription'.[27] The main part of the text then narrates the story of

[25] The text mentions at the end the establishment of the Bobbili *zamindari*, but ends shortly before the war itself with the construction of the Bobbili fort by Raṅga Rao, the tragic hero of the Bobbili war.

[26] This line is not included in my Telugu text, but is to be found only in Rajaguru's translation

[27] *Kaifiyat of* Gajapati *Kings*, p. 2 of Rajaguru's translation.

Bobbili yuddhamu which is of no consequence here except that it is noteworthy that the text never uses the title 'Gajapati' again between the introductory part and the victory over Bobbili. The first king who was to use the title was Pūsapāṭi Ānanda Rāju II alias Ānanda Gajapati (1758-60 or 63), from whence the title is routinely attached to the name of every king of the Pūsapāṭi family till the present day. It is this king who started the war against Parlakimedi in which the Pūsapāṭis for the first time became directly involved in the affairs of the districts adjacent to the Orissan Mogulbandi. The Pūsapāṭis used the title Gajapati only after they had achieved two important successes: (1) after their victory over Bobbili in 1758 (and in another context: over the French in the battles of Rājāmandri and Masulipatnam, 1758 and 1759) they had won the hegemony over Kaliṅga and were virtually independent rulers and (2) after their successful campaign against Parlakimedi 1760 when they had defeated Gajapati Jagannātha Nārāyaṇa Deva of Parlakimedi. Only then, it seems, they felt themselves qualified to use the title.

Langulesvara Itihasa

The rise of the Pūsapāṭis of Vizianagaram as the dominant military power in the Northern Circars in the eighteenth century is also represented in *Langulesvara Itihasa*, a history of the three Kimedi estates. The text mentions frequently that the rulers and the people of the Kimedi area turned to the Rājā of Parlakimedi for arbitration of dispute.[28] According to the text, this function was appropriated by the *Faujdars* of the Chikakole province in the middle of the eighteenth century. The text mentions the Golconda *Faujdar* for the first time in the year 1742, when Nizam-ul-Mulk Mir Qumuruddin Khan Āsaf Jah I (1671-1748) appointed Jaffar Ali Khan as Faujdar of Chikakole.[29] The next two decades are said to have been times of turmoil: The Rājā of Parlakimedi, Jagannātha Nārāyaṇadeva, tried to regain his family's political position by waging war against the

---

[28] For example *Langulesvara Itihasa*, 64.

[29] Ibid., 77.

provincial authorities; the Carnatic wars brought French and English troops into the country, and the Rājā of Vizianagaram, Pūsapāṭi Vijayarāma Rāju I, ensured that his family was the one which influenced most the politics in the region. All this is told without referring to the title 'Gajapati', even though other symbols of royalty can be found in the text. The most plausible explanation for this could be that the writers of the text[30] grudgingly acceded supremacy to the Pūsapāṭis after their victory over the former Gajapati, the king of Parlakimedi. Instead, the text introduces the name of a lady called Gaṅgā and the dynasty named after her in order to outline the rank and age of the Kimedi ruling families. This is done in a poetical style closer to a Purāṇa or Māhātmya than to a typical Mackenzie Kaifiyat, and the names mentioned in the text suggest that the writers had known the Mādaḷā Pāñjī of Puri. The text also contains legendary themes such as the immigration of the Gaṅgas from Kolahalapura which is mentioned in the *praśasti* of the Gāṅga copper plate inscriptions as early as Coḍagaṅga Anantavarma (r. 1077-1142). All this may have been used in this Mackenzie text to prove that despite the lost war against the Pūsapāṭis, the Kimedi Rājās were still more refined, older than, and superior in rank to, the upstart dynasty of Vizianagaram.[31]

It becomes clear from this that even though the present paper concentrates on the title Gajapati, the said title is only a fragment in a multi-dimensional network of challenges and responses in which various elements can be used to make one's point.

Gajapati Vṛttāṃtamu

Despite its title, the main characters in this text are not the kings of Orissa, but the Reḍḍis of Rājāmandri. Here, as in other instances already mentioned, the title is taken over by former enemies/little kings of the Orissan rulers. When the Reḍḍis of Koṇḍavīḍu,

---

[30] The text has two parts which tell the histories of Pedda Kimedii and Cinna Kimedi respectively.

[31] For instance in a context were Pūsapāṭi Vijayarāma Rāju decides the successorship of Chinna Kimedi in the way of a great king (ibid., 31).

formerly little kings under the Gaṅgas, conquered the southern part of the Gaṅga empire during the rules of Narasiṃha IV (1378-1414) and Bhānudeva IV (1414-34), the foundation for the claim for the title was laid. Shortly afterwards, two historical events followed which made it possible for the Reḍḍis to assume the title: first the foundation of a minor branch of the family in Rājāmandri (*c.* 1430) and the conquest of Koṇḍavīḍu by Vijayanagar (*c.* 1450), and second the end of the Gaṅga empire in 1434. Historically, this newly found independence should have been a very short episode because Kapilendra and his son Hamvīra conquered the Koṇḍavīḍu province around 1450/60, but the memory of the victories against the Gaṅgas seems to have been still fresh around 1800 when the text was written.[32]

In the *Gajapati Vṛttāṃtamu* we also encounter the already mentioned 'division of the earth' between the ruler of the north, the *aśvapati* who is a Turuṣka (Muslim), the ruler of the west, the *narapati*, the kings of Vijayanagara, and among them most prominently Kṛṣṇadevarāya, and the ruler of the east, the Gajapati. In this context, the name of Hamvīra, the eldest son of Kapilendra and viceroy of the south, is mentioned.

The Kāñcī-Kāverī Legend

This popular legend was used by at least two of the families mentioned (Jaypur and Parlakimedi) to claim a right to the highest rank of traditional kingship in the region.[33] Winning an actual or propagandistic war against the holder of the title and/or stealing the

---

[32] The text has not been edited or translated and the extant copy is very corrupt. Even though the text needs to be analysed more thoroughly, it is clear that except for the title Gajapati itself, no further connection with Orissa is mentioned.

[33] Schnepel 1997, 141-3; Berkemer 1993, 202-8; cf. also Mohapatra 1996; Mukherjee 1946; Subrahmanyam 1950. The originally tribal goddess Maṇikeśvarī is very popular in parts of central and south Orissa where her cult unites the local people and their little kings. The royal legend (e.g. *Kaṭakarāja-vaṃśāvali* ch. 64) connects the goddess with Jagannātha and thus with the highest layer of royalty in Orissa. Recent research in Keonjhar indicates a wider distribution than previously assumed.

symbol of imperial rulership in combination with marriage relations with the overlord might very well have been a strong legitimation to claim the highest rank after the downfall of the empire. One has therefore to look for hints and hidden symbolisms in the Mackenzie texts as well as in oral traditions to see how widespread the network of rivalling versions of this legend was between the sixteenth and the eighteenth centuries.[34]

Inscriptions

The title Gajapati was attributed to the kings of the Orissan empire from the beginning of the Gaṅga rule. But it seems that the title was not used systematically for legitimatory purposes. N. Mukunda Rao mentions several inscriptions in which titles such as *gajādhīśa* and *kuñjarādhīśvara* are used from the time of Coḍagaṅga Anantavarman (1077-1142).[35] At the temple of Siṃhācalam King Narasiṃha I (1238-1264), the Gaṅga king who not only built Konarak but also had Siṃhācalam thoroughly renovated, is shown mounted on an elephant as well as on a horse. Thus, he is both Gajapati and *aśvapati* according to Siṃhācalam iconography.[36] According to M. Krishna Kumari he was also the first Gaṅga king to explicitly use the title 'Gajapati' in an inscription,[37] but in the main Gaṅga inscriptional 'archive' of Siṃhācalam the title is mentioned only from the fourteenth century onwards. The title

---

[34] There are for instance two unpublished Telugu manuscripts of the sixteenth and eighteenth centuries mentioned in secondary literature as associated with the Pūsapāṭi family (Dattatreya Sarma 1983, 35; ibid., 1985, 5). The *Kṛṣṇavijayamu* and the *Uṣābhyudayamu* refer to a king named Tammi Rāju who is said to have won a battle against the king of Orissa near Nandapur and thus 'conquered' the title Gajapati. Narrative plot and location are identical with the Kanaka Durgā story of the Jaypur kings.

[35] Mukunda Rao 1991, 91-2.

[36] Krishna Kumari 1994, 109.

[37] Ibid. This is the second of Narasiṃha's Kapilas-inscriptions which are engraved on a stone vase, originally an adornment of a temple at Kapilas, Dhenkanal District, Orissa. In line 4 of the text occurs the title '[Gaja]tti' which seems to be intended to mean 'Gajapti', the Oriya form of Gajapati (cf. the Kapilas Inscriptions of Narasimhadeva, Sircar 1959).

appears in the time of Gaṅga Narasiṃha IV (1378-1414).[38] His successor Bhānudeva IV (1414-34) used the title from his first inscription onwards. Unfortunately, Siṃhācalam inscriptions from after 1600 are not published so that we cannot verify whether the title was used thereafter. During the reign of the Sūryavaṃśa Gajapatis (1434-1568) the title occurs in both temple and copper plate inscriptions at various places.[39] After the end of the Orissan empire, Gajapati Narasiṃha (d. 1590) of the Bāhubalendra family used the title in an inscription near Khallikota dated AD 1590. This text was actually issued in the name of his overlord, Muhammad Quli Qutbshah. In the nineteenth century Vijayarāma Gajapati Rāju of the Pūsapāṭi family[40] had a *praśasti* inscribed at Śrīkūrmam in which he not only claims to be the Gajapati, but also holds besides the title 'Gajapati' the British title 'His Highness' and the Muslim title 'Manya Sultān'.

IV

The texts discussed above give us an insight not only into the way in which a royal title is claimed and used by a group of rival little kings after the downfall of an empire. They also mention other symbols, titles and rituals that provide a view of the network of status claims in which the use of the title 'Gajapati' is one of the many symbols of royalty. The texts also make it evident that the use of this title goes beyond mere claims of status and power. Can we say that the imperial power pyramid still exists in the latter half of the eighteenth century when most of the texts were written, even though there is no paramount sovereign now? The political and ritual structures on which these texts are based seem to be more or less intact, or at least to be remembered very vividly by the

---

38 Inscription of Peda Narasiṃhyadevarājulu, dated Śaka 1305 (*South Indian Inscriptions* 6, No. 752; Mukunda Rao 1987, 87-8).

39 Subrahmanyam 1986.

40 This is either Vijayarāma Rāju III (r. 1845-79) or Vijayarāma Rāju IV (r. 1897-1922).

protagonists.[41] The Gajapati as the first servant of Jagannātha is a ritualistic figure at the head of the 'sacrificer state'[42] and thus, transcending person and office of the king, he is a part of the deep structure of the regional tradition of Orissa. The context in which the title of the Gajapati of Orissa is meaningful shows that, even after the empire, the traditional power pyramid of the no longer extant overlord of Orissa remains at least partially functional as a phenomenon of slow-flowing structural changes behind historical facts.

In the context of these narrations the title 'Gajapati' is perhaps the shortest 'text' among the well known symbols of royalty, such as royal patronage over local temples and the role of the first devotee in the cults of the great deities in Puri and Siṃhācalam, the usage of one's own era (*aṅka*), titles of Cāḷukya and Sūryavaṃśa origin, claims of Gaṅga or Rājput descent, etc. The title 'Gajapati' can be taken as a narrative abbreviature and thus contains the whole traditional discourse outlined in this paper. For the little kings who claim the title as their own it functions as a repository of knowledge. But it has to be explained to others from outside, especially to the officers of the British East India Company and the envoys of Colin Mackenzie.

41 Cf. Frenz 2000, 160 for a discussion of the possibility of a regional power pyramid of little kings after the disappearance of the great king. She introduces the notion of the *virtual great king* for this situatuion.

42 Tanabe 2000.

The inheritance of Vīrakṛṣṇadeva's sons and sons-in-law according to Bārabāṭi Vīrakṛṣṇadev (p. 23-8)				
kinship relation	**capital**	**size of realm**	**name of taluks**	**remarks**
eldest brother	Jaypur	nine taluks	Pārvatipura, Sālur, Aṇḍrāi, etc."	exiled; fights for jungle kingdom no use of the title Gajapati ? Kanaka Durgā featuring prominently in legitimation myth
second brother	Khimundi	nine taluks	Meraṅgi, Kurupām, etc."	exiled
third brother Bhimadeva	"Vijayanagara in the same Khimundi" (modern Sanakhimundi)	twelve taluks		exiled
youngest son by a Sūdra concubine (*antara*-son)	capital in Kaṭaka	imperial rule, i.e. overlord over the Garhjat kingdoms		selected by Jagannātha parallel to Puruṣottama Gajapati
Mukunda Bāhubalendra, first son-in-law	Potnuru	first all of coastal Kaliṅga, later one village (Macamara)		holder of military fief killed by Pūsapāṭi Vasavarāja
Pūsapāṭi Vasavarājā, second son-in-law	Bhogapuram, later Vizianagaram	"some towns" near Potnuru, later Visakhapatnam and Srikakulam districs (16 or 18 taluks)	Khimundi, Palakonda, Saluru, Parvatipura, Makkuvapalipentha, Merangi, Kurupāmu, Aṇḍra, Oḍḍādi, Māḍagula, Golagoṇḍa, Āṭhagaḍa, Gumusara, Chikati, Mahuri, Jalantara	title stolen; holder of military fief; also overlordship over Peddapuram and Bobbili

The title's second context is the new order in which the British East India Company plays the role of the arbitrator between the contestants. But the frequent cases of armed rebellion against the EIC show that the two main contexts, the traditional network of the Orissan power pyramid and the 'one-dimensional' administrative structure of the EIC are without an interface at the level of deep structure. The claiming of traditional titles and privileges by the Orissan little kings and their generation of 'endo-historical' texts are insufficient to make themselves understood in the colonial context. The traditional strategy to make the opponents 'one's own' before being able to successfully engage with them, as demonstrated in the case of *Barabāṭi Vīrakṛṣṇadev* in which all the opponents are made into relatives, is no longer valid. The new 'total books' in the form of British law and scientific discourse replace the traditional network of texts which are meaningful only in the specific social and historical context of the sacrificer state.

References

Abū al-Fadl ʿAllāmī. 1989. *A'īn i Akbarī*. 3 volumes, English translation, by H. Blochmann, D.C. Phillott and H. S. Jarrett. Calcutta: The Asiatic Society (rpt).

Account of Gajapati *Kings of Kimidi*, copied from Mackenzie vol. 405 (fol. 60a), preserved in the Govt. Oriental Manuscripts Library, Madras, English translation by S.N. Rājāguru.

Assmann, A. 1993. 'Zur Metaphorik der Erinnerung', in A. Assmann and D. Harth (eds.), *Mnemosyne: Formen und Funktionen der kulturellen Erinnerung*. Frankfurt am Main: Fischer Taschenbuch Verlag, 13-35.

Bārabāṭi Vīrakṛṣṇadev, copied from Telugu Local Records vol. 6 (pp. 1-41), preserved in the Govt. Oriental Manuscripts Library, Madras, English translation by S.N. Rājāguru.

Basu, P., P.M. Joshi and C.S. Srinivasachari. 1952. Report on the Mackenzie Collection of Manuscripts at the Government Oriental Manuscripts Library, Madras: Indian Historical Records Commission.

Berkemer, G. 1993. *Little Kingdoms in Kaliṅga. Ideologie, Legitimation und Politik regionaler Eliten*, Stuttgart: Steiner.

Berkemer, G. 1998. 'Literatur und Geschichte im Vormodernen Hinduistischen Südasien', in J. Rüsen, M. Gottlob and M. Mittag (eds.), *Die Vielfalt der Kulturen. Erinnerung, Geschichte, Identität 4*. Frankfurt am Main: Suhrkamp, 145-90.

Berkemer, G. 2001. *Banausia and Endo-history: European Conceptions of Indian Historical Consciousness*. Kyoto: Graduate School of Asian and African Studies (ASAFAS), Kyoto University, 2001.

Chandrasekharan, T. 1952/58. *A Descriptive Catalogue of the Telugu Manuscripts (Mackenzie Local Tracts Volumes) in the Government Oriental Manuscripts Library, Madras. Vol. 1. Telugu Local Tracts Nos. 1 to 150; Vol. 2. Nos. 151 to 250*, Madras: Government Press.

Cotton, J.S., J.H.R.T. Charpentier and E.H. Johnston (eds.). 1992. *Oriental and India Office Collections: Catalogue of Manuscripts in European Languages belonging to the Library of the India Office. Volume I, Part II. The Mackenzie General and Miscellaneous Collections*, with an Introduction by David Blake, London: British Library.

Dattatreya Sarma, A.V. 1983. *Vijayanagaraṃ jillā caritra-saṃskṛti*. Vijayanagaraṃ: Mansas.

Dattatreya Sarma, A.V. 1985. *Life and Times of Mahārājā Ananda* Gajapati, Vizianagaram: Mahārājā's College.

Dirks, N.B. 1993. 'Colonial Histories and Native Informants: Biography of an Archive', in C.A. Breckenridge and P. van der Veer (eds.), *Orientalism and the Postcolonial Predicament: Perspectives on South Asia*, Philadelphia: University of Pennsylvania Press, 279-313.

Dirks, N.B. 1994. 'Guiltless Spoliations: Picturesque Beauty, Colonial Knowledge, and Colin Mackenzie's Survey of India', in C.B. Asher, T.R. Metcalf (eds.) *Perceptions of South Asia's Visual Past*, New Delhi: Oxford & IBH, 211-32.

Eichinger Ferro-Luzzi, G. 1987. *The Self-milking Cow and the Bleeding Liṅgam: Criss-cross of Motifs in Indian Temple Legends*, Wiesbaden: Harrassowitz.

Eichinger Ferro-Luzzi, G. 1989. 'The Polythetic-prototype Approach to Hinduism', in G.D. Sontheimer and H. Kulke (eds.), *Hinduism Reconsidered*. New Delhi: Manohar, 187-95.

Frenz, M. 2000. *Vom Herrscher zum Untertan. Spanungsverhältnis zwischen Lokaler Herrschaftsstruktur und der Kolonialverwaltung in Malabar zu Beginn der britischen Herrschaft (1790-1805)*, Stuttgart: Steiner.

Gajapati *Vṛttāṃtamu*, copied from Telugu Local Records vol. 50 (pp. 302-12), preserved in the Govt. Oriental Manuscripts Library, Madras.

Hill, D. 1834/5. 'Biographical Sketch of the Literary Career of the Late Colonel Colin Mackenzie, Surveyor-General of India. Comprising some particulars of his Collection of Manuscripts, Plans, Coins, Drawings, Sculptures &c. illustrative of the Antiquities, History, Geography, Laws, Institutions and Manners of the Ancient Hindūs; contained in a letter addressed by him to the Right Hon. Sir Alexander Johnston, V.P.R.A.S. &c. &c.', in *Journal of the Royal Asiatic Society of Great Britain and Ireland* 1 (1834), 333-64, 2 (1835) 262-90, 354-69.

History of the Rulers of Kimidi, copied from Telugu Local Records vol. 47 (p. 150), preserved at the Govt. Oriental Manuscripts Library, Madras, English translation by S.N. Rājāguru.

Kaifiyat of Gajapati *Kings*, copied from Telugu Local Records Vol. 6 (pp. 42-105), preserved in the Govt. Oriental Manuscripts Library, Madras, English translation by S.N. Rājāguru.

Kaṭakarājavaṃśāvaliḥ: A Traditional History of Orissa, edited by G.C. Tripathi and H. Kulke, Allahabad: Vohra, 1987.

Krishna Kumari, M. 1994. *Studies on Medieval Andhra History and Culture*. Delhi: Kanishka Publishers.

Langulesvara Itihasa, etc., copied from Telugu Local Records vol. 37 (pp. 409-98), preserved in the Govt. Oriental Manuscripts Library, Madras, English translation by S.N. Rājāguru.

Mackenzie, W.C. 1952. *Colonel Colin Mackenzie: First Surveyor-General of India*, Edinburgh, London: W. & R. Chambers Ltd.

Mahalingam, T.V. 1972/6. *Mackenzie Manuscripts: Summaries of the Historical Manuscripts in the Mackenzie Collection.* 2 vols. Madras: University of Madras.

Mohapatra, B.N. 1996. 'Ways of Belonging: The Kanchi-Kaveri Legend and the Construction of Oriya Identity', in *Studies in History,* n.s. 12 (2), 187-217.

Mukherjee, P. 1946. 'Historicity of the Kāñcī-Kāverī Tradition', in *Indian Historical Quarterly* 21, 34ff.

Mukunda Rao, N. (ed.)l 1986. *Simhāchalam Temple Inscriptions.* Simhachalam: Simhachalam Devasthanam.

Mukunda Rao, N. 1991. *Kaliṅga under the Eastern Gaṅgas. Ca. 900 A.D. to ca. 1200 A.D.*, Delhi: B.R. Publishing Corporation.

Rājāguru, S.N. 1972. *The History of the Gangas. Vol. II*, Bhubaneswar: Orissa State Museum.

Richman, P. (ed.). 1991. *Many Rṟmāyaṇas: The Diversity of a Narrative Tradition in South Asia.* Berkeley: University of California Press.

Richman P. (ed.). 2000. *Questioning Rṟmāyaṇas: A South Asian Tradition.* New Delhi: Oxford University Press.

Rüsen, J. 1882. 'Die vier Typen des historischen Erzählens', in R. Koselleck, H. Lutz ad J. Rüsen (eds.), *Formen der Geschichtsschreibung*, München: dtv, 514-603.

Rüsen, J. 1990. 'Der Teil des Ganzen. Über Historische Kategorien', in K. Acham and W. Schulze (eds.), *Teil und Ganzes*, München: dtv, 299-324.

Sahlins, M. 1983. *Islands of History*, Chicago and London: University of Chicago Press.

Schmid, A. 2001. 'Lord Jagannatha in Pictorial Representations: A Collection of Cloth Paintings (Pata Citras) from Orissa', in B. Schnepel and H. Kulke (eds.), *Jagannath Revisited: Studying Society, Religion and the State in Orissa*, New Delhi: Manohar.

Schnepel, B. 1997. *Die Dschungelkönige. Ethnohistorische Aspekte von Politik und Ritual in Südorissa / Indien*, Stuttgart: Steiner.

Seshagiri Rao, B. 1947. 'The Ganga Vamsavali of Parlakimedi', *Journal of the Kalinga Historical Research Society* 2, 250-8.

Shulman, D.D. 1980. *Tamil Temple Myths: Sacrifice and Divine Marriage in the South Indian Śaiva Tradition*, Princeton: Princeton University Press.

Sircar, D.C. 1859. 'Kapilas Inscriptions of Narasimhadeva', in *Epigraphia Indica* 33, 41-5.

Subrahmanian, T.N. (ed.) 1953-7. *South Indian Temple Inscriptions*. 3 vols. Madras: Government Press.

Subrahmanya Aiyer, K.V. (ed.). 1928. *South Indian Inscriptions. Vol. VI.* Madras: Archaeological Survey of India.

Subrahmanyam, R. 1950. 'Kāñci Kāverī Expedition of Purushottama Gajapati - Its Probable Date', in *Indian Historical Quarterly* 26, 67ff.

Subrahmanyam, R. 1986. *Inscriptions of the Suryavamsi* Gajapatis *of Orissa*. New Delhi: Indian Council of Historical Research.

Tanabe, A. 1999. 'Kingship and Caste: the Relationship between King/Dominant Caste and the Brahman Reconsidered', in Steering Committee of the Research Project Institutions, Networks and Forces of Changes in Contemporary South Asia (eds.), *Rituals as Popular Culture: Towards Historico-Anthropological Understanding of Modern Indian Society*. Tokyo: Steering Committee of the Research Project, 201-30.

Tanabe, A. 2000. *Early Modern and Colonial Transformation: Rethinking the Role of the Little King in Eighteenth and Nineteenth Century Orissa, India*, ASAFAS Special Paper no. 4, Graduate School of Asian and African Studies (ASAFAS), Kyoto University.

Tekkali Zamindar, copied from Telugu Local Records vol. 59 (pp. 144-62), preserved in the Govt. Oriental Manuscripts Library, Madras, English translation by S.N. Rājāguru.

Wilson, H.H [2]1882. *The Mackenzie Collection: A Description of the Oriental Manuscripts, and Other Articles Illustrative of the Literature, History, Statistics and the Antiquities of the South of India; collected by the late Lieut. Col. Colin Mackenzie, Surveyor General of India. To which is prefixed a brief outline of the life of Col. Mackenzie and of the steps taken to catalogue and utilize his collection*. Madras: Higginbotham & Co.

5

Anecdotes of History: Reflections on Contexts and (Hi)stories

Heiko Frese

The study of Indian Chronicles often proves to be a difficult topic of Western historical research.[1] So, apart from the question as to whether their contents can be taken as historical facts, it is not easy to decide whether the past described in – or conveyed by – chronicles should be the topic of research, or the period in which the Vaṃśāvalī-s, Kaiphiyat-s, etc., were written. What kind of impact could this double refraction, looking at (con)texts which look at other (con)texts, have on one's work? Could the insight that not only different contexts but also different qualities or kinds of contexts exist, change the historian's view on history in general?

This paper is in two rather different parts. It starts off with a short excursion to Nepal and shows how I 'came across' a number of contexts while working on documents from the nineteenth century. Then it switches to Orissa and tries to theoretically categorize and reflect what I found could be such contexts, adding an example from the Mackenzie Collection. Finally it deals with the character of a certain kind of historical sources and points to their possible connection with literary studies.

The Beyond: Nepal and its Chronicles

Between 1769 and about the end of the nineteenth century, in the Kathmandu valley quite a number of chronicles – the so-called *later chronicles* – emerged, which deal with the history of the dynasties and rulers of this place from the earliest, mythical beginnings up to their present time. In my research I focused on passages in these chronicles which deal with the famous king Jayasthitimalla, who

[1] Cf. e.g. Fleet 1895/6.

ruled in the fourteenth century, is known as the founder of a dynasty, and is supposed to have reunited the valley and reformed the social system: even several caste lists exist, some integrated into certain chronicles, some as single documents.[2]

So the first context I came across consisted of the different versions of chronicles and their 'treatment' of Jayasthitimalla. I wondered if the information given conveyed a coherent picture. It turned out that it did not. Only two versions contained a list of 64 caste names. In other manuscripts lists with 55 – completely different – Jātis could be found, whereas in most of them there was no list at all (though Jayasthitimalla was mentioned as a reformer). Also the passages devoted to Jayasthitimalla differed in length enormously. There were differences from one sentence to many pages, and so, while some manuscripts consisted only of a few pages, others consisted of several hundred folios.

Consequently I grouped the different versions according to the manner in which they mentioned the reform of castes: the first group consisted of chronicles in which Jayasthitimalla had not at all been in any way connected to a caste reform; in the second there were no lists, but Jayasthitimalla was mentioned as a caste reformer; the third group contained the list of 64 castes; and the fourth a specification of 55 castes. This classification also did justice to the varying size of the manuscripts, so that the fourth group was the one of the most elaborate versions. In addition a fifth group was found necessary, as this contained manuscripts consisting only of a caste list (ascribed to Jayasthitimalla).

Obviously these structures made a 'normal' critical analysis impossible – I had to develop other tools to deal with these texts, to define anew and restructure the intratextual context. That is why I divided the passages about Jayasthitimalla into 'contential' parts, which in each case contained one topos (an event or a group of events). This meant that although the first group (containing pure or almost pure genealogies) had to be disregarded for the time being, a kind of contential archetype nevertheless developed: a text consisting only of those parts which could be found in *every*

[2] On Nepalese chronicles and Jayasthitimalla cf. Frese 2002.

passage, i.e. the smallest possible unit which was common to all the passages concerning Jayasthitimalla. This was not, as it could seem, just a theoretical construction, because in the second group, which did not contain caste lists but mentioned Jayasthitimalla as a caste reformer, such archetypes were actually present.

My assumption was that this archetype consisting of eight elements served as a pre-text (*Vorlage*) for the more elaborate versions – simply because the similarity of the passages excluded independent authorship. A comparison of the different versions showed that the eight elements were always there, sometimes identically worded and only adorned in groups three and four with further details.

This sounded like a first hierarchy; but to give it a linear shape would have been too rash; for example, in a 'Hinduistic context', it seemed strange to find a Śloka of 64 caste names in the obviously older version, while the younger 'only' contained a specification of 55 Newar castes – because the metrical form, the language (of the names, Sanskrit) and of course the ideal number 64 would have been the more normative and pretentious way of presentation. Why actually two lists? Later it became clear that the list was a later addition, a conclusion arrived at by looking at the structure of certain manuscripts and from the fact that also external caste lists (group number five) exist.

But coming back to the eight elements and their elaborations: now it seemed necessary to change the context and leave the text for the first time. Which of the facts given in the chronicles could be dated to the fourteenth century and, also, which sources did the chroniclers use in the nineteenth century, and why did those chronicles appear only in the nineteenth century and not earlier?

To begin with, until today no source – from an extratextual context – has been detected which shows that one or more of the elaborations belong to the fourteenth century. Of course it was possible that the authors simply wrote down what had been the oral tradition before, but the more elaborate chronicles contained a number of indications, above all the language, that they belong to the nineteenth century. The later chronicles are written in Gorkhali, whereas the traditional languages of the Kathmandu valley are

Newari and Maithili; only after the conquest of the valley in the year 1769 by the Gorkhali their language, today known under the name Nepali, became relevant in documents there. That is why it seemed very unlikely that the oral tradition appeared first of all in a written translation, without being recorded in Newari before: and such a step did not exist.

So from this extratextual context I could conclude that the elaborations were interpolations of the nineteenth century, only projected on Jayasthitimalla. Also an analysis of the two caste lists showed that they could not be dated back to the fourteenth century.

A comparison, i.e. an analysis of the intratextual context, yielded no results. Of course both lists were ascribed to Jayasthitimalla, and both were supposed to be arranged hierarchically, but only few names of one list could be found in translation in the other, the rest was too different, sometimes unintelligible. But another context was at hand: a document from the seventeenth century turned out to be very revealing, where the author had tried to translate those 64 Sanskrit castes into Newari. Though the document was incomplete it could clearly be seen that the author actually had not *translated*, but *contrasted* Sanskrit and Newari names (this could also mean creating pairs which only *sounded* similar, e.g. Naṭijīva – Naḍi).

Nevertheless it could be shown that this 'translation' had been used as a pre-text (*Vorlage*) for the Newari caste list, as a number of details indicated, so that two results remained. First, already the indigenous translator from the seventeenth century had obvious difficulties in understanding the list of 64 names; second, the list of 55 names could not have been the work of Jayasthitimalla's time. Though it represented the structure of a probable society, it was not authentic enough to belong to the fourteenth century (it was an interpretation of the seventeenth century), and not representative of the nineteenth century (some important caste names were missing).

A thorough analysis of the other list – again the intratextual context – helped me to move a step further. It turned out that the list of 64 castes consisted of fragments of probably *two* lists transmitted in other texts which had been rearranged and combined. When this had happened and who had been its author is as unknown as the origin of the fragments. But it was now clear that this enumeration of 64 castes could neither have come from Jayasthitimalla's time nor represent the structure of the society of fourteenth century Nepal.

This left me with the eight elements, the contentional archetype. And it soon became clear that they too did not mirror fourteenth century reality. But to prove that, it was necessary to 'try' several contexts which had not been consulted so far. Did other sources, like architectural ones, confirm the statements of the chronicles, or did they not? What did the chronicles have to say about other rulers and their deeds? How did other chronicles present their rulers?

One example: the passage says that Jayasthitimalla had a Trimūrti erected on the bank of a river. But in a manuscript of the first group the erection of this very sculpture is ascribed to a certain Bhīmadeva. Other manuscripts do not mention this sculpture at all, and some versions of the second group talk about a Viśvadevavarma in this context. The Gopālarājavaṃśāvalī, a chronicle or bunch of chronicles from the fourteenth century,[3] says Viṣṇugupta was the donor. Last but not least, Slusser and Vajrācārya, relying on art-historical and geographical research, claim that it had indeed been Viṣṇugupta.[4]

Finally, after applying 'all those' contexts, actually nothing seems to have been left for Jayasthitimalla, at least no historical fact in terms of Western history, though another, further context will soon make clear that this was not the point. But before that I had to think about a number of inscriptions which did not mention Jayasthitimalla at all, because this, as another context outside the 'immediate' chronicles, was yet another pointer towards the disintegration of the 'famous' king. In short, it seemed that his origin, which was not clear, and local tradition played a decisive role, and the power structures of the Kathmandu valley, which at times was divided into three little kingdoms, had led to different

---

[3] Cf. Vajracharya and Malla (eds.) 1985.

[4] Slusser and Vajrācārya 1973.

traditions. Of these – in the chronicles – Jayasthitimalla's was most successful.

So I had to deal with different qualities of sources: inscriptions which do not mention Jayasthitimalla, genealogies which do mention him with first attributes ascribed to him, and then extensive descriptions of rituals and land reforms. However, the external caste lists were still missing; the lists which were required to complete a series of documents which would enhance his importance more and more. For had it not been sure in the beginning whether he would occur in the genealogies at all, in the end he served as legitimation. First the attributes confirmed him, finally he confirmed the attributes: at the end of the external lists one finds the sentence: 'These castes were made by Jayasthitimalla.' Whereas the evidence makes the ruler vanish, he is nevertheless everywhere. How can all this be explained?

As a possible answer served, of course, another context, the political situation in the eighteenth/nineteenth century. In 1769 the Kathmandu valley had been conquered by the Gorkhas, and it seemed that besides the geographical the mental space, too had been occupied by them. By uniting the past of the conquered with the present time of the conquerors in the later chronicles, the Gorkhas healed, as H. Kulke called it, the break of tradition. Here one encounters the next context, which consists of theories of a metaregional level. In Kulke's opinion, in the Hinduistic realm, conquest necessarily leads to integrative processes: 'there seemed to have been a strong, common need to heal the forced break of tradition and to link up the present time with the "not-yet-fully-destroyed" old tradition. In many societies the rise of legends and historical writing has been an appropriate method of coming to terms with the past.'[5]

A fascinating picture emerges if one looks at the different versions as a whole. Obviously conditioned by each other, the variations could not have developed in a linear series. What comes into view is an exemplary genesis of historiography, where history is not fixed and unchangeable, but in a steady flow, corresponding

[5] Kulke 1998.

to the needs of the society which produced it, interspersed with details of its present world. These details can be seen in the structure, the composition and the development of this passage, in the language. But, with the exception of the language, these elements are in no way striking, they are even more of secondary significance. One can recognize neither the efforts to hide nor to stress them. What is important is that the world still worked according to the rules of Dharma.

And this is the final, the Dharmic, context. Historical facts are of less importance, so it is no lie if Jayasthitimalla is said to have carried through reforms interspersed with details from other times. It will not be historically incorrect to say that he created a caste system of 'these 64 castes', even if the list is an unintelligible one. This is beside the point. The point which needs to be kept in mind is that Jayasthitimalla had been a ruler who acted according to the Dharma, and that had been demonstrated. It is just natural that there are data in the texts which belong to the time of the authors, the chroniclers. Also in last century Nepal the viewpoint of the author is present in the text, and if in the Western world certain ideologies and theories illustrate the author's contemporary world, then here certain facts stand out from the ideal descriptions. Yet to feel annoyed by the lack of historical facts is left to others, to another context: first of all these texts transport the standard, then the time of the chronicler, and only then and by chance something valuable for the Western understanding of history.

But it would be too easy to dismiss these histories as pure fiction or chance which, as an act unaware of their importance and weight, do not touch anybody. Do these texts really contain fewer facts than – for example – the papers presented here? Many a Nepali would doubt that. Only the context within which one acts presents a firm footing and displaces 'the Other'.

Coming Closer to Orissa and Structuring Theory

Among the so-called *Unbound Translations* of the Mackenzie Collection, a part of a report or letter of the Mulliah Brammy in the Kalinga Circars to Col. Mackenzie has been preserved (Trans Class XII, Vol. 7, No. 69) which generally reads as follows:

> …Limitted by East Vangam, by south Ganjam, by West Amey Bundah, by north Balecotah from 1411 to 1430 of AS had reigned for twenty years, on his death his son Tapanasoroo Mahapatrooroo, his son Shree Rama Kristna Suru, his son Shree Madhava Suru, his son Vanamali Suroo, his son Bhumi Sarana Sastrooroo, his son Ramachundra Soroo, his son Jagunnaud Soroo, his son Madhudoodana Sooroo, his son Veswimbhur Sooroo, his son Shundra Sakur Sooroo, are ruled, one of his successor is now managing the districts-
>
> The God Bhouda Eswer was on the hill worshipped by the sages. Formerly in this age it was appeared to one of the ancient king called Dhurmasarana patrooroo, desired him to reestablish, he had done so, & continued the devine services to be performed permanently on a other hill near Mullada Village, is a God Cumbala Eswer, was seated by Poroshotama Deo on his going to possess the Canchimundalum-
>
> Early Drona Achary had been performed the devotion for his Archery erected a lingum on the Hill of Culendapah & worshipped on his meeting the desire by the grace of Eswer, blessed the people may get the archery that does chose for-
>
> In the age Vanamali Patrodoo had erected the temple to that God & continued the allowances, performed different ceremonies-
>
> On the 27th March, He proceeded to Homahi towards 30th was copeing the accounts in order to dispatch them to Madras…

A number of thoughts may occur to the – exasperated – reader of this passage: What is the text about? What kind of language does the author use? What were his sources for the dates? What was the purpose of this text? Who used it?

In addition, the order of things and the way the author puts them across makes the reader laugh; his language and thoughts seem difficult to comprehend and one is reminded of the famous list of Jorge Luis Borges in his essay 'The Analytical Language of John Wilkins' which purports to describe a Chinese encyclopaedia's categorization of animals:

> …animals are divided into: (a) belonging to the Emperor, (b) embalmed, (c) tame, (d) sucking pigs, (e) sirens, (f) fabulous, (g) stray dogs, (h) included in the present classification, (i) frenzied, (j) innumerable, (k) drawn with a very fine camelhair brush, (l) et cetera, (m) having just broken the water pitcher, (n) that from a long way off look like flies…[6]

Both texts hardly fit into any familiar mould. Foucault asks where the strange typologies could be juxtaposed, other than in the 'non-place of language', in the 'unthinkable space' that language spreads before us. He talks about 'the common space in which encounters are possible'; about 'the table upon which ... language has intersected space'; about the 'space of order' within which knowledge is constituted; about the 'space of knowledge', 'sites' and 'the already "encoded" eye' that is forcibly confined by 'linguistic, perceptual, and practical grids'.[7] And in a similar way the report of the Mulliah Brammy represents a non-place, because it is both a report and a chronicle, but at the same time it is neither; because it uses a language one expects to understand, but does not. By using a kind of private grammar, it makes one read the text twice.

Both texts report something historical or at least pretend to do so. But either the form or the contents make the historical essence

[6] Borges 1984. Cf. also Foucault 1973, xv.

[7] Foucault 1973, xv–xvii.

almost stand back and reduce the text's value as a source. Though causing amusement both texts cause a certain uneasiness (it may be that this uneasiness makes one laugh). The order these texts are based on, the codes of culture which made them appear, are not those one 'normally' deals with. These texts are less transparent, not easily 'transgressable': They present problems for historians.

Towards the end of the 1980s, a new theoretical paradigm, the *New Historicism,*[8] came into being. Its main assumptions are:

1. 'every expressive act is embedded in a network of material practices;
2. every act of unmasking, critique, and opposition uses the tools it condemns and risks falling prey to the practice it exposes;
3. literary and non-literary 'texts' circulate inseparately;
4. no discourse, imaginative or archival, gives access to unchanging truths nor expresses inalterable human nature;
5. ... a critical method and a language adequate to describe culture under capitalism participate in the economy they describe.'[9]

Every text as 'culture in action' is not only a portrayal of reality, but is also embedded in a dynamic socio-cultural and aesthetic network which is both synchronic and diachronic in nature. This network is relevant because of its connections, i.e. its 'communication', with other, also non-written texts and cultural practices.[10] This of course also applies to historical sources, so that every *Tradition* must also, or even primarily, be seen as unintentionally providing information about its emergence (its author, its times).[11] The value and the

[8] Mainly represented through S. Greenblatt, S. Bercovitch, J. Dollimore, C. Gallagher, J. McGann, F. Lentricchia, H.A. Veeser.

[9] Veeser (ed.) 1989, xi.

[10] Nünning (ed.) 1998, 402.

[11] The technical terms *Tradition* and *Überrest* used in German historiography to my knowledge do not have any equivalent in English. Both stand for historical sources or remains; a *Tradition* is created specifically for the purpose of informing future generations, whereas *Überrest* denotes all sources which 'unintentionally' remain – as opposed to *Tradition*, cf. Brandt 1996, 56-64.

'volume' of a *Tradition* change if its historiographical contents become subject of only secondary importance. Uncovering the crucial contexts for the emergence of a text leads to important findings concerning its cultural connotations.[12]

Thus *New Historicism* refers to contexts of texts and the linguistic or cultural surroundings which basically define their meaning. It refers to the plurality of contexts, since the history of reception of every literary work (and in a broader sense this includes written historical sources) shows that and how contexts shift. They decisively influence the reception and production of texts, fundamentally define the presuppositions of author and reader, form expectations and the way the world and written texts therein are seen. The context is always influenced by culture, so that it changes in the course of history and depends in its valence on the consensus of the ruling stratum of society. Several different contexts will always present themselves for interpretation, and preference for only one dominating context normally demands explicit reasons.

Not only the quantity, but also the quality of contexts is an object of discussion, ever more so since Jacques Derrida with his famous '*il n'y a pas d'hors texte*'[13] radically questioned the unity and separability of texts. It is since possible to differentiate between 'conventional' and 'textual' contexts, and with respect to history they may also be called 'classical' and 'postmodern' contexts. One may distinguish between three kinds of context:

1. The first kind of context consists of the documentary and other artifactual sources from the past and texts (in a broader sense) which fit into the field of research the historian has defined for himself. From the texts of the past, historians hope to infer the contexts that make sense of these texts so they can present them as part of their histories.

---

[12] Incidentally, the demands for a careful handling of the 'facts' presented by a *Tradition* ironically met with an unexpected response in the fundamental critiques of historiography, intensely discussed since the 1970s – at least in the United States. Cf. e.g. White 1994 and 1991.

[13] Derrida 1974, 227.

2. The second kind of context is precisely the one which has been constructed through the use of these sources and the 'stories' which circulate among the bones of this skeleton of sources: they convey pictures of the world people lived in, carry the imaginations of historians (built on sources); but they are limited to a certain time and a certain locality, generalizations are rare. It is the context formed by secondary sources, taken as a true representation of the past it deals with.
3. The third kind of context is the construction or interpretation (by a historian) of the past as the larger framework of past beliefs and behaviours. It is – as opposed to the second context – not limited to a certain time and locality and not only open to generalizations but even defined as such. It is the context of the grand histories.

So-called postmodern theories challenge this scheme of classifying contexts by broadening the definition of text considerably. Text, whether appearing in a written, oral or other form, is no longer limited to the status of a (phenomenological) object with a fixed meaning. Texts are now regarded as sites of intersecting meaning systems receiving diverse readings and various interpretations. Texts are 'read' as systems or structures of meaning flowing from the semiotic, social, and cultural processes by which they are constructed. Such a perspective also allows paintings, films, clothing styles and even societies and cultures to be read as texts, in addition to the written sources that historians customarily consider documents.[14]

This point of view has considerable implications for traditional historical methodology. It not only adds to the complexity of analysis of a documentary *Tradition* or *Überrest* by inquiring as to the process of signification displayed by the source, it may also supplement or even dissolve the notion of authorship into the cultural or other practices that have produced the *Tradition* or *Überrest*. So terms like intention and authorship, which had been

[14] Cf. Young (ed.) 1981 as one example for the numerous approaches to this problem.

necessary premises for the traditional interpretation of documents and reconstructing the past, may be rejected. In this perspective past and present, text and context, converge. Is it no longer possible to distinguish between them?

After these remarks it may be easier to understand that the kinds of contexts relying on such reflections differ considerably from those mentioned above. They both begin and end up with the notion of the text itself, even when it seems to extend beyond it.

1. The first context remains within the text by comparing one part to another or one part to the whole. It is so reduced to the system or structure of words or signs and normally examines the internal consistency of a story.
2. The second context comes, or is constructed from, other texts. Intertextuality may mean that one text refers to several other texts as its pre-text(s), or that it is referred to by others as their pre-text. Interpretations are necessarily intertextual because they refer to other interpretations or monographs; annotation refers to other works and thereby enters into a dialogue with other texts. Every text of the historical profession depends in many ways, even for its form and content, upon the discursive practices of the profession. Historians deal with the past as this is defined by their discipline. Texts are also only treated as sources if the discipline allows this, even the facts therein and how they might be used is a matter of agreement within the profession.
3. The third context emerges (or: is constructed) outside the 'classical materiality' of texts. The antipositivist premise of this approach leads beyond the past historians customarily presume for their research and representations. Texts are produced through social interaction and human behaviour, and moreover humans and their societies can be understood as texts. Only through collective interpretation are theoretical structures generated. If a set of behaviours is defined through interpretation, its components are bundled into a new structure and – as a text – integrated into or constructed as a new context. Thus all past behaviour in historical practice is

> interpreted as texts, and is only (re)constructed by means of textualized evidence. Abstractions such as society, culture, and polity play an important role, because as textual constructions they not only contain textualized contexts, but also serve as elements – as texts – in superordinate contexts.

This perspective may radically alter an interpretation and generate a reality dependent on the cultural constructions created by historically conditioned discourses. No other human structures can be identified which are not in a way constructed; text and context are collapsed into one broad vein of discursive production.

The above mentioned reasons for the choice of a context very quickly lead into the fields of philosophy and comparative literature, where historians and philologists do not generally feel at home. Also, reflections on the kind of reality one's work touches do not seem to contribute to a rewarding discussion, but rather to generally question the work of historians and philologists. However, doubting the idea that language is a transparent tool for the registration and communication of reality does not automatically imply a 'revolution' (because in the end the consequent textualist referent is reduced to the signified or, worse, to the signifier itself),[15] but rather it is an invitation to reflect one's own methods.

Let me now return to the passage from the report to Mackenzie. The story this report relates is incomplete. Apart from the additional fact that the text terminates abruptly *in medias res*, it can hardly be called a chronicle (or several chronicles, because there are a number of beginnings of (hi)stories in this document), because it lacks literary density. Annals[16] on the other hand would

---

[15] Cf. especially Rorty (ed.) 1992, 371-4.

[16] 'Annals normally completely lack a structure, an order of meaning, that they do not possess as mere sequence. The chronicle, by contrast, often seems to wish to tell a story, aspires to narrativity, but typically fails to achieve it. More specifically, the chronicle usually is marked by a failure to achieve narrative closure; it does not so much conclude as simply terminate. It starts out to tell a story but breaks off in medias res, in the chroniclers own present: it leaves things unresolved, or rather, it leaves them unresolved in a storylike way.' White 1987, 5.

demand clear-cut borders to those parts of the text which show the structure of a report (and these passages do not possess much by way of contents). In other words, there is no structure of relationships by which the events related are endowed with a meaning by being identified as parts of an integrated whole. In short, there is no plot.[17] A plot does exist for each individual story contained in the text, but not for the whole.

Nevertheless the text represents a unity, it is *one* text. And one is also not dealing with an oneiric or infantile discourse, not with the words of a person in a state of confusion. The text unfolds (one could say 'adds' itself) within the realm of reality. It is wrong to ask why the author did not manage to create a narrative structure with which others are familiar. Rather, the question is what kind of notion of reality authorized construction of a narrative account such as his. Why did he select just these facts? Why did he choose this form of narrative discontinuity?

These questions quickly recoil on us: it is surely the 'need or impulse to rank events with respect to their significance for the culture or group that is writing its own history that makes a narrative representation of real events possible'.[18] It is important to ask what kind of order prompted the author to choose this form, but the question as to what kind of order forms our expectations is every bit as interesting. Again, 'what kind of notion of reality authorizes construction of a narrative account of reality in which continuity rather than discontinuity governs the articulation of the discourse'?[19] Do texts perhaps have to 'speak' through a certain order to be history? Are in the end reality and truth influenced or determined by the form in which things are presented?

The historical narrative 'speaks' in a different way than annals do. Reality in historical narratives is more inviting, since it easily lends itself to reading. In between these two are the chronicles, with their failure to achieve narrative closure, 'leaving things unresolved

---

[17] Cf. ibid., 9, but also Schweikle (eds.) 1990, 352.

[18] White 1987, 10.

[19] Ibid.

in a storylike way'.[20] Annals and chronicles have quite often been transformed into narratives, as they have a form which, with its central subject, appropriate beginning, adequate middle and proper end, presents a coherence corresponding only to an ideal reality. In other words, one will find the fullness, integrity and closure displayed in narrative histories only in the imaginary. The world and, with that, the past hardly presents itself to somebody in the form of well-made stories, but rather as fragmented, distorted or dim structures, often as a mere sequence with no beginning or end, or as a sequence of beginnings. Above all, it never comes to us in a narrated form, nor does it 'speak' by itself and does not invite anyone to do this. Could it be possible that annals and chronicles, with their obvious failure to narrativize reality 'adequately', represent reality in a form which is closer to actual perception?[21]

This is precisely the case with the report of the Mulliah Brammy. With its unarranged sequence of different parts of annals, chronicles and personal remarks, with its English which seems to function along the lines of Telugu grammar, it does not do justice to any claim of a historical narrative. No picture will emerge from the many fragments, no story can be written from the facts. In the end one is left with an uneasy smile, assailed with the question what to do with this text. It may make sense to look for other similar texts and to question the reasons for its irritating uniqueness – but what about its contents?

> 'And even if it isn't fine to-morrow,' said Mrs. Ramsay, raising her eyes to glance at William Bankes and Lily Briscoe as they passed, 'it will be another day. And now,' she said, thinking that Lily's charm was her Chinese eyes, aslant in her white, puckered little face, but it would take a clever man to see it, 'and now stand up, and let me measure your leg,' for

---

[20] Ibid., 5.

[21] Ibid., 24-5.

> they might go to the lighthouse after all, and she must see if the stocking did not need to be an inch or two longer in the leg.[22]

With this quotation from Virginia Woolf's *To the Lighthouse,* Erich Auerbach begins the last chapter, entitled 'Der braune Strumpf', in his famous work *Mimesis.*[23] Auerbach continues the quotation for a couple of paragraphs, before he enters into a close examination of Woolf's book. The other 19 chapters of *Mimesis* all begin with a short excerpt from a text, and then proceed to unpack them, mostly by intense close reading, i.e. by examining style, diction, tone, rhetorical strategies, and latent philosophical and sociological assumptions. In this way he provides insights into the literature of the 'occident', as he calls it, from the beginnings to the present.

Mimesis is an unusual book. Not only because of the place and history of its origin: it was written by Auerbach while in exile in Istanbul, where he emigrated after he had been expelled from academic life in Germany in 1935. At that time there was no well-equipped archive in Istanbul (by European standards),[24] so that he had to do without reliable critical editions of the texts. But above all *Mimesis* is unusual because of its ambitions and the range of its contents. There is no (theoretical) introduction, no methodological foreword, and it does not seem to follow any programmatic course. Each chapter is self-contained and Auerbach avoids any gesture towards an integrated account, though the chapters reveal a profound sense of historical process and a rich awareness of complex intertextual relations. Apart from interpretation of reality through literary representation or 'imitation',[25] as he referred to the subject of his work, one is dealing here with a book with no specified purpose, consisting of a number of – almost lonely – sequences and episodes.

---

[22] Woolf 1996, 42.

[23] Auerbach 1994, 488.

[24] Ibid., 518.

[25] Ibid., 515.

Although the topics are only loosely unified, the book nevertheless revolves around the term 'reality', though the author steadfastly refuses to define the term. Here, Auerbach presents a series of fragmentary, anecdotal passages which are nevertheless a study of the European literary world of representations of reality. He writes that he tries to create space for diversity and give his formulations flexibility,[26] but also that with the help of a well-equipped archive he would have written a different book. He thus confirms that in *Mimesis* he has published statements of a kind which he would not have dared to publish under different circumstances. The strength of this book is surely its convincing representation: not only of historical 'places' through texts, but also of the texts through the excerpts. In the end an entire culture is represented through a small excerpt in such a way that the tiny fragments could apparently only have been written at particular moments, moments of representational plenitude, in which a culture's apprehension of reality, its experience of reality, and its representation of reality all converge.

Auerbach is brilliant in locating these moments, even if one gets the impression that towards the end of the book, when he starts dealing with the literature of the nineteenth century, the excerpts become more and more arbitrary, almost unimportant. But the idea of convergence of apprehension, experience and representation implies that language has access to (historical) reality, mirrors it mimetically and provides the reader with direct access to foreign and past worlds. For Auerbach, textuality is a concrete and precise mirror of the world.

The passages, the moments of reality one finds in *Mimesis,* bear witness to a change of reality. Auerbach suggests that reality must have changed parallel to the evolution of literature, if one is to be a true portrayal of the other. That is why the excerpts lose their character of seclusion in the course of the book, do not tell a story of their own any longer. Because in the nineteenth century literature begins to enter the spheres of everyday life, everyday life with its fragmented, ordinary character begins to determine literature. And

[26] Ibid.

so in the end the author of *Mimesis* is confronted with his own work: in a world where multiple viewpoints, discontinuity and aimlessness have made their way into literature, his loose-knitted chapters no longer need a foreword or a proper end. Auerbach's book is obviously a child of his times.[27]

And so the passage from *In the Lighthouse*, which begins with the above cited excerpt, displays a fragmented picture. As an anecdote,[28] **as the concentrated representation of a story that a culture would like to tell about itself**,[29] Auerbach created its representativity by demonstrating its fullness and showing how the elements that he was able to analyse tell at least one more story beyond the one narrated by Woolf. It is this confidence that in any randomly chosen part of life, at any time, the wholeness of fate is contained and can be portrayed[30] that guides Auerbach, even though he adds another, a 'real' legitimization: 'etwas wie eine Geschichte des europäischen Realismus hätte ich nie schreiben können; ich wäre im Stoff ertrunken'.[31]

Even more clear is the following paragraph where he says that also the modern writer is lead by the idea

---

[27] For more details on this topic cf. Greenblatt and Gallagher (eds.) 2000, 20-48.

[28] The term 'anecdote' has a number of definitions. Normally 'bezeichnet Anekdote vor allem eine *epische Kleinform*, die auf eine überraschende Steigerung oder Wendung (Pointe) hinzielt und in gedrängter sprachlicher Form (häufig in Rede und Gegenrede) einen Augenblick zu erfassen sucht, in dem sich menschliche Charakterzüge enthüllen oder die Merkwürdigkeit oder die tieferen Zusammenhänge einer Begebenheit zutage treten.' Schweikle (eds.) 1990, 14. Fineman describes anecdotes as complete little stories which produce 'the effect of the real, the occurence of contingency, by establishing an event as an event within and yet without the framing context of historical successivity'. Fineman 1989, 61.

[29] Cf. e.g. Greenblatt and Gallagher (eds.) 2000, 49-74; Fineman 1989, 49-76. Lentricchia 1995, 429-46.

[30] '...das Vertrauen, das in dem beliebig Herausgegriffenen des Lebensverlaufs, jederzeit, der Gesamtbestand des Geschicks enthalten sei und darstellbar gemacht werden könne...', Auerbach 1994, 509.

[31] Ibid.

> …daß es hoffnungslos ist, innerhalb des äußeren Gesamtverlaufs wirklich vollständig zu sein und dabei das Wesentliche hervorleuchten zu lassen; auch scheuen sie sich dem Leben, ihrem Gegenstand, eine Ordnung aufzuerlegen, die es selbst nicht bietet. Wer den Gesamtverlauf eines Menschenlebens oder eines sich über größere Zeiträume erstreckenden Ereigniszusammenhanges von Anfang bis zu Ende darstellt, schneidet und isoliert willkürlich; jeden Augenblick hat das Leben längst schon begonnen, und jeden Augenblick läuft es immer noch weiter fort; und es geschehen mit den Personen, von denen er erzählt, weit mehr Dinge als er je hoffen kann zu erzählen. Aber was wenigen Personen im Verlauf weniger Minuten, Stunden oder allenfalls Tage begegnet, kann man hoffen, mit einiger Vollständigkeit zu berichten; und hier trifft man auch die Ordnung und Deutung des Lebens, die aus ihm selbst entsteht….[32]

Does this passage not perfectly characterize historiography? And is it not also a plea for the fragmentary, a legitimization of the anecdote? Not the completeness he mentions in the last sentence, for this is historically impossible even with shorter periods of time. Crucial is the order and interpretation of life one meets in every hour and minute, which is also (and in many a culture mostly) shaped and represented through discontinuity. There is no need of grand (hi)stories to represent the order of a given culture. On the contrary, this tool of representation of our civilization will often create a more distorted picture of reality. There is no need (and no possibility) for a ‘completeness’ of sources, and creating it quite often means inventing culture or history.[33] The short fragment, the accidental remain in all its unwieldiness and inscrutability surely represents a different, but not a lesser quality of a historical document.

This is what the short paragraph from Woolf's *To the Lighthouse* stands for. The casual glance of Mrs. Ramsay at the

---

[32] Ibid., 510.

[33] Cf. e.g. Dirks 1993, 279-313.

passing Bankes and Briscoe and the one thought she happens to think, nevertheless indicate the perception of a certain kind of order. It is a fragment at the border of her momentary activity which conveys a picture, a 'secondary context' which takes just an instance to open and close, leaving an insight behind, in this case a characterization of Lily Briscoe. In this context it is my metaphor for secondary areas and documents of 'marginal importance' which now move into the centre, standing for small texts which sometimes seem unintelligible and 'amorphous', as for example a strange report of a Mulliah Brammy in the Kalinga Circars to Colonel Mackenzie. Texts which may convey substantial facts or structures, if one lets or makes them speak.

There is no longer any unitary history, no superordinate concept of human behaviour through which everything is interpreted and arranged. Every individual culture, however complex and elaborated it may be, can experience and leave but a small part of its possibilities for expression and experience, in comparison with the whole of mankind. Thus every culture will only preserve a fraction of all its possible perspectives, i.e. only those which it is able to perceive, just as the cultures of our own time will preserve their conclusions of history. These perspectives of scientific historiography, which does not exist independently of other human sciences, have moved away from the grand (hi)stories in the last decades. Perhaps, in accordance with literary studies, marginal forms and structures have come to the fore; contexts have changed and created new rooms for encounters and intersections. In this multiperspectival landscape, even a text like the report of the Mulliah Brammy contains rich material for the attentive reader. To a certain extent as a pendant to the so-called 'little kings',[34] I would name these texts 'little chronicles'. Through their form and their contents they question normative texts, but cannot exist independently of them; though (through) belonging to the peripheries of the discourse, they gain appropriate attention and rise to a possible main subject: as anecdotes of history.

---

[34] Cf. especially the works of Berkemer 1993 and Schnepel 1997.

References

Auerbach, E. 1994. *Mimesis. Dargestellte Wirklichkeit in der Abendländischen Literatur,* Tübingen: Francke.

Berkemer, G. 1993. *Little Kingdoms in Kalinga,* Stuttgart: Franz Steiner.

Brandt, A. v. 1996. *Werkzeug des Historikers,* Stuttgart: Kohlhammer.

Borges, J.L. 1984. 'The Analytical Language of John Wilkins', in J.L. Borges, *Other Inquisitions 1937-1952,* Fort Worth: University of Texas Press.

Derrida, J. 1974. *De la Grammatologie*, Paris: Minuit.

Dirks, N.B. 1993. 'Colonial Histories and Native Informants: Biography of an Archive', in C.A. Breckenridge and P. v. d. Veer (eds.), *Orientalism and the Postcolonial Predicament*, Philadelphia: University of Pennsylvania Press, 279-313.

Fineman, F. 1989. 'The History of the Anecdote: Fiction and Fiction', in H.A. Veeser (ed.), *The New Historicism,* New York: Routledge, 49-76.

Fleet, J.F. 1895/96. 'Records of the Somavaṃśī Kings of Katak', in *Epigraphia Indica* III, S. 338.

Foucault, M. 1973. *The Order of Things: an Archaeology of the Human Sciences,* New York 1973.

Frese, H. 2002. *Variationen von Wirklichkeit*, Hamburg: Verlag Dr. Kovac.

Greenblatt, S. and C. Gallagher (eds.) 2000. *Practicing New Historicism,* Chicago: University of Chicago Press.

Kulke, H. 1998. 'Geschichtsschreibung als Heilung eines Traditionsbruches? Überlegungen zu Spätmittelalterlichen Chroniken Südasiens', in M. Gottlob, A. Mittag and J. Rüsen (eds.), *Die Vielfalt der Kulturen. Erinnerung, Geschichte, Identität,* Frankfurt: Suhrkamp.

Lentricchia, F. 1995. 'In Place of an Afterword – Someone Reading', in F. Lentricchia and T. McLaughlin (eds.) 1995, *Critical Terms for Literary Study*, Chicago: University of Chicago Press, 429-46.

Nünning, A. (ed.) 1998. *Lexikon Literatur- und Kulturtheorie,* Stuttgart: Metzler.

Rorty, R. (ed.) 1992. *The Linguistic Turn*, Chicago: University of Chicago Press.

Schnepel, B. 1997. *Die Dschungelkönige.* Stuttgart: Franz Steiner.

Schweikle, G. and I. (eds.) 1990. *Metzler Literatur Lexikon,* Stuttgart: Metzler.

Slusser, M.S. and G. Vajrācārya 1973. 'Some Nepalese Stone Sculptures: A Reappraisal within their Cultural and Historical Context', in *Artibus Asiae* 35, S. 79-138.

Vajracharya, D.V. and K.P. Malla (eds.) 1985. *The Gopālarājavaṃśāvalī*, Wiesbaden: Steiner.

Veeser, H.A. (ed.) 1989. *The New Historicism,* New York: Routledge.

White, H. 1973. *Metahistory: The Historical Imagination in Nineteenth-Century Europe,* Baltimore: John Hopkins University Press.

White, H. 1978. *Tropics of Discourse: Essays in Cultural Criticism,* Baltimore: John Hopkins University Press.

White, H. 1987. 'The Value of Narrativity in the Representation of Reality', in H. White, *The Content of the Form*, Baltimore: John Hopkins University Press, 1-25.

Woolf, V. 1996. *To the Lighthouse,* London: Penguin.

Young, R. (ed.) 1981. *Untying the Text: A Poststructuralist Reader*, Boston: Routledge & Kegan Paul.

6

Devotion, Poetry and Healing: Exploring Bhīma Bhoi's *Stuticintāmaṇi*

Johannes Beltz

In this paper I attempt to examine the relationship between a particular text and its many contexts, i.e. instances of reading.[1] Exploring a text means analysing not only its semantics but also its transmission, diverse interpretations and ritual dimensions. The text I address is the famous *Stuticintāmaṇi*, an Oriya poem composed by Bhīma Bhoi. This text is not only the most fabulous of his poetic creations; it is also one of the most authentic texts. Compared to other rather mysterious texts such as *Mahimā Vinod* or *Padma Kalpa* (whose authorship, though attributed to Bhīma Bhoi, remains highly questionable), there is little doubt regarding *Stuticintāmaṇi*'s authenticity. What also makes this text very important is its philosophic content. Bhīma Bhoi provides an elaborate overview of how he imagines and understands Mahimā Dharma, the new religion revealed to him by his Guru, Lord Mahimā. In other words, this text is not only an expression of Bhīma Bhoi's personal spirituality but also a compendium of Mahimā Dharma theology. Indeed, it represents a foundation of this new religious doctrine. In this paper, I attempt to explore its transmission within different contexts, *i.e.* the religious community of Mahimā Dharmīs, the general public in Orissa and the academic community. I will explore how these diverse contexts cause divergent interpretations of the same text and how the shift in meaning can be understood.

[1] This research could not have been done without the help of my Indian friends and colleagues. I am especially grateful to Kedar Mishra and Sanjeeb Kumar Nayak from Sonepur for their transliteration and translation assistance and Dr Gourang Charan Dash from Anugul for providing me with numerous documents.

The Author

Though the life of Bhīma Bhoi requires a separate study, some basic information should be provided.[2] Very little is known about him, since reliable documents are lacking. Bhīma Bhoi did not provide any autobiographic details in his writings, and the very few references about his life are difficult to understand and allow contradictory interpretations. Newspapers and administrative reports are quite contradictory and confusing.[3]

However, it is generally accepted that Bhīma Bhoi was born somewhere in western Orissa, in an area located within the present districts of Sambalpur and Sonepur, probably between 1855 and 1860. It is widely believed that he was a foster child, adopted by a tribal couple. In his *Stuticintāmaṇi*, Bhīma Bhoi confirms having been an Orissa Research Programmehan with 'neither friends nor relatives, neither father, mother nor close friends'.[4] He also calls himself a Kandha.[5] Could these passages be read as autobiographical? One should keep in mind that this text is poetic and religious in its nature and that Bhīma Bhoi has no interest in

---

2 In a separate project, I attempt to collect biographies as well as legends, hagiographies and strange stories about Bhīma Bhoi. It goes without saying that these stories tell us more about how Bhīma Bhoi is imagined and less about him as an authentic historical person.

3 Cf., for example, Debendra Dash's (1997) re-edition of articles on Bhīma Bhoi published in Oriya newspapers of the period.

4 In my paper I refer to the edition published by the Dharmagrantha Store in Cuttack, which has a wide circulation but has often been criticized for being inaccurate. However, this edition was the basis for the first integral English translation by Aniruddha Dash. Interestingly it was during the first phase of the Orissa Research Project (ORISSA RESEARCH PROGRAMME) that Anncharlott Eschmann undertook that project and asked Dash to translate *Stuticintāmaṇi*. The manuscript, which was never properly edited (probably because of Eschmann's tragic disappearance), remains till today in Heidelberg. I should indicate that this translation is problematic. The text being very difficult, the translator whose mother tongue is not English was not always faithful to the poet's art. The manuscript remains in the Orissa Archive (MSS 798). The quoted passage is from *Stuticintāmaṇi* 21, 15-16.

5 *Stuticintāmaṇi* 7, 20.

revealing his origin. The quintessence of this autobiographical passage lies in depicting his experiences of misery. Bhīma Bhoi claims that at the age of 12 he had to herd cattle in the forest. He wandered in the woods everyday, often overtaken by hunger and thirst.[6] According to him, this misery changed only after Mahimā Gosain initiated him into Mahimā Dharma.

Indeed, the contact with Mahimā Gosain changes the live of the herdsman. Different stories circulate about their first meeting and the resulting initiation. It is generally believed that Bhīma Bhoi received a visit by Mahimā Gosain. Some think that it would have been around 1862, when the writer was still very young. According to Biswanāth Bābā,[7] one of the most important promoters of Mahimā Dharma of this century, it was about late in the night when Mahimā Gosain and Govinda Bābā, the Guru's first disciple, came to meet Bhīma Bhoi. They knocked at the door and waited for Bhīma. Bhīma Bhoi arose immediately and rubbed his eyes, but it wasn't a dream. He greeted them, asked the Guru about his companion, and was told that he was Govinda Bābā, the reincarnation of Puri's Lord Jagannātha. Bhīma Bhoi was offered vision and initiated into Mahimā Dharma. If we search for this story in Bhīma Bhoi's own writings, we do so in vain. He told a similar story about the origin of his *Nirvedasādhana*, when his Guru revealed him the text.[8] In fact, the initiation might have occurred at another time altogether. The fact remains that Bhīma Bhoi started at some point to compose religious poetry in order to spread the new *dharma*.

After joining the new movement, he became an adept preacher. Composing songs, he left the place of his origin and moved around, staying at places in western Orissa. Nagendra Nath Vasu[9] quotes a story according to which Bhīma Bhoi originally

---

[6] Ibid., 21, 2; 21, 17; 22, 1.

[7] Biswanāth Bābā 1991, 53.

[8] *Nirvedasādhana*, I quote from Aniruddha Dash's translation, which can be consulted in the Orissa Archive (MSS 854). The Oriya text is published in K. Sahu's *Granthāvalī*.

[9] Vasu 1911, 163-4.

adopted an ascetic life and he married later. But this is hypothetical, since the poet never mentions this. He had male and female disciples who offered their daughters in order to serve him as followers. Two Brahmins joined him to become his scribes. Finally, he settled in the village of Khaliapali in the independent kingdom of Sonepur. There he founded his own *āśrama* in 1877 under the patronage of the local king. The local village headman offered the land. Bhīma Bhoi soon attracted many people. As the prominent historian Chittaranjan Das[10] correctly points out, 'although Mahimā Gosain was the founder of Mahimā Dharma, it was really the works of Bhīma Bhoi ... that brought home to all people the essence and excellence of the new doctrine'. Indeed Bhīma Bhoi's importance cannot be underestimated. He contributed the major part of the widespread devotional poetry that characterizes Mahimā Dharma. He was often erroneously assumed to be the actual founder of Mahimā Dharma.

As already mentioned, it is often said that Bhīma Bhoi was blind from his birth. This idea, though it might have an older or different origin, was canonized by Biswanāth Bābā.[11] He declared Bhīma Bhoi to be blind. In his history of the Mahimā Dharma movement, Biswanāth Bābā narrates in detail how Bhīma Bhoi, blind from his birth, could have gained his eyesight during his first meeting with Mahimā Gosain. According to Biswanāth Bābā, Bhīma Bhoi refused the offer, preferring to remain blind in order to dedicate his entire life and devotion to his Lord. As argued earlier, this interpretation became authoritative. This story has largely influenced even the academic perception.[12]

But how could a herdsman do his job if he were blind? More and more voices nowadays claim that Bhīma Bhoi played with blindness as an allegory and he was not blind at all.[13] This is

---

[10] Das 1951, 160.

[11] Biswanāth Bābā 1991, 53.

[12] Das 1951, 160, and Eschmann 1978, 382 accepted this statement to be true.

[13] According to Mahapatra 1983, 10-1 and Nepak 1997, 96, Bhīma Bhoi was not blind at all.

confirmed by his poetry.[14] I should add here that his blindness could also be seen in terms of a hagiographic topic.[15] The eye after all can also be a source of sin and illusion.[16] Cannot blindness be a form of higher knowledge? The poets of the *nirguṇa-bhakti* tradition think that God is in essence without form and quality. Accordingly, the visible world is only an illusion! I also think that Bhīma Bhoi may have called himself blind because he could not see in the darkness of his day's *Kaliyuga.* Darkness and sin damaged his vision. Given such insights, we may now have gained a better understanding of Bhīma Bhoi's significant 'blindness'.

One must also add that some of his writings criticize the society in which Bhīma Bhoi lived: he questioned Vedic rituals,[17] caste inequalities, the Brahmanic hegemony and the idol worship of Jagannātha, Orissa's *rāṣṭra devatā* in Puri. However, his alleged involvement in the 1881 attack on the Jagannātha temple in Puri remains questionable. Instead it seems that some of his followers, coming from a radical group of western Orissa, did it without his guidance.[18] It is also important to recall that Bhīma Bhoi represents the lay branch of Mahimā Dharma and voluntarily kept himself apart from the monastic orders in Joranda. He even criticized them and protested against their strict ascetic rules. He accepted women in his *āśrama* and had more than one female consort.

One must note that Bhīma Bhoi's role and significance became debatable within the Mahimā Dharma movement.

---

[14] In *Stuticintāmaṇi* 71, 13-14 he says that he has seen sinful things with his eyes. He reports on having seen beauty, fair complexion of ladies, beautiful and colorful things with both eyes.

[15] I refer to the story of Sūr Dās, the blind Braj poet. He also falls into a well and voluntarily renounces the return of his vision. The choice of blindness strikes a parallel with the story of Bhīma Bhoi. Both stories use blindness as a religious issue.

[16] In *Stuticintāmani* 71, 17-8. Bhīma Bhoi says that seeing things causes sin. As the sky is covered with mist, so are his eyes. Only when the sun's rays fall into mist then the sin disappears.

[17] *Stuticintāmaṇi* 14, 20.

[18] For further details, cf. the articles by Eschmann 1978; Nepak 1997; D. Das 1997; and Banerjee-Dube 2001.

Documents concerning the judicial debate between the two main ascetic orders, the Balkaladhārīs and Kaupīnadhārīs, are especially revealing for our investigation.[19] It is not a question of superiority or the struggle concerning temple management, property, money, influence, or domination which attracts me. Nor do the arguments, rebuttals, and court decisions. What makes this controversy interesting is the fact that Bhīma Bhoi becomes a reference point in the ongoing fight for influence among these two groups. There seems to be a different reception to Bhīma Bhoi: while the Kaupīnadhārīs claim to admire Bhīma Bhoi's poetry such as *Stuticintāmaṇi* as the main source, as their holy books, the Balkaladhārīs seem to take Bhīma Bhoi as one among many. They fail to accord him a special position. In an open letter Biswanāth Bābā, who was a main actor in this debate, presents his point of view. Speaking for the Balkaladhārī community, he says that Bhīma Bhoi's books are not regarded as laying down regulations or a code of conduct but are accepted as religious books and are read along with others. On the other hand, the Kaupīnadhārīs accept Bhīma Bhoi's writings as a code and authority.[20] Bhīma Bhoi is either considered as the absolute authority, the mouthpiece of Mahimā Swāmī, or as just another writer among others. The final judgment of the court stated that the Balkaladhārīs were legitimate owners of the temple complex in Joranda and their authority should be respected. They are now officially recognized as legitimate representatives of the Mahimā Dharma religion. The Kaupīnadhārīs have lost. Biswanāth Bābā's argument has been accepted and the predominant role of Bhīma Bhoi as projected by the Kaupīnadhārīs

---

[19] The Balkaladhārīs wore the bark of the Kumbhi-tree, claiming that their vestment signifies spiritual superiority. According to them, every novice (*tyāgī*) first gets a *kaupīna* cloth from his guru, and if he is approved, the *balkala*. The Kaupīnadhārīs wear loin-cloths dyed in red ochre because, according to them, Mahimā Gosain gave the *balkala* only to a limited number of disciples. In brief the Balkaladhārīs claim to be atop a sacred hierarchy, but the Kaupīnadhārīs do not recognize this claim and fight for equal recognition.

[20] Deposition by Abadhut Biswanath Baba before the Commissioner of Endowments, Orissa, Cuttack, 28 March 1961, South Asia Institute, Orissa Archive, MSS 175.

has been nullified. The Biswanāth Bābā group not only recognizes other Hindu scriptures such as the *Manusmṛti* as equally – or even more – important but also argues that Mahimā Dharma's philosophy is in full accordance with the Vedas, the Purāṇas and the Bhāgavadgītā. According to them, Mahimā Dharma is nothing else but true Vedānta. Bhīma Bhoi's revolutionary and challenging positions are neutralized and annihilated. Due to the challenging positions and extraordinary creativity of Bhīma Bhoi, the particularity of Mahimā Dharma becomes less visible. In other words, the challenging appeal of the Mahimā Dharma movement is misleading, since it let some people conclude that the Mahimā Dharmīs are a separate, *i.e.* non-Hindu sect. It is impossible to consider Mahimā Dharma different from Sanātana Dharma. It is always emphasized that Mahimā Dharma fulfils Hinduism.

I should add that the text and its author possess an importance that goes clearly beyond this. I have already noted that Bhīma Bhoi is not only known as the founder of a new religious movement in Orissa. Today he is seen as one of Orissa's most interesting literary and religious figures of the nineteenth century. He is identified as a revolutionary who protested against almost everything that generally characterizes 'orthodox' Hinduism, that is, the reference to the Veda as a sacred scripture, idol worship, temple cult, pilgrimage, and Brahman priesthood. One should keep this development in mind in order to imagine the divergent stands people take regarding Bhīma Bhoi's significance. However, it must also be recalled that very little is known about the institutional conflict between Kaupīnadhārīs and Balkaladhārī in the daily practice of common people. Bhīma Bhoi is largely appreciated. One could even say that the chanting of the *Stuticintāmaṇi* (or of any other of his texts) is done in non-Mahimite contexts. Being very popular, his poems, for example, are recited by professional artists.[21]

[21] Some *bhajans* of Bhīma Bhoi are available on audio-cassettes: *Mahima Alekh (Bhimabhoi Bhajan)*, presented by Arabinda Mudul, recorded at J.E. Studios Cuttack, produced and distributed by Jagannath Electronics Cuttack; *Bhimabhoi Bhajan*, presented by Mana Mahapatra, recorded at J.E. Studios Cuttack, produced and distributed by Jagannath Electronics Cuttack.

The Text

The *Stuticintāmaṇi* ('The Praise of a Spiritual Jewel') is not the only work of Bhīma Bhoi.[22] But it is probably one of his most significant and beautiful compositions. As in his other work, Bhīma Bhoi presents himself as a devoted servant of his Guru who only articulates what the latter tells him.[23] He calls him his master and identifies him as God, as Brahma, as majesty. Indeed Bhīma Bhoi develops a theology similar to the Pañcasakhā or other medieval devotional *bhakti* movements. He advocates a God without form (*arūpa*), the one who cannot be described (*alekha*), without name (*anāma*), without attributes (*nirguṇa*), who is unlimited, shapeless, with desire, void (*śūnya*). This God is indescribable, without colours (*avarṇa*), beyond light (*ajyoti*), inaccessible (*durgama*), without limbs. Still the deity is the source of everything[24] and is in fact the Dharma. God's names are Alekha, Nirañjan, Nirākāra, and Nārāyaṇa. The emphasis on *śūnya* has often been taken as a proof of Mahimā Dharma's connection with Buddhism. Nagendra Nath Vasu[25] even concluded that Mahimā Dharma is a form of new Buddhism in Orissa. But a closer look into both doctrinal texts shows that they are actually distinct. The great Mādhyamika philosophers Nāgārjuna and Candrakīrti advocate *śūnyatā* as a principle of nothingness and emptiness, whereas Bhīma Bhoi uses *śūnya* to designate a divinity and all pervasive power.[26]

---

[22] However, his *Cautiṣā Madhucakra* and *Cautiṣā Rasarkeli* are interesting poetic texts whose stanzas are arranged so that the first word of each line starts with a letter in alphabetical order. These works possess some quite erotic passages. Interestingly, they are often ignored by Mahimā Dharmīs or believed to be composed before his conversion. Bhīma Bhoi also wrote the *Ādianta Gītā* which deals with the sexual union of man and women in metaphysical terms. Both texts are also included in Sahu's *Granthāvalī*. No English translation has been done so far.

[23] This is, again, a common characteristic of *nirguṇa* poets, *i.e.,* to dedicate their entire inspiration and creation to their spiritual guide.

[24] *Stuticintāmaṇi* 1,10; 2,14; 6,7; 6,8; 6,12; 14,17.

[25] Vasu 1911.

[26] Cf. for instance Huntington 1992, 55-9.

Let us move to the text in question, *Stuticintāmaṇi*. As mentioned earlier, this text is of particular interest because it is probably his major work. Composed in 100 *bolis* ('chapters') of 20 verses two lines each, it contains 4,000 lines. The text consists of cosmological speculations and hymns about the Lord Brahma, Lord of the Void, the one without form.[27] Yet the main theme is the miserable situation of the world (*duḥkha*). The world suffers from guilt and sin. According to Bhīma Bhoi, this is because the world ignores the right path and the grace of God. In this sense the text is apocalyptic; often Bhīma Bhoi gives a threatening picture of the world's degeneration. This owes to the inherent concept of time: Bhīma Bhoi thinks himself at the end of the *Kaliyuga*, which is marked by decline, the loss of moral values and compassion. The result is chaos and anarchy. At this juncture Mahimā Gosain offers a way out. Mahimā Dharma offers salvation, a solution to misery. Lord Alekha, the one without beginning, knows all sorrows. Being endless and omniscient, the deity can destroy sins.

Combining the idea of cosmic cycles (*yugas*) and divine descents (*avatāra*) with the appearance of his Guru, Mahimā Gosain, Bhīma Bhoi, articulates an interesting eschatology. According to him, the present era is about to end. Again and again, he reminds readers that the present *Kaliyuga* is going to vanish and that a new era has already begun. The Lord of the Void has come to save the world of disorder, diseases, disasters and moral degradation. In this way, Bhīma Bhoi's *Stuticintamani* is both threatening and evangelic.[28] The future conjures up frightening thoughts; there is relief in knowing that an escape beckons. Still a paradox remains: Indian cosmology is basically cyclical. Each *yuga* is followed by another one. In other words, the notion of a purifying

---

[27] Regarding Bhīma Bhoi's notion of *śūnya*, cf. Dhiren Sahoo's dissertation (2000).

[28] Of particular interest is another text, *Padmakalpa*, also attributed to Bhīma Bhoi. Though it might not be his own poetic creation, the text enjoys high popularity, is widely circulated, and not only among Mahimā Dharmīs. In this text, Bhīma Bhoi is believed to have predicted the 'Super Cyclone' which hit Orissa in 1999. His *Padmakalpa* is quoted: 'All of a sudden a cyclone will come and swallow all villages, towns, and countries', cf. *Ghora Kali Yuganta 1999-2010* (Oriya) edited by A.K. Sahu, Cuttack 1999, Dharmagrantha Store.

apocalypse needs not be the final state of affairs either or the age of deliverance. Other cycles of ages will follow.

It goes without saying that this text must be analysed within a wider context of apocalyptic writing in Orissa (*mālikās*). However, though other texts express anger and fears of a particular historic era, they are permanently re-actualized and reread as prophecies.[29] They also function as an important rhetoric tool to enforce the absolute authority of Mahimā Dharma: all previous dharmas, Vaiṣṇava, Śaiva, or Tantrika are outdated. It is the new Mahimā Dharma which will reign in the *Satyayuga*.

In fact one could consider *Stuticintāmaṇi* as a theological programme. Bhīma Bhoi explores how one can achieve the real devotion (*bhakti*) of the Brahma. He asks himself how he can cleanse himself from sins (*pāpā*) accumulated in previous births. It goes without saying that Bhīma Bhoi refers to the idea of *karma* as a cause of rebirth. The ultimate aim is to view the supreme reality. But this aim includes the salvation of humanity, for which personal life could be sacrificed. To repeat, *Stuticintāmaṇi* addresses the sinful situation of the world and the way to leave it. But the text is more than abstract theological speculation. It reflects personal suffering and concern. Indeed the beauty of the text is the person, the individual appearing between the lines. Bhīma Bhoi addresses his Guru in terms of devotion but also in anger. He blames him for being unjust, for not helping him. He feels abandoned.[30] Still Bhīma Bhoi reaffirms that his Guru is 'everything' for him.[31]

In order to illustrate the differing interpretations of *Stuticintāmaṇi* and the contexts in which they are articulated, a crucial passage in the text should be presented and interpreted. I chose *bolis* 71 to 77 because they are remarkable if one wants to explore the ritualistic performance of this text. Hardly any other passages can compete with the extraordinary diversity of possible interpretations (i.e. as poetry or healing verse).

---

29 Mohapatra 2000.

30 *Stuticintāmaṇi* 15, 8-10.

31 *Stuticintāmaṇi* 11, 4.

Elimination of Sorrow and Sin

To start with, the following passages can be seen as a unit since their composition and theme is similar. Each deals with the removal of sin from the human body. What makes this so interesting is the expressive poetic imagery. Bhīma Bhoi proves himself to be a master of language, allegories and comparisons. Let us start with a general introduction to the content. Bhīma Bhoi addresses himself to his Lord and preceptor:

> You are my preceptor, oh Divine God, you are like fire. Burn them all (the sins) with the fire of the divine. Let this body be clean. Now remove my diseases both from my skin and the hairs of my skin. Let this body remain at this stage. Let the sorrow and disease get away from my body and go wherever they like.... I have heard sinful matters, faulty matters, crooked matters, false things, matters relating to anger, envy, lust, greed and delusion. They have filled both my ears. Kindly remove them. As the mire covers the water and bank covers the trees, likewise I am covered by sins on my entire body. Oh Lord of the void, consider this and be merciful so that they can all be removed.[32]

What is important is that Bhīma Bhoi uses a wide range of images to explain how he is exposed to sins, which are basically moral. His images refer to nature, such as a tree covered by dust, to human feelings like sorrow (*duḥkha*) or to diseases (*roga*). Throughout the text, Bhīma Bhoi repeatedly wants his sin to be burnt by the grace of his Lord. At this point he lists the organs of the human body and describes their exposure to sin. After having talked about the skin and the hair, as well as the ears, the nostrils become a special object of his consideration: 'Oh Alekha, kindly burn all the sins which I have in both of my nostrils. In the Kali age there are sins every where. The nostrils receive all smells good or bad, all obnoxious

---

[32] *Stuticintāmaṇi* 71, 5 – 10.

smells and scents. These are sins which are striking to the nostrils. Oh Lord, clean the sins by casting your kind eyes towards them.'[33]

Sin is compared to scents entering the nostrils. One could argue that smell is not only used as a metaphor but that aging itself leaves a bad odour. However, a glance from the Lord would be sufficient to evaporate this: 'Oh preceptor, somehow remove the sins which might have accumulated from the time of birth. If the preceptor casts his kind glance, they will evaporate. I indulged in the enjoyment of the scents and have been greedy to get them. For this I have repeatedly submitted to the preceptor to burn them by divine fire and forgive me.'[34]

I emphasize here the repetitive use of aging, the 'divine fire'. Elimination of sin is imagined as a fire. We will have to discover that fire plays an important role in the Mahimā Dharma rituals. From the nose and the obnoxious scents it detects, Bhīma Bhoi shifts to the mouth as a possible source of impurity.

> I cannot account for the sins which I have acquired by speaking words through the mouth. At the tip of the tongue I have spoken so many sinful words.... These sins are sticking to me like the mire which sticks to water. Kindly burn them by the divine fire and purify my body. I might have lied some time previously from the day of my birth. I might have spoken sinful words. Like the flood in the river, the mouth utters innumerable words. Oh preceptor Alekha, kindly remove all the sins which have been accumulated on the tip of the tongue as well as in the throat.[35]

It is remarkable how Bhīma Bhoi alternates from the human body to nature. The mouth utters sinful words, but they flow 'like a river'. Thus, his images remain complex and paradoxical. In one verse, sin takes on the vile nature of a disease. Then it turns into 'mud'

[33] *Stuticintāmaṇi* 72, 1-5.

[34] Ibid., 4-6.

[35] Ibid., 7-10.

something quite natural and less evil in itself. Time and again Bhīma Bhoi asks his Lord to pardon him. He wants to be forgiven for his mistakes:

> Let me be forgiven for these faults and let my body be purified. Let all the old rubbish be removed from my body. Let the poison of sin be removed from my heart. I do not know any God or Goddess. You are my all the great God. Therefore, with all sincerity I am submitting my grievances.... I have followed my Lord Alekha who is the king of all the kings and emperor. He will consider my virtues and vices. The servant will find out a way out if so ordered. I have expressed all my virtues and vices and my preceptor is competent to give remedy. In all humility I have seen the face of my preceptor and have submitted every thing and hope for the good with folded palms.[36]

This passage clearly describes the total submission of Bhīma Bhoi to his Guru. He is his servant as well as his *malu* (patient). He has no other master, god or goddess. Alekha is his only Lord. In the 73rd *boli*, Bhīma Bhoi continues to use the metaphor of disease to describe how the human body is affected by sin. He systematically notes all parts of the human body and asks that they be purified: 'The waist, the belly, the naval centre area are full of diseases due to wind causing paralysis bites. Cold, cough, heat, and extreme cold are causing pain to the body as if out of rage. Fever, headache, side pain, pain of throat, lips, tonsils, head, joints, fist are found in the limbs. The diseases have occupied even the blood, the flesh, the skin, the hair of the skin and the entire body.'[37]

I emphasize the use of medical terms and anatomical knowledge. In enumerating organs and their typical pain, Bhīma Bhoi reveals quite a good knowledge of medicine. He also has a certain idea about diet: 'Like a parasite creeper the great sins possess the entire body. Like enemies, they are giving pains to the

---

[36] Ibid., 14-20.

[37] *Stuticintāmaṇi* 73, 1-4.

body day and night.'[38] Sin is a parasite. It attacks the body like a creeper (*latā*), a vine. Likewise a net of sin covers all the body. This is why the human soul cannot show any improvement. Sin is an enemy to be defeated. It causes pain and must therefore be eliminated. The following paragraph deals with food preparation and digestion, concluding with the plea to be rescued from the sin attached to his intestines. One rediscovers that this text is not primarily a medical analysis of diseases and their cure. Bhīma Bhoi uses medicine as a metaphor for salvation. The intestines need to be cleansed (*mājibā*, *dhoba karibā*). Likewise he asks to be rescued from human birth and relieved from sin: '... oh disease-free Lord, be kind to me and purify me. Kindly light the celestial fire and burn the vices so that I will get rid of the worries. Oh preceptor forgive my sins.... I am repeatedly praying your Majesty not to leave any sin in my body. In order to be purified, this sinful man has been serving the Lord regularly.'[39] Bhīma Bhoi also proves his intimate knowledge of the yogic theory of the *cakras* which constitutes the human body:

> Remove all the diseases that I have inside my belly and in my heart. There are very many sins in the place called *liṅgacakra*.[40] This place is covered up by male and female fluids and urine. It is the place of 11 sex openings. I think and also fantasize about the images and the nature of illusion and know that all the sins caused by nature cover the place called *liṅgacakra*. Kindly forgive me for these faults and save me from the world which is compared for its difficulties with the sea. Oh pious preceptor, burn them by the divine fire and save this creature.... Bhīma Bhoi has meditated at the feet of the preceptor and fixed his mind at Brahma. He expects that all his faults will be forgiven.[41]

---

[38] Ibid., 5.

[39] Ibid., 9-10, 12.

[40] The part of the body where the genitals are located. Another term is *svādhiṣṭhānacakra*

[41] *Stuticintāmaṇi* 73, 13-16, 20.

Completing the map of the body, Bhīma Bhoi refers to the *guhyacakra*.[42] He explains that it is covered with soil and also full of sins and asks his preceptor to be kind and burn them by his divine fire. From the anus, Bhīma Bhoi moves to the feet. They pose the same problem. He asks the preceptor to forgive the sins committed by his feet. Bhīma Bhoi fears to have trampled down many creatures under his feet while walking, knowingly or unknowingly. He thinks that when he was ignorant in his babyhood and childhood, he must have placed his feet on the bodies of his parents. Though his parents might have excused it because he was still a small boy, he feels now guilty and wants the Resident of the void to forgive him. Bhīma Bhoi prostrates himself 100 times, folds his hands, and promises that his two legs will commit no more wrongs. Then the sins committed at the *liṅgacakra* are mentioned, and these too need to be forgiven by the preceptor. Bhīma Bhoi promises not to have unnatural intercourse with animals and to abstain from intercourse with prostitutes. From there he moves to the heart, which he wants to be free of crookedness and meanness. Back to the mouth, Bhīma Bhoi prays not to let his tongue speak falsehood.[43]

In asking the Lord of the Void to remove sin, Bhīma Bhoi uses symbolic language. He works with metaphors of light and darkness. Darkness is identified as sinful and light as liberation. Needless to say, this symbolic language can be found in many ancient philosophical and mystical treatises. Though these symbols are not his own invention, his handling of them reveals his poetic creativity: 'With the fall of the rays of the sun, the darkness vanishes. Likewise, oh Lord, kindly destroy the sins by your sword and wisdom. When the moon rises in the night, the night becomes bright. Likewise, oh Lord, remove the burden of my sins.'[44] And suddenly, Bhīma Bhoi moves from heaven to earth, to an animal closest to the earth, the snake. The vocabulary changes drastically

---

[42] The *guhyacakra* signifies the anus. Another term is *mūlādhāracakra*.

[43] *Stuticintāmaṇi* 74, 1-15.

[44] *Stuticintāmaṇi* 75, 1-2.

and turns medical. Here Bhīma Bhoi reveals quite a profound knowledge of medicine, pills and the process of curing a person:

> When there is snake biting, the *guṇika*[45] chants mystic words and removes the poison. Over my body, the creepers of sins have grown. Let them be removed. At the stage of collapse of a patient, the physicians administer poisonous tablets. As a result, a big quantity of the water which circulates in the body of the patient dries up. Likewise, kindly remove the sins and sorrows from my body which are as vast as a sea. Administer medicine and wisdom and remove them.[46]

Again, while Bhīma Bhoi asks for a cure, he plays with different semantic contexts. As medicine dries up a human body, his sin should dry. After identifying God as a healer, Bhīma Bhoi invents a new picture. He addresses God as a *rajaka,*[47] which is an uncommon comparison. As one washes dirty clothes, the Lord removes the sin of mankind: 'As the washer man washes the dirt from the dirty cloth near the water like wise oh Lord remove the sins from my body and purify me. When gold is burnt in fire, it shines more. Likewise, burn me in divine fire and let my dirt be burnt and removed. When man enters into the water, he is purified by taking bath. The dirt and mire are washed away immediately. Likewise see that sins which equally stick on my body are removed.'[48]

Sin reappears here as dirt and dust (*dhulimali*) which must be removed from the body. But sin is also compared to clouds that block out the light and must therefore disappear. Sins are described as ornaments which cover the body during a dance, but which must be discarded when the dance is over. Sin is imagined as cold in the winter, which causes pain and troubles the body.[49] Again, he uses

[45] Oriya *guṇika* or *guṇiā* is a witch doctor, shaman, or magician.

[46] *Stuticintāmaṇi* 75, 3-5.

[47] *Rajaka* means washerman.

[48] *Stuticintāmaṇi* 75, 6-9.

[49] Ibid., 14-7.

medical language: 'In this Kaliyuga, the sins are immense. How can I get over them? ... Oh imperishable Lord, destroy them so that I will have no suspicion. Sins and falsehood have grown like parasite creepers. Kindly remove all these sins and dangers and fulfil my desire.... All these may kindly be removed ... like a *baidya*[50], kindly cure me.'[51]

I would like to underscore the last line, because Bhīma Bhoi makes very clear that he wants God to act as a doctor who cures diseases. The sin is like accumulated *karma* and needs to be removed.[52] However, the image is a paradox, because a doctor usually struggles with a disease; he rarely is its master. In this sense, the Lord is more than a simple physician: He has the power over sin. He rather resembles a witch doctor with magical powers, one mightier than the disease. The important conclusion is that the Lord is above all. He can order sins to leave Bhīma Bhoi's body. The sun and the moon carry out his orders by rising and setting in the sky. Under his orders the stars rise, and Indra showers rain. One is reminded that God alone removes sin. He alone saves the world. Bhīma Bhoi is so sure about this, so confident that his Lord will help him, that he changes his language. From a person who prays, Bhima Bhoi transforms himself into somebody who gives orders. He calls on his sins to get out and to go away:

---

[50] *Baidya* (skr. *vaidya*) is a traditional āyurvedic doctor.

[51] *Stuticintāmaṇi* 76, 1-6.

[52] It should be added here that the idea that *karma* causes disease, can be found within the Buddhist scriptures as well as in the *Caraka Saṃhitā*, the famous āyurvedic medical compendium.

> If the Guru will be kind, my sins will be removed. If the preceptor will so order, the sins will follow its fate and will go away to the place from where it had come. Oh sins, you have caused sufferings to me by force till now carry out the orders of the preceptor over your head now and get out and hide yourself. Bhīma Bhoi has remembered all the sins which he committed for 100 births and says that he has surrendered them at the feet of the Guru.[53]

Again, it is argued that only total submission at the feet of the Lord can help. Bhīma Bhoi may make a command, but what good would it do, since it is only 'the Lord' that can carry it out? Wouldn't this be an exercise in futility? 'Oh sins which are like disease ... of my body. If you disobey orders and stay by force, you will get curse. From the nail to the nose of my body, get out. For you I have already submitted before His Majesty, My Guru. From my joints and fists, as well as from my head, Oh sins, you are like the mouth of the Death God, get out!'[54]

This paragraph is also similar in form to a *mantra* uttered by a traditional shaman healer. It remains the magic recitation of a witch or shaman who likewise orders diseases to get out of the patient's sick body. Bhīma Bhoi also addresses himself to the sin personally, just as if he could talk to it as a person:

> If you are fortunate enough, fly away, go away.... If you do not obey, you will be put into disaster and danger and punished.... It is the Guru's oath that you must leave the limbs the skin and the hairs of the skin. Accept the words of the Divine. Why you are showing a temper of disobedience? It is an oath in the name of Alekha Brahma that you must leave anybody. If you do not, you will be like a piece of foam, tussled away when it is driven by the wave of the divine.[55]

---

[53] *Stuticintāmaṇi* 76, 18-20.

[54] *Stuticintāmaṇi* 77, 1-3.

[55] Ibid., 4. 6-7.

We reach the end of this passage. Bhīma Bhoi gets irritated and asks the sin to leave. He appeals to it to understand. He even threatens it. If it does not go, it will vanish or be destroyed. This too is a very interesting rhetoric figure. Bhīma Bhoi plays with words and meanings. He uses the same language as the traditional healer. He also speaks directly to the disease and gives order. Like a witch doctor, Bhīma Bhoi appeals first politely and than gets firm.

At the end we deal here with a multitude of meanings and references. But all verses, all discourse, stylistic figure, rhetoric element, metaphor finally has only one aim: to announce the new age which changes everything. All lies within the Lord of the Void. Let the formless Brahma be kind to everybody, and let all have the opportunity of seeing Him. Prayer and devotion will save. Brahma will surely destroy the sins of endless birth and give deliverance.[56] When Bhīma Bhoi reasons about sin, illness, and cure, he does it within the context of his apocalyptic visions about the final *Kaliyuga*.

Still the theme of healing is more then a metaphor. Bhīma Bhoi did possess a good knowledge of āyurvedic medicine. He frequently mentions āyurvedic diagnostic terminology such as *pitta* (bile), *kapha* (phlegm), *āma* (acidity), *sarpāghāta* (snakebite), *jvara* (fever), *saṃnipāta* (high fever, coitus, death), *vāta* (rheumatism) or medicines such as *biṣāna* (poisonous pills). He knows about yogic practices and theories. It is further recorded that Hari Panda and Basu Panda, his two scribes, and his spiritual consort Labanyabati were *kabirājās.*[57] Labanyabati's maternal uncle was even one of the most famous *kabirājās* at the royal court of Patnagarh. One can, therefore, conclude that āyurvedic medicine was part of Bhīma Bhoi's preaching. However, this is not a treatise about medical plants or specific medical practices. The medical references are embedded in the theological discourse on how the human state is sinful and must be changed. Bhīma Bhoi explores the importance of

---

[56] *Stuticintāmaṇi* 77, 19.

[57] *Kabirājā* is a traditional physician.

past *karma*, referring, for instance, to the *Caraka Saṃhitā,* which explained that the *karma* determines the state of health at the time of birth.

However, Bhīma Bhoi does not talk about postures or breathing practices; he advises the patient to surrender himself to the Lord of the Void. In the strict sense, Bhīma Bhoi did not write a medical text. I further suggest that Bhima Bhoi was familiar with yogic concepts and practices. Especially repeated references to channels (*nāḍī*) of the subtle body and energy points (*cakra*) might be noted. In addition, Bettina Bäumer recently observed that the use of terms like *cakra*, *padma* and *dvāra* indicates Bhīma Bhoi's fondness for Tantric sexual symbolism.[58]

However, Bhima Bhoi's work reflects many streams of religious traditions, and it is not difficult to imagine that some devotees attribute healing power to *Stuticintāmaṇi*. In the following paragraph I will show how this text is indeed recited to promote healing. A new dimension of the text is discovered, which could hardly be expected if one looks only into the literary meaning. In other words, we see how necessary it is to combine philological research with ethnographic fieldwork.

Ritual Recitation and Healing

Before discussing in detail the healing dimension connected with recitation of the quoted passages from *Stuticintāmaṇi*, I have to remind readers that this text is still largely transmitted orally, though there are a limited number of palm-leaf manuscripts. When and on which occasions is the text recited? The recital context of *Stuticintāmaṇi* as well as of other Mahimā Dharma texts is a ritual called *dhuni*. That is the ritual fire dedicated to Alekha Prabhu. It is usually conducted on full moon days or on any other auspicious occasion. In Sonepur I attended a *dhuni* organized at a *śrāddha*[59] ceremony. It must be stressed here that only a Bābā can perform *dhuni*. Common layman cannot do it; a special religious authority is

[58] Bäumer 2002.

[59] Rites dedicated to honour ancestors.

needed. The way the ritual is performed is almost the same. There always exists a special place in a village where the ritual is performed. In the evening a Bābā will come and prepare the firewood. As soon as the fire is burning well, he will pour ghee into it. The ritual will be accompanied by recitation of *mantras*. Collective singing will follow. The *bhajans* of Bhīma Bhoi as well as the *Stuticintāmaṇi* are recited with accompaniment by instruments like *khañjaṇi.*[60] Diverse traditional, popular and local tunes are used as melodies.

I observed during my fieldwork that the *dhuni* ritual is used for healing. It is evident that a major reason why people join the Mahimā movement is to be cured of diseases. Mahimā Dharma indeed offers more effective means of healing than traditional healers and doctors. I discovered that healing was not only a minor but a basic feature of Mahimā Dharma in Orissa. Again and again Mahimā Dharmīs told me how they had miraculously been cured of snake bites, sickness and diverse diseases. People claimed to have been cured of possessing evil spirits.[61]

Bhīma Bhoi's *Atha Bhajans* and the *Stuticintāmaṇi* are considered to be his most powerful texts. People recite them by heart or read them from small, widely circulated booklets. By reciting these texts and praying to Mahimā Alekha, barren women claim to have become pregnant. *Bibhūti*, the remaining ashes of a fire ritual, are considered to be a very effective medicine. A 33-year-old man from Putupada, Bolangir district, narrates that he was severely ill and he had gone to many doctors and occultists. But it was the *Bibhūti* given to him that gradually healed his illness. I was given a small box with holy ashes to use in case of a sudden illness. I experienced another rather funny incident when a Bābā asked me about my wife and children. As I told him that I had a wife but no children, he took his bag and handed me some holy ashes. He told me to mix it with water and give it my wife to drink after her period

---

60 A small drum normally used to accompany the singing of *bhajanas*. Often they are also accompanied by *gini* (small bell-metal cymbals) and *kāthi* (castanets).

61 This is confirmed by a survey conducted by the Tribal Research Institute in Bhubaneswar and published in 1969. The survey reported that 35 per cent of all interviewees had accepted Mahimā Dharma in order to be cured from diseases.

following her first bath. My wife would get pregnant with a son shortly afterwards. However, we did not try it. Many others confirmed that *Bibhūti* can prevent women from miscarriages.

I have to add here that healers are mostly the Bābās, not laymen. But one should keep in mind that most Mahimā Bābās – like their counterparts in other Hindu sects – are not properly trained as healers. They do not even pretend to be so. Their healing capacity is part of their *śakti*, an expression of their sacred power obtained through renunciation of the world and their direct contact with the divine. Given this background, one is not surprised to see lack of special analytical tools. The Bābās do not examine diseases as such. No special treatment is required for healing. Barren women, pain and all kinds of sufferings are cured in the same way. The Bābās perform *bhajana* and *kīrtana*. Sacred formulas are recited and holy ashes are smeared on the patient or swallowed with water. Simultaneously, the 'patient' is required to participate in the healing process by reciting *mantra*s and offering affirmations of faith to Alekha Mahimā. Only then can the healing succeed.

When I conducted my interviews, I was surprised by the way that certain Bābās rationalized their healing capacity and the possible effects. Let me quote an interview with Dasharathi Dās Bābā from Julunda to illustrate my point. He told me: 'By reciting the *bolis* 71 to 77 of *Stuticintāmaṇi* with wholehearted sincerity and purity, one can be cured of snake bites and many other diseases.' There is no doubt that the powerful effect lies in recitation of Bhīma Bhoi's poetry. However, after asking the Bābā how healing is performed, he told me that poison has to be sucked out. In other words, merely reciting the *Stuticintāmaṇi* is not enough. What is even more striking is the formulation of 'wholehearted sincerity'. The patient's total devotion is required. The Bābā knows very well that healing is not magic which works without the patient's participation. Thus, he asks his patient to believe in what he does and to submit himself totally to Lord Mahimā. Only then can he gain relief from sorrow and disease. It is the notion of *bisvāsa*[62] that emerges as crucial in understanding the meaning of healing in this

[62] *Bisvāsa* (kr. *viśvāsa*) means 'faith'.

particular context. One places his full trust in the healer and hands over his body to him. This phenomenon reminds me of what is commonly called the 'placebo effect'. It hardly matters if you take *Bibhūti* or any substitute for medicine. If you recite a *mantra*, you must have faith in what you are doing. If you do, it may help. Though this is not meant as support for the Bābās' anti-medical position, the positive effect of what one could call 'auto-suggestion' cannot be denied. The devotee must recite *kīrtanas* and *bhajanas* and worship the wonderful Lord Mahimā. Indeed the important point is that the healing stories are embedded in a deep faith and intensively lived religiosity: they are an expression of an interaction between the Lord and his devotees. The topics are the same: miraculous healing, charismatic Bābās. The power of the narrative is always reinforced by dramatic moments: medicines that do not work and a sudden, unexpected healing.

Finally I should add that the practice of healing is not a recent phenomenon. After looking into historic reports, I discovered that healing has been a fundamental part of the emerging Mahimā Dharma movement from the start, not only a side aspect. In a report submitted by the manager of Dhenkanal State, Babu Banamali Singh, to the superintendent of the Tributary Mahals, dated as early as 8 October 1881, it is affirmed that Mahimā Swāmī, when residing at the Kapilash hills, relieved people of their diseases.[63] An article published in 1908 in a literary magazine called *Mukur* reconfirms this. The essay's author, Damodar Mohanty, who was a senior officer of the court of Sonepur Maharaj, stated that Mahimā Swāmī was assisted by his wonderful healing power and that he cured people of many diseases only through the power of his words.[64] Bhīma Bhoi was also said to possess the power of healing. Daya Sagar Das from Khaliapali told me the following story: 'Once an old woman from Patnagarh, who was a leper, came to Bhīma Bhoi seeking refuge. He told her, 'One cannot get any fruit without offering anything at the door of the Guru.' The old woman answered, 'I have nothing, what can I offer you?' Bhīma Bhoi

---

[63] A transcribed copy of this text is kept in the Orissa Archive in Heidelberg.

[64] The complete Oriya text is reproduced by Debendra K. Dash 1997.

replied, 'You bring some leaves and tooth brushing sticks.' After the old woman had brought it, she was completely cured of leprosy by the blessings of Bhīma Bhoi.'

Similar stories circulate. It should be recalled that miraculous powers are attributed to the founder of a particular religious sect as a common fact. That is how sainthood is conceptualized and justified. The founder of a religious movement is bound to be different from his common fellows.[65]

I would like to conclude with three points. First, I argue that healing power is conceptualized as an attribute of a sacred person. It is a crucial hagiographic topic. Mahimā Gosain, Bhīma Bhoi and certain Bābās are commemorated as healers. Healing is used as a metaphor to describe the supernatural and sacred nature of these persons. Second, healing is more than a metaphor. It was – and still is – a widespread practice among Mahimā Dharmīs. Physical wellness and spiritual liberation are interwoven. Or, to put it in more general terms, medicine and devotion are part of healing, just as healing is a fundamental part of religion. But this finding needs a rectification. Healing is not a specific practice of Mahimā Dharmīs. We must recall that faith healing is a widespread phenomenon among religious groups all over India, across borders of sectarian affiliation and belief. Yet this very fact shows how similar Mahimā Dharma is to other ascetic traditions.[66]

More Contexts

Bhīma Bhoi has become an object of intellectual discussion. During the last decades he has been politically appropriated as a great freedom fighter and a vehement critic of communalism. He is cast as the forerunner of women's emancipation and a great protagonist of Oriya language. He is celebrated as Orissa's Kabīr. For others, he

---

[65] Chittaranjan Das 1951, 168 has noticed the importance of miracles in the legends about Mahimā Dharma. He pointed out that the capacity of healing characterizes the 'charisma' of a prophet, referring probably to Max Weber's sociology of religion.

[66] Cf. Kakar 1998; Lewis 1992; and Zysk 2000.

manifests Orissa's contribution to the Indian cultural heritage. For instance, when New Delhi's Sahitya Akademi asked for a poetic passage from each of the 14 Indian languages, a couplet of Bhīma Bhoi's *Stuticintāmaṇi* was chosen.[67] These lines are well known today. They signify the humanism of Mahimā Dharma.

The associations, schools and colleges operating in Orissa in the name of Bhīma Bhoi are numerous and many research institutes and trusts are created in his name. Indeed Bhīma Bhoi has become a vehicle of affirming a specific cultural Oriya identity. Bhīma Bhoi is promoted as a founding father of Oriya literature. He is considered to be a national integrator. Tribal and Vedic culture became united and harmonized through him. He preached universal love, a message uniting rich and poor, kings and tribal populations of the jungle. As a saint, Bhīma Bhoi is considered to offer solutions to contemporary problems. Let us paraphrase Sudhakar Das, a reader from Sonepur College who notes that age-old problems like casteism, ignorance and poverty still persist but holds that the thinking of the revolutionary, visionary philosopher and poet Bhīma Bhoi might provide a solution.[68] G.N. Sahu, a lawyer and journalist from Sonepur, also states that one could apply the great thinker's philosophy to find a solution for problems plaguing society.[69]

Bhīma Bhoi is also becoming increasingly an object of diverse political discourses. Congress politicians have appropriated Bhīma Bhoi as the direct precursor of Gandhi and a prophet of Indian independence. Ancharlott Eschmann quotes a booklet that culminates in identifying Bhīma Bhoi as a fighter for a unified India under the banner of Sanātana Dharma.[70] One must keep in mind that the Mahimā Dharma has always been viewed as an indigenous

---

[67] The couplet reads (*Stuticintāmaṇi* 27, 7): ***Prāṇiṅka ārata duḥkha apramita, dekhu dekhu kebā sahu, mo jībana pache narke praḍithāu, jagata uddhāra heu.*** Sitakant Mahapatra 1983, 27 translates: 'Boundless is the anguish and misery of the living. Who can see it and tolerate? Let my soul be condemned to hell, but let the universe be redeemed.'

[68] Das 2000.

[69] Sahu 1999.

[70] Eschmann 1978, 407.

reform movement which developed independently from Christian influences. It should also be recalled that this thesis always culminates in affirming Bhīma Bhoi's 'Indianness'. It is argued that Bhīma Bhoi *resisted* Christianity. Being a tribal man, he did not convert to Christianity but reformed Hinduism. Doing so, he saved the masses from becoming Christians. In this way Bhīma Bhoi is a true nationalist, defending the Hindus against foreign missionaries. The anti-Western and anti-Christian tone of this discourse is significant.

Thus far we have seen the nationalistic interpretation of Bhīma Bhoi. But there are other voices to be heard. I must add that Bhīma Bhoi also represents the significance of western Oriya culture in a pan-Indian context. He is easily integrated in the separatist discourse that these days demands an independent Koshal Pradesh. More and more intellectuals reclaim Bhīma Bhoi as a man of the soil demanding that his writings be published in their original language, Sambalpuri. Bhīma Bhoi is cited as a critic of coastal hegemony and a forerunner of western Orissa's fight for recognition.

As I have already argued, Bhīma Bhoi is a matter of ongoing negotiations between different socio-religious groups. In Sonepur I interviewed a Christian pastor, and it culminated in the question of whether Bhīma was a Christian or not. He argued, quoting from *Stuticintāmaṇi,* that Bhīma was Christian, having converted due to some divine visions. But he was a secret Christian. He could not declare it openly because people would have tortured him.[71] The pastor argued that he had already suffered too much when people had tried to kill him. While not particularly appreciating this argumentation, it does reveal a new context in which *Stuticintāmaṇi* is read and used as a sectarian argument. This context is quite specific and different from the contexts quoted earlier. The pastor

71 The pastor quoted a passage from *Stuticintāmaṇi* (68, 9) which can be translated as follows: 'Why do you make me Christian just before my death? Nobody would come to shoulder my dead body.' However, there are other passages indicating that Bhīma Bhoi was indeed accused of being a Christian. Read, for example: 'I'm termed as a Christian by the people, and I'm abused by them as such, and I'm blamed' (20, 3).

belonged to the Gaṇḍa-Paṇa caste and had heard that I was interested in Mahimā Dharma. By telling me that Bhīma Bhoi was Christian, he tried to awaken my curiosity. And I became the target of his missionary zeal.

This leads me to another point. I have to repeat that the research project on Mahimā Dharma is also a new context in itself, a new area in which Bhīma Bhoi's text is re-actualized. It is the focus on Bhīma Bhoi as the most authentic, historically original and most fascinating poet, which forms my perception of *Stuticintāmaṇi* as a religious text. My research is not only a context of this particular text, but it will produce further texts: in the second phase of the ORISSA RESEARCH PROGRAMME, plans call for editing, translating, and commenting on significant parts of Bhīma Bhoi's poetry as well as studying his hagiography.

Conclusion

What can we conclude from my findings? Let me present some preliminary conclusions, although further systematic research and investigation is required. From a reading of certain passages of *Stuticintāmaṇi* it becomes clear that Bhīma Bhoi should not only be seen in the context of Orissa's philosophic and devotional tradition but also within its medical tradition. One is reminded of the complex relation between popular religion and healing. But this is not the end. Looking into contemporary representations, one discovers that Bhīma Bhoi is viewed as a poet, a religious prophet, a social reformer, a magic healer, a *bhakta* and a saint. The question then is how to analyse this amazing (and often contradictory) diversity of interpretations. Yet let me recall that *Stuticintāmaṇi* remains the main source of argumentation, discursive creations and projections.

This leads to understanding the relationship between text and context. It became clear that this text is not only appreciated for its poetic quality, which follows from my close reading. Shifting attention to its *ritual performance*, one discovers that it is sung in order to heal. I must add that the list of contexts is far from being complete; more contexts could be added. It goes without saying that this article represents a new context for Bhīma Bhoi's poem, as does the academic discourse on Mahimā Dharma.

Instead of presenting a concluding argument I would like to end by raising a question: taking into account the many divergent interpretations of Bhīma Bhoi, could one consider one as more authentic than others? Should one adopt a rigid perspective, declaring certain interpretations and appropriations as false and misleading? Can one argue in terms of authenticity and struggle for imaginary 'objectivity'? I rather think that no meaningful text exists without its context. The *Stuticintāmaṇi* becomes significant when sung by devotees, when quoted within academic discourse or referred to by politicians. For me, this is the most interesting aspect of my research: the discovery of new contexts in which *Stuticintāmaṇi* is read, recited or quoted.

References

Banerjee-Dube, Ishita. 2001. 'Issues of Faith, Enactment of Contest: The Founding of Mahima Dharma in Nineteenth-Century Orissa', in H. Kulke and B. Schnepel (eds.), *Jagannath Revisited*, New Delhi: Manohar, 149-77.

Bäumer, Bettina. 2002. 'Tantric Elements in Bhima Bhoi', paper presented at the conference Mahimā Dharma Reconsidered, Utkal University Bhubaneswar, February 2002.

Bhoi, Bhīma. 1991. *Stuticintāmaṇi*, Cuttack: Dharma Grantha Store.

Biswanāth Bābā, Abadhuta. 1991 [1935] *Mahimā Dharma Itihasa* (Oriya), Mahimāgadi Dhenkanal: Mahimādharma Granthakosa Samiti.

Das, Chittaranjan. 1951. 'Studies in Medieval Religion and Literature of Orissa', in *Vishva Bharati Annals*, 3, 107-94.

Das, Sudhakar. 2000. 'Communalism versus Bhīma Bhoi', in *Bhīma and National Integration, Smaranika 1999-2000*, Sonepur: Sonepur College.

Dash, Debendra Kumar. 1997. 'Bhīma Bhoi o Mahimā Dharma' (Oriya), in *Eshana*, 34, 120-52.

Eschmann, Anncharlott. 1975. 'Spread, Organization and Cult of Mahimā Dharma', in Nilamani Senapati (ed.), *Mahimā Dharma*, Cuttack: Dharmagrantha Store, 9-22.

– 1978. 'Mahimā Dharma: An Autochtonous Hindu Reform Movement', in Eschmann/Kulke/Tripathi (eds.) *The Cult of Jagannath and the Regional Tradition of Orissa*, New Delhi: Manohar, 375-410.

Gross, Robert Lewis. 1992. *The Sadhus of India*, New Delhi: Rawat Publications.

Guzy, Lidia. 2000. '"On the Road with the Bābās". Some Insights into Local Features of Mahimā Dharma', in *Journal of Social Sciences* 4 (4), 323-30.

– 2001 (unpublished). 'Voices of Gods. Ecstatic Alekhs and Local Configurations of Mahimā Dharma', paper presented at the ORISSA RESEARCH PROGRAMME Conference, Salzau, May 2001.

Huntington C.W. 1992 (1989). *The Emptiness of Emptiness, An Introduction to Early Indian Mādhyamika,* Delhi: Motilal Banarsidass Publishers.

Kakar, Sudhir. 1998 [1982]. *Shamans, Mystics and Doctors, a Psychological Inquiry into India and Its Healing Tradition,* Delhi: Oxford University Press.

Mahapatra, Sitakant. 1983. *Bhima Bhoi*, New Delhi: Sahitya Akademi ('Makers of Indian Literature').

Mohapatra, Bishnu. 2000, '"Fish Will Swim over the Twenty-two Steps of the Jagannath Ttemple', Time, Order, and Cosmology: Exploring the Career of an Apocalyptic Imagination"', paper presented at the ORISSA RESEARCH PROGRAMME Conference, Salzau, May 2000.

Nepak, Bhagirathi. 1997. *Bhima Bhoi: The Adivasi Poet Philosopher*, Bhubaneswar: Bhagiratha Prakashan.

Sahoo, Dhirendra Kumar. 2000. *Bhīma Bhoi's Concept of Śunya*, unpublished PhD dissertation, Bhubaneswar: Utkal University, Department of Philosophy.

Sahu, Gorek Nath. 1999. 'Bhīma Bhoi's Ideals Prescribed for Social Problems', in *Asian Age*, 11 February.

Sahu, Sri Karunakar (ed.). 1991. *Bhīmabhoi Granthāvalī*, Cuttack: Dharmagrantha Store

Tribal Research cum Training Institute (Bhubaneswar) 1968-69. 'Impact of Satya Mahimā Dharma on Scheduled Castes and Scheduled Tribes in Orissa', in *Adibasi,* 10 (1), 41-76.

Zysk, Kenneth G. 2000 [1998]. *Asceticism and Healing in Ancient India, medicine in the Buddhist monastery*, Delhi: Motilal Banarsidass Publishers.

7

Mantra-Recitation as a Religious Institution: Śrī Kalpataru Sevā Āśrama in Bhubaneswar

Angelika Malinar

Time and again monks and devotees, and even occasional visitors to the Kalpataru Sevā Āśrama (popularly called 'Bāyā Bābā Maṭha') in Bhubaneswar point to the *akhaṇḍa-nāma-kīrtana* as the special feature of this place. *Akhaṇḍa-nāma-kīrtana* means the 'uninterrupted chanting of the name of god' through the repetition of one *mantra*-text in various melodies. Monks and devotees are proud of the fact that they have managed to uphold this continuous, 24-hour-chanting since it was started by Nāmācārya Bāyā Bābā, the founder of the *āśrama*, in 1973. The institutionalization of the *mantra*-recitation thus provides an important point of reference for the self-perception of the residents of the *maṭha* as well as for the description of the religious ambitions of individual devotees.

What is called *mantra* or *nāma* cannot easily be subsumed under current notions and classifications of textuality and textual genres, it rather constitutes a genre of its own. Explanations, translations and definitions of the term cover a rather large spectrum. Gonda,[1] for example, lists amongst others, the following translations: 'prayer', 'liturgical formula', 'incantation', 'sacred sentence', 'Spruch', 'spell', etc. This diversity points to the 'plurivalent character'[2] of *mantra*. In this essay, I shall deal with *mantra*s which consist of a sequence of names of god(s)[3] and constitute a fixed linguistic unit. As the sequence of names is fixed, the *mantra* has a specific wording which might be commented

---

[1] Gonda 1975, 249ff.

[2] Ibid., 249.

[3] These *mantra*-texts are closely related to the genre of '*nāmastotra*', hymns in praise of a god consisting of his different names. Cf. Gonda 1970, ch. 14.

upon, recited, repeated, written down, etc. The text of the *mantra*, i.e. the wording which constitutes a unified whole,[4] thus serves as the stable and unchanging point of reference in different contexts, e.g. scholarly interpretation, meditation, ritual and performance. And although the text is codified in its wording, it is not destined to be treated and understood as a self-contained entity; rather the theological impact which is ascribed to the text can only be realized in the context of practice. It is claimed by practitioners as well as by authorized interpreters of *mantra* that the text can unfold its efficacy only when placed in contexts as those indicated before. These contexts explore the power (*śakti*) and truth (*satya*) ascribed to the text.

In the present case one is confronted with a notion of text in which the text is seen as being, on the one hand, dependent on its contextualization, and on the other hand, as stabilizing the context through its codification, i.e. its being a persistent point of reference in divergent contexts. 'Meaning' as well as 'power' are created in this very interplay between text and context. This implies that neither the text nor the context(s) can be treated as containers or media of meaning, which are per se complete and self-referential and thus ready for learned interpretation. Rather, one is confronted with the phenomenon that context does not create or imply more sense than the text apart from – or prior to – its contextualization; and conversely that the text, in spite of its self-validity, has no life apart from those who practice and perform it. This, however, does not imply that its wording can vary according to context. Thus, in this case, what for a long time has been called in literary criticism (Literarkritik) the question of the 'Sitz im Leben' of a text has to accompany the analysis of the text from the very start. The following analysis of the interplay between text and context(s) thus might show that text and context, in this case, appear as mutually

---

[4] In this regard it fulfils one of the criteria of 'textuality' discussed within linguistic parameters: textuality does not first and foremost depend on the length of a passage or on a certain number of sentences. Cf . Halliday, Hasan 1976, 1, Vater 1992, 15.

constitutive.[5] In order to explore this interplay between *mantra*, *mantra*-recitation and its institutionalization as *akhaṇḍa-nāma-kīrtana* the following contexts shall be dealt with.[6]

(1) Context of genre: The text which is continuously recited in Bhubaneswar is called '*kīrtana-mantra*'. It has been introduced in the middle of the nineteenth century and is characteristic of a specific *guru*-affiliation. An intrinsic relationship between the text and its practice as well as its performance is implied in its being designated as *mantra*. The features of this genre of texts will be discussed by dealing with the specific theological interpretation and the practical importance of *mantra*-recitation within the Caitanya tradition and its monastic affiliations.

(2) Context of *guru*-affiliation: While *mantra*-practice is common to all the branches of the Caitanya tradition, the institutionalization of the performance of the *kīrtana-mantra* as *akhaṇḍa-nāma-kīrtana* in Bhubaneswar is closely related to the charismatic personality of Nāmācārya Bāyā Bābā. He not only initiated *akhaṇḍa-nāma-kīrtana* in Orissa in 1953. In his approved mastery of *mantra* he has become for his followers an addressee of veneration as well as proof of the efficacy of devotional *mantra*-practice.

(3) Context of setting: *akhaṇḍa-nāma-kīrtana* can be regarded as an institutionalization of individual *mantra*-practice as well as of occasional *kīrtana*-performance. Not only is the text thus contextualized in new ways through the establishment of a permanent setting for the performance (i.e. the *kīrtana-maṇḍapa* or

[5] For a critique of a reification of both text and context and a plea for considering also processes of 'contextualization' and 'detextualisation' cf. Baumann and Briggs 1990. For a discussion of the limits of 'deconstruction' with regard to the analysis of text and context cf. Spiegel 1994, esp. 191-5.

[6] The analysis of these contexts is based on the study of classical texts as well as on data collected by interviews, participation in gatherings and festivals as well as on an analysis of the publications available in the *maṭhas*. I am grateful for the hospitality that was offered to me in all the *maṭhas* and for the numerous conversations with members as well as devotees. Also, I am indebted to Prabin Kumar Tripathy for his assistance during my fieldwork. I am especially grateful to the German Science Foundation, whose grants allowed me to conduct this research.

kīrtana-hall), but also through other contexts of text practice. This 'setting' shall be analysed by dealing with the spatial arrangement as well as with the visual and audial impact of the different 'sacred spaces' within the *maṭha*-compound.

1. Context of Genre: *Mantra*

The loud and even public chanting of the name(s) of god *(nāma* or *mantra)* is characteristic of religious groups and institutions that claim to follow the specific tradition of *bhakti* established by Caitanya (1486-1533). This tradition aims at a realization of 'selfless love' (*prema*) for the divine pair Rādhā and Kṛṣṇa. The practice of chanting is different from the more or less silent recitation (*japa*) of *mantra*-s as part of meditative practices. Both practices, loud chanting and more or less silent recitation are stages in the process of salvation taught in the Caitanya school. What is chanted or recited is called '*mantra*', a term which connects the practice to traditions of text-recitation since Vedic times.[7] Amongst these traditions, both (1) the ritual application of *mantra*s in the context of sacrifice or temple-worship, and (2) the usage of *mantra* in Yoga-practices form important contexts for the understanding of the specific features of *mantra*-practice and -performance in the Caitanya tradition. Therefore, I shall briefly deal with both: The recitation of *mantra*s is necessary in order to successfully carry out Vedic sacrifices (*yajña*) and, in later times, the worship (*pūjā*) of gods and goddesses in temples. They serve to invite the godhead to the ritual. Also, they indicate the completion of individual ritual activities, as for example, when each libation is accompanied by the recitation of a *mantra*, the completion of both might be marked by interjections like '*svāhā*', etc. In contrast, the usage of *mantra*s or the silent recitation of the different names of gods (*nāmajapa*) in the meditative practices in various traditions of asceticism and Yoga either aims at achieving a vision (*darśana*) of the god or goddess named in the *mantra* or at appropriating the power ('conquest';

[7] For an overview of these traditions and of the research on the genre of *mantra* cf. H. Alper (ed.) 1986.

jaya) which is ascribed to the godhead of the *mantra*. This is possible because the forms (*rūpa*) of the gods, which appear during meditation, are said to consist of *mantra*s. Seen from this perspective, *mantra*s are crystallizations of the power (*śakti*) of gods. Successful *mantra*-practice thus results in the mastery of the *mantra*, i.e. gaining and controlling the power of the *mantra* (*mantraśakti*). Therefore, the practice of *mantra* is a means of gaining access to the realm of godhead. The form of the gods, i.e. their iconographic representation, and their respective '*mantra*-body' depend on their position in the cosmological hierarchy, which is integral to the respective religious tradition. For this reason, the soteriological status of the practitioner can be determined by the *mantra* which he or she tries to master. As the efficacy of *mantra*s is linked to the context of practice (*sādhana*), in which mastery of the *mantra*s mostly goes along with a (physical) transformation of the adept, the mere utterance of the text makes no sense, i.e. has no effect. This does not imply that *mantra*s have no meaning (*artha*) as a linguistic unit or that they have no self-validity at all; rather, it is claimed that the evocative dimension of their meaning tends to evade the grasp of linguistic analysis. When traditional interpreters claim that in the *mantra* the signifier and the signified converge, i.e. the name of a godhead actually *is* the godhead, the *mantra*s are also called *vācaka*; they are evocative. This is why they differ from written texts, as has been pointed out by Padoux: 'à la difference de l'écrit, le mantra suppose toujours la présence de l'émetteur. Il n'est jamais coupé de sa production, de son origine, comme peut l'être l'écrit. … Il est inseparable … d'une énonciation'.[8] In the context of these practices, *mantra*s are regarded as texts which primarily aim at evoking the godhead named in the text and to receive a vision of his or her being.

---

[8] Padoux 1995, 134.

1.1. Theology of *Mantra*: *Japa* and *Kīrtana*

As already mentioned, *mantra*s also play a prominent part in the religious practice taught in the Caitanya School. This corresponds to traditional accounts of Caitanya's teachings in which it is said that chanting the name of god (*nāma-saṃkīrtana*) was regarded and propagated by him to be the only means of salvation in the present age of decay, the *kaliyuga*. In fact, reciting the name of god was Caitanya's main teaching; at least, if one accepts the traditional ascription of his being the author of a text comprising eight verses (*Śikṣāṣṭaka*).[9] As already indicated, the two contexts of *mantra*-s practice discussed before (see section 1) are important also in the Caitanya tradition: Firstly, the ritual application of *mantra*s of different gods and goddesses during temple-worship, and secondly, the silent recitation (*japa*) of *mantra*s during meditation. While these *mantra*-practices can be also encountered in other Hindu religious communities, the loud and public chanting and recitation of *nāma* and *mantra*, their performance as well as the institutionalization of this performance in the form of *akhaṇḍa-nāma-kīrtana,* can be regarded as characteristic of the Caitanya tradition.

As discussed earlier, both silent recitation (*japa)* and loud chanting (*kīrtana*) signify different stages on the way to salvation. *Japa* is mostly practised with the so-called '*mahāmantra*', which is traced back to Caitanya himself. The text reads as follows:

> '*Hare Kṛṣṇa, Hare Kṛṣṇa, Kṛṣṇa, Kṛṣṇa, Hare, Hare*
> *Hare Rāma, Hare Rāma, Rāma, Rāma, Hare, Hare*'.

This *mantra* consists of vocatives only, so that its recitation becomes a permanent invocation of Hari-Kṛṣṇa and Rāma as well as of Rādhā, when 'Hare' is interpreted as the imperative of Harā (and

[9] These verses are quoted in Caitanyacaritāmṛta (3.20.3-10), which became the most influential of all hagiographical accounts of the life of Caitanya, written by Kṛṣṇadāsa Kavirāja. Compare Stewart 1985, cf. also De 1961, 113ff. On Caitanya and the practice of '*nāma*' cf. Hein 1976.

not of Hari) in the *mantra.*[10] It is supposed to be recited in silent murmuring (*japa*) during meditation. Moreover, it is a controlled practice, since the number of recitations ought to be counted with the help of a *mālā* (rosary) made of *tulasī*-beads. The authorization (*adhikāra*) for practising this *mantra* is conferred to the adept during the first initiation (*mantra-dīkṣā*). It is a pre-requisite for becoming either a lay-devotee or a *sevaka*, a novice, and it is said to be open to all, i.e. restrictions of caste and gender do not apply.[11] In comparison with *mantras*, which are used in temple-ritual, it can be pointed out that the *mahāmantra*, apart from its rhythmic structure, does not contain any marking of its completion. Vedic as well as tantric *mantras* used in rituals often show such markings (like *svāhā*, etc.), a fact that suits their ritual application insofar as it corresponds to the individual segments of the ritual which are limited in time. In contrast to this, the *mahāmantra* seems to be especially suitable for endless repetition during *japa*, where recitation is first and foremost controlled by the counting of the beads of the *mālā.* It comes to an end when a fixed number of *mantra*-repetitions (108, 1008, etc.) is completed.

The practice of the *mahāmantra* is part of the meditation (*smaraṇa*, lit. bringing to one's mind) on Rādhā and Kṛṣṇa, which in its final stage results in a vision (*darśana*) of what is happening between the two in the highest heavenly region (*Vrajaloka*). *Japa* is thus claimed to be effective in bringing about the decisive transformation of the devotee: He becomes a participant in the eternal play (*līlā*) of love between the two addressees of his veneration, between Rādhā and Kṛṣṇa. The devotee then gains access to the *līlā* by playing the part of a female attendant of Rādhā (*sakhī* or *mañjarī*). This transformation into a participant in the play

[10] There are different views as to the identity of 'Rāma' and, to a smaller extent, to that of 'Hare' and 'Kṛṣṇa' in the *mantra*. This leads to the question of the divergent interpretations of text within the Caitanya tradition, which will be dealt with in a future publication. Compare the brief remarks by Beck 1992, 271-72.

[11] The second initiation, the *bheka-dīkṣā*, implies a change of name, dress, etc., and the initiation into secret *mantras* given by the initiating *guru*. In receiving this initiation, one renounces the world.

continuously performed in *Vrajaloka* is equivalent to salvation.[12] Ideally, successful *japa*-practice results in loud *kīrtana* or *saṃkīrtana* and testifies to the achievement of the highest form of *bhakti* (i.e. *prema-bhakti).* Loud and ecstatic singing is seen as a consequence of a preceding successful *japa*-practice: it is thus an indication of the mastery of the practitioner. He or she has become an actor in the play (*līlā*) that centres on those who are invoked in the *mantra*. For the male adept this is accompanied by a change of gender as he enters the realm of Rādhā and Kṛṣṇa as one of the female attendants of Rādhā. Also, *kīrtana* reflects the state of the arts in the eternal love play which is endlessly re-staged in *Vrajaloka*: The participants collectively chant those very names which the individual adept repeats during his or her *japa*. And it is an endless chanting (the true *akhaṇḍa-nāma-kīrtana*), which one can join only if one has acquired some mastery in *japa*. The highest form of mastery is achieved when persistent *japa*-practice results in permanent *japa*. This is called '*ajapa-japa*': *japa* which is not-*japa*. This means that *japa* has become a self-processing activity, a natural fact like breathing, so that the *mantra* repeats itself continuously. Therefore, the renowned *guru*s of the Caitanya tradition are often characterized as always having the name of god on their tongue. This is corroborated by stories that deal with the problem of stopping *ajapa-japa* in inappropriate situations, i.e. situations of impurity (as defecation, etc.).[13]

In the end, the *ajapa-japa* merges with the collective *kīrtana.* Thus, the *kīrtana* reflects a higher stage in which *japa*-practice is absorbed in ecstatic performance. In both cases, however, the mechanisms of control which were required in meditative practice, as counting with the help of the *mālā*, are suspended. Neither *ajapa-japa* nor *kīrtana* are any longer controlled as they have become continuous, i.e. endless. This reflects the condition in the heavenly regions: There, the endless repetition (re-performance) of the

---

[12] Compare on this inter alia Dimock 1966, Haberman 1988 and Rosen 1996.

[13] As for example the account of a conversation between Caitanya and Gopāla Guru Gosvāmin, in which is related that Caitanya used to stick out his tongue during the *śauca*, as it would otherwise continue to recite the name of god even during the course of impure activity.

eternal love-play between Rādhā and Kṛṣṇa is accompanied by the likewise endless chanting of the name of gods by participant observers. The absence of this kind of control is characteristic of *kīrtana*-performance, which makes it a rather unusual form of 'performance' as in most cases temporal limitation, and, thus, the prospect of termination, is regarded as one of its pre-conditions.[14] However, control or at least limitation is established through a different set of boundaries created by specific spatial settings as well as temporal frames that serve to structure endlessness according to certain time-rhythms. This applies even to the eternal *kīrtana* in *Vrajaloka*, where the *līlā* is measured according to a certain sequence of events (for example, as reflected in the *aṣṭa-kāliya-cakra*[15]); and it holds even more true for earthly *nāma-kīrtana.*[16] The latter not only varies due to the usage of different melodies, it is also terminated, for example, after the expiration of the projected duration of *nama-kīrtana* (mostly one or three days). Only in the case of institutionalized *akhaṇḍa-nāma-kīrtana* termination is suspended. Nevertheless, other boundaries are set up, as will be shown with regard to the spatial arrangement in the *maṭha* in Bhubaneswar (see section 3). Also, another difference between 'heavenly' and 'earthly' *akhaṇḍa-nāma-kīrtana* can be noticed. In the case of the institutionalized *mantra*-recitation, no congruity between mastery of *japa* and ability for *kīrtana* is indicated. The mere performance of the *mantra*-text by professional singers or musicians, who are engaged for special *kīrtana*-festivals or for *akhaṇḍa-nāma-kīrtana,* does not necessarily imply their having achieved the highest stage of *bhakti*. In this case, the performer does not become the sign of spiritual fulfilment, but a reminder of the necessity of *mantra*-practice. The performance might then be seen as a continuous invitation to also practice the *mantra* for all who happen to listen to it.

---

[14] Compare Schechner 1994, 6-16 and 106-52.

[15] Haberman 1988, 123ff.

[16] For an analysis of different forms of *kīrtana*-performances cf. M. Singer 1966 and T.K. Venkateswaran 1966.

Japa-practice and *kīrtana*-performance are contexts of and for the *mantra*, which are, to a certain extent, mutually dependent on and even constitutive of each other. This mutual dependence is, in turn, based on an ambiguous interpretation of the self-validity of the *mantra*-text: on the one hand, on the stability of the wording of the recited text and continuous repetition of this wording; on the other hand, on the fact that the efficacy, the evocative value of the text, is dependent on the mastery of the practitioner. Both aspects, if taken together, also allow for the recitation or utterance of *mantra*s even by those who are not primarily engaged in a religious life. Thus, the *mantra*, self-contained as it is, is not harmed by unskilled usage, as it only becomes effective if placed in the suitable context or if spoken by its 'masters'.

1.2. *Mantras* in the Context of Monastic Affiliations

These *mantra*-practices are transmitted and enacted by members of religious communities following the Caitanya tradition not only in Orissa but also in other parts of India. In order to specify the position of the text used for the *mantra*-performance in the Kalpataru Sevā Āśrama in Bhubaneswar within the larger context of the dissemination of the Caitanya tradition in Orissa, it is necessary to briefly point to the structures of monastic affiliations within the Caitanya tradition. The religious institutions (*maṭha*, *āśrama*) which follow the tradition of Caitanya in contemporary Orissa identify themselves in the larger, i.e. all-Indian context of their 'religious school' (*sampradāya*)[17] by referring to a specific family (*parivāra*) to which the respective *maṭha* belongs. Although members of *maṭha*s occasionally refer to sixty-four *parivāra*s, the *maṭha*s visited so far can only be listed under seven *parivāra*s. Five of these seven accept the same so-called 'great *mantra*' (*mahāmantra*, see section 1.1), which is traced back to Caitanya himself. Each family

[17] The majority of the *maṭha*s visited claim to belong to Brahma Mādhva-Gauḍīya *sampradāya*, whereas some specify their *sampradāya* as Mādhva Gaureśvara *sampradāya*. For a discussion of the connection between the followers of Caitanya and their inclusion in the *guru-paramparā* of Madhva cf. Mukherjee 1940, De 1961 and Deadwyler 1992.

(*parivāra*) traces itself back to Caitanya's time as it is claimed that either one of his companions (*pārṣada*) like Nityānanda or one of his disciples' disciples (Śyāmānanda, for example) has been its founder. Each family is again divided into several branches with different *guru*-lines (*guruparamparā*). Each family may include sub-families (*gaṇa*) that emerge through the fission of *guru*-disciple-affiliations or due to the appearance of a charismatic *guru*.[18] The *maṭha*s, which have been founded or taken over by Nāmācārya Bāyā Bābā, all belong to Nityānanda-*parivara*. Members of this *parivāra* trace themselves back to Nityānanda, an elder companion of Caitanya. Whereas Caitanya is viewed as the incarnation of both Rādhā and Kṛṣṇa, Nityānanda is seen as the incarnation of Kṛṣṇa's elder brother Balarāma. He is also called Nitai. As he is also viewed as the incarnation of the principle of guruship (*guru-tattva*), he receives utmost veneration as the divine *guru*.

In addition to the inclusion in the Nityānanda *parivāra*, Nāmācārya Bāyā Bābā and, in consequence, the *maṭha*s associated with him, belong to a specific *gaṇa*, a sub-family, within the *parivāra*: the so-called Rādhāramaṇa *gaṇa*. Rādhāramaṇa Caraṇa Dāsa (1853-1905) is one of the most important *guru*s of this *parivāra* in Orissa as well as in Bengal.[19] Amongst his disciples Rām Dās Bābājī became very influential and it was he who also gave the *mantra*-initiation (*mantra-dīkṣā*) to Nāmācārya Bāyā Bābā. Rādhāramaṇa Caraṇa Dāsa introduced the text and the practice of a new *mantra*, which is accepted by his followers besides the *mahāmantra* mentioned above. It is said that he received the *mantra* during a *kīrtana*-performance[20] and propagated it as a means for revitalizing the *bhakti* taught by Caitanya. The propagation of this *mantra* was also one of the main concerns of Rām Dās Bābājī. It was with his permission that Nāmācārya Bāyā Bābā started the

---

18 This genealogical model of transmission is detailed by Malinar (in print).

19 For more information on Rādhāramaṇa cf. Kapoor 1993, Malinar 2002. On the religious institutions, which were established by him and his followers cf. Malinar (in print).

20 For an analysis of the account of this incident in the sacred biography of Rādhāramaṇa, the Carita Sudhā, cf. Malinar 2002.

akhaṇḍa-nāma-kīrtana in Vṛndāvan. The text is referred to as the *kīrtana-mantra* or the *kīrtanīya-mantra*, the formula destined for public or loud chanting, or as *nāma*. This new *kīrtana-mantra* is neither performed by other *parivāras*[21] nor by those members of Nityānanda-*parivāra*, who do not follow Rādhāramaṇa Caraṇa Dāsa. It is also this *mantra* that is chanted in the *maṭha* in Bhubaneswar since 1973. The text reads as follows:

(1) *bhaja Nitai Gaura Rādhe Śyāma, japa Hare Kṛṣṇa, Hare Rāma*

Adore (by singing): 'Oh Nitai (Nityānanda), oh Gaura (Caitanya), oh Rādhā, oh Kṛṣṇa';
recite: 'Oh Hari, oh Kṛṣṇa, oh Hari, oh Rāma'.

In addition to this, the text in its printed version is sometimes also rendered as follows[22]:

(2) *(bhaja) Nitai Gaura Rādhe Śyāma, (japa) Hare Kṛṣṇa, Hare Rāma*

---

[21] One example is the Rādhākānta Maṭha in Puri, which belongs to Vakreśvara-*parivāra*. Here, *akhaṇḍa-nāma-kīrtana* is performed in front of the room, in which Caitanya lived during his stay in Puri. The *kīrtana-mantra* is different from the one performed in Bhubaneswar.

[22] As for example on the title page in the compilation of texts dealing with the right conduct of the devotees, ascribed to Nāmācārya Bāyā Bābā under the title 'Sadācāra'. It is also written in this way on the entrance gate to the shrine of the Gopaljew Maṇḍir of the Gopal Jew Maṭha in Darakhapatana, Cuttack. This *maṭha* also belongs to the *maṭha*s established by Nāmācārya Bāyā Bābā and which are now administered by a trust board, the Kalpataru Śacīnanda Trust. Compare Malinar (in print).

If seen against the background of the structure of *mahāmantra* discussed before (see section1.1) the following features of this text seem to be remarkable:

(1) In contrast to the *mahāmantra* quoted earlier, Nityānanda (Nitai) and Caitanya (Gaura) are included in the vocatives of the divine names. Thereby, the prominence of Nityānanda as the elder brother as well as the *guru* par excellence is signalized to the extent of invoking him before Caitanya, Rādhā and Kṛṣṇa.

(2) The names are preceded by imperatives (*bhaja*, adore, love; *japa*, recite) which address not the god as in traditional *mantra*s (i.e. *mantra*s taught in Āgamas and Tantras), but the (potential) reciter-performer as well as the listener. Thereby, *nāma-kīrtana* is recommended and this very recommendation allows for a continuous chanting of the *mantra*, which is in fact done in *akhaṇḍa-nāma-kīrtana*. This recommendation thus points, in addition to an endless repeatability, to another aspect of the *mantra*: The *mantra* has not only to be repeated again and again because it is the ideal form of veneration of god, but also because there always might be someone who is not already on the way to salvation, who is not aware of Nityānanda and Kṛṣṇa-Caitanya. This special feature of the text may also explain the second version of the text, in which the verb-forms are put in brackets. Somehow, these verb-forms are apparently felt to be a peculiarity of the text, not exactly matching the style of a *mantra*.

(3) The text recommends the recitation (*japa*) of another text, i.e. the *mahāmantra* text (in an abbreviated form referred to by '*Hare Kṛṣṇa, Hare Rāma*'). This can be taken as a hint that Rādhāramaṇa Caraṇa Dāsa did not mean to replace the *mahāmantra* by the new text, a fact which may serve to reject allegations of heterodoxy and defectiveness (as raised for example by Bhaktivedānta Sarasvatī and his followers[23]) against this text.[24]

Thus, apart from declaring the affiliation with and the importance of Nityānanda and his *parivāra*, the reciter also propagates and recommends the recitation of this text to the

---

[23] This debate will be dealt with in a publication under preparation.

[24] Cf. Kapoor 1993, 159, note 1.

audience. The structure of the text allows for its infinite repetition as it is independent of the ritual schemes of *pūjā* as well as of *japa*-count. It is this *mantra* which is chanted in the *maṭha* in Bhubaneswar since 1973, when *akhaṇḍa-nāma-kīrtana* was inaugurated by Nāmācārya Bāyā Bābā.

2. Context of *Guru*-Affiliation: *Nāmācārya Bāyā Bābā* (1891-1981)

While the text of *kīrtana-mantra* declares the affiliation of Nāmācārya Bāyā Bābā and his followers with Nityānanda *parivāra* and the *gaṇa* of Rādhāramaṇa, Bāyā Bābā himself is regarded as an important context of and for the recitation: Firstly, he is responsible for the institutionalization of *akhaṇḍa-nāma-kīrtana* as he inaugurated the *kīrtana*. Also, his followers gave donations for the construction of the *maṭha*-compound. Secondly, his charismatic personality is taken as a living proof of the power of chanting the name of god. Thus, he is the point of reference in the spiritual quests of his devotees. His mastery of *mantra* is indicated in the name: Although he was initiated with the name Śacīnanda Dās, his devotees rather refer to him as Nāmācārya Bāyā Bābā, the 'mad' (*bāyā*) Bābā, who is the teacher as well as the master (i.e. having realized the goal of the practice as well as the power associated with it) of the name of god (*nāmācārya*). 'Mad' indicates that he has achieved the highest spiritual level of ecstatic *bhakti*,[25] his distance from the regular code of behaviour, and also the special power ascribed to him. It is reported that he also did not use his name or the personal pronoun 'I', but referred to himself only as 'Bāyā'. His veneration as the *guru* and the veneration expressed by reciting and chanting the *mantra* are thus intertwined. The attractiveness of the

[25] This ecstatic 'madness' (*divya-unmada*) is an inevitable sign of having achieved the highest form of *bhakti*. Its symptoms are the so-called *sāttvika-bhāvas* like horripilation, tremor, fainting, etc.

institution is also rooted in the charisma of its initiator, for which biographical accounts provide a narrative structure.[26]

Nāmācārya Bāyā Bābā was born in 1898 in Balisahipatana, Kerada, Distr. Kendrapara (Orissa). He had a rather difficult childhood dominated by periods of disease and the early death of his father. Turning soon to the worship of Kṛṣṇa[27] (possibly after the *nāma-kīrtana* which was performed in Cuttack in 1915 during a cholera epidemic), he was initiated into the practice of this *mantra* by Rāmdās Bābājī in Jhāñjapitā Maṭha in Puri in 1917. However, he only dedicated himself completely to his religious pursuit in 1934 when he gave up his job and stepped out of a rather unhappy marriage. In the following years, he toured India and stayed for some time in the Himalayas, where he is said to have acquired *siddhi*s or *vibhūti*s, the super-human powers of a Vaiṣṇava (Tantric) Yogin. After his return to Orissa he stayed in several places with disciples and devotees and demonstrated his powers whenever necessary. Apart from his ability to predict future events and to read the mind of those around him, his ability to heal is especially noticeable. There are also reports that he resuscitated the dead. He recommended the chanting of the name of god and gave specially consecrated leaves of the *tulasī* tree to those in need as the appropriate medicine. From 1937 until 1961, he kept to the observance of silence (*mauna-vrata*), a period in which he

---

[26] The 'textualization' of Nāmācārya Bāyā Bābā directly contributes to establishing a specific tradition as well as to the continuation of devotion to him. This topic, however, cannot be detailed within the scope of this paper. Apart from the 'oral tradition' of stories about him documented in several interviews, biographical information has also been collected from Guna (Akshaya Kumar Das) 1984 and Chaudhurī 1996. These oral traditions have now also become written texts. Thus, several books have been published by devotees and disciples. Three volumes, for example, have already appeared under the title 'Bāyā Bani' 1981, a compilation of questions and answers and discourses roughly arranged according to time and place. Another collection of teachings of Bāyā Bābā has been published in two parts under the title: *Śrīkalpataru Kathāprasaṅga* 1995-6.

[27] In the centre of his worship stood Kṛṣṇa as *Ṣaḍbhuja*. The six-armed Kṛṣṇa is popular amongst the Caitanya followers as Caitanya gave the Brahmin Sarvabhauma a *darśana* of this *rūpa* in Puri.

communicated by writing only.[28] In this period he also visited Vṛndāvan, where he stayed in the Āśrama of one of his *guru-bhāī* (co-disciple of his *guru*). In 1951, he started *akhaṇḍa-kīrtana* in Vṛndāvan, where it continues until today in the Akhaṇḍa Kīrtana Bhāvan, Ramaṇareti. After that, he returned to Orissa where he began to establish a net of *maṭha*s that now amounts to 14 *maṭhas*. The Nṛsiṃha Tikiri Maṭha in Kendrapara was the place where in 1953 *akhaṇḍa-kirtana* was started for the first time in Orissa in the context of the *samādhi*-ceremonies performed for Bāyā Bābā's *mantra-guru* Rām Dās Bābājī (who had passed away the same year).[29] Rām Dās Bābājī had made a will in which he conferred the *maṭha* to his disciple. In the following years, Bāyā Bābā was busy enlarging the *maṭha* in Kendrapara. In addition to this, new *maṭha*s in Jajpur, Puri, Cuttack and Bhubaneswar and elsewhere were established. With the establishment of *akhaṇḍa-kīrtana* in several of his *maṭha*s, Nāmācārya Bāyā Bābā institutionalized what he viewed as the central and 'simple' teaching of Vaiṣṇavism. At the same time, he also created a space where veneration could be extended to him as well. Thus, life-size statues of him have been set up in several of the *maṭha*s, and pictures of Bāyā Bābā are also among the pictures in the hall in which *kīrtana* is practised. *Akhaṇḍa-kīrtana* has thus become a tribute to Bāyā Bābā as well. In this way, the institution of text-performance is also connected with the 'institutionalization of the charisma' of its initiator. The interplay of the contexts pointed out so far will now be put in more concrete terms by turning to both the locality itself and the mutual contextualization of the different sacred spaces within the *maṭha*-compound.

[28] A facsimile reproduction of letters is offered in Amiya līlā 1997.

[29] The *samādhi-pīṭha* of Rām Dās Bābājī has been established in the Pathbādī Āśrama in Calcutta.

3. Context of Setting: *Mandira*, *Kīrtana*-hall and *Guru*-Shrine

The *maṭha* is located in the New City of Bhubaneswar in Unit IX, a quarter inhabited mostly by people belonging to the (lower) middle-class. Construction started in 1971, with a small hut for Bāyā Bābā and the construction of a hall (*maṇḍapa*) for *akhaṇḍa-nāma-kīrtana*. Bāyā Bābā was able to raise funds mostly from people of the middle- and upper-classes,[30] who were dedicated to him, in many cases after having benefited from his healing powers. In 1975, two years after *akhaṇḍa-kīrtana* was started, the construction of a rather large temple compound began. The temple compound is not directly attached to the Akhaṇḍa-Kīrtana Hall. Behind the temple are the kitchen, store-rooms and rooms for the about 30 monks (i.e. *sevaka*s and *bābājī*s) who live at present in the *maṭha*. Inbetween the temple-compound and the *akhaṇḍa-kīrtana-maṇḍapa* is located a shrine with a life-size white marble statue of Bāyā Bābā in a sitting posture. Attached to this shrine is the room in which he stayed. The *maṭha* compound thus houses three 'sacred spaces' that have separate but nevertheless interrelated lives:

(1) The temple: The main shrine of the temple is dedicated to Rādhārāṇī and Kṛṣṇa-Gopīnātha. Figures of Nityānanda (to the right) and Caitanya (to the left) are placed in front of the shrine. To the right of the main shrine, a shrine for Śiva is placed, to the left one for Lakṣmī-Annapūrṇā. Between the main shrine and the one for Śiva there is a small, wooden shrine containing pictures of the *guru*s of Bāyā Bābā (i.e. Rādhāramaṇa Caraṇa Dās and Rāmdās Bābājī) and of the Jagannātha trinity. In 1993 a shrine for Rāma, Sītā and Lakṣmaṇa to the right in front of the Śiva shrine and one for Hanumān to the left in front of the Annapūrṇā shrine were added. The procedures in the temple basically follow the daily routine of worship in Hindu temples. *Pūjā* is performed by a Brahmin priest with a distinction between Śaiva and Vaiṣṇava

---

[30] A part of the constructions was, for example, sponsored by the industrialist Bhramarabati Agarwal (Kalinga Food Products). Cf. Guna, (Akshaya Kumar Das) 1984, 231.

pūjāris. Also, the main festivals of the resident gods and goddesses are celebrated with the majority of the participants coming from the surrounding neighbourhood. In fact, the *maṭha* is used by the neighbours as 'their', i.e. the nearest temple. With the instalment of Rāma and Hanumān now all the services demanded from the visiting neighbours can be provided by the *maṭha*. Visitors time and again stress the convenience of the institution giving the opportunity to worship so many important gods and goddesses in one place.[31] Although many of them are not devotees of Bāyā Bābā or do not follow the Caitanya tradition, they point out that the special feature of the *maṭha* is the performance of *akhaṇḍa-kirtana*, which makes the place unique in Bhubaneswar. This perception reflects the self-perception of the members of the *maṭha* as well as of the devotees of Bāyā Bābā: For them, both the efficacy and the necessity of the text-performance are reconfirmed in the response as well as in the non-response of those who do primarily visit the temple but cannot help but listen to the *kīrtana* while paying homage to their deities. Both monks and devotees express their conviction that the power of the performed text as well as the persistence of its performance will inevitably rouse the interest also of those who come here primarily for another purpose, i.e. for *pūjā*. The manager of the *maṭha* reported that the *maṭha* has already been called by visitors 'Vaikuṇṭha of Bhubaneswar', because the *akhaṇḍa-nāma-kīrtana* goes on and on like in the Heaven of Viṣṇu.[32]

---

[31] Thus, the *maṭha* offers services similar to those in the much larger Rāma Mandir, which is about 2 km away from the *maṭha*. The existence of this temple seems to have been one motive for the instalment of the additional shrines for the Rāma-'family' in the Bāyā Bābā *maṭha*. However, shrines for Śiva and Lakṣmī-Annapūrṇā can also be found in other *maṭhas* of the Śrī Kalpataru Trust, as can be seen, for example, in Darakhapatana Maṭha in Cuttack or the Mālā Āśrama in Keshol, Distr. Kendrapara.

[32] On the one hand, this view mirrors an attempt to classify the institution; on the other, it indicates the distance of the occasional visitors to the Caitanya tradition, according to which the place of the *līlā* is not Vaikuṇṭha, but *Vrajaloka*.

(2) Akhaṇḍa Nāma Maṇḍapa: as in other *maṭhas* too, a special area is reserved for *akhaṇḍa-nāma-kīrtana*. In the *kīrtana*-hall two to four singers are engaged in chanting, with members of the *maṭha* incidentally joining in. There are four groups of performers who chant for six hours per day. Half of the singers are permanent residents of the *maṭha* as they joined the institution as *sevaka* (novice) or *bābājī* (renouncer) respectively. The other half are householders (*gṛhastha*) who have received the first initiation (*mantra-dīkṣā*). They earn part of their living from their performances. Both housholders and residents of the matha regard the *akhaṇḍa-nāma-kīrtana* as a service (*sevā*) to god. The chanting is accompanied by the playing of drums (*mṛdaṅga*) and cymbals (*jhāñja*) and varies in melody and rhythm. The *chandas,* i.e. metrical pattern, as well as the melody for the *mantra* vary according to the respective time of the day and the sequence of *bhoga* and *āratī*: *kuñjabhaṅga* (midnight); *prabhāta āratī* (dawn); *prabhātī* (morning); *madhyama* (midday) and *sandhya āratī* (evening).[33] The sequence of rhythms and melodies thus corresponds to these times. Variations of the *kīrtana* in-between these fixed times do not follow a fixed plan or sequence, but seem to depend on the singers.[34]

In the middle of the *kīrtana* hall a free-standing, small pyramidal construction is placed. It is called *gaddi* or *pīṭha* and is typical of other *kīrtana* halls as well as for special *kīrtana*-performances.[35] On the four sides of the *gaddi* pictures of different gods and goddesses and of the main *guru*s of the tradition are placed. The *gaddi* should be circumambulated (*parikrama*) by visiting *bhakta*s during *kīrtana*. The main side of the *gaddi* can be identified by the *pūjā*-utensils placed in front of it. In Bhubaneswar

---

[33] I am grateful to some of the member of the Āśrama in Bhubaneswar for allowing me to record their performance of this sequence.

[34] On this point there was no agreement between the statements of the different persons interviewed.

[35] This construction is thus also temporarily put up, when *kīrtana* is organized as a special function, as for example the celebration of a festival or on the demand of a devotee. In this case, it usually, lasts for 24 hours (*aṣṭaprahara*) or 3 days (*caubisprahara*). Cf. also section 1.1.

it consists of oleographs arranged one above the other of (1) Rādhā and Kṛṣṇa on top, (2) the Jagannātha trinity in the middle, and (3) Caitanya and Nityānanda below. Here also *pūjā* is performed regularly, following, however, a timetable which is slightly different from the temple. *Pūjā* starts from the main side of the *gaddi* and proceeds clockwise. Thus all the other images are also worshipped. Apart from those belonging to the Caitanya tradition, pictures of Śiva, Rāma, Sītā, Lakṣmaṇa and Hanumān are also included. Important for the contextualization of the *kīrtana* with regard to the temple and the orthodox service offered there to the important gods of Hinduism, is the fact that the *pūjā* is here performed by a non-Brahmin priest. He performs the so-called '*vaiṣṇava-pūjā*' with the *vaiṣṇava-mantra*s ordained in the *paddhati* (authoritative manuals), first of all in the *Haribhaktivilāsa*. This practice represents and testifies to the interpretation of Vaiṣṇavism, favoured in the Caitanya tradition, as a creed transcending the borders of caste, creed and race. However, he belongs to a touchable caste, and it was pointed out that untouchables are, contrary to any touchable caste, not entitled (*adhikāra*) to perform the *vaiṣṇava-pūjā* even after they have received the final initiation (*bheka-dīkṣā*); a fact which theoretically results in having left behind their past and, along with it, also their former untouchability. On the other hand, the entitlement (*adhikāra*) for *vaiṣṇava-pūjā* does exceed the *adhikāra* of the Brahmin priests in the *mandira*. While the *vaiṣṇava-pūjāri* is allowed to perform *pūjā* with the *vaiṣṇava-mantra*s in the temple, the Brahmin priest may not perform *pūjā* in the *akhaṇḍa-kīrtana*-hall. In this case, the rights (*adhikāra*) of the ascetic exceed those of the Brahmin. This implies also that the gods in the temple may be included in the *vaiṣṇava-pūjā,* even if they are not installed in the *kīrtana* hall. If installed there, they receive the *vaiṣṇava-pūjā* only.

Moreover, according to the devotees, *akhaṇḍa-kīrtana* in itself demonstrates the non-violent and universal character of *vaiṣṇava-dharma* as lived in the *maṭha*: One does not have to engage in public missionary activities or other attempts to spread the faith. Rather, the *mantra* practised in *kīrtana* is self-efficient and therefore needs no additional support apart from its performance. Its content, which is its power, enfolds itself in the course of practice and performance. Therefore, it is said that people become spontaneously attracted and every visitor is a proof of this. This corresponds to the power that Nāmācārya Bāyā Bābā is said to have had on everybody, be it Hindu or Muslim, as the result of his successful text practice. Reports and *kathā*-s (stories) on this power are included in several publications by his followers. The creative power of the *mantra* is thus amply demonstrated by the miraculous powers of its master. Thus, Bāyā Bābā is, apart from his position in the larger *guru*-tradition of Nityānanda-*parivāra*, also on this level a context for the text-performance. This is again implied in the spatial arrangement of the *maṭha*, in the mutual contextualization of the sacred spaces.

(3) Shrine with the statue of Bāyā Bābā: As already mentioned, the marble-statue of Bāyā Bābā is placed inbetween the two other localities. It is, however, directly attached to the *kīrtana* hall. The shrine is opened only at specific times for *darśana* and offering *bhoga*. These timings correspond to the *pūjā*-schedule in the *akhaṇḍa-kīrtana* hall. Thus the *prasāda* milk-coffee is offered to the devotees, as this had been Bāyā Bābā's favourite beverage. The priest is also the same non-Brahmin priest who is in charge of the *gaddi* in the *kīrtana* hall. Thus, Bāyā Bābā is affiliated to the specific form of Vaiṣṇava worship not only as the founder of the whole institution, but also by having himself become an object of worship, his own image having been established in a separate shrine. The shrine, however, serves an additional purpose for the community: every Sunday afternoon the lay-devotees of Bāyā Bābā meet for '*satsaṅga*', communal gathering (lit. 'the company of the god men'), in front of the shrine. The community consists, as far as I could make out, largely of those who have known Bāyā Bābā personally or had at least interacted with him. Parallel to the on-going *kīrtana* in the hall close-by, members practice the collective singing of *bhajana*s, followed by the recitation and explanation of authoritative sacred texts by one of them. The texts that are used include canonical texts of the Caitanya tradition like the *Bhāgavata-Purāṇa* (however, not the Sanskrit *Purāṇa*, but the Orīya *Bhāgavata* by Jagannātha Dāsa) and the *Bhagavadgītā*.

Furthermore, texts indicating the affiliation with the *guru*-tradition of the *maṭha* are dealt with, like the *Carita Sudhā*, the hagiography of Rādhāramaṇa Caraṇa Dās and extracts from Bāyā Bāṇī, the collection of sayings and teachings of Bāyā Bābā. The communal dimension becomes also manifest in the existence of a *satsaṅga*-diary, in which attendance is documented by the signature of the participants. The *satsaṅga* extends until the evening service begins in the temple. It is thus an additional attraction for the visitors, some of whom drop in and pay their respect to the marble image of Bāyā Bābā. All the time, needless to say, the *akhaṇḍa-kīrtana* continues next door.

4. Concluding Remarks: Text, Performance, Institution

The present analysis of the interplay between a *mantra* and its different contexts shows that (1) text and context(s) are mutually constitutive of each other, and (2) that there are remarkable differences between what is seen by different participants and interpreters in a given situation as 'text' and 'context' respectively. This variability of the contextual framework, however, does not result in blurring the boundaries between both categories or in a 'fluidity' of the text. Rather, the canonical authority and the semantic implications of the text remain stable, a fact that is, however, not contrary to its being largely dependent on the contexts of its practice. As has been shown already, both the individual practice as well as the different modes of performance can be regarded as contextualizations of the very same text whose significance depends on the mastery of the practitioner. The institutionalization of the *mantra*-recitation reflects decisive aspects of the generic as well as of the theological contexts of *mantra*-texts. The timelessness suggested in the continuous chanting takes shape through the specific impact of the charismatic *guru* and through spatial and audio-temporal settings created within the *maṭha*-compound. The spatial arrangement of the *maṭha*-compound testifies to the mutual contextualization of its sacred spaces. The different contexts dealt with in the foregoing analysis are variably used by devotees (practitioners as well as performers) as well as occasional visitors to the *maṭha* as points of reference in explaining the impact of the institution of *akhaṇḍa-nāma-kīrtana* and in realizing their respective spiritual ambitions. The *maṭha* is also a temple which is, however, perceived to be unique because of the *akhaṇḍa-kīrtana* by the neighbours and by visitors dropping by. Seen from the perspective of the residents and devotees of the *maṭha,* the *mandira* might serve as an entrance for those who use it primarily for their daily *pūjā.* Therefore, they may not have any particular interest in the activities of the *maṭha.* The residents of the *maṭha,* however, hope that one day the visitors will become attracted by the chanting and find their way to the *kīrtana*-hall, or join the *satsaṅga* in front of the Bāyā Bābā shrine. This hope is based on the notion that the chanting of the name of God is efficient in itself. Nevertheless, its efficacy is dependent on its performance. The *kīrtana*-performance audially pervades the *maṭha* and thus accompanies all other activities.

The spatial contextualization of this performance mirrors not a 'centre' or an essential meaning, but rather the divergent demands and expectations of those who are in contact with the institution. The performed text fulfils this purpose perfectly as it belongs to a genre of texts which is made to evoke and satisfy religious ambitions. The institutionalization, therefore, is not understood as a preservation of a codified and memorable truth. Rather, the truth-claims implied in the text and its performance have to be realized in the various contexts which are created by the very people who take it as the basic text for their comments on the identity of the *maṭha* and their own aspirations. As a religious institution the text-performance not only constantly re-creates a codified text, but rather aims at activating its creative dimensions, i.e. the powers which the performed text might enfold in each and every individual's practice – a practice, however, that reaches its final goal when the individual practitioner joins the *kīrtana* performed by the community of *bhakta*s, be it in heaven or on earth. Thus, text performance in this case is neither just a specific mode of contextualization of a text nor is it a master context that displays some ultimate meaning. Rather, it is an ensemble of arrangements which aims at inviting the listeners to practice a codified text and to become able to play a role in another performance. The institutionalized recitation not only bridges the gap between listening and doing, between continuous repetition and eternal chanting, but also makes it visible. Thus, neither the text nor the performance are self-referential, rather, their mutual dependence invokes diverse referential frameworks; and the very play with endless repetition allows for the contingency and discontinuity of individual perspectives and demands.

References

Alper, H. (ed.) 1986. *Understanding Mantras*, Albany: State University of New York Press.

Amiya līlā. 1997. Bhubaneshwar: Kalpataru Ashrama.

Bauman, R. and C.L. Briggs. 1990. 'Poetics and Performance as Critical Perspectives on Language and Social Life', in *Annual Review of Anthropology* 19, 59-88.

Bāyā Bāṇī. 1996. *Prathama bhāga, saṃpādanā maṇḍalī Kalpataru śākhā saṃgha* (1st. ed. 1981); *Dvitīya bhāga, saṃpādanā maṇḍalī Kalpataru devā saṃgha. Tṛtīya bhāga, upasthāpanā Śrī Akṣaya Kumāra Dāsa*, Bhubaneśvara: Kalpataru Saṇgha.

Beck, G. 1992. 'Sonic theology', in Steven J. Rosen (ed.) *Vaiṣṇavism: Contemporary Scholars Discuss the Gauḍīya Tradition*, New York: Folk Books, 261-81.

Beeman, W.O. 1993. 'The Anthropology of Theater and Spectacle', in *Annual Review of Anthropology* 22, 369-93.

Chakrabarty, R. 1985. *Vaiṣṇavism in Bengal: A Historical Study, 1486-1900*, Calcutta: Sanskrit Pustak Bhandar.

Chaudhuri, K.C. 1996. *Amlā-jyoti nāmācāryya śrīmad śrī bāyābābā viracita. Saṃgrāhaka o lekhaka śrī kiśorī caraṇa*, Kaṭaka: Dakṣiṇa Kālī Presa.

De, S.K. 1961. *Early History of Vaisnava Faith and Movement in Bengal from Sanskrit and Bengali Sources,* Calcutta: Firma K.L. Mukhopadhyay.

Deadwyler, W. 1992. 'The Sampradāya of Śrī Caitanya', in Steven J. Rosen (ed.), *Vaiṣṇavism: Contemporary Scholars Ddiscuss the Gauḍīya Tradition,* New York: Folk Books, 127-40

Dimock, E.C. 1966. 'Doctrine and Practice among the Vaiṣṇavas of Bengal', in M. Singer (ed.), *Krishna: Myths, Rites, and Attitudes*, Chicago, London: University of Chicago, 41-63.

Duranti, A. and C. Goodwin (eds.). 1992. *Rethinking Context. Language as an Interactive Phenomenon,* Cambridge: Cambridge University Press.

Gonda, J. 1970. *Notes on Names and the Name of God in Ancient India,* Amsterdam, London.

Gonda, J. 1975. 'The Indian Mantra', in J. Gonda, *Selected Studies. Vol. IV: History of Ancient Indian Religion*, Leiden: Brill, 248-301. [originally published in: Oriens 16 (1963, 244-97)].

Goodwin, C. and A. Duranti. 1992. 'Rethinking context: an introduction', in A. Duranti and C. Goodwin (eds.), *Rethinking Context. Language as an Interactive Phenomenon*, Cambridge: Cambridge University Press, 1-42.

Gumperz, J.J. 1992. 'Contextualization and Understanding', in A. Duranti and C. Goodwin (eds.), *Rethinking Context. Language as an Interactive Phenomenon,* Cambridge: Cambridge University Press, 229-52.

Guna (Akshaya Kumar Das). 1984. *Reminiscences of my Master,* Cuttack: Kalpataru Sacinandana Trust.

Haberman, D. 1988. *Acting as a Way to Salvation: A Study of Rāgānugā Bhakti Sṟdhana,* New York, Oxford: Oxford University Press.

Halliday, M.K. and R. Hasan. 1976. *Cohesion in English,* London: Longman

Hein, Norvin J. 1976. 'Caitanya´s Ecstasies and the Theology of the Name', in B.L. Smith, *Hinduism. New Essays in the History of Religion*, Leiden: Brill, 15-32.

Kapoor, O.B.L. 1993. *The Life of Love. Biography of Sri Srimat Radharamana Charana Das Deva the Veritable Embodiment of Sri Caitanya Mahaprabhu's Uuniversal Religion of Love,* Vrindavan: Paramartha Prakasana.

Kennedy, M. 1925. *The Caitanya Movement,* Calcutta: Association Press.

Malinar, A. (in print). 'Genealogy and Centres: Communities of the Caitanya Tradition in Orissa', in Georg Pfeffer (ed.), *Periphery and Centre: Groups, Values, Categories*, Delhi, Heidelberg: Manohar.

Malinar, A. 2002. 'Rādhāramaṇa Caraṇa Das und die Caitanya Nachfolge in Orissa: Zur Textualisierung von Charisma', in Dirk Lönne (ed.), *Toḥfa-e-Dil. Festschrift für Helmuth Nespital*, Reinbek, 295-313.

Mukherjee, P. 1979. *History of the Chaitanya Faith in Orissa,* Delhi: Manohar.

Padoux, A. 1995. 'L'oral et l'écrit. Mantra et mantraśāstra', in *Puruṣārtha* 18, 133-45.

Rosen, S.J. 1996. 'Rāgānugā Bhakti: Bringing out the Inner Woman in Gauḍīya Vaiṣṇava sādhana', in S.J. Rosen (ed.), *Vaiṣṇavī. Women and the Worship of Krishna*, Delhi: Manohar, 113-32.

Sadācāra 1995. *Sadācāra nāmācāryya śrīśrīmad bāyābābāṅka dvārā saṃpādita,* Bhubaneśvara: S.S. Prinṭars.

Schechner, R. 1994. *Performance Theory.* Revised and expanded edition, New York, London: Routledge.

Singer, M. 1966. 'The Rādhā-Krishna Bhajanas of Madras City', in M. Singer (ed.), *Krishna: Myths, Rites, and Attitudes*, Chicago, London: University of Chicago Press, 90-138.

Spiegel, Gabrielle M. 1994. 'Geschichte, Historizität und die Soziale Logik von Mittelalterlichen Texten', in C. Conrad and M. Kessel (eds.), *GeschichteSschreiben in den Postmoderne. Beiträge zu einer Aktuellen Diskussion*, Stuttgart: Reclam, 161-202.

Śrīkalpataru Kathāprasaṅga (Nāmācāryya śrīśrīmat bāyābābāṅka upadeśāmṛta). Saṃkalana Śrī Bipin Vihārī Dāsabābājī. Prathamakhaṇḍa, 1995; Dvitīyakhaṇḍa 1996. Kaṭaka: Śrī kalpataru āśrama.

Stewart, Tony Kevin. 1985. *The Biographical Images of Kṛṣṇa-Caitanya: A Study in the Perception of Divinity,* Chicago (PhD-thesis).

Vater, H. 1992. *Einführung in die Textlinguistik*. München: Fink

Venkateswaran, T.K. 1966. 'Rādhā-Krishna Bhajanas of South India: A Phenomenological, Theological, and Philosophical Study', in M. Singer (ed.) *Krishna: Myths, Rites, and Attitudes,* Chicago, London: University of Chicago Press, 139-72.

8

Creating Performative Texts: The Introduction of *Maṅgaḷā pūjā* in Southern Orissa

Beatrix Hauser

During my first few weeks in Berhampur, the main town of Ganjam district in southern Orissa, women discussed with me the worship of the goddess *Maṅgaḷā*. According to the Hindu calendar this worship is observed in the month of *āśvina*[1] (September/October). On every Tuesday of this particular month married women fast and worship *Maṅgaḷā* in order to insure the well-being of their husband and children. To my surprise I found that this ritual was quite new to the region. It only became popular about ten years ago. My curiosity was awakened. I became interested in the phenomenon why women feel attracted to such a ritual, whereas similar traditions in urban contexts are dying out, and how they learn to perform this new ritual. The common ways of acquiring ritual knowledge and agency in Hindu India are usually through either continuous observation and imitation and/or through the study of scriptures with the help of a guru, the latter requiring to be of the proper sex, i.e. male, and caste. How would women dedicated to goddess *Maṅgaḷā* perform the *pūjā* (worship)? 'Ah, it will be written in a book', Oriya friends answered to my enquiries. This seemed to me quite natural since it corresponded to my own view of how to learn something.

After having regularly watched a group of women performing the *Maṅgaḷā pūjā* and discussing their approaches to it in individual lengthy interviews, my view of this ritual observance had changed completely. In fact, I was quite confused as (1) important sequences of the *Maṅgaḷā pūjā* were explicitly invented; (2) the sacred books

---

[1] If not stated otherwise the Indian terms used in this article refer to Oriya and are given in their specific spelling and transliteration. Some of them do exist in other more frequent spellings, drawn from Hindi or Sanskrit.

consulted seemed to be hardly related to the ritual event; and finally (3) the given motive for the performance of the ritual, i.e. the particular well-being of husband and children, appeared to be rather unimportant. However, the confusion was obviously on my side only. These features did not match my naive view of faithful wives unreflectively carrying out what had been transmitted from the past. The *pūjā* itself was perfectly valid, the elderly lady who played the leading role did a sincere job and the participating women were all truly pious. I had to revise my assumptions.

The scholarly discourse on ritual is, no doubt, a complex one. There is an abundance of anthropological, religious and sociological studies on the nature of rituals, their symbolism, structure, functions, meanings, performance, intention, etc.[2] So the observations mentioned above could serve as the starting point for a whole range of arguments and discussions. In this article I wish to concentrate on the role of texts in *Maṅgaḷā pūjā*. I should like to examine how far written documents determine the ritual process. How do they contribute to the enactment of the ritual and the establishment of religious agency? In brief, I should like to analyse the relation between text and context. Moreover, I should like to view the issue of text and context in a wider and post-modern sense: As a consciously created cultural document I consider the ritual itself to have textual qualities in its own right in reference to several contexts (i.e. 'co-texts') including, for instance, other events or the biographies of its attendants. Naturally, in contrast to printed texts, these 'cultural texts' are in continual flux. However, even though they may be reflected upon, disputed and altered, they are still characterized by their constancy.[3] Accordingly, my analysis will

---

[2] For some more recent theories on ritual cf., for instance, Bell 1992 or Humphrey and Laidlaw 1994.

[3] It is not the aim of this essay to concentrate on theoretical issues of text and context. In Social Anthropology, however, matters of 'text', 'texture' or 'entextualization' are dealt with in basically three overlapping domains: (1) the study of verbal arts/folklore as ethnopoetics; (2) the debate on writing culture, i.e. ethnographers as authors; and (3) the controversy on culture as discourse (cf. Baumann and Briggs 1990, Berg and Fuchs, eds. 1993, Clifford and Marcus, eds. 1986, Rapport 1997, Tyler 1987).

focus on the imagined, remembered and staged composition of the ritual which I shall call the 'performative text'. Although this kind of screenplay suggests authority, it is not a *pre*-script; rather it is composed *during* performance by one or more authors/actors. Its inventions and alterations are legitimized through their convincing performance itself, and may – or may not – imply a reference to previous events (like devotional experiences). In other words, I aim at analysing by what means women create performative texts (the worship of *Maṅgaḷā*) and how far they refer to printed documents or other cultural texts in this process.

I wish to discuss this matter by examining the *Maṅgaḷā pūjā* conducted by a particular group of women from the lower strata in the urban setting of Berhampur (250.000 inhabitants). Their *pūjā* is part of a religious observance in honour of the goddess *Maṅgaḷā*. It is called *Niśā maṅgaḷābāra oṣā,* lit. 'the fasting on Tuesday night', and takes place in the Hindu month of *āśvina* (September/October).[4] On this occasion the story of *Khulaṇā Sundarī* (The Beautiful *Khulaṇā*) is read out. Besides there are also other written sources. So in this paper I will explore the interrelations and interactions of the *Khulaṇā Sundarī,* the performance of the ritual and its socio-cultural environment.[5]

[4] The data on *Maṅgaḷā pūjā* were collected in the months of September and October 1999. This fieldwork was part of a larger study on women's cultural performances and their constructions of socio-cultural identities in southern Orissa. I am grateful to the German Research Foundation for financing this research.

[5] I would like to thank Burkhard Schnepel and Angelika Malinar for their comments on an earlier draft of this paper.

1. Women's Religious Observances

Hindu women are excluded from a range of rituals and religious practices. At many ceremonies they remain in the background or play minor roles only.[6] This is usually justified by the explanation that women cannot avoid pollution since they menstruate and give birth. The nature of women's religion is regarded as the fulfilment of their *strīdharma*,[7] i.e. in accomplishing their specific duties as females they contribute to the well-being, prosperity and procreation of their in-law's family.[8] Part of it is the regular observance of fasts and rituals for the benefit of one's husband and sons (Oriya: *brata*, *oṣā*).

On the other hand, women play a key role in performing the daily religious activities in a household. They do not only regularly worship the household deity but are also considered to be responsible for the organization of most life cycle rituals (for which they might order a male priest to come) and also to celebrate the different religious holidays and festivals throughout the year. In spite of this, female religious specialists and their contribution to the enactment, transmission and alteration of Hinduism have been largely ignored in scholarly discourse on South Asia.

As already mentioned, these religious chores are conveyed by the idea of *brata* and/or *oṣā*.[9] Both terms refer to a specific worship which includes fasting, possibly for the fulfilment of a wish, which in English is commonly translated as 'ritual observance' or 'votive ritual'. In colloquial Oriya both terms are used synonymously, even

---

[6] According to religious law (*dharmaśāstra*) they cannot even obtain religious liberation without first being reborn as a man (McGee 1991, 76).

[7] Even though this term originates from Brahminical discourse it embodies values relevant to all women, the only exception being female ascetics.

[8] Leslie (ed. 1991) and others have elaborately discussed the specific roles for Hindu women.

[9] Hindu women's rituals focusing on family, procreation, etc., have been discussed in detail by Bennet 1983 for Nepal, by Fruzetti 1982, Gupta 1983, Gupta 1999 and Ray 1961 for West Bengal, by McGee 1989, 1991 for Maharasthra and by Tewari 1991 for Uttar Pradesh.

a combination is possible.[10] Still '*brata*' implies the idea of a voluntarily taken religious vow (Sanskrit: *vrata*) while '*oṣā*' refers explicitly to fasting (Sanskrit: *upavāsa*). The votive rites differ according to their aim, their date and the status of the women participating. Most *oṣā-bratas* address married women, some are specified for unmarried girls, and some are followed by postmenopausal women and widows. Some are carried out alone, some are observed in a group of twenty or more women. Both individual and group rituals are rarely distinguished since in a joint household rituals to be done on one's own are also in fact shared by all the women of the respective marital status or age. Just as the worship of a deity is considered to be most fruitful and appropriate on a specific day of the week, each month has its own rituals. Accordingly, the votive rites are distributed throughout the year. Miśra (1994) in his collection of *oṣā-bratas* of Orissa has mentioned altogether 83 different types. Some of them are hardly known these days; others have been altered to meet changing lifestyles (working hours, increased age of marriage). The *oṣā-bratas* also vary according to their degree of difficulty. Depending on the scheduled time of *pūjā*, breaking of the fast will be either at noon or as late as after sunset. During some fasts even the drinking of water is prohibited.[11]

Throughout Orissa the goddess *Maṅgaḷā* (lit.: 'the Bestower of Well-Being') is very popular. People worship her as their protector, defender and saviour. She is considered to be a form of *Caṇḍī* (*Durgā*) and as such is identified with a group of goddesses

---

[10] However, which votive rite is to be called by either of these names is fixed by convention.

[11] Our knowledge of women's religious practices in Orissa is only fragmented. Marglin [1985] 1989 in her study on the *devadāsis* of Puri has discussed a variety of female values and concepts. Freeman 1980 studied postmenopausal women gathering in Puri in the month of *kārttika* to perform the *habiṣya*-fasting. Tokita-Tanabe (1999b) has discussed the celebration of a girl's first menstruation. Some scholars have focused on *Raja parba*, the festival of the menstruating earth (Behura 1963, Marglin 1995, Tokita-Tanabe 1999a). All studies so far have been conducted in coastal Orissa (Puri and Khurda districts).

such as *Śāraḷā*, *Bimalā*, *Samaḷāi*, *Birajāi*, *Hiṅgulā*, *Carchikāi*, *etc.*[12] All of these belong to a kind of independent (i.e. without a male consort), often fierce goddess who 'travels at midnight'.[13] Some of these require animal sacrifices, always of male victims. However, nowadays 'non-veg.' offerings are disliked or even prohibited in many places. In Orissa this type of goddess is classified as '*ṭhākurāṇī*' (great mistress, our lady). *Maṅgaḷā* is often associated with female deities who both cause and cure illness, especially a variety of pox and fever diseases of the hot season.[14] As will become clear below, the women in this case study approach her for other reasons. Generally speaking, they invoke *Maṅgaḷā* for immediate personal or material gains, such as the fulfilment of cherished desires, and to overcome a present crisis in life.[15] Even though *Maṅgaḷā* is cherished all over Orissa, it is only in her temple in Kakatpur (Puri District) that she is worshipped by Brahmin priests. In the scholarly discourse of Orissa this temple is basically known in connection with the ritual of *nabakalebara*, i.e. the replacement of the statues in the *Jagannātha* temple of Puri which takes place approximately every nineteen years.[16] In the

---

[12] There is a varying list of either eight or twelve goddesses. Even though all are considered to be different representations of the same goddess, one can distinguish them by their individual attributes. Nevertheless appearances, names and epithets intermingle. Thus, what is given as an epithet in one place signifies an independent goddess somewhere else (on the problem of naming Hindu goddesses cf. Hauser 1990).

[13] The prototype of the fierce goddess is often contrasted with the benign one which reflects the ideal female role model. Anyhow, this dichotomy is not an exclusive one.

[14] Marglin [1985] 1989, 268 and Eschmann 1978a, 86 mention the offering of *paṇā*-juice to *Mā Maṅgaḷā* on the roads in the month of *caitra* (March/April). This type of worship should protect the family and the village from all kinds of diseases. In and around Berhampur I have not come across this practice. Instead, women offer *paṇā* in the temple of *Buṛhī Ṭhākurāṇī* for the same purpose. Cf. also Marglin and Mishra 1991, Preston 1980, 12.

[15] Cf. also Mahapatra, ed. 1981, 30.

[16] Cf. Hardenberg 1998, 240, Marglin 1985, 70, Tripathi 1978, 233.

search for new logs the priests have to visit her temple and it is *Maṅgaḷā* herself who conveys to them in a dream how to locate the appropriate logs.[17]

2. The Performance of the Ritual

The maidservant's 12-year-old daughter shows us the way. It is the second Tuesday of *āśvina*. At about 9 o'clock in the morning we reach a typical Oriya house. We leave our shoes at the front door, close to 3 or 4 cows which are kept there. In the first room we pass a big wooden bed, some trunks and a TV. In the main room, which is about 12 square metres in size, we meet *Māusī*.[18] She is 52 years old and a mother of six grown-up children. Her appearance is bucolic: she is wearing neither blouse nor petticoat and the sari only roughly covers her body. On one side of the room there is an altar in the lower portion of a wall cupboard. I can recognize the image of a four-handed goddess, pasted in a thick layer of ground turmeric onto the wall. The relief is decorated with silver eyes, jasmine flowers, vermilion, *kajal* and a red dress. 'This is *Mā Maṅgaḷā*,' she is introduced to us, 'she lives on the hilltop (*pāhāṛa*)'. In the same manner a pile of red cloths (*pāhāṛā*) is kept on a low wooden stool, one piece given by every woman who observes the *Niśā maṅgaḷābāra oṣā*. On top of it, a bowl of consecrated betel nuts, lemons and a bunch of red bangles have been placed. Besides there are twenty-

[17] This temple is the focus of a study by the Anthropology Department of Utkal University, Bhubaneswar (Mahapatra, ed. 1981). In addition there are a number of other publications on *Maṅgaḷā*: Fischer 1996 as well as Fischer and Pathy 1996 look at her as the main motive of *oṣākoṭhi*-murals, Marglin and Mishra 1991 compare oral and textual versions of her story by Brahmin and non-Brahmin priests and mediums; and Eschmann 1978a mentions the goddess in her discussion on the Hinduization of tribal deities. However, none of these studies deals with the women's worship of *Mā Maṅgaḷā* or ritual observances in her honour.

[18] Lit.: 'auntie'. Since there is no term in Oriya to signify a female ritual specialist, I am using this common way to address an elderly lady. Most of the women joining the *pūjā* addressed her like this.

three auspicious *kumbhas*, i.e. earthen jars with coconuts on top, all decorated with a pair of red bangles, some cloth, flowers and vermilion. Each participant has to give one decorated *kumbha*, a betel nut and a cloth. The *kumbhas* contain water which has to be replaced every Tuesday. This is done like all the other preparations by *Māusī*. Only she is supposed to approach the goddess, and nobody may touch her at this time since this would cause her, *Māusī*, to be polluted. Along with a bunch of peacock feathers *Māusī* also keeps some lithographs of *Maṅgaḷā* and of *Gaṇeśa*. While she twists cotton to be put into a small ghee-filled lamp, she doesn't seem to listen to my question as to how she has learned to perform the *pūjā*. Her son explains how she had made a wish some ten years ago and started the worship at that time. 'I knew the *pūjā* from myself, I never asked anybody', she answers finally. 'I had been to Puri in the month of *kārttika*.[19] Everyone talked about *Maṅgaḷā pūjā* there. They told me to go to Kakatpur, to offer and take back a betel nut for worship.' This was about seven years ago; subsequently more and more women joined *Māusī's pūjā*. Meanwhile some of the women have arrived, bowed down in front of the goddess and placed their offerings on a brass plate in front of the altar. I am told that there should be eight types of fruits, eight stalks of *duba*-grass, puffed rice (*liā*) and flowers, preferably hibiscus (*mandāra*). However, most plates contain a coconut, bananas, apples, guavas, etc., mostly less than eight pieces. The goddess takes only 'uncooked' food.[20] *Māusī* gets some coloured powder, and by letting it trickle through her fingers draws a beautiful diagram in the shape of a flower on the floor. All the lamps are lit, it is 11 o'clock. *Māusī* rushes to

[19] In *kārttika* (October/November), the most auspicious month of the year, many older postmenopausal women gather in Puri for a specific fast (*habiṣya*), cf. Freeman 1980.

[20] The category of *kañcā*, i.e. uncooked, raw or dry food, also includes pre-processed sweets which are not offered in this case. In her temple in Kakatpur *Maṅgaḷā* is either offered six types of fruits or cooked food, the latter to be prepared by temple cooks in the temple premises (Mahapatra ed. 1981, 53)

get dressed in a new sari. She comes back with some smouldering coire and incense to offer to the deity. The *pūjā* starts in the presence of ten participants (out of twenty-three) with a shrill and auspicious *huḷahuḷi*-sound. All married women cover their heads with their sari. An elderly lady invokes hymns in praise of different goddesses, the others join in: 'Glory to Thee, oh *Mā Maṅgaḷā*! … If one remembers you, all sorrows will be erased!' After a while somebody starts reciting the story of *Khulaṇā Sundarī*. A few women listen. Yet more participants arrive. There is hardly any space left to sit, the air is hot and filled with smoke. The recitation goes on. Whenever the word *huḷahuḷi* is mentioned in the story, all participants hoot it loudly. After singing and listening for about half an hour, pieces of dried turmeric are collected, seven pieces per person. All are put into an iron mortar. While listening to the *Khulaṇā Sundarī*, one by one the women grind it. 'If you crush it well, you'll get a good husband', *Māusī* teases one of the few unmarried girls in the group. The girl had sighed, exhausted from moving the heavy pestle. Now the others laugh at her. The grinding takes almost an hour. Even though the *Khulaṇā Sundarī* is still sung the attention has turned to the preparation of some *paṇā*-juice. Calls such as 'Stir in the puffed rice!', 'Why don't you call for …?', 'Where is the other plate?', etc., interrupt the recitation. Some women chat about where to get fancy bangles and the like. Laughter. Again all join to sing hymns. *Māusī* crushes some coconuts and sprinkles a bit of their water over the idol and the offerings. She also offers *duba*-grass and some grains of rice with milk. Once again *Māusī* brings some smouldering coire and camphor. For this *āḷati*-ceremony we have to get up and try to touch *Māusī's* body. She speaks some sacred formulas on our behalf and offers smoke to the deity. A gong is beaten and one lady blows a conch. We shout a high-pitched *huḷahuḷi* and finally wave the camphor smoke towards our foreheads. Then flowers are offered in the same manner. Afterwards *Māusī* goes outside and gives water to the sun god. Everyone follows her. Finally all the women go back

> inside. The sacred *bhoga* (the offerings left over by the goddess) and the *paṇā*-juice are distributed. The morning session of the *pūjā* is now over. It is 1.30 p.m.[21]

When the participants leave for their respective houses *Māusī* takes the crushed turmeric powder, mixes it with water and replaces the old idol by a new one. When the women return in the evening they will see the newly decorated goddess with lots of fresh flowers attached. Then the evening session begins. It is a bit more grand, and the offerings, the number of participants and the time spent reciting the *Khulaṇā Sundarī* are more elaborate. It is the main and name-giving part of the *Niśā* (nocturnal) *maṅgalābāra oṣā,* since the goddess is thought to 'travel by night'. It will not finish before 10 p.m. I shall not describe this *pūjā* in detail since it resembles the morning session to a large extent. The major difference is that instead of crushing turmeric, each woman has to join eight strands of thread by making eight knots, each in one of *Maṅgaḷā's* names. With this sacred thread they fix eight pieces of *duba*-grass and eight grains of rice which are wrapped into *barakoḷi*-leaves onto a cucumber. At the end of the *pūjā* the thread is removed and tied to the upper arm of the respective woman.[22]

While watching the *pūjā* I thought these women to be from a lower caste or strata. There were some striking differences to those rituals I had seen in houses of Brahmin friends and in temples. First of all, *Māusī's* place was very small, a two-room-house with a kitchen had to serve as a home for about eight people. There was no space to maintain the strict separation of the sacred domain which I had noticed in many other houses. At night *Mā Maṅgaḷā*'s room definitely had to serve as the usual sleeping place, used garments were hanging on the wall, even small kittens crossed the room while the *pūjā* was on. All these features are considered to be polluting

---

[21] Revised excerpt from my fieldnotes, dated 5 October 1999.

[22] The ritual differs slightly on each of the four or five Tuesdays of the month. On the first Tuesday the *kumbhas* are prepared, on the third Tuesday some green grams are put to sprout. The evening section of the last Tuesday is followed by the immersion of the idol, the *kumbhas*, sacred threads and the sprouted green grams.

and should be avoided where a religious ritual takes place. I was very much surprised when I found out, that *Māusī* herself and many of the 23 women participating in the *pūjā* were actually Brahmins.[23] At first glance, caste did not seem to matter. Some women belonged to the *Khaṇḍāyata* (*Kṣatriya*), others to the *Baṛhei* (carpenter, i.e. *Śūdra*) caste. Only later I learned that women of lower castes like *Bhaṇḍārī* (barber, i.e. *Śūdra*) or *Dhobā* (washermen, i.e. Scheduled Caste) were not supposed to join the *Maṅgaḷā pūjā*. But this was not a matter of dispute since many different groups of women observed their *Niśā maṅgaḷābāra oṣā* in that neighbourhood anyhow. Also some middle class Brahmins preferred to do the worship among themselves. *Māusī's* house would certainly not be considered proper, even though her religiosity was respected. Economically most of her attendants were from the lower strata. Their families ran small workshops or other small businesses. Apart from the (impure) state of the sacred site there were other differences between the *Maṅgaḷā pūjā* and priestly dominated rituals. The agency of conducting the *pūjā* seemed to be shared among the women: more than five or six felt responsible for the proper procedure, all of them had to prepare the required items and many shouted here and there what had to be done in their opinion. This feature, however, applies to other votive rites as well.

Furthermore, the ritual process derives its character from a certain structure. On the one hand, the *Maṅgaḷā pūjā* consisted of many common sequences which are part of other Hindu rituals as well, whether a male priest is involved or not, such as the prostration in front of the idol, the ringing of a bell or gong, the blowing on a conch, the offering of incense, light, camphor, water and flowers, the composition of the *kumbhas* and so on. On the other hand, one can identify some specific sequences which do not occur in other *pūjās*. First, the collective crushing of the turmeric and the renewal of the approximately 70 cm sized relief of the

[23] *Māusī* belongs to the *Haluā*-Brahmins who were traditionally farmers (*haluā*, lit.: 'plough'). In Orissa there is a large variety of Brahmins and one will find many status differences within this category.

goddess is unique.[24] Second, the particular number of eight items is striking. For several ritual observances a specific number of offerings such as flowers, fruits, threads or knots is prescribed. The number eight is justified by the eight names of *Maṅgaḷā*.[25] Third, the tying of *duba*-grass, rice and *barakoḷi*-leaves onto a cucumber as such is not found in any other ritual. However, sacred threads are used in many votive rites and sometimes even fastened round cucumbers.[26] Fourth, while the recitation of sacred texts is a must in many *pūjā*s, the particular story of *Khulaṇā Sundarī* is recited only on the occasion of *Niśā maṅgaḷābāra oṣā*.

Watching the performance of the ritual I felt tempted to assume the existence of a kind of screenplay in the background. The carefully structured procedure of this *pūjā* almost suggested that it was borrowed from some kind of normative original. Even though I knew that the ritual had been introduced only recently, it seemed to repeat or refer to something. I was wondering to what extent written documents prescribed those sequences. Did they serve as a manual? Hence, let us turn to the scriptural sources used in the *Maṅgaḷā pūjā* and examine their contribution to the enactment of the ritual.

3. The Written Sources

For the *Maṅgaḷā pūjā* two kinds of written sources are used. First of all, one person recites the story of *Khulaṇā Sundarī*. This story (*kathā*) is divided into five parts to be read out on the four or five Tuesdays of *āśvina*, half of it in the morning and half of it in the evening session. In this way the story develops throughout the respective Tuesdays. Second, the devotees sing different hymns (*stuti*) in praise of various gods and goddesses.[27] The most

[24] Turmeric itself is quite commonly used in Hindu religious practice for the decoration of idols, to rub other women's feet, to be crushed during initiation, to represent *Gaṇeśa*, etc. In women's rituals even the usage of kitchen utensils is nothing specific.

[25] The list of those eight names varies.

[26] For instance at *Somanātha brata*.

[27] One may recite *stutis* for *Durgā*, *Ṭhākurāṇī*, *Śiba*, *Mahālakṣmī* and so on. A hymn is always welcomed, no matter who starts singing. However, only those

important of these is obviously the *Maṅgaḷā stuti*. These hymns are repeated on almost every Tuesday and also on other occasions. They are easily recognized by some of the women who spontaneously join the main singer. Some of the hymns are transmitted orally. Additionally, most of them are available in cheap booklet form in the local bazaar.

In the *Maṅgaḷā stuti* the goddess is praised as the saviour from evil, sorrow, suffering, pain and danger. The verses express the plea of the devotee to rescue her/him from difficult situations. Calls such as 'Oh *Mā Maṅgaḷā*, save me! I have no friend, brother, nor strength. Oh great Mother, save me from this danger!' are no mere sacred formulas. They actually substitute the voices of women performing the *pūjā*, a point I will come back to later.

In addition, the hymn describes *Maṅgaḷā* as a red dressed woman with terrifying teeth and tongue, riding on a lion at night. In her hands she holds weapons like a sickle-shaped sword, a curved dagger, a conch, a discus and a club. Apparently, *Māusī's* and the other women's idea of what the goddess looks like was not influenced by this description. Nor did they follow the iconography of *Maṅgaḷā* in her main temple in Kakatpur, where the four-armed goddess holds the full moon, a lotus and prayer beads.[28] I once asked *Māusī* what kind of items *Maṅgaḷā* usually keeps in her hands. I was astonished to hear her answer: 'She holds the earth, nothing else. She has four arms. She is holding only the earth. She holds neither conch, nor discus, club or lotus.' Even though the hymn and the Kakatpur discourse is familiar to her, she follows her own vision as to what *Maṅgaḷā* should look like. However, the turmeric representation of *Maṅgaḷā* made by her was not holding a single item. This image actually corresponded to figurines of the mother goddess (*ṭhākurāṇī*) which I had seen several times in those areas of a temple compound where women perform their rituals independently, i.e. near a tree or stone next to the main building (where the performance of a *pūjā* usually is under the authority of a

---

hymns which are considered appropriate for Tuesdays are recited, i.e. there won't be a hymn for *Santoṣī Mā* who is worshipped preferably on Fridays.

[28] According to Tripathi the present image is evidently substituted and represents *Tārā* (cited in Eschmann 1978b, 281).

male priest). So we might assume that *Māusī* was referring to a different cultural (visual) text, which could be defined in terms of gender, ritual hierarchy or other criteria. At any rate, the women who participated in *Māusī's Maṅgaḷā pūjā* were very much aware of her specific turmeric image. As one participant explained: 'No one does it the way we do.' The devotees did not only appreciate *Māusī's* individual talent to mould and fix the relief onto the wall, but also their collective crushing of turmeric in the morning sessions of their *pūjā*. In that way all contributed to the installation and replacement of the goddess. This collective identification became especially clear by a statement of an elderly lady who spoke in plural: '(First) we paste the image onto the wall … for the eyes we fix silver ones and we also stick a tongue of silver. Then, like we fold pleats in our sari, we fix a dress to the image.'

The *Maṅgaḷā stuti* also describes how the goddess is worshipped in different areas of Orissa as *Caṇḍī*, *Śāraḷā*, *Bimalā*, *Rāmacaṇḍī*, *Carchikāi*, *Birajāi*, *Hiṅgulā*, *Gaurī*, *Bhagabhatī* and *Samaḷāi*.[29] In this way *Maṅgaḷā* is related to a group of other goddesses who shape and characterize the *Śākta* topography of Orissa. Besides, the women I watched doing the *pūjā* identified *Maṅgaḷā's* appearance as *Samaḷāi* with a goddess phonetically almost similar: the goddess *Śyāmaḷāyi*. This is significant since in the last twenty years many of them have migrated from Hinjilikatu (near Aska) where there is a big temple of *Śyāmaḷāyī* (The Dark One, i.e. *Kāḷi*). Even though the *Maṅgaḷā stuti* mentions *Samaḷāi* residing in Sambalpur, the attendants of the *pūjā* are convinced that *Samaḷāi* refers to *Śyāmaḷāyī* at Hinjilikatu. In this respect *Maṅgaḷā* connects them with their native place, represented by the goddess *Śyāmaḷāyī*. Her prayer is liked by everyone and dominates the ritual. One might also view it as the transfer of their own local goddess down to Berhampur.

In contrast to the *stuti*-hymns which might be sung with the help of a booklet, the story of *Khulaṇā Sundarī* (The Beautiful *Khulaṇā*) is considered to be too long to be remembered orally.

[29] Cf. Marglin [1985] 1989, 331 for a quite similar sequence of the '*Māḷāśrī* of *Sarbamaṅgaḷā*', sung by the *devadāsīs* during *Bimalā's* festival.

Even though all the participants roughly know the story plot (which has been made into an Oriya feature film as well), the episodes will be remembered only after the participants have listened to it once more. The *Khulaṇā Sundarī* contains 62 verses (*chānda*) to be recited in different melody types (*rāga*) in altogether four or five parts (*pāḷi*). Each round is introduced by the poet with a prayer.[30] Depending on the publisher the verses cover up to 156 pages.[31]

In brief, the story goes as follows:

(1) There was a childless king with the name of *Dhaneśvara*. None of his riches could cheer him up. So his chief queen *Nayanā* suggested to him to gamble with her brother to win her sister *Khulaṇā* as a co-wife. The king won the game, *Khulaṇā* joined the palace and became pregnant. Still, the king left his country. Only after the news of the birth of a son he would come back. At the time of his departure he prayed to Lord *Jagannātha*. Goddess *Maṅgaḷā* became angry and decided to teach him a lesson. On *Dhaneśvara's* voyage she made him see a vision of a beautiful lady sitting on a lotus about whom he enthusiastically told *Sudarśana*, the king of *Birupā*. *Sudarśana* was eager to see this image but could not recognize anything. He accused *Dhaneśvara* of being a liar and put him into prison. Meanwhile the jealous *Nayanā* had started to treat *Khulaṇā* not only as her servant but to torture her in various ways. However, *Khulaṇā* was a sincere devotee of *Mā Maṅgaḷā* and with her help she could bear all the burdens and sufferings with ease. So even *Nayanā's* attempt to poison both *Khulaṇā* and, later on, her son failed. Finally *Khulaṇā* and her son *Śrīdhara* left the palace. Years passed, *Śrīdhara* grew up and set out on a voyage in search of his father.

---

30 In *chānda* 1, 2, 3, 14, 26, 39, 51.

31 I would like to thank Bandita Panda and Ranjan Das for their assistance in summarizing and/or translating the *Khulaṇā Sundarī*.

(2) Just before he left, he worshipped the village deities, *Śiba* and *Mā Maṅgaḷā*. All blessed him and gave him a sword, an arrow and *duba*-grass respectively to defend himself in times of trouble. Since at that time *Śrīdhara* was only a boy of seven years he was accompanied by *Somanātha*. With great difficulties they crossed dangerous oceans and were attacked by hundreds of leeches, the demon-goddess *Kāḷi*[32], big prawns and huge crabs. Only due to the magic weapons given by the gods, *Śrīdhara* and *Somanātha* survived. Finally they arrived in *Birupā*. But since *Śrīdhara* defied king *Sudarśana* he was immediately arrested by his troops.

(3) Twenty-seven soldiers were ready to execute *Śrīdhara*. Once again he prayed to *Mā Maṅgaḷā*. So at every attempt to behead him the soldiers were killed by their own swords. One by one they died. Only a single soldier was left to inform the king. Now *Sudarśana* ordered to hang *Śrīdhara*. But by the time he was led to the gallows, his ropes had been already opened by the goddess. Then *Maṅgaḷā* in the disguise of ugly old women went to the king's palace. When she was thrown out brutally, she showed her real appearance. The king asked for forgiveness and *Maṅgaḷā* demanded that he should give his daughter to *Śrīdhara* for marriage. The king had to agree. At the same time she made *Śrīdhara* ask for the royal prison as his dowry. The king was surprised by such an unusual request. He learned about *Dhaneśvara* and set him free. Finally the marriage was celebrated with pomp and splendour.

(4) Three months had passed when *Śrīdhara* dreamed that his mother was very ill. He decided to return to his own country. First *Somanātha* went as his messenger to give *Khulaṇā* the happy news. This time goddess *Maṅgaḷā* sent eight ghosts to build a new palace. Meanwhile *Nayanā* visited *Khulaṇā* and wondered with whose help she might have got this new palace and all those riches. *Khulaṇā* had to prove her

[32] The identity of *Kāḷi* is confusing: at first the text seems to refer to the snake demon *Kāḷiya* and later to goddess *Kāḷikā* who requires human sacrifices daily.

virtue in a series of tests: walking on water, converting iron into rice, staying in a burning house and the like. Finally and with the help of *Maṅgaḷā* her fidelity was proven.

(5) When *Śrīdhara*, his wife and his father arrived at the new palace *Khulaṇā* told them how *Nayanā* had tortured her during all the years. *Dhaneśvara* became very angry and wanted to kill *Nayanā*. Luckily *Śrīdhara* could dissuade him from committing such a great sin. Finally, *Nayanā* died a natural death and received her punishment in heil. *Śrīdhara* became the new king and performed all the rites required to thank god *Śiba*.

At the end of the book, the narrator introduces himself as the poet. By this time the reader is already familiar with his name, *Dhībari Bhikārī*, which he mentions at the end of each verse. In his biography he describes himself as a 19-year-old orphan from the fishermen caste (*dhībari*), who was asked by his teacher to write down the story of *Khulaṇā Sundarī*.[33] Such a reference to the poet is well known in many epic traditions even though the story was actually transmitted orally for many generations and finally written down by a number of authors.[34]

---

33 In many works we also find the author tending to be self-depreciatory and excusing any mistakes he might have made while describing a deity's greatness. Even this could be the case with the fisherman *Bhikārī* considering his name which means nothing but 'beggar' (*bhikārī*).

34 According to the description in the *Khulaṇā Sundarī* the myth was composed during the reign of the *Sūryyabaṁśa* dynasty, i.e. in the fifteenth/sixteenth centuries AD. In the history of Orissa this period is known for its renaissance of art, music and literature. However, it is one of the features of Hindu mythology that we find one and the same theme, story or legend in a multitude of versions, from orally transmitted folk poetry to different *purāṇas*. Thus, some Bengali storytellers in the neighbouring district of Midnapur (W.B.) narrate a quite similar myth which they trace to the sixteenth century *Caṇḍī maṅgal* (cf. '*Śīmantas* Hinrichtung' in Hauser 1998, 123). It would be stimulating to investigate this link further since it would contribute to the development of goddess devotion in eastern India (compare Eschmann 1978a, 85; Fischer and Pathy 1996, 527).

Even though the recitation of the *Khulaṇā Sundarī* constitutes an extensive part of the *pūjā*, at first glance there does not seem to be any relation between its content, the ritual itself and its meaning. Strictly speaking, *Khulaṇā* does not worship *Maṅgaḷā* for the well-being (and safe return) of her husband but to be saved from her own sufferings. Yet the women are told to do so on the first page of the book: 'If you sincerely worship *Mā Maṅgaḷā*, it will be for the well-being of husband and sons. Friends, you won't come across any troubles in life,[35] sisters, do this *oṣā-brata*!' Furthermore, in the interviews I conducted with the participants after the *pūjā*, it turned out that most of them were not really familiar with the story. Taking rest from housework, chatting with friends and busy with preparing offerings they did not follow the recitation. In response to my question none of them was able to remember the poet's name which is mentioned at the end of each of the sixty-two verses. Equally, nobody could recollect how *Khulaṇā* actually worshipped *Maṅgaḷā* even though there are several hints in the book. The goddess should be worshipped on Tuesdays, on an empty stomach, with some incense, lights and offerings, *mandāra*-flowers and a piece of cloth.[36] However, most of these descriptions might apply to the worship of other deities as well. Also, the frequent references to specific *rāgas* (melody types) to be used for recitation were ignored. In fact the only way the book influenced the ritual process was through the regular invitation to hoot the shrill sound of *huḷahuḷi* and through the prayers which interrupted the story plot again and again. When I asked some of the participants to explain the story, they mostly narrated the conflict between the two sisters, how the son was born, and how *Khulaṇā* had to suffer. Nobody took the initiative to tell the events after *Śrīdhara* left on his voyage, i.e. from the second part onwards. Obviously, when speaking about the *Khulaṇā Sundarī* women had only the very beginning in mind. Did they perceive only those sequences of the story with which they

[35] Lit.: 'You will not get any thorns in your feet while walking.'

[36] *Khulaṇā Sundarī*, 2, 11, 27, 70, 79.

could identify? In any case, the convention of the act of recitation at a *pūjā* site seemed to be far more important than the content of the sacred text.[37]

Yet, to presuppose a kind of manual for the performance of *Maṅgaḷā pūjā* was not entirely misjudged. There are several booklets available which describe different kinds of worship and prayers in honour of the goddess *Maṅgaḷā*. Some of these manuals are aimed at scholars and priests well-versed in Sanskrit,[38] some, in fact, address lay devotees.[39] There are even audio tapes with prayers, as well as booklets which tell further stories (*kathā*) about this goddess.[40] However, neither these stories nor any of the *pūjā*-instructions were known to or followed by the women I met. In other words, even though there is a genre of written *pūjā*-instructions (*pūjā bidhi*, *oṣā bidhāna*), it seems that women's rituals are constituted and legitimized in a different manner.

---

[37] This phenomenon does not come as a surprise. For the use of written texts in cultural performances cf., for instance, Blackburn and Flueckiger (1989, 11) in their introduction to Blackburn et al., eds. 1989.

[38] For instance, the *Mā Maṅgaḷā Mahāpurāṇa/Śrī Maṅgaḷā Mahimā* (Paṭṭanāyaka n.d.) deals with the temple in Kakatpur, different kinds of worship, the annual *jhāmu yātrā* (walking on glowing charcoal), several legends and prayers (cf. also Marglin and Mishra 1991). Being written partly in Oriya and partly in Sanskrit it is a compendium for the faithful Brahmin scholar and/or priest. Its style of writing does not appeal to female devotees. Similarly there is the *Śrī Mā Maṅgaḷāṅka pūjā o melā*. It contains a whole range of prayers, directions for meditation, including orders for the performance of *Maṅgaḷā pūjā*. Also this booklet is mostly in Sanskrit and for this reason hardly accessible to women. Anyhow, it refers to a different ritual than the one I discuss here. None of these booklets mentions the story of *Khulaṇā Sundarī*.

[39] The *Mā Maṅgaḷāṅka stuti o melā* (Dīkṣita, n.d.) contains not only some prayers and *mantras* but also a summary of various legends about the goddess, including some lines about *Khulaṇā Sundarī*. In the end it describes rules for the collective worship of *Mā Maṅgaḷā* and mentions general features as well as specific offerings. However, these do not correspond with the *Maṅgaḷā pūjā* as I had watched it.

[40] Booklets like *Caitra Maṅgaḷā oṣā kathā* or *Niśā maṅgaḷābāra oṣā kathā* contain legends relating to ritual observances in honour of *Maṅgaḷā* in the month of *caitra*, respectively *āśvina*. Yet, even the latter does not refer to the *Khulaṇā Sundarī* but depicts two different legends.

4. The Goddess who Guides Through Troubles

The goddess *Maṅgaḷā* is not worshipped for only one particular reason, like progeny or health. Certainly, as for other deities, her devotees might have a specific wish in mind when they approach her. Such a wish usually serves to reach individual goals or to overcome personal crises. While interviewing the women from the *pūjā* site, it turned out that quite a few of them approached *Maṅgaḷā* to solve major economic problems of their families. Virtually none of them worshipped her explicitly for the well-being of their husband or children. In any case, it is rarely possible to distinguish the *pūjā* for personal matters from those for the benefit of the whole family. The fate of a woman basically relies on her husband and in-laws. I would not dispute that in other circumstances women might pray solely for the well-being of their husbands and children. However, in this context of *Maṅgaḷā pūjā* the given motive seems to be more of a general plea which can be utilized by women. It gives them the freedom to move outside the household compound. I was surprised to hear that the male family members often did not appreciate their wives and mothers to engage in these fasts. While women stated that they did not feel any pain or difficulty in going without food – moreover, they gained self-esteem by doing so – men objected to it, claiming how harmful it might be for their wives' health. Since they seemingly showed little care about it otherwise, this argument appeared to be more an effort to keep them at their disposal. Women are supposed to remain indoors and even shopping is usually done by men only. But to observe an *oṣā-brata* and to leave the premises for the purpose of praying for the well-being of one's husband and sons provides an occasion which can hardly be declined. Obviously, this feature does not apply to *Maṅgaḷā pūjā* only. With reference to Rajasthan, Minturn has pointed out that since there is no indigenous concept of leisure time all forms of recreation are realized in the religious domain, i.e. in domestic ceremonies and public festivals.[41] Indeed collective rituals serve to strengthen female relations and friendships beyond kinship ties.

Only after interviewing the participants in regard to their religious motivation did I learn that the *Khulaṇā Sundarī* and its performance are interrelated on another level. When discussing the devotees' approaches to the goddess *Maṅgalā* concerning their feelings and aims towards the *pūjā*, I noticed how they responded in a somewhat standardized manner. Initially, I was confused. But after a while I recognized some similarities between their way of expressing personal problems and how *Khulaṇā's* suffering was narrated in the book. There seemed to be a relation between the framing and interpretation of events in the *Khulaṇā Sundarī* and the way women assessed their own experiences. On the other hand, I had to admit that even though I doubted the women's knowledge of the book, they were convinced that they faced no difficulty in understanding it: 'No, anyone can understand it. Anyone who reads *Khulaṇā Sundarī* will understand it. It contains everything, about the sister's pain and suffering, about her son, their departure.' Did we talk about different stories? I suggest that we were not only reading one and the same written text from a different perspective, we perceived two different cultural texts altogether. While I was searching for the story-plot the women at the *pūjā* site objectified the *Khulaṇā Sundarī* as a thematic entity. Their subject matter was how women are capable of bearing their sufferings. Once more I went through the written text, this time looking for those passages which might serve women to explain and tolerate their constraints.

First of all, *Khulaṇā* is praised for her ability to bear more distress than her husband: '(*Dhaneśvara*) had taken so much pain while living in the prison. How did you (*Maṅgalā*) save him from his suffering! His wife's name was *Khulaṇā*. As a human being she tolerated so many troubles. There is no one in this universe who bore so much pain. How you managed to save her, like that do help us!'[42] Here we get introduced to the fundamental theme of the

---

[41] Minturn 1993, 178.

[42] *Khulaṇā Sundarī*, 5.

Khulaṇā Sundarī: *Maṅgaḷā* helps to bear the sufferings. She does not solve the problems. She neither guards her devotees from difficulties nor does she punish the culprits. She guides her devotees through all the troubles. The poet *Dhībari Bhikārī* repeatedly explains how the women can assure *Maṅgaḷā's* support: 'With a lamp, incense, offerings and in a happy mood pray to the goddess. Whom she graces, she gets wealth, sons, happiness. All the desires will be fulfilled. She is the eradication of sorrows.'[43] He invites the audience to commemorate *Mā Maṅgaḷā* 'at her feet', i.e. to pray and meditatc in front of her idol. No matter what troubles made the women pray to the goddess, like in the written text, they always stressed on performing the *pūjā* in a happy mood.

Like many women, wives and young daughters-in-law *Khulaṇā* has to face an enormous number of physical and emotional burden. Neither for her work load nor for her mental stress is she shown respect. She becomes a servant to her elder sister cum co-wife who gives her all kinds of inhuman orders. For instance, *Nayanā* forces her sister to carry a water jar of about 150 litres: '(In despair *Khulaṇā*) raised her hand and hit her forehead. "Let it burn, my unlucky fate, who I am going to tell about it?" She prays to *Mā Maṅgaḷā*. *Mā Maṅgaḷā* will know about her pains.'[44] The book describes many situations of such injustice. In her question as to whom she should talk to, *Khulaṇā* expresses how useless it would be to complain to someone since nobody would be in a position to change her situation. More than that, the only one to understand her is goddess *Maṅgaḷā* herself. Only she will help to cope with such ill-treatment in the in-laws' house. She advises *Khulaṇā* to keep quiet and to continue to carry the heavy water jar and it will appear to her 'as light as a small flower'. In this way, *Maṅgaḷā* reduces *Khulaṇā's* pains on many other occasions. Along the same lines the devotees also approach the goddess not to solve their problems but to help them go through the troubles. For instance, one woman tells: 'So I called upon *Mā Maṅgaḷā* for the repayment of loan and to get more orders in our business. I am not asking god to give me

[43] Ibid., 70.

[44] Ibid., 18.

(money) to repay everything. Let my children grow up under good conditions so that they will study well, and let us get more work so that we can repay the loan.' However, not all those wishes were fulfilled, as another devotee expressed: 'For so many years I have been performing this *pūjā*. Nothing was fulfilled. And as you have seen, everything went wrong … . I keep on doing it because I have been performing it for five years. Even now I am doing it happily. What I had in mind, did it materialize? No. I thought of repaying the loans, but instead they increased. They multiplied. For one year we have been in this miserable state now. Doesn't god know about this, the way we are living?' The women are quite aware that they cannot expect miracles from *Maṅgaḷā*. They worship her to get support in times of crisis. Since women feel responsible for their family's well-being they call upon the goddess and seek nothing else but help to bear their fate. Otherwise they would have to justify themselves as *Khulaṇā* has, confronted by her sister (co-wife): 'I don't know any trick. I only have the blessing of *Mahāmāyī* (*Maṅgaḷā*). Besides her I don't know anyone else. Whatever difficulty and pain you have given me I tolerate it all because this will count for my *dharma*. Let my body suffer like this, as you are the elder one, let this right be always with you.'[45] In anger *Khulaṇā* asks her sister to continue with her tortures. She communicates to the audience that bearing suffering will 'count for their *dharma*', i.e. positively recognized as the fulfilment of one's (female) religion and duty. She embodies the idea that women are able to do so and that they will be rewarded on the spiritual level. Even more than that: by bearing sufferings women can prove their faith. In this way, the *Khulaṇā Sundarī* reflects the yearning of a female devotee that someone might help in her hopeless situation. On the other hand, it conveys that she should accept her fate in a positive way. *Khulaṇā* cries: 'The fate written on my forehead gives me continuous pain and I try to bear it also. Yet, if you do not rescue me I may drown deeper into it.'[46] Only *Maṅgaḷā* can save them. The other choice for a woman to escape ill-treatment would be to leave for her parents'

---

[45] Ibid., 20.

[46] Ibid., 23.

house which in fact is no alternative at all. Since it is considered to be the wife's fault if she cannot adapt to her in-laws, her return is associated with dishonour and shame. Even *Khulaṇā* considers this option:

> (That sorrow) which is written in my fate is unlimited. You are the one who (always) helped me get out of it. All my sorrow would immediately stop if I go to my parents' house. But I cannot bear to be considered unfaithful by the whole world, so I won't go. Let her (*Nayanā*) give me as much punishment (as she likes), as it is my fate, my body will bear it. In my parents' house everybody will ask why my husband left. They will blame me for coming back as such a poor *Alakṣmī*.[47] By hearing this my blood will heat up. (These abuses) will leave black spots on my reputation.[48] I can bear the sufferings but I can't bear these abuses. So I won't go back to my parents' house.' While thinking about all these things she cried and prayed to *Mahāmāyī*. Immediately *Maṅgaḷā* appeared before her: 'Why are you crying *Khulaṇā*, it is written in your fate. It is the nature of women to tolerate more pain (than men) and that is why you can cope with it. Since you had so many pains, oh *Sundarī* (beauty), I will free you from all the troubles. Within a few days all your pains will disappear and you will feel happiness in your mind. You will have a son who will free you from all the sorrows. Let crores[49] of troubles come upon you, at last you will come victorious out of it.[50]

---

[47] The opposite of *Lakṣmī*, the goddess of wealth.

[48] *Badana*, lit.: 'face'.

[49] 1 crore = 10.000.000.

[50] *Khulaṇā Sundarī,* 24.

Following *Maṅgalā's* explanation that women can tolerate more pain than men, the sacred texts not only call on the female devotee to bear her own burden but they also actually consider suffering to be a fundamentally female quality. Besides, the book suggests that only a son is able to help a woman to escape from her sorrow. However, on the textual level this turns out to be an illusion: When leaving upon his voyage *Śrīdhara* leaves his mother with the same message: 'We have to bear our sorrow. So mother, please endure all sufferings by chanting (the name of) *Maṅgalā* at her feet. She will protect you from all sorts of dangers. Always keep your mind at the feet of *Mā Maṅgalā*.'[51]

For women listening to the *Khulaṇā Sundarī* the character of *Khulaṇā* provides a figure to identify with. Her suffering, crying, prayers and calls upon the goddess reflect their own experiences made in everyday life. With the character of *Śrīdhara* there are also sequences in the text which could serve for male identification. However, the main character remains *Khulaṇā*. Even in the further development of the story-plot her sufferings are emphasized, partly since *Nayanā* continues to threaten *Khulaṇā* even after her departure from the palace, and partly because *Khulaṇā's* previous experiences are repeatedly narrated (for instance to *Dhaneśvara* in part five). Yet, the relation between the written text and its audience is more complex. By either taking the position of the narrator or letting the characters speak for themselves the book does not only reflect the devotees' sufferings. It also suggests to its audience how to perceive and classify their own feelings of distress and powerlessness. While discussing the motives to observe the *Niśā maṅgalābāra oṣā,* women often responded in somehow standardized phrases. 'Whatever is in our fate, it will happen. If we have bad luck why should we curse *Mā* (*Maṅgalā*)? … But by condemning god nothing will happen. It is our bad luck. We have this hardship because it is written in our fate.' I would suggest that the formulae in the sacred text serve as a kind of vocabulary, grammar and syntax for women to understand and to conceptualize their own experiences: It (1) prompts the *terms* to assess individual

[51] Ibid., 51.

sensations, (2) mediates how to *relate* these towards one's self and to its origin, as well as (3) how to *assemble* one's experiences in terms of destiny (*bhāgya*). In this way, it communicates culturally accepted and appreciated values for dealing with (female) subordination. The written text itself becomes an agent in constructing reality. By gathering, reading and listening to the *Khulaṇā Sundarī* women revive and embody those virtues. They convince each other that there is hope of gaining the goddess *Maṅgaḷā* as an ally. Moreover, the ritual suggests that even in hopeless situations the devotee is capable of agency: she can go through the troubles by praying to the goddess and, even without taking food, she might enjoy it. One could also interpret the joint physical effort of crushing turmeric in the morning session of *Maṅgaḷā pūjā* as a somatic experience of *Khulaṇā's* sufferings being rewarded in the afternoon by the presence of a newly visualized goddess. I should add and make the point that I do not assume this quality of the text to be exclusive to the *Khulaṇā Sundarī*. Still, in this case, I believe this text – like many other written and cultural sources – might serve as a framework to perceive, assess and reconsider individual emotions and experiences.[52]

5. Conclusion

In south Orissa the basic things women need to be able to worship goddess *Maṅgaḷā* are a small picture of her, a consecrated betel nut and the book of *Khulaṇā Sundarī*. Besides the general conventions of how to perform a *pūjā* or an *oṣā-brata*, there are no further instructions for her worship. Most devotees install a sacred pot (*kumbha*) and recite some verses of the *Khulaṇā Sundarī*. But only *Māusī's* group regularly prepared and replaced a goddess image and tied a sacred thread onto a cucumber. The case study presented here does not give any cause to assume that women in southern Orissa follow the *pūjā* in an identical fashion. Quite the reverse happens to be the case: the ritual does not only permit individual interpretation,

[52] Regarding the anthropological debate on emotions cf. Lynch 1990.

the latter also adds to its value. The more women identify with 'their' *Maṅgaḷā pūjā*, the more devoutly they call upon her. I have demonstrated how the ritual is not just carried out as an unreflected practice of tradition. Moreover, even the reason to pray to *Mā Maṅgaḷā* as the saviour from sorrow, distress or difficulty might be disputed in another ritual context. However, in this case study she helps the devotees to cope with their misery and to make their burden 'as light as a flower'. Her blessings work like a pain-killer.

Let us return to the aim of this essay and distinguish the different strands of argumentation concerning the intermingling of written and cultural texts and contexts (i.e. co-texts). Let us consider by what means written documents contributed to the enactment of *Maṅgaḷā pūjā* and, since its performance was hardly dependent on those, what actually outlined the ritual process. How was *Māusī's* ritual agency and authority established? How did she and other women create their performance?

Text and Ritual

As we have seen, the sacred texts determine the ritual process only to a very limited extent. Certainly the *Khulaṇā Sundarī* tells the women to hoot the *huḷahuḷi* at appropriate moments. It also describes here and there how characters of the story worship the goddess. But these depictions are not taken as a kind of instruction. Apart from that, neither the book nor the prayers mention any of the peculiarities characteristic for the *Maṅgaḷā pūjā* in this case study. In this respect, the emphasis is on the act of reciting, not on its content. This also becomes apparent when considering the devotees' limited knowledge of the story-plot. But then again the *pūjā* manuals available for the worship of *Maṅgaḷā* did not influence the women's performance either.

Nevertheless, the *Khulaṇā Sundarī* affects the ritual indirectly. Even though there is no immediate relation between its story-plot and the ritual context of its recitation (i.e. between the sacred and the performative text), it influences the participants of the *Maṅgaḷā pūjā* in essentializing their feelings of distress and as such their approach to the goddess. The sacred text's main character

Khulaṇā serves as a female role model and demonstrates how women can bear any kind of suffering and injustice. Moreover, the book provides women with a vocabulary, grammar and syntax to evaluate and express their emotions and sorrows. In this respect, the recitation of the sacred text serves to reproduce and embody those feelings in the ritual context of *Maṅgaḷā pūjā*. However, the influence of the written text on its performance is by no means a one-way process. Even though none of the devotees will be able to change the printed book, they might focus their attention on different aspects or parts of it. In this way, the performance of the *pūjā* not only stages but also limits the written source. In addition, the devotees also influence the further selection of sacred texts. And, as we have seen in the case of the *Śyāmaḷāyī* hymn, this might be for the sake of regional identity as well.

Last but not least, the analysis of *Maṅgaḷā pūjā* demonstrates its relevance for the understanding of the *Khulaṇā Sundarī* as a text. Like other written documents it needs a context-sensitive interpretation or, in other words, it reveals its meanings only in relation to other cultural texts.

Ritual and Performance

The performance of the *Maṅgaḷā pūjā* is mostly influenced by the way rituals are done in general, i.e. not a specific but various performative texts served as examples. Some elements were borrowed from other votive rites, some were considered particularly important for the goddess *Maṅgaḷā*. The most elaborate and time-consuming sequences of the *pūjā* I observed, however, were introduced in the last three to five years: the making of a goddess image out of turmeric paste in the morning and the tying of a sacred thread onto a cucumber in the evening. This selection was by no means accidental. It reflects ideas that *Māusī* and the participants had acquired through oral transmissions at places where women meet: at relatives' houses, at the local pond, at pilgrimage sites. In many respects the women adapted the *pūjā* to their individual expectations, liking and needs. They 'personalized' the ritual. It became a vehicle for their expression and a medium to reinforce their identity. Such inventiveness follows culture-specific rules. In India, it often works metaphorically, i.e. by the translation of analogous items and actions.[53] This process, I suggest, was based on shared and embodied experience rather than on conscious decision-making. Since the collective crushing of turmeric matched their routine of tiring housework, they might have sensed it as being appropriate. Since the hymn of *Śyāmaḷāyī* coincided with their memories of the goddess in Hinjilikatu, they continued chanting it. Still, those sequences could be altered and disputed since the responsibility for the performance of the *pūjā* is shared by many of the attendants. Of course, individuality is underplayed and difficult to pinpoint in a society where the major ideological emphasis is on faithful adherence to tradition. Nevertheless, when one listens to the women and how they stress their particular way of worship, one can make out that their performance is a consciously created cultural document. There was no example to follow, no historical paradigm. Thus, there is a big difference to the *Maṅgaḷā pūjā* performed in her temple in Kakatpur, where priests explicitly perform the ritual in the 'Vedic style' – whether or not such a ritual was carried out in those times. Corresponding to that idea of invariability in tradition *Māusī* too tries to place her *pūjā* in the timeless sphere of ritual. Alterations from year to year remain unmentioned. However, the *Maṅgaḷā pūjā* she started with about seven years ago is not the same as the one she does today and this process is still not concluded. One day I brought a couple of booklets on *Maṅgaḷā* with me for a discussion with *Māusī*. It turned out that none of them was known to her. She spontaneously selected one with *pūjā*-instructions and asked me to get her a copy.[54]

---

[53] As such, in many rituals one item can be substituted by another: red hibiscus (*mandāra*) can replace a blood sacrifice, a pile of cloth (*pāhāṛā*) can replace a mountain (*pāhāṛa*).

[54] Significantly it was the *Mā Maṅgaḷāṅka stuti o melā* (Dīkṣita, n.d.), cf. footnote 39.

Performance and Agency

In the case of a temple priest the question of ritual authority is straightforward. By being born into the proper Brahmin caste (or perhaps as a barber in subaltern contexts) he is already qualified to be trained in sacred scriptures. After being initiated and after some years of study he will be authorized to do the *pūjā*. Even if his performance is criticized by the devotees as superficial and business-minded, his authority will remain untouched. In the *Maṅgaḷā pūjā* textual knowledge does not provide this aura of authority. The woman to recite the sacred verses is chosen because of her good voice. She does not have any further ritual tasks or rights. And *Māusī*, the ritual specialist, proves her authority to a large extent through her convincing performance of the *pūjā*. The participants appreciate her ritual inventions as a sign of her devotion to the goddess. However, these inventions have to meet their ideas of authenticity. Hence there is discourse about the blessings *Māusī* received from *Maṅgaḷā*. How she miraculously found significant items for the *pūjā*, how she had a vision of the goddess, how *Maṅgaḷā* 'lives' in her house, though not in her body. Women talk about what they have heard to be meaningful, and they affirm others in their perceptions of the supernatural. In terms of ritual authority these examples of evidence of the grace of a goddess serve as the counterpart to the legitimization by birth and textual knowledge which is prevalent in Brahmin discourse.

Text and Co(n)text

In relating my observations about *Maṅgaḷā pūjā*, its attendants and the *Khulaṇā Sundarī* I have tried to demonstrate how perception and meaning of a sacred document changes according to its written and cultural contexts/co-texts and how the performance of a ritual is related to written sources. For this purpose I have distinguished three distinct levels: written texts, performance of the ritual (i.e. their context) and context of the ritual (i.e. other cultural texts). We have seen that every level might consist of a plurality of 'texts' which influence each other as well as other levels. If one analyses the ritual process, one feels tempted to assume a kind of prescript. If one focuses on some written sources, one might conclude that there are matching performances. As I have demonstrated, the additional meaning of the written source (*Khulanā Sundarī*) for this specific performance of *Maṅgaḷā pūjā* (i.e. its ritual context) has revealed itself only after considering the background and motives of its attendants. The selection as to which specific text is stressed at a particular moment is based on human agency. By means of the example of the female ritual specialist described in this case study we have learned that this can be a very creative process. More than once I have suggested examples of the intermingling with other frames of reference. This web of texts and 'co(n)texts' could be drawn further and further. It has been my aim to stress the possibility and ambiguity of variations, since I believe that a rather conscious selection like this from a plurality of meanings and sources should not be confined to *Maṅgaḷā pūjā* alone. I suggest that it applies to all rituals, and especially to those with shared agency, i.e. most if not all rituals performed by women as well as by many folk or subaltern religious movements.

To conclude, let us also consider whether or not it was useful to introduce the category of a 'performative text'. Did it just serve as another metaphor to construct social reality (like language, theatre, play …). Or did it meet the post-modern challenge to understand each and everything as some kind of text? In this essay which aimed at analysing an ethnographic case study it was certainly an advantage to presume such a category. It helped to grasp the ritual as a rather independent composition and suggested an agent-centred view of the ritual. Moreover, it reminded us that the enactment of a ritual was not only characterized by previous events of this kind, but implied a reference to forthcoming performances as well. As soon as one identifies a particular performance, it already serves as a performative text.

References

Baumann, R. and Ch. Briggs. 1990. 'Poetics and Performance as Critical Perspectives on Language and Social Life', in *Annual Review of Anthropology* 19, 59-88.

Behura, N.R. 1963. 'Rajaparba: The Festival of Fertility Cult in Orissa', in *Eastern Anthropologist* 16, 186-90.

Bell, C. 1992. *Ritual Theory, Ritual Practice*, Oxford: Clarendon Press.

Bennett, L. 1983. *Dangerous Wives and Sacred Sisters. Social and Symbolic Roles of High Caste Women in Nepal*, New York: Columbia University Press.

Berg, E. and M. Fuchs (eds.). 1993. *Kultur, Ssoziale Praxis, Text. Die Krise der Eethnographischen Repräsentation*, Frankfurt: Suhrkamp.

Blackburn, S.H. et al. (eds.). 1989. *Oral Epics in India*, Berkeley: University of California Press.

Bruhat Khulaṇā Sundarī bā Niśā maṅgaḷābāra oṣā, Kaṭaka: Bīṇāpāṇi pustaka bhaṇḍāra napani, n.d.

Caitra Maṅgaḷā oṣā kathā, Kaṭaka: Dharmagrantha ṣṭora, n.d.

Clifford, J. and G.E. Marcus (eds.). 1986. *Writing Culture. The Poetics and Politics of Ethnography*, Berkeley: University of California Press.

Dīkṣita, R. (n.d.). *Mā Maṅgaḷāṅka stuti o melā*, Kākaṭapura: Siṁhabāhinī pres.

Eschmann, A. 1978a. 'Hinduization of Tribal Deities in Orissa: The Śākta and Śaiva Typology', in A. Eschmann, H. Kulke and G.C. Tripathi (eds.), *The Cult of Jagannath and the Regional Tradition of Orissa,* Delhi: Manohar, 79–97.

Eschmann, A. 1978b. 'Prototypes of the Navakalevara Ritual and their Relation to the Jagannātha Cult', in A. Eschmann, H. Kulke and G.C. Tripathi (eds.), *The Cult of Jagannath and the Regional Tradition of Orissa,* Delhi: Manohar, 265-83.

Fischer, E. 1996. 'Oṣākoṭhi. Murals for the Invocation of Goddesses and Gods in Ganjam District, South Orissa. A Research Report', in A. Michaels, C. Vogelsanger and A. Wilke (eds.), *Wild Goddesses in India and Nepal. Proceedings of an International Symposium Berne and Zurich, November 1994*, Bern: Lang, 513-27.

Fischer, E. and D. Pathy. 1996. *Murals for Goddesses and Gods: The Tradition of Oṣākoṭhi Ritual Painting in Orissa,* Delhi: Indira Gandhi National Centre for the Arts.

Freeman, J.M. 1980. 'The Ladies of Lord Krishna. Rituals of Middle-Aged Women in Eastern India', in N.A. Falk and R.M. Gross (eds.), *Unspoken Worlds. Women's Religious Lives in Non-Western Cultures*, San Francisco: Harper & Row, 110-26.

Fruzetti, L.M. 1982. *The Gift of a Virgin. Women, Marriage, and Ritual in a Bengali Society*, New Brunswick, NY: Rutgers.

Gupta, E.M. 1983. *Brata und Alpana in Bengalen*, Beiträge zur Südasienforschung 80, Wiesbaden: Franz Steiner Verlag.

Gupta, S. 1999. 'Hindu Woman, the Ritualist', in H. Tambs-Lyche (ed.), *The Feminine Sacred in South Asia/Le sacre au Feminin en Asie du Sud*, Delhi: Manohar, 88-99.

Hardenberg, R. 1999. *Die Wiedergeburt der Götter. Ritual und Gesellschaft in Orissa*, Hamburg: Verlag Dr. Kovac.

Hauser, B. 1990. 'Göttinnenverehrung im Modernen Indien. Eine Bestandsaufnahme (Teil 1)', in *Mitteilungen aus dem Museum für Völkerkunde Hamburg*, Neue Folge, Bd. 20, 65-108.

Hauser, B. 1998. *Mit irdischem Schaudern und Göttlicher Fügung: Bengalische Erzähler und ihre Bildvorführungen*, Indus 4, Berlin: Das Arabische Buch.

Humphrey, C. and J. Laidlaw. 1994. *The Archetypical Actions of Ritual*, Oxford: Clarendon Press.

Leslie, J. (ed.). 1991. *Roles and Rituals for Hindu Women*, London: Pinter Publishers.

Lynch, Owen M. (ed.). 1990. *Divine Passions. The Social Construction of Emotion in India*, Berkeley: University of California Press.

Mahapatra, L.K. (ed.). 1981/82. *Man in Society. Bulletin of the Department of Anthropology, Utkal University* 2, Bhubaneswar: Department of Anthropology, Utkal University.

Marglin, F.A. 1985. 'Types of Oppositions in Hindu Culture', in J.B. Carman and F.A. Marglin (eds.), *Auspiciousness and Purity in India*, Leiden: E.J. Brill, 65-83.

Marglin, F.A. (1985) 1989. *Wives of the God-King. The Rituals of the Devadasis of Puri*, Delhi: Oxford University Press.

Marglin, F.A. 1995. 'Gender and the Unitary Self: Looking for the Subaltern in Coastal Orissa', in *South Asia Research* 15 (1), 78-130.

Marglin, F.A, and P.C. Mishra. 1991. 'Death and Regeneration: brahmin and Non-brahmin Narratives', in D. Eck and F. Mallison (eds.) *Devotion Divine: Bhakti Traditions from Regions of India. Studies in Honour of Charlotte Vaudeville*, Groningen/Paris: Egbert Forsten, 209-30.

McGee, M. 1989. *Feasting and Fasting: The Vrata Tradition and Its Significance for Hindu Women*, Ann Arbor, Michigan: University Microfilms.

McGee, M. 1991. 'Desired Fruits: Motive and Intention in the Votive Rites of Hindu Women', in J. Leslie (ed.), *Roles and Rituals for Hindu Women*, London: Pinter Publishers, 71-88.

Minturn, L. 1993. *Sita's Daughters: Coming Out of Purdah. The Rajput Women of Khalapur Revisited*, New York: Oxford University Press.

Miśra, N. 1994. *Oṣā brata gapa*, Brahmapura: Tārātāriṇī pustakāḷaya.

Niśā maṅgaḷābāra oṣā kathā o stuti pāṭha, Brahmapura: Raghunātha pustakāḷaya, n.d.

Paṭṭanāyaka, T. (n.d.). *Mā Maṅgaḷā mahāpurāṇa/Śrī Maṅgaḷā mahimā*, Kaṭaka: Śrī Śāradā ṣtora.

Preston, J.J. 1980. *Cult of the Goddess. Social and Religious Change in a Hindu Temple*, New Delhi: Vikas.

Rapport, N. 1997. *Transcendent Individual: Essays Toward a Literary and Liberal Anthropology*, London: Routledge.

Ray, S.K. 1961. *The Ritual Art of the Bratas of Bengal*, Calcutta: Firma K.L. Mukhopadhyay.

Sarba Maṅgaḷā stuti, Kaṭaka: Pustaka bhaṇḍāra, n.d.

Śrī Mā Maṅgaḷāṅka pūjā o melā. Kaṭaka: Pustaka bhaṇḍāra, n.d.

Tewari, L.G. 1991. *A Splendor of Worship. Women's Fasts, Rituals, Stories and Art*, Delhi: Manohar.

Tokita-Tanabe, Y. 1999a. 'Play and Eros. Girls' Swing Play and Swing Songs in Orissa, India', in *Journal of the Japanese Association for South Asian Studies* 11, 25-50.

Tokita-Tanabe, Y. 1999b, 'Women and Tradition in India. Construction of Subjectivity and Control of Female Sexuality in the Ritual of First Menstruation', in M. Tanaka and M. Tachikawa (eds.), *Living with Śakti. Gender, Sexuality and Religion in South Asia*, Senri Ethnological Studies, 50, Osaka: National Museum of Ethnology, 193-220.

Tripathi, G. C. 1978. 'Navakalevara: The Unique Ceremonies of the "Birth" and the "Death" of the "Lord of the World"', in A. Eschmann, H. Kulke and G. C. Tripathi (eds.), *The Cult of Jagannath and the Regional Tradition of Orissa,* Delhi: Manohar, 223-64.

Tyler, S.A. 1987. *The Unspeakable. Discourse, Dialogue, and Rhetoric in the Postmodern World*, Madison, Wis.: University of Wisconsin.

9

'Facing the Trial by Fire Every Day' Text and Performative Context in South Orissa

Burkhard Schnepel

I

In this paper I would like to address the complex, dynamic and multi-faceted interrelationships between text and context by focusing on one particular specimen of text: 'The story of the fowler'. I have collected examples of this text in the form of scripts and songs, and have myself witnessed them as dramatic performances while doing research on village theatre in south Orissa. In this paper I want to discuss how the fowler-story is related to various other texts, and how it interacts with a number of contexts, in particular with two kinds of the performative context, namely, song and theatre. Some final, more theoretical statements concerning the problem of text and context, as it appears from a predominantly anthropological perspective, will conclude the paper. Let me start by citing two passages from the story of the fowler:

> FOWLER: My Queen, the wealth of my life! I will bring a bird for you. You will kill it and prepare a curry out of it by adding turmeric.
>
> WIFE: How much food you ask for, my dear! There is neither spice nor oil. So how can I cook?
>
> FOWLER: So much pride you express! I shall beat you and see if any father of yours can protect you.
>
> WIFE: So much vanity you show! You have no rice to eat. And yet you dance so much. You have no home and you always remain in the jungle.

FOWLER: You witch, you have lice in your hair. Your sister wanders the streets. You live in the bazaar.

WIFE: Your caste is that of the bird hunter. I recognize you. You don't have any fear in your mind.

FOWLER: You quarrelsome woman! You eat from the cooking-pot. Your sister walks in an unchaste style.

WIFE: You have no caste and no family, my darling; but how cunningly you speak.

FOWLER: You shake your earring so much! With a single blow I shall make all your teeth drop out. You will cry because of me.

WIFE: I swear I shall not remain in this house. You famine-stricken man, you shameless person.

FOWLER: How strongly you speak! With a kick I shall break you down. You are trying to annoy me.

WIFE: How much you lie! There is a goddess in our village, and you do not fear her! You forget my love and beat me.

FOWLER: You quarrel without any reason and scold me without looking me in the face.[1]

Finally, the wife departs, leaving the fowler alone moaning in his misery:

FOWLER: Where have you gone, my darling?
How can I live without you now?
I got you by worshipping a crore of linga,
And I also observed the Hari-Gauri fasting to get you.
O my companion, my companion of many births!
Because I was afraid of my younger brother,
I brought you to the jungle with me.
My friend, come quickly if you are hidden
O trees, creepers, river, hill! You are all my friends.

---

[1] *Bīṇā Daṇḍa* 1980, 18-9. I am very much indebted to Mr R.K. Das for his help in translating this text, and the other Oriya texts that follow.

Have you seen my wife?
My dear friends, why are you silent?
There are thieves, robbers and ferocious animals in the forest.
Has anyone violated her?
My queen, my jewel! All my deeds have gone wrong.
I see darkness in ten directions.
My darling, your eyes are like that of a deer.
How can I live without you? I am blind without you.
What shall I say to your parents?
How can I show my face to the villagers?
My wealth, you have made me restless.
I cannot think what to do and where to go.
My darling, the jewel among the women!
Leaving me, where have you gone?[2]

The content of the fowler story as a whole can briefly be summarized as follows. Chadheiya, the hero of the story, is a fowler who lives in the jungle. He catches birds using a snare given to him by Siva (who got it from Yama, the god of death), but only under the explicit instruction not to kill various types of birds dear to the deities, namely, pigeon, peacock, parrot, mina and swan. After a time, however, Chadheiya repeatedly transgresses these prohibitions, until one day he even kills a peacock in the precincts of a temple. Infuriated by this, Siva and Parvati make him die of snake bite. When the fowler's consort Chadheiyani finds her husband dead, she laments greatly and attempts to bring him back to life in various ways. She asks a witch-doctor and a village doctor, but they fail. In the end, however, Chadheiya is revived when his desperate wife prays to Vana Durga, who in turn appeals to Siva and Parvati. These two deities relent and send Dhanwantari, the physician of the gods, in the form of a snake charmer, who casts a

---

[2] Ibid., 19.

spell in the name of Siva and Parvati. In the end, it is perseverance, love and deep faith on the part of Chadheiyani which does the trick. This basic storyline is often subjected to embellishments and variations. For example, sometimes there are two fowlers, resulting in a comedy of errors. Many humorous situations are created by the fact that Chadheiyani and Chadheiya frequently quarrel with each other, revealing some secrets of their domestic and erotic lives to the amusement of spectators. It seems that the two cannot live together, but then equally they cannot bear to be apart. In other versions Chadheiya has a lame and ugly brother, who wants to marry his sister-in-law on learning that his brother is dead. In yet other versions, the fowler has two wives. These variations of a common theme indicate that the fowler story is to be understood, in essence, as a dynamically changing creative process rather than as a fixed product.

The various passages from the fowler story cited so far come from a little booklet obtained in Berhampur market called *Bīṇā Daṇḍa*. This was written, or rather compiled, by one Sanyasi Nayak of Berhampur, who pays tribute to an older book written by Srinivas Bharati. This latter author is constantly referred to in ways that ascribe not only temporal priority to his text but also, implicitly and explicitly, to greater truth and sanctity. Srinivas is presented by Nayak as his guru and great devotee of the goddess. At one point, we find, for example, the lines: 'I, Srinivas lie at your (the goddess's) feet',[3] or: 'Srinivas narrates this story with the worship of Siva, Gauri and Brihaspati',[4] or he even 'interferes' with the action, such as when, at the end of the first passage cited above, we read: 'Srinivas says: "Let this quarrel stop"'.[5] Hence, the text I have cited is put in chronological order and a hierarchical relationship with yet another text of the same kind and style shown. Thus, we encounter a text which legitimizes strategy by referring to another text as more ancient, more valuable and divine, and to another

[3] *Bīṇā Daṇḍa* 1980, 1.

[4] Ibid., 58.

[5] Ibid., 18

author as having greater authority and the status of a guru.[6] As rhetoric, this *paramparā*-strategy is about the transmission of authority, not information. Ultimately, all *human* authorship is denied. The story of the fowler is not a figment of human imagination, but a true story known to us through divine communication.

On a more interpretive or theoretical level, the two passages cited above could well stand, and be interpreted, on their own. The first passage or fragment of the story of the fowler addresses the theme of quarrelling spouses, the second the theme of the love a couple bear each other.[7] The fact that in both passages the two parties, whether quarrelling or romantically longing, are one and the same couple shows that these fragments are interrelated and combined into a higher level of fragment, albeit in dialectical ways. Alternatively, one might take just one fragment of the story, identify it as a specific type of literary genre and compare it with other specimens of that kind. For example, one might take the second fragment and view it as an example of love poetry which could be compared with other love poems of Orissa and beyond. Alternatively, it might be illuminating to pursue the matter of variation as a context-sensitive interplay between various sorts of reflexivity and/or as a manifestation of the diversity of narrative traditions in South Asia.[8] Hence, this story itself (including its variant forms) may be subjected, in its manifestation as a written text, to various linguistic investigations.

---

[6] In Hinduism, in general, it is often not the author of a text who is considered important *per se*, but his being a disciple in a master-disciple line of succession (*paramparā*), the Sanskritic *guru-śiṣya* relation. On this point, cf. among others Michaels 1997, 119-23. More generally, on the performative function of such 'disclaimers of originality' and 'appeals to tradition', cf. Baumann 1977, 21.

[7] More precisely, many passages of the fowler story speak of the anguish of separated lovers (*virah*) and of the romantic longing rather than of romantic love 'in fulfilment'. Hence, these passages can be seen to belong to a sub-genre of Indian love poetry which prototypically belongs to, and expresses the mood of, the monsoon season. Cf. Lutgendorf 1991, 101-10.

[8] For an elaboration of this point, cf. Berkemer 1998, 174-6, Doniger (ed.) 1993, Ramanujan 1988, Richman (ed.) 1991.

There then appears to be a lot of work just by sticking to the given written text, work that would include at one stage or another serious reflections on how, and under which linguistic premises, the task of translation (not only of the text, but also of the culture in which it is embedded) has been done. To add to this, one might then compare this text not only in its variant forms but also with other stories, different but of the same kind, for example, with other hunter stories from Orissa and beyond. Finally, one might move to a higher level and view the story of the fowler as an example of the universal myth of the 'dying and resurrected god'. However, while these lines of 'intratextual' and 'transtextual' inquiry[9] represent possible ways of pursuing the matter further, I wish to proceed in other directions.

II

So far we have encountered the story of the fowler only in its form as a text in the narrow sense of the term, i.e. as a script, as something written in a book or on a palm leaf or something similar. To most people in Orissa, however, the story of Chadheiya is known, not by reading it, but by having heard it sung and/or seen it performed. I wish to discuss these two performative manifestations of the story of the fowler – let us call them 'the song of the fowler' and 'the drama of the fowler' – in the sections that follow, starting with a discussion of a song recorded during the performance by the Sri Nāṭya Samsad or Sri Dramatic Society based in Aska and directed by Sri Choudhury Parida.[10]

Having sung several devotional songs and songs in which the fowler laments the loss of his love and praises her virtues, this

[9] I am aware of the existence of a considerable number of publications – some stimulating and thought-provoking, others steeped in obscurity and saturated with esoteric terminology – which have been produced in 'postmodern' schools of thought. As I cannot and do not wish to enter into this debate, at least not on an exclusively meta-discursive level, I adapt some of the main 'technical' terms used here from just one source, namely, Genette 1993. By and large I follow this author in distinguishing the five types or forms of 'transtextuality': intertext, paratext, metatext, hypertext (respectively hypotext), and archetext.

[10] Recorded by the Samrat Cassette Company.

group proceeds to deliver a song in an Oriyan dialect and idiom spoken by the common man from Ganjam District. The content of this song differs in one basic respect from what has been presented so far: the main characters are not a fowler and his wife, but a washerman and his wife. The song goes thus:

The washerman comes in quick steps, being angry.
He has tied a red cloth around his head.
Being drunk he walks tottering.
There is no hair on his head.
He twists his moustache bravely.
He fears none, cares for none and dances swiftly.
He sings at a high pitch and laughs.
His wife is not with him.
She has gone to her father's house.
Jogi says, 'His heart is wailing due to this separation'

As far as the actual performance of this song is concerned, in this passage and in the ones to follow, there is basically only one singer, though this single person assumes different roles. Thus, in lines 1-9 he functions as an outside spectator and narrator, describing the arrival and state of mind of the washerman. In line 10, however, he suddenly assumes the role of a specific person, not a character within the story but someone who is described as the author of what he has sung (and will be singing), namely, a man called Jogi. We are thus confronted with a situation which somehow parallels that found in the *Bīṇā Daṇḍa* text in the relationship between the compiler Nayak (here, the singer as narrator of the story) and Srinivas (here, Jogi). In fact, almost every song ends with the word: 'Jogi says'. The washerman's plight continues: [11]

Hey, washerman!
Yes, master.
Have you become a rich man?
No, sir! I have become the victim of liquor.

[11] As opposed to the spoken passages, I have set the narrative line in italics.

What do you drink?
Red Horse, White Horse, etc., like this I am addicted to four types.
OK. Then you won't wash my clothes?
What shall I do, sir. My daughter is dying for a rice-miller and my son for a banana-eater (i.e. both are busy with amorous affairs). My wife is not at home. How can I do the work alone?
Is it so?
Yes, sir.
The washerman weeps. He is worried.
His wife has gone to her father's house.
O, drummer! She has already been gone four months, making me sad; she has forgotten me.
We had a relationship like that of milk and water.
That has changed now.
Being sad because of her departure, I have become frail.
O, drummer. She is like the garland of my neck, the pupil of my eyes. She is a soft woman whose face is like the moon.
When I think of her virtues, my heart is cut.
Even if I am separated from her for just a moment, my mind becomes restless.
Now, she who has thick hair on her head, has forgotten me ... (inaudible)
In this dense forest ... (inaudible) what a shame for me.
Her love is sweeter than honey, cream and nectar.

Thus, after some music, another dramatic strategy occurs in lines 11-20, for this passage is not sung by one person but presented as a spoken conversation between two different performers impersonating a village-style patron and the washerman. In lines 20 and 21 – and there is no pause or musical interlude between these passages – we are back to singing and to the soloist as narrator. Suddenly, however, in the following lines, up to line 37, this very same singer, without changing his voice, impersonates the washerman, who is lamenting about the absence of his wife, praising her beauty, etc. While doing so he talks to the drummer and, hence, to a person outside the play proper (lines 23, 27). It also seems that, for a brief moment at least (line 31), we have left the streets of ordinary village/town life and are back in the mythological, somewhat Arcadian scene of the fowler story. The song continues :

The washerman's cunning wife swiftly comes out. She smiles gently. Her coy look steals the heart. What a nice gait she has.	
WIFE:	O brother. How far is your brother-in-law's house?
BROTHER:	It is there, just a little further on.
WIFE:	Fate has decided like this. What can we do? But I cannot forget his memory, says the washerman's wife.
BROTHER:	Sister, don't cry. I feel weepy with you.
This song in metres and styles was sung by Jogi. Swiftly and gracefully comes out the fisherman's wife.	

After a short musical interlude, we thus return to the singer as narrator, who describes the washerman's wife (lines 38-41). Note that here, as elsewhere before and after these lines, there is an emphasis on the description of the character's gait, a point which will become important when we turn to the 'drama of the fowler'. This passage is followed by a short conversation between the washerman's wife and her brother, in which it is indicated that she is longing to go back home (lines 42-3). Thereafter, the dramaturgy becomes rather complicated, because there are two lines of song and one line of conversation (lines 44-6), in which the singer assumes the role of brother and sister, followed by one line of song in which he refers to the superior author, Jogi, as the one who is saying this. Without any interruption, one then hears the same voice, but this time as narrator (line 48), before the following sequence of conversation starts with some repetition:

WIFE:	O brother! How far is your brother-in-law's home?
BROTHER:	It is very near. Only a little further on. Sister, see! The man coming towards us seems to be the brother-in-law. Oh, yes, he is drunk. Hey, brother-in-law. Welcome!
HUSBAND:	Who are you?
BROTHER:	Don't you recognize me? I went to work in the colliery, doing digging work.
WIFE:	He is my brother.
HUSBAND:	I see. He has grown up. You take your sister back. I don't need her. You keep her.
BROTHER:	Won't you keep her? If you don't, then your father will have to keep her. And whenever you come to our place, I'll give you a proper thrashing.

The story continues in the form of a sung conversation between husband and wife as follows:

HUSBAND:	O, mean woman, I know you. Ignoring my words, you went to your father's home. You will therefore have to face the consequences.
WIFE:	Master of my life, my husband! Please listen to me.

	What mistake have I committed that makes you so angry? Please tell me, my husband.
	O, my master! Consider my words.
	Short musical interlude
HUSBAND:	You have become unchaste, you sinner. What were you thinking of?
	I have been able to size you up.
	When you went to your father's house, you did not think of me.
	You stayed there, you mean woman. I know you.
WIFE:	Don't be mad, my husband. Calm down.
	When a daughter goes to her father's place, is that wrong?
	My master, please consider my point of view.
HUSBAND:	You sinner, get out of my house.
	Now I'll divorce you. You get out of my house.
	I'll not see your face.
	You mean woman. I know you.

This passage is followed by a dialogue in which the vernacular becomes even more colloquial:

WIFE:	Hey, won't you see my face?
HUSBAND:	No, never.
WIFE:	You'll divorce me?
HUSBAND:	Certainly!
WIFE:	How can you do that?
	Five men of the village will sit and decide the matter.
	You will have to take out all the

	property that I have brought from my father to the road.
	I will be anointed with oil and turmeric and will sit on a bullock cart.
	You will sit under that cart.
	Twenty-one buckets of water will be poured on my head.
	You will take a bath in that dirty water.
	Only after that can you divorce me.

In this passage, we see that the wife ultimately takes up the quarrel with her husband, even showing herself superior to him. She threatens him with a *panchayat* and invents a ritual of inversion, a symbolic reversal of the newly married woman's procession to her in-law's house. This also turns out to be a ritual of humiliation for the divorcing husband, exposing him to the impure water with which she was bathed earlier. This passage is followed by a short song which indicates a change of mood on the part of the wife:

HUSBAND:	Those days are gone. Get quickly out of my house!
WIFE:	Dear husband! Is there any king greater than Rama?
	The grandson of Paulastya (i.e. Ravana) took Rama's wife and kept her in Lanka for fourteen months.
	My dear master, consider what I am saying.

After this somewhat poetic linking of domestic strife in the streets of Berhampur to the *Rāmāyaṇa* tradition, there follows another dialogue between husband and wife in which the 'Great Tradition' is further referred to by the two antagonists, though in a rather earthy manner:

HUSBAND:	Hey, Ravana kept Sita for fourteen months in Lanka. She did not become unchaste.
WIFE:	But I stayed in my father's home for three days and became unchaste and you are throwing me out of the house?
HUSBAND:	Lo ... sinner! Sita underwent the trial by fire and came out unscathed. Can you be equal to her? I know you, mean woman.
WIFE:	Rama went to Lanka, killed Ravana and rescued Sita. Then Sita underwent the trial by fire. But Sita underwent such a trial only once. I face it every day.
HUSBAND:	How can that be? Can you explain that?
WIFE:	You go to the jungle and collect wood. I use it to make fire. Is that not a trial by fire?
HUSBAND:	I do not accept that. Go back soon.

But finally the quarrel ends, and a romantic and an amorous situation arises:

WIFE:	Dear husband. For a long time I have not done my duty. My mind is restless day and night, tears flow from my eyes. Hey! In which family does this sort of thing not happen? Let's go, or else people will laugh at us.
HUSBAND:	OK. Let us go! Come quickly.

Holding the husband's hand, the enticing woman says: 'Excuse me. Let us go to the forest. It is so beautiful. There is a light breeze. Deer, bison, boar, and other animals can be seen in the forest. The whole land looks beautiful. Deer are happily grazing in pairs. There are so many flowers. Who can count them? They have a strong fragrance. I shall use them to adorn my hair'.	105

With images like this, the happy couple moves deep into the serene forest and, so it is implied, towards an erotic encounter. And the audience moves back from the mundane life that they are familiar with towards the Arcadian setting of the story of the fowler, which, it must not be forgotten, is the theme of the songs preceding and succeeding the story of the washerman and his wife.

As far as the performative side of this song or, rather, group of interrelated songs is concerned, the performers confront the audience with a number of different angles to and levels of the story. On the one hand, they make use of the two most direct ways of communicating a story by either taking the position of narrator, or by letting the characters speak for themselves. This latter angle usually takes the form of a dialogue, but we also have monologues or 'trialogues' (when the brother joins in). In all such cases the songs are sung by one character. Only when we have spoken dialogues are there two different voices. These scenes and songs are sometimes interspersed with musical interludes. On yet another level, we find the main singer taking up a meta-level (albeit not a meta-commentary) in as much as he pays tribute to yet another speaker, i.e. Jogi. In other songs performed by the same group, which will not be discussed here, there is yet another level: it is not another human who is being referred to as the original author, but someone called Sudharma. Sometimes it is also said that 'the sound came from the horizon', implying that its source is not known or that it came from Siva.[12] And we find in other songs that sometimes the role of female characters is sung by a chorus at a higher pitch. Variations can, of course, also be found in the rhythm and mood, though I am not able to discuss these with sufficient ethnomusicological expertise.

As far as the content of the songs is concerned, we find that the song of the washerman parallels the story of the fowler as regards the interconnected themes of domestic strife and reunification of the couple, though this parallelism takes place on a more mundane level. While such a shift in the frame of reference may detract some of the mythological and divine aura from the story and lead to a certain transformation of the fowler-hypotext into a parody, it also brings it closer to the day-to-day experiences and imaginations of the audience and adds many subtleties and performative possibilities, especially as far as the comic side of the performance is concerned. This shift to the mundane lived-in reality of the people does not mean, however, that the washerman variant is understood by the actors or spectators as mirroring their own lives, nor does it mean that they view the fowler variant as being 'only fiction'. Both stories are accorded some kind of reality, though they refer to different levels in actors' and spectators' conceptions of reality and vary in their respective degrees of closeness to what the actors and spectators themselves experience daily. Sati's trial by fire is as real to them as the common housewife's experience of daily chores, though it is also more remote from the latter.[13]

Moreover, in both versions it is the woman who is the real hero or, rather, heroine, since it is she who 'faces the trial by fire every day'. While the husbands are at fault – the fowler kills birds,

---

[12] The idea of Siva as 'primal narrator' is not uncommon in Hindu thought, as Lutgendorf (1991, 24) points out in connection with the *Rāmāyaṇa*. Hence, from an emic point of view, Siva's narration is the archetext. Furthermore, the use of the term 'sound' stresses that, in connection with the story's origin, it is essentially understood as conveying an oral/aural experience rather than the one transmitted by silent reading.

[13] It appears that washerman/washerwoman can be substituted by other 'subaltern couples', such as fisherman/fisherwoman, as indicated in line 48 of the song.

the washerman is a habitual drunkard, and both husbands roam around neglecting their domestic lives, at the same time expecting their wives to keep them up and to comply instantly with their wishes when they return – it is thanks to the wives that both stories end happily. In the fowler's story, it is Chadheiyani's persistence in finding help and her devotion to Vana Durga that brings the fowler back to life. As for the washerwoman, she clearly surpasses her male counterpart in wit and the ability to quarrel. But it is also she who opens the way for an amicable settlement by showing herself to be more flexible and submissive at the right moment, and by knowing the *dharma* of the housewife. Hence, her heroism is ultimately that of Sita, not that of, for example, Phoolan Devi or other war-like heroines (*vīrāṅganās*) of Indian folk tradition.[14]

III

The song of the washerman and those belonging to the fowler tradition are embedded in a more varied and larger performative context. Booklets and audio recordings are only secondary, modern-day offshoots of 'the drama of the fowler'. In its dramatic form, the audience can enjoy not only its lyrics and songs, but also dances, histrionic arts and all things related such as costumes.[15] Hence, in viewing the fowler story as a theatrical play, it can be seen that the verbal messages discussed so far intermesh with a variety of multivalent non-verbal images and actions. For the audience watching such performances, the content of the story (which is known by and large) and the semantic meaning of the words become less important than the style and quality of the performance – its performativity and theatricality. This fact requires that the external observer, who in many cases comes from a script-oriented cultural background and will himself produce a script of what was observed, ought to pay greater attention to the way this story is actually performed and to the way performer and audience

[14] Cf., for example, Flueckiger 1996, Ch. 3.

[15] This use of a mixture of media is a characteristic feature of South Asian theatre in general. On this point, cf. Wadley 1989.

interact.[16] As a matter of fact, the affective quality and effect of the performance and the ensuing interactive milieu, so vivid in many forms of Indian village theatre, are major new components which emerge when one progresses from the written text to the performance of this text in song or recitation, but especially in drama.

As is customary in many Indian theatre genres,[17] in dramatic performances of the fowler story, the various characters of the play enter the stage one by one. Each character enters in his or her own inimitable style, be it steps, costume, song, rhythm or music. For, in dramatic performances of the fowler story, the plot as such is not acted out like the dramaturgy of a story-line in Western theatre. Rather, it is enacted piecemeal or as a series of sequences, by successively presenting the various characters, with the dances, songs and types of acting characteristic of them. Thus, the dramaturgy of the narrative is subordinated to the presentation of the play's characters who appear and enact their roles either individually or in pairs.

One of the main protagonists in these proceedings is a man known as *pata bhakta or* 'chief devotee'. This person plays a role similar to that of the *sūtradhāra* of classical Sanskrit theatre.[18] He might be considered an actor, but not a 'character' or *veśa* (lit.: 'costume'), because he appears at the performative level of the fowler story and not at the textual level. During the performance he appears without a particular costume, standing at the edge of the

[16] In recent years fokloric and anthropological studies have experienced a re-orientation from text-centred to performance-centred investigations and interpretations, both in general [e.g. Bauman (ed.) 1992, Hughes-Freeland (ed.) 1998, Parkin, Caplan and Fisher (eds.) 1996] and as far as Indian studies in particular are concerned [e.g. Appadurai, Korom and Mills (eds.) 1991, Flueckiger and Sears (eds.) 1991, Frasca 1990, Hansen 1992, Kapur 1990, Lutgendorf 1991, Sax (ed.) 1995, Schnepel 2000].

[17] For examples, cf. Hawley 1981, Vatsyayan 1980.

[18] *Sūtradhāra* literally means 'holder of a string', and indeed, metaphorically speaking, this person weaves the 'Ariadnean thread' of the play. On preliminaries, entry dances and the role of the *sūtradhāra*, cf., among others, Mathur 1964, 39-47, 112-13, Richmond, Swann and Zarilli (eds.) 1994, 36-7, 66, 173, Varadpande 1990, 19-20.

stage and assumes a role which is comparable to that of the chief singer at the level of the song. Actually, since these two levels are usually combined, the songs of the fowler only rarely being performed outside their dramatic contexts, he *is* the chief singer. Apart from singing songs which belong to the genre of the fowler story, the *pata bhakta* also sings songs of salutation (*vandanā*) in praise of Ganesh, the elephant-headed god of auspicious beginnings, and in praise of Saraswati, the goddess of learning and art.[19]

Moreover, during the play, he functions as a sort of master of ceremonies and as a commentator of what is going on in the play, thus standing both inside and outside it. In this role he acts as a mediator between the actors and the audience, asking questions about and talking to the *veśas* as well as the spectators. This 'communication about communication', or 'meta-communication', represents a significant performative technique by means of which the audience is provided with clues for the interpretation of the drama's meanings and by which the dramatization of the story is punctuated and structured.[20]

Of the different characters within the play itself, Chadheiya and Chadheiyani, that is, the fowler and his wife, are the most important ones. The former enters with a turban-like head-dress to which a number of feathers are attached. In one hand he holds a pole, in the other a snare (*khanjākāthi, phāśa*), and he introduces himself with a vigorous style of dancing. Then the *pata bhakta* asks him several questions as to who he is, what is the purpose of his coming and other things that introduce his role and the theme of the story to the spectators.

One of the most important characters in the sacred drama of the fowler is Binakara, 'the man who plays the harp (*bīṇā*)'. He wears a red shirt and necklaces of beads. In his right hand he holds the harp shaped like a bow, in his left an arrow to which peacock

---

[19] Lutgendorf (1991, 183) argues that the *vandanā* 'is so common a feature of South Asian Hindu performance, both religious and 'secular', that we may identify it as a characteristic 'performance marker" for this culture – a sign to the audience of the moment of transition in the performance frame.'

[20] On the question of framing, cf. Bauman 1977, 15, Lutgendorf 1990, 18-29.

feathers are tied. He recites Sanskrit verses, also explaining their meanings. He sings a story adapted from one of the *purāṇas* or one of the two great epics of Indian tradition. Using song form, he also answers various questions put to him by the *pata bhakta*. This Binakara is none other than Siva himself. When he dances, the cobras, which he wears like a garland around his neck, hear it and become excited, so that they join in his dance, raising their hoods and hissing along to the tune of his song – or rather, this is what draws the attention of the audience. Karuani is the consort of Binakara, who acts as co-singer and co-dancer. She is none other than Parvati. They too quarrel in what turns out to be a wordy battle of wits and which, of course, also ends amicably with images of romantic love. The sequence with Binakara and his wife is often the longest in this drama. At the end of the performance, Binakara also sings the final song known as *melāni*.

Another important couple are Saura and Sauruni. Just like the fowler, Saura is a hunter who lives in the jungle. He hardly wears any clothes and, in a way reminiscent of the tribal Sora people living in the Orissan hinterland, he holds a bow and arrows as well as an axe in his hands. Moreover, he wears a turban with feathers stuck in it. His dance style is vigorous. His consort is Sauruni, who decorates herself with jungle flowers, holds a basket, wears bangles and sings 'berry songs' while selling birds and berries of various kinds. She is an illegitimate child. It is said that a low-caste man was wandering in the forest, where he met the pretty daughter of a Sabara/Sora named Ksyati. The young man made love to her and she conceived, delivering a baby girl. The mother left the child in the forest, where another Sabara found her and took her to his hut. She grew up into a beautiful girl, but nobody wanted to marry her because of her unknown parentage. However, Saura liked her and married her. Saura and Sauruni are both devotees of Siva and Vana Durga. They also narrate mythological and religious stories. Just like the fowler and his wife, they quarrel among themselves, but here too there is a romantic and happy ending to their story in the play.

Then, there are the 'snake-charmer brothers' (*sāpuā bhāi*), Taxak and Kulina. When Siva became angry with the fowler, he called upon eight different species of cobra (*nāga*) and asked them to bite and kill the fowler. Of these, Taxak and Kulina took the image of snake-charmers, carried the conch- and lotus-cobras with them, and killed Chadheiya. Yet another character is the snake-charmer Kela, who is sometimes believed to be none other than Dhanwantari, the physician of the gods, in disguise. His role is to bring Chadheiya back to life. He brings with him a variety of snakes, sometimes real ones. As a great devotee of Siva and with this god's blessings, he is able to cure Chadheiya. Kela is a master of many forms of black magic (*guṇi*), for he knows how to benumb, delude, subdue, attract, kill, and is able to fly. He plays a wind instrument and a small drum, produces snakes and makes them dance, and often he too breaks into dance. He sings songs about snakes and about Krishna plucking a lotus. Other songs relate to mountains and rivers, or they contain snake-bite curing *mantras*. Kela, too, has a consort called Keluni, who does tattoos and sings songs about them. Again, these two quarrel and then make up, thus providing a lot of comic relief.

In the fowler play we also come across Jogi, a mendicant who lives off that which he receives when begging. After wandering from place to place and begging, he comes home, searching for his wife Jogiani in order to ask her to serve him food. Yet again, there is a quarrel and even a fist-fight. Sometimes a group of *jogis* enter the stage. Their scene is satirical, for it is shown that it is not their detachment from the world and their faith but their laziness which has driven them to take on the fake appearance of *jogis*.

It can be seen that all these main characters appear as couples. In this aspect, they (and with the exception of the snake-brothers Taxak and Kulina) mirror the dominant theme of domestic strife, separation and re-union prototypically exhibited by the fowler and his wife. Even the divine couple Siva and Parvati act in this way at one end of a scale from divine to mundane, while the washerman and his wife stand at the other end of this (universal?) aspect of married life. In other words: Siva-Parvati, Chadheiya-Chadheiyani, Saura-Sauruni, Kela-Keluni, Binakara-Keruani, Washerman-

Washerman's wife, Fisherman-Fisherman's wife, Jogi-Jogiani, all these couples are not so much different characters, after all. Rather, in their resemblance, they impersonate different aspects, qualities or levels of being a couple.

Apart from these main characters, there are a number of single or spouseless *veśas*, who appear in supporting roles. It is only through their appearances that the performance of the fowler story achieves its particularly rich dramatic flavour, providing the opportunity for many satires and comic interludes. These characters might even be considered so important for the overall success of the performance and for the progress of the plot that their characterization as 'side characters' whose appearances are mere 'interludes' can only be made with reservations.

Among these single characters we find a fortune-teller, who is sent by the gods to warn the fowler before his death of the grave consequences of killing 'tabooed' birds. This man is understood to be Brihaspati, the 'teacher of the gods', in disguise. He goes to the fowler, looks at his hand and predicts that he will die of snakebite. He, the fowler, could only remain alive by worshipping Siva and Parvati. However, as we know by now, the fowler ignores his words and continues to kill the birds indiscriminately. Another character is 'Brother Dear' ('Bhaidhana') who carries two bundles of peacock feathers, swirling them gracefully while he dances. Then there is a witch-doctor (*guṇia*) and a village doctor (*vaidya*), both depicted as nothing more than charlatans trying to cheat the simple folk. Then there is Manginath, who acts as a mediator in the various domestic strifes; or, rather, tries to do so, his (comic) intervention often making things worse. Moreover, as can be expected in the Indian social context, the various couples are not without relatives, in-laws and offspring. Hence, Saura and Sauruni have a daughter and a father-in-law/father; Kela and Keluni have a son; Chadheiya has a lame and ugly brother as well as a son; both Chadheiya and Binakara have younger second wives (*sano* or little Chadheiyani and *sano* Keruani). In some areas the Sora/Sabara is replaced by a Kandha in a sequence called 'Khanda Khanduni'. Then there are performances in which Vaishnava *sadhus* appear singing devotional songs, which is made fun of during the performance and interspersed with humour. Or we find Brahmins being caricatured and mocked. Such minor characters and new characters are introduced in the story from time to time, depending upon where the performance is staged. In some stories a policemen (*jamadār*), a village watchman (*chowkidār*), and even Muslim and/or British officials are introduced. They enquire into the fowler's death, suspecting it to be murder, thus turning the story somewhat into a Hindi film drama. Last but not least are various deities, of whom Siva, Parvati, Kali, Vana Durga, Ganesh and Ganga are the most important ones, while in some plays or local variations Krishna may take centre stage. Siva and Parvati also appear in the guise of other characters, namely, Binakara and Keruani. Ganga, too, most often appears not as Ganga, but as Binakara's second wife. Kali does not appear in the play but can be said to preside over the performance in the form of a bamboo painting called *prabha*, which stands at the side of the stage.[21]

IV

A typical dramatic performance of the fowler story consists of dialogues and songs in Oriya, though at times Sanskrit verses are also recited. As far as spoken dialogues and scenes are concerned, some characters even speak in Hindi, Bengali, Telugu, Urdu, in local dialects of colloquial Oriya or mixtures thereof. Humorous passages and scenes are interspersed throughout the performance, the humour being expressed through puns, battles of wit, slapstick, exaggerated scenes of quarrelling, clumsy dancing, funny movements and other theatrical ploys, such as when someone assumes the role of a clown (*vidūṣaka*).[22]

Thus, in the 'drama of the fowler', verbal messages, music, dramatic arts and numerous diverse and polyvalent non-verbal images are seen to be combined into a rich and multi-facetted

---

[21] For a discussion of the characters of the play and their roles in it, cf. also Dash n. d., 9-13.

[22] For the role of the *vidūṣaka* in classical and popular Indian theatre, cf. Bhat 1959, Goldberg-Belle 1989, Vatsyayan 1980, 26-30.

Gesamtkunstwerk. Written texts, songs and dramatic performances closely interact with each other and form three levels of ever-wider encompassment, with the third constituting the all-encompassing level. The actual performance of a fowler-drama would traditionally take a whole night, from around midnight till the early hours of the morning. However, these days it usually does not last longer than an hour or two, and I even saw one which was over within half an hour. We, therefore, have to distinguish between a full-scale performance and its (in most cases) considerably synthesized and abridged versions.

In contemporary south Orissa, therefore, the whole story as outlined in the preceding sections is only rarely performed. At this point, it becomes necessary to emphasize that this story is enacted during the festival of Daṇḍo Nāṭo. This festival takes place once a year over a period of thirteen days in the month of *Chaitra* (March/April), and as far as I am aware the fowler story is enacted *only* during Daṇḍo Nāṭo. These days, the shortened version is followed by night-long performances of melodramatic plays. Some priests and actors told me that the drama of the fowler need be performed only every thirteenth year or on special occasions, such as when some incident or misfortune occurred and a stricter adherence to tradition seems to be demanded. In normal years, sponsors and audiences nowadays tend to opt for modern theatre performances, so-called 'social dramas', which are very much influenced by the well-known plots, ways of acting and dancing, and songs from present-day Hindi films. Hence, the drama of the fowler is no longer merely transformed into something else in the way a text (or rather hypotext) is transformed into a hypertext (such as when the Chadheiya-Chadheiyani hypotext is transformed into the story of the washerman and his wife). Rather, it is by and large pushed aside and substituted by another text genre, namely, Hindi films or, more correctly, by a village-theatre style hypertext transformation of the hypotext 'Hindi film'.

The fowler story and its performance are then not unaffected by the shifting tastes, creative imaginations and expectations of the audiences. Modern media indirectly or directly influence and change the story's traditional boundaries regarding narrative content, performativity and meanings (and the wider religious context within which the story is placed). This shift in taste is well captured in a letter sent to me in 1997 by one of my Oriya research assistants:

> I noticed that if one of these groups is showing a social drama (which contains murder, rape, emotions, etc.) people will come in large numbers whereas other groups showing traditional stories (mythological) will be watched by only few people.... I watched a social drama which was just like a new Hindi film. This drama was based on corruption, rape, murder, love, etc. No traditional dresses were used. Here you can see jeans, T-shirts, mini skirts. Weapons were quite different too. Swords and bows were replaced by artificial pistols, knives, etc. Stages are also different. The light and sound systems are spectacular. The director does not rely on the harmonium. He sits in front of a Cassio. Moreover, real ladies also take part, which is amazing. So you see that customs do change as time passes.

Apart from illustrating the issue of changing tastes, I have reproduced this letter pertinent to our problem of text and context, as it enables me to highlight another point, i.e. that texts and contexts are always objects of commentary or interpretation, resulting in metatexts (and occasionally new texts belonging to the fowler genre). It is obvious that among these metatexts, one has to distinguish carefully between emic comments, opinions and interpretations on the one hand and etic ones on the other. Furthermore, within the category of emic interpretations in themselves, one has to distinguish between inside and outside views. Had I presented the comments of actors or priests connected with this play, other pictures or aspects would have emerged.

All this raises further and possible lines of inquiry which I would like to touch upon briefly. If rituals, theatre and art are social constructs, they are certainly also subject to historical changes, are embedded in changing frames of production, interpretation and reception of meaning. What happens, one might ask, if the fowler story is commercialized by private entrepreneurs or by government cultural agencies who produce cassettes, brochures and booklets and invite troupes to perform plays outside their traditional socio-religious settings? Moreover, how does a change in the medium in which a work of art or ritual is produced change its message, its understanding or exegesis by the people and, ultimately, the thing itself? A consideration of these changing frames must also take into account new technological developments. Thus, what would happen to the story if it were not just sung or orally transmitted any longer but enters new forms of modern electronic media such as television, film or even the Internet and is then 'consumed' by viewers sitting at home?[23]

V

In conclusion I would like to add that my discussion of text and context has neither been exhaustive nor conclusive. For a fuller understanding of the story, one could and indeed ought to look more closely at the 'setting context', i.e. at the setting, stage, seating of spectators, etc., of actual performances in village streets, at crossroads, in the courtyards of temples or sponsors' houses, or on local cricket grounds. Moreover, for a comprehensive understanding of the fowler story, it would be imperative to look at the (broader) 'event context'[24] in which performances are embedded, i.e. the yearly festival of Daṇḍa Nāṭo. As this festival is most probably the only occasion during which the fowler story is performed, it would be absolutely necessary to probe more deeply into this festival as a whole and find out what role the fowler story plays in it, both as mythology and as performance.[25] The very fact that this festival is a religious one makes the fowler story, in the

---

[23] For a discussion of the role of modern media in Indian religion, cf. Babb and Wadley (eds.) 1995.

[24] I have freely adapted the concepts of 'setting context' and 'event context' from Briggs 1988, 13.

[25] A first introduction into the ethnography of Daṇḍa Nāṭo can be found in Schnepel 2000 and 2001.

eyes of both actors and spectators, more than mere entertainment, imbuing it with an aura of a 'true story' with religious significance. Further insights might come from comparing this Daṇḍa Nāṭo with other important religious festivals and theatre genres dominant in the sub-region of south Orissa (for examples, Thakurani Yātrā and Prahlāda Nāṭa). Investigating some such 'genre-context' of Daṇḍa Nāṭo and thus focusing on 'systems of genres' would also enable us to understand better indigenous principles in the identification and classification of genres as well as the complex ways in which these in turn give identity to groups and communities.[26]

Needless to say, there still remain a large number of other kinds of context, e.g., social, religious, theological, economic, historical and political – which cannot be explored here, though they are by no means unimportant. Only a consideration of these contexts (in combination with a closer consideration of the subjective intentions of writers, compilers, singers, priests and actors) will allow us to reveal the illocutionary force behind the written, sung, spoken, danced or performed utterances discussed here and enable us to grasp more fully the intentional meanings or 'points' behind their lexical or locutionary meanings. As a matter of fact, these contexts are exactly those at which the proper task of a social anthropologist would seem to start. So why did I choose to ignore these contexts and only hinted at them here, while, in the first section of this paper, I have only briefly and no doubt insufficiently indicated possible lines of inquiry of a traditional text-oriented Indologist or folklorist? The answer is: I have by and large held onto and elaborated upon the precarious middle level of the *drama* of the fowler, because I think that the complex and dynamic nature of the interrelationship between text and context can best be demonstrated on that performative level and because this is the level where the work of Indologists and anthropologist can meet sensibly and complement each other in fruitful ways.

In concluding this paper, the various types of text and context which we have encountered deserve closer scrutiny from a

---

[26] For an elaboration of these points on 'genre context', cf. Flueckiger 1996, esp. xiii, 2, and 16.

theoretical point of view. The script on which my discussion was initially based is the *Bīṇā Danḍa* text, which comes closest to our conventional understanding of text. However, the *Bīṇā Danḍa* is not a storybook in the traditional sense. It contains a lot of loosely connected poems, prayers, lyrics, myths, bits of purāṇas, theological explanations, moral admonitions and ritual prescriptions. From within the *Bīṇā Danḍa*, I identified and filtered out one particular kind of text, which I called the 'story of the fowler'. While this story constitutes the main topic of the *Bīṇā Danḍa*, it is, to repeat, far from being its only theme. Moreover, in the *Bīṇā Danḍa*, the fowler story is itself dispersed in bits and pieces throughout the booklet. The story's unity is only a thematic one: in form it is fragmented, not only when performed, but also in writing.

As the various fragments of the story in its written form are nevertheless interrelated (e.g. domestic strife is followed by and turns into the longing for the absent lover) and as these combined fragments are connected with others (e.g. re-unification arguments lead to happy, amorous encounters in the jungle) and as the story is in itself only a (dispersed) section of the *Bīṇā Danḍa*, we are faced with both more inclusive and more exclusive levels in the fission and fusion of the *Bīṇā Danḍa*. If we take the story of the fowler as our guiding text, it could be argued that the *Bīṇā Danḍa* represents a compilation of several texts rather than a single, unified one.

By giving this fragmented group of texts the title 'the story of the fowler' and by thus assuming (or even 'inventing') the existence of a thematic unity under this title, I added other dimensions of the text which are not unproblematic. Using this title, I created a paratext with which I type-cast the phenomenon under discussion. While this paratext helped me give stringency and coherence to my own metatext (in the form of the article presented here), it also implicitly assumed that there is an identifiable particular archetext – the tradition or genre of the fowler – which exists and can be studied in its own right. The question of whether this archetext also exists as such in the minds of the actors and spectators, and, if so, the question of the ways in which these perceive and experience the fowler tradition, is of course extremely important. As far as I can see, the fowler story is indeed perceived in indigenous views as an archetext in its own right, commonly known as 'Chadheiya-Chadheiyani'. However, this apprehension derives mainly if not solely from the performative level or manifestation of the text. In addition, the unity and unique characteristic of the said tradition is not seen as a story with a plot that gradually unfolds itself in Aristotelian ways from a beginning through a middle to the end, but rather in the form a theme (or, rather, an interconnected bundle of themes) and its variants. This consideration of the emic point of view leads us to the importance of sub-texts: What does the washerwoman really want to tell her husband, what is her point, when she utters: 'I face the trial by fire every day!'? Or, rather, what do members in the audience understand her utterances to mean? And are there different understandings of this utterance by different spectators, for example men and women? Some such 'sub-texts' represent the most important kind of text for the actors and spectators. They are also the most difficult ones to unveil for the outside interpreter, who needs to combine extensive participant observation with the collaborative production of emic metatexts by means of conducting interviews with actors and spectators alike.

Finally, the ways in which I have come to consider text and context as being interlinked in the particular socio-cultural phenomenon discussed here lead me to suggest a number of more abstract propositions with regard to the problem of text and context in general:

1. Text and context should not be understood as being something like a script/written text on the one side and life/culture/society or lived-in reality on the other.
2. Rather, 'text' needs to be understood in its widest possible sense as something meaningful (including culture and material objects, such as archaeological remains, earthen pots or temples) which can be 'read', experienced, observed, understood and interpreted, while 'context' is yet another text, albeit one which is specified by the prefix 'con-'.
3. This 'con-' can have (at least) two meanings: (a) as a surrounding text of a higher, more encompassing order; and

(b) as an accompanying text, i.e. a text that goes together with another text and interacts with this in various ways.

4. This also means that the relationship between text and context is less one of dichotomy than of interdependence and mutual influence.
5. Moreover, the question of what is text and what is context is dynamic and relational, depending on the social situation and the interpretative focus (of both actors and outside interpreters) at hand.
6. As situations and interpretative foci change, so do the ontological status of texts and contexts.
7. It would then be erroneous to consider which came first, text, then context, or vice versa, for there is no (temporal or ontological or logical) primacy of text in relation to context, nor is there any primacy of context in relation to text.
8. Texts (even in the narrowest sense of the term as script) do have agency; they themselves (as texts) influence the social construction of realities no less than contexts influence the production of texts (and, of course, of realities).
9. In this capacity, texts do not represent realities in mirror-like ways. More often than not, they distort and misrepresent them, and they do so deliberately. (What would be their point if they did not add anything to, or do anything with, realities?)
10. Not surprisingly, then, texts are often agents in, and objects of, conflicting negotiations concerning power, property, influence, honour, order, justice, prestige, domination and the exegesis of the world.[27]
11. As far as contexts are concerned, there is no prime mover (for instance, economy), and as far as texts are concerned there is no *Urtext* (for instance, the *Ṛgveda*), which would have all the agency, while other contexts (for instance, politics) and other texts (for instance, pamphlets from a Berhampur bazaar) would

[27] For a fuller elaboration of propositions 8, 9, and 10, cf. Schnepel 1997, esp. chs III and IV. For negotiation as an important element in the text-context interplay, cf. the *New Historicism* school of thought, as can be retraced in Greenblatt 1988 and Veeser (ed.) 1989.

only represent dependent variables and derivative (or even corrupt) products.

12. There is no beginning and no end when it comes to unreeling this interconnected whole of movers and moved, causes and results, *Urtexts* and pamphlets, texts and contexts, *Basis* and *Überbau*, realities and (mis)representations of realities, at least not a priori or as a general presumptive rule.
13. Hence all kinds and types of text and context should be seen as being connected to, interacting with and influencing everything else.
14. This does not, however, exclude the possibility that in actuality or concrete reality one or the other context/text may have become a prime mover, respectively *Urtext*, and as such have achieved a stronger force in moving instead of being moved.
15. Temporal primacy may be a factor for a certain kind of context or text in achieving stronger agency, but this is not necessarily so.

Finally, I would like to add that I do not wish to promote the postmodernist view that all performances are text, nor do I wish to argue, in the wake of the performative turn which many cultural studies have taken during recent years, that all texts are performances. However, I hope to have shown that in a perspective which acknowledges the dynamic, relational and situational character of text and context (both independently and as far as their interaction is concerned), all texts have a performative quality and energy, while all performances have a textual quality and energy.

References

Appadurai, A., F. Korom and M. Mills (eds.). 1991. *Gender, Genre and Power in South Asian Expressive Traditions,* Philadelphia: University of Pennsylvania.

Babb, L. and. Susan S. Wadley (eds.). 1995. *Media and the Transformation of Religion in South Asia*, Delhi: Motilal Banarsidass Publishers.

Bauman, R. 1977. *Verbal Art as Performance*, Rowley: Newbury House.

Bauman, R. (ed.) 1992. *Folklore, Cultural Performances and Popular Entertainments*, New York: Oxford University Press.

Berkemer, G. 1998. 'Literatur und Geschichte im Vormodernen Hinduistischen Südasien', in Rüsen, Gottlob and Mittag (eds.), 145-90.

Bhat, G.K. 1959. *The Vidusaka*, Ahmedabad: The New Order Book Co.

Bīṇā Daṇḍa. 1980. Compiled by Sanyasi Nayak, Berhampur: Sanyasi Pustakalya.

Blackburn, S. H. et al. (eds.). 1989. *Oral Epics in India*, Berkeley: University of California Press.

Briggs, C. L. 1988. *Competence in Performance: The Creativity of Tradition in Mexicano Verbal Art*, Philadelphia: University of Pennsylvania Press.

Dash, D. n. d. *Danda Nata of Orissa*, Bhubaneswar: Orissa Sangeet Natak Akademi.

Doniger, W. (ed.). 1993. *Purāṇa Perennis: Reciprocity and Transformation in Hindu and Jaina Texts*, Albany: University of New York Press.

Flueckiger, J. B. 1996. *Gender and Genre in the Folklore of Middle India*, Ithaca and London: Cornell University Press.

Flueckiger, J. B. and L. J. Sears (eds.). 1991. *Boundaries of the Text: Epic Performances in South and Southeast Asia*, Ann Arbor: Center for South and Southeast Asian Studies.

Frasca, R.A. 1990. *The Theater of the Mahabharata: Terukuttu Performances in South India*, Honolulu: University of Hawai Press.

Genette, G. 1993 (1982). *Palimpseste: Die Literatur Zweiter Stufe*, Frankfurt: Suhrkamp.

Goldberg-Belle, J. 1989. 'Clowns in Control: Performances in a Shadow Puppet Tradition in South India', in Blackburn et al. (eds.) ,118-39.

Greenblatt, S. 1988. *Shakespearean Negotiations: The Circulation of Social Energy in Renaissance England*, Berkeley: University of California Press.

Hansen, K. 1992. *Grounds for Play: The Nautanki Theatre of North India*, Berkeley: University of California Press.

Hawley, J.S. 1981. *At Play with Krishna: Pilgrimage Dramas from Brindavan*, Princeton: Princeton University Press.

Hughes-Freeland, F. (ed.). 1998. *Ritual, Performance, Media*, London: Routledge.

Kapur, A. 1990. *Actors, Pilgrims, Kings and Gods: The Ramlila at Ramnagar*, Calcutta: Seagull Books.

Koepping, K.-P. and U. Rao (eds.). 2000. *Im Rausch des Rituals. Gestaltung und Transformation der Wirklichkeit in Körperlicher Performanz*, Münster: Lit Verlag.

Lutgendorf, P. 1991. *The Life of a Text: Performing the Rāmcaritmānas of Tulsidas*, Berkeley: University of California Press.

Mathur, J.C. 1964. *Drama in Rural India,* New York: Asia Publishing House.

Michaels, A. 1997. *Der Hinduismus: Geschichte und Gegenwart*, München: Beck Verlag.

Parkin, D., L. Caplan and H. Fisher (eds.). 1996. *The Politics of Cultural Performance*, Oxford: Berghahn Books.

Ramanujan, A.K. 1988. 'Where Mirrors and Windows: Toward an Anthology of Reflections', in *History of Religions* 28, 187-216.

Richman, P. (ed.). 1991. *Many Rāmāyaṇas: The Diversity of Narrative Tradition in South Asia*, Berkeley: University of California Press.

Richmond, F.P., D.L. Swann and P.B. Zarilli (eds.). 1994. *Indian Theater: Traditions of Performance*, Honolulu: University of Hawai Press.

Rüsen, J., Gottlob, M. and A. Mittag (eds.) 1998. *Die Vielfalt der Kulturen: Erinnerung, Geschichte, Identität 4*, Frankfurt a. Main: Suhrkamp.

Sax, W. S. (ed.). 1995. *The Gods at Play: Līlā in South Asia*. Oxford: Oxford University Press.

Schnepel, B. 1997. *Die Dschungelkönige. Ethnohistorische Aspekte von Politik und Ritual in Südorissa/Indien*, Stuttgart: Franz Steiner Verlag.

Schnepel, B. 2000. 'Der Körper im "Tanz der Strafe in Orissa"', in Koepping and Rao (eds.) 2000, 141-56.

Schnepel, B. 2001. 'Blurred Genres: The Internal Dynamics of the "Dance of Punishment" in Orissa', in *Adivasi* 39: 12-34.

Varadpande, M.L. 1990. *The Mahabharata in Performance*, New Delhi: Clarion.

Wadley, Susan S. 1989. 'Choosing a Path: Performance Strategies in a North Indian Epic', in Blackburn et al. (eds.) 1989, 75-101.

Vatsyayan, Kapila. 1980. *Traditional Indian Theatre: Multiple Streams*, Delhi: National Book Trust.

Veeser, H.A. (ed.). 1989. *The New Historicism*, London: Routledge.

10

Entering the Realm of Durgā: Pāṭkhaṇḍā, a Hinduized Tribal Deity

Cornelia Mallebrein

The multitude of deities with a tribal origin form a characteristic and at the same time fascinating and distinguishing feature of the religious landscape of Orissa. Although most of these deities have found their way into the realm of pan-Indian Hindu gods and goddesses, their character and the rituals and 'texts' associated with them continue to reveal more or less traceable features of their tribal origin. [1]

One of the pioneers in bringing to light the historical development of Hinduized tribal deities was Anncharlott Eschmann.[2] Already in the early 1970s she began her research on this topic as part of the first Orissa Research Project. Whereas in those days her pioneering efforts were in line with the analysis of the historical development of the cult of Jagannātha, her attention being focused on the original iconographical model of the Trias, her research on the Hinduized deities still reverberates with her outstanding insight into the complex and gradual process of

---

[1] The present paper is part of a wider study on the Hinduized tribal deities of Orissa financed by the German Research Council (DFG) within the Orissa Research Programme. I would like to thank the DFG for making this research possible. I am grateful to Miss Bibasini Rath (M.A.) and Mr. Devdas Mohanty for their assistance.

[2] For a critical discussion of the terms 'Sanskritization', 'Brahmanization', 'Kshatriyaization', 'Rajputization' and 'Hinduization', cf. Urhahn 1985, 38-65, Srinivas, 1955, Staal 1962/63, Kulke (b) 1993, 83, Schnepel 1993, 338. In this paper, the term 'Hinduization' is used in the sense of A. Eschmann 1978 (a), 82: 'Hinduization may be defined as a continuum operating in both ways between the two poles of tribal religion and codified or „High" Hinduism... the process of Hinduization acts in both ways...tribal elements are incorporated into Hinduism, but also implies that features from Hinduism are integrated into tribal cults'.

assimilation into the realm of 'codified Hinduism' (Eschmann).[3] Still today in Orissa, this process of assimilation and adaption of tribal deities has not lost any of its dynamics but has rather increased during recent years. Whereas A. Eschmann focused on the religious, historical and iconographical development of tribal deities, H. Kulke draws attention to their political and legitimizing function within the process of early regional state formation. With the help of indigenous deities worshipped by the tribes in the newly conquered areas, rājas from outside tried to reconcile the tribes to their rule by elevating their gods to the status of royal tutelary deities.[4] Since the 1990s, B. Schnepel has carried out extensive studies on the development of tribal deities in the course of his research on the 'little kingdoms' and regional traditions of Orissa.[5] C. Pasayat focuses on the folk and tribal traditions mainly of western Orissa,[6] while H.C. Das[7] includes them in his study of the *śāktā pīṭha* of Orissa.

The present paper must be seen in the context of this previous research. The different 'texts' connected with this deity, such as myths, oral accounts, written descriptions and historical data, are interpreted and analysed within their social, cultural and historical contexts. The paper aims to show how the tribal deity Pāṭkhaṇḍā enters the realm of Durgā, that is, the sphere of 'codified Hinduism', while preserving her characteristic traits as a tribal deity. This double aspect only emerges through the various types of texts associated with her. Therefore, one of the questions I shall be addressing is how the memory of her origin from the forest, the world of the tribes, and her later movement into the plains, the sphere of Hinduism, is kept alive and thus the 'cultural memory' of the Mutkīā Kondh. In what form – verbal, non-verbal, symbolic or performative – is this 'cultural memory' stored and preserved in the

---

[3] Eschmann 1978 a and 1978 b, 1994.

[4] Kulke 1978, 1992, 1993 b, 1995.

[5] Schnepel 1993, 1997 a.

[6] Pasayat 1997, 1998.

[7] Das 1999. He discusses important goddesses of tribal origin from Orissa. For further information on this topic cf. Mishra 1992, Mishra 1983.

community of her followers and devotees? Who are the carriers of this and how and through which agents is it handed down from one generation to the next? What are their aims? According to Assmann, the cultural memory does not simply continue, it has to be negotiated every time anew, established, mediated and acquired. Individuals and cultures build up their memory interactively through communication in language, pictures and ritual repetitions.[8] The cultural memory forms a sphere in which the mimetic memory, the memory of things and the communicative memory more or less without a break pass over.[9] As this memory is only orally retained, it does not leave the sphere of 'ceremonial communication'. Within this collective memory, it is the Pāṭkhaṇḍā *yātrā* performed every year at Jarasingha and her different rites which function as the custodian of memory. According to Assmann rites are part of the realm of the cultural memory because they represent a form of a tradition and do recall the cultural sense.[10] The five-day festival in honour of Pāṭkhaṇḍā must be interpreted as a huge 'performative text', the visible expression of the 'collective memory' of the Mutkīā Kondh clan, transformed into an impressive performance of their history. This 'collective autobiography' is performed by various actors, such as the main priest of the deity, his entourage and the deity's devotees. The stage for this play includes a vast geographical area and historical time frame, linking the past with the present.

The following analysis of the historical development of Pāṭkhaṇḍā attempts to interpret the different texts in the broadest sense of the term. As such 'text' does not refer only to 'literary text', it means in the sense of Geertz 'culture as text'.[11] According

---

[8] Cf. A. Assmann 1999, 19.

[9] Cf. J. Assmann 1999, 20-1.

[10] Cf. ibid., 21.

[11] It is not possible to deal at length with the concept of Clifford Geertz, for more information, literature and critics on this theory cf. Gottowick 1997, Fröhlich 1998, Moore 1984. Singer 1972, speaks of 'textual approach' and 'contextual approach' in referring to two different approaches that various disciplines adopt for the study of culture. The first deals with written texts whereas the latter, the contextual study, means in its broader sense oral texts.

to him culture is a text to be read and the different structures of its meaning can be examined. Culture is formed by a multitude of texts, such as symbols and signs. In their sum they can form different condensed texts. The subject of ethnography is an 'ensemble of texts', a 'montage of texts', which can be read like a manuscript. All members of this culture are authors of these texts which are open for different types of reading and interpretation. The texts are part of the changing historical context and are therefore subjugated to constant changes. We thus deal with textures of socially shared meanings interwoven among those aspects of social expression which, for analytical reasons, the observer often chooses to isolate as religion, politics, economics, art, play, etc.[12]

As noted earlier, the process of the incorporation of tribal deities into Hinduism has lost none of its dynamics. The extent to which the religious milieu has changed within only few years can be seen by comparing the published field notes taken by Eschmann in the 1970s with my own field notes from 1999 and later. The former wooden shrines and temples (*guḍī*) housing the characteristic aniconical *mūrti* of tribal deities have been exchanged for large cement buildings. The walls of the new *mandir,* constructed in the 'Cuttack style', are decorated with modern wall paintings depicting major Hindu gods and goddesses and their deeds. As a result, the deity is presented in another context, within a new 'visual text', the 'text' of modern Hindu deities. The former aniconical image is now endowed with anthropomorphic traits or replaced by a modern cult statue. Through the innovation of regularly performed worship, the deity is visually experienced in her anthropomorphic image and now has a place within the iconographical concept of Hinduism. The 'performative text' visible in the various rituals has also changed: the buffalo sacrifice practised earlier, a striking reminder of her tribal origin, has been replaced by goat sacrifices, the former tribal priest by a Hindu priest; the deity has ceased to possess the medium and thus stopped appearing as a visible, immediately amenable and responsive deity. Her cults are pacified, the formerly 'uncontrolled, wild' and

---

[12] Cf. Martin 1984, 21.

'dangerous' deity has been brought under control, and she has left the human sphere in this world to go to a remote puranic heaven. [13]

The following contribution, which aims to analyse the gradual integration, adaptation and assimilation of Pāṭkhaṇḍā into the context of Hinduism, is divided into five sections. Each section must be seen as a unity, with one or more actors and the texts they have presented. However, the five sections do not stand in isolation from one another but form the parts of a larger puzzle. In its complete form the puzzle portrays the historical evolution of the deity Pāṭkhaṇḍā.

The different actors and stages are:

1. Two priestly families *Pātra* I and *Pātra* II in Mahasinghi, the place of origin of Pāṭkhaṇḍā. They compete with each other. Their texts deal mainly with ritual supremacy over Pāṭkhaṇḍā and its legitimation. In their texts it is the deity who grants this favour.
2. The priest (*thānāpati*) from the main temple at Jarasingha (Bolangir District). His text deals with the origin of Pāṭkhaṇḍā from the forest area, her arrival at Jarasingha and the part she played in the war between the Chauhan king and the king of Bastar.
3. Paraśurām Siṅgh Deo, formerly Zamindar of Jarasingha, still much honoured by the people, and still called rāja. Pāṭkhaṇḍā is his family's tutelary deity. He presides over the annual Pāṭkhaṇḍā *yātrā*. His text links the *yātrā* and the role of Pāṭkhaṇḍā with the *daśaharā* festival of Durgā.

---

[13] On the temple of goddess Bāralā Ṭhākuraṇī in Balasgumpha (Phulbani-Distrikt) A. Eschmann writes: '... the shrine is...on the verge of the temple level. ...the outer appearance is that of a usual tribal shrine of this region...an open mud house with thatched roof, a wooden post'. One can still see the old, now dilapidated posts of the former mud shrine. In 1992, a new concrete cement temple in the 'Cuttack style' was constructed in front of these posts. The walls are decorated with modern paintings. In 1999 they stoped the traditional buffalo sacrifice when it was banned by the Collector of Phulbani. This same year they began to construct a temple to Lakṣmī, with financial support from business people in the area.

4. The priest called Sāhāṇi. He is the king's *rājpurohit* on behalf of Pāṭkhaṇḍā. In his text Pāṭkhaṇḍā is addressed as a form of Durgā who kills the buffalo demon.
5. Members and devotees of the Pāṭkhaṇḍā *yātrā*, performed annually at the end of *daśaharā* in Jarasingha.

1. Introduction

Pāṭkhaṇḍā is a clan deity of the Muṭkiā Kondh, a subsection of the Mājhi Kondh from the Kondh Hills. Her place of origin lies in a dense forest grove near Mahasinghi, a village about 7 km south-east of Balliguda, a subdivision of Kondhmal District. In course of time her worship extended towards the north, and today she is widely worshipped in villages ranging from the Balliguda-Mahasinghi region up to the southern part of the Bolangir District around Tusra and Guduvella. There are two major centres of Pāṭkhaṇḍā worship: the village of Mahasinghi, from where she originates, and the village of Jarasingha, about 25 km from Bolangir. In the former village her roots as a tribal deity are still evident, whereas in the latter she enjoys the status of a *rājadevatā,* the tutelary deity (*iṣṭadevatā*) of the local Zamindar, who is still addressed as rāja by the people.

During her progress towards becoming a *rājadevatā*, kingdoms of two regions in Orissa tried to patronize this powerful deity: first the rāja of Badakimedi and Sanakimedi, prominent 'little kingdom' in Ganjam and Gajapati districts; and later, hand in hand with the expansion of their imperial power, the Chauhan kings of Patnagarh, in present-day Bolangir District.[14]

[14] In the year 1607 the Parlakimedi-rājā, the largest and most important kingdom in Ganjam in South Orissa gave to his younger son one part of his kingdom the area of Baḍa (groß)-kimedi. This kingdom was later, in 1776, split up into Baḍakimedi and Sana (small)-kimedi. The Sanakimedi-maliahs, e.g. the mountain regions had 1.975 square miles. In the 19th c. the area was occupied by the British. According to Dr. U.N. Deb (personal communication), present Raja Saheb of Sanakimedi the shrine of Mahasinghi was under their dominion. Their territory extended till Tumribandha in the Kondhmals. For further information, cf. Schnepel 1997 (a), 104 -05, fn. 67, and Berkemer 1993, 200-2.

Although she is one of the most prominent deities in these areas, with thousands of devotees flocking to the yearly Pāṭkhaṇḍā *yātrā* at Jarasingha and Bhuanpada, there is no written documentation on her apart from a few short notes.[15] The information gained during field studies in 1999 to 2000 form a group of different texts presenting the deity Pāṭkhaṇḍā in different contexts.[16] They provide valuable information about different phases in the process of her Hinduization. They also reflect the struggle between powerful regional kings over her patronage in their attempts to control the area, and they mirror the migration of various Kondh clans to the plains. The five-day Pāṭkhaṇḍā *yātrā* is a striking example of how a former tribal deity develops the dynamic force and capacity to integrate and thus to unite not only different villages, but also different social groups, such as tribes, caste Hindus and members of the Scheduled Castes under the umbrella of her realm. Although the *yātrā* nowadays tends to adopt modern forms of *daśaharā*, such as the installation of different Durgā shrines, the performance of the various rituals reflects the original quality of Pāṭkhaṇḍā as a deity of fertility. One of the main attractions for devotees in participating is her healing power and her

---

[15] The information presented here is based on oral information collected during two field trips to the Kondhmals and Bolangir District in October 1999 (documentation on the five-day Pāṭkhaṇḍā festival at Jarasingha) and January to February 2000 (various centres of Pāṭkhaṇḍā worship). All important sites associated with Pāṭkhaṇḍā have been visited and documented up to now.

[16] The original tribal name of the goddess Pāṭkhaṇḍā is not known. The name means 'the best of all swords'. Pāṭkhaṇḍā is the name of the main royal ceremonial sword used by the ruling rāja, it is a symbol of power and victory. As such it embodies the power of Durga, the deity of war and victory par excellence. The Pāṭkhaṇḍā sword is kept in the *iśāna*, a special room in the palace where the weapons and the ancestors receive regular worship. No one besides the close family members are allowed to enter this very sacred room.
As the name of deity Pāṭkhaṇḍa suggests she is worshipped in all her shrines in the Bolangir district in form of a sword. It is said, that the sword worshipped in her main temple in Jarasingha was given to the deity by the Chauhan king. The moment the tribal deity entered the realm of royal patronized Hinduism her former tribal symbol, the vegetable chopper (*paniki*), was replaced by the sword, a symbol of war and victory.

capacity to cure barrenness. As a Kondh deity – the Kondh are considered to be skilled in magic – she also has the power to control and drive away evil ghosts and spirits, and therefore the knowledge to cure her devotees from mental illness.

2. Different Phases in her Development

2.1 Mahasinghi: the Place of Origin of the Goddess Pāṭkhaṇḍā

Today there are two major centres of Pāṭkhaṇḍā worship, Mahasinghi and Jarasingha. The site at which Pāṭkhaṇḍā originated lies in a small forest grove near the hamlet of Jakeripada. A rough stone marks the spot. Only rarely does worship take place there. Very close to it is the sacred site of Barālī, Pāṭkhaṇḍā's mighty sister, and of Jenābuḍhā, an old Kondh deity, considered to be her brother. But Kandhenbuḍhī, the autochthonous village deity, also has a place of veneration there.

In former times, before the village was shifted to its present site, this area was the sacred centre of Mahasinghi. Mahasinghi was once an extremely important sacred centre within the Kondhmal region. Two major deities of this region originate there, Pāṭkhaṇḍā and Barālī. Because of its importance it was always a contested centre.[17] This is evident in the oral texts of the two priestly families, *pātra* I and *pātra* II, who are in charge of the worship of Pāṭkhaṇḍā. Their accounts reflect the religious as well as political rivalry between the two families to gain supremacy and throw light on the great interest the Hindu kings had in controlling these deities, exercising influence and power over the tribes of this area through their appointments of the priests. Besides their ritual duties, the

[17] The goddess Barāḷī is mainly worshipped in the present Phulbani district. Her main place of worship is Balasgumpha. In most of the villages she has her place of worship, may it be a small shrine or just an open platform. The famous goddess Bhairavī from Puruna Cuttack is considered as her older, Pāṭkhaṇḍā as her younger sister. Very frequently Barāḷī is worshipped together with Pāṭkhaṇḍā.

priests were entrusted with the task of collecting revenue for the rāja. Thus, the priests and their patronized deity formed the major link between the ruling rāja and the tribal population.

Pātra I tells why and how his family was entrusted with the worship of Pāṭkhaṇḍā. According to him the deity was formerly worshipped by a Kondh priest. But she refused to accept offerings from him, since he had become polluted by eating meat and drinking alcohol.[18] To show her anger she withdrew her activity as a goddess of fertility by causing a drought and barrenness in both nature and human beings. She demanded to be worshipped by a clean, high-caste priest wearing a sacred thread.[19] The Kondh sought and found Biśmoṇī *pātra*, a Kṣatriya (*pāika*) staying near Pudamari, and they brought him to Mahasinghi as the new priest. But first the goddess demanded the sacrifice of a pregnant woman.[20] The flesh of the tribal woman was distributed to the villages of twelve *mūṭhā* (a group of villages), and in each *mūṭhā* the priest set up a place of worship (*dhārnī*). Besides being the main priest, he became the head of the twelve *mūṭhā*. He also brought twelve kinds of seeds to sow on the barren land. Thanks to him, the land became fertile again. On behalf of the king, he carried out the function of a

---

[18] I thank Shridev *pātra* from Mahasinghi Jakeripada for his valuable information.

[19] The area where the Kondh stayed was called Gosiṅgha daitya pṛthivī, the name of a demon king who ruled the area before Biśmoṇī *pātra*. According to Śrīdev *pātra*, all the tribal inhabitants at that time, like Nākburā and Kānburā, were dangerous cannibals.

[20] The sacrifice of a pregnant woman is a common subject. It signifies the greatest of human sacrifices and is a sign of fertility and prosperity. According to *pātra* I, the first *pātra* Biśmoṇī told the Kondh: 'there is so much barrenness everywhere. Give me a pregnant woman, I will sacrifice her and thus rescue the country'. The Kondh Mānsiṅgh gave his sister Sikbāduṅgā to be sacrificed and thus save the country. This subject is in line with the martyr *iṣṭadevatā*. The future ruler of an area performs the ritual killing of a member of the tribe in that region, a sign of virile power over a territory. On the subject of the martyr *iṣṭadevatā* cf. Kulke 1992. On the tradition of performing a human sacrifice (a member of a tribal group) in connection with the coronation ceremony of a king cf. Carrin-Bouez 1978.

pātra, that is, collecting revenue from the tribes.[21] According to the priest, this incident took place about thirteen generations ago.[22]

The text reflects the great interest of the Bada- or Sanakimedi king in increasing his influence over this area. By replacing the local Kondh priest and establishing the *pātra*, the king ensured that he would receive revenue from the local tribes. As head of the twelve *mūṭhā* and priest of a dangerous tribal deity, the *pātra* gained great power and controlled the fertility of the land. His descendants established various shrines in villages around Mahasinghi.

According to *pātra* II, who at present is in charge of the deity, the former priest *pātra* I also failed by becoming polluted through consuming meat and alcohol.[23] The deity was angry, and as a result the land and all human beings again became barren, and the Kondh suffered from hunger and drought. The deity demanded a new *pātra* as priest from another family. The Kondhs gathered together and asked Chintāmoṇīguru, a mythical man of great knowledge and a blacksmith, to make four arrows, as the deity had appeared to the Kondh in their dreams and told them to shoot an arrow to each of the four cardinal points. They were then to follow the direction that was marked with blood, which would guide them to the place from which the new *kṣatriya* priest should come. It was the arrow towards the north that left the blood marks. Following them, they reached Jarasingha and saw the arrow stuck in the wall of the fort. There they met the king's sons, who were called Subhāscāndra and

---

[21] The *pātra* (kṣatriya) are a king's chief executive officers. According to Kulke 1997, 257, the rulers of larger imperial kingdoms tried to improve the central administrative apparatus by introducing the ministerial *pātra* and *parīkṣā* systems in the 12th and 13th centuries, that means to have officers at hand who could be controlled from the centre.

[22] According to Śridev *pātra* their family originated from Pudamari near Taptapani and they came to this area 13 generations, i.e. around 300 years, ago. This would mean that the area was still under the control of Badakimedi and a littlelater was taken over by Sanakimedi. However, historical data based on orally transmitted genealogies are very vague.

[23] I would like to thank Bindika *pātra*, priest of Pāṭkhaṇḍā shrine in Mahasinghi, for his valuable information. It was Patu *pātra*, the grandson of Eiśmoṇī *pātra*, who had already failed as a priest. According to *pātra* I, they are the victims of a conspiracy against his family.

Bāhanacāndra. The Kondh delegation requested them both to come to Mahasinghi and take over the worship of all their gods. But the two brothers were suspicious and demanded a test to see the real power of the Kondh deity for themselves. First, they asked the Kondh to bring water in a sieve, and then to cook rice in an unbaked earthen pot on a hearth made out of a goat's head. The Kondhs succeeded in these tests, thus demonstrating the presence and power of their deities. The Kondh in their turn tested the truthfulness of Subhāscāndra and Bāhanacāndra by asking them to cut seven bamboo poles with one stroke of an axe. They also told them to urinate on the top of a pile of seven plates, so that the urine should pass down to the bottom plate by the power of their faith. The brothers performed their test satisfactorily too, and it was confirmed that the deity had accepted them as their priests. Before the delegation reached Mahasinghi, Subhāscāndra, the elder brother married a Brahmin widow from the royal house of Puruna Cuttack.[24] At Mahasinghi they performed a human sacrifice to please all the gods and goddesses. The land became fertile again, and the barrenness came to an end.

The texts reflect the fact that there was a shift in supremacy over Mahasinghi from the former dynasty of Sanakimedi to the royal house of Jarasingha in present-day Bolangir District, from which the new priest came.[25] To strengthen their influence and power, the descendants of Subhāscāndra established Pāṭkhaṇḍā shrines in all the villages of the area.

The texts of both *pātra* I and *pātra* II try to justify their assumption of supremacy over this contested centre with reference to the wish of the deity for change. Change here means an opening towards the plains, the sphere of Hindu culture. The legitimizing element for this change is pollution: first the original Kondh priest, then *pātra* I became polluted by drinking wine and eating meat. Whereas *pātra* I's text about the assumption of power is quite

---

[24] According to the *pātra* priest Kanhu Charan Singdeo, formerly in charge of the shrine in Badagaon, near Balliguda, King Subhaschandra brought with him people from all sorts of service castes, and it was through him that Hindu civilization and culture was brought to the Kondh.

[25] According to Bindika *pātra* this took place eleven generations before him.

simple in its structure, *pātra* II's presents a long and complex story.[26] But both texts have the aim of justifying the adoption of supremacy by the different families with respect to religious as well political power. In these texts it is the deity who demands the change in the priesthood. Out of anger she withdraws her capacity to ensure fertility, and thus withdraws herself as a deity of prosperity. Without her existence and influence, no human being can exist. The main actors in the texts are the Kondh in their search for a new priest. As both texts are mainly meant to justify the take-over of ritual worship by one *pātra* family, they do not play an active role in the present-day ritual or daily life of the devotees.

They do not function as 'performative texts' and are therefore handed down from one generation to the next only within the priestly families.

Pāṭkhaṇḍā in Jarasingha

2.2 The main temple priest (thānāpati) of Pāṭkhaṇḍā

In contrast to the priestly families of Mahasinghi *pātra* I and *pātra* II, the present priest at the main temple in Jarasingha stresses other aspects of the deity.[27] His text has the character of a legend. Its content is not concerned to legitimize his religious and worldly power but to throw light on the identity-creating potential of the deity in the social and religious life of the Kondh. In his text the deity appears as the main actor, her stage being this world, among humans. There is no separation between the worldly sphere of the Kondh and the heavenly realm. In her function as the clan deity of the Muṭkīā Kondh, Pāṭkhaṇḍā guides them from the dense forest

---

[26] His text is a long and detailed account giving the names of all the places the delegation passed through. He also mentioned a detailed genealogy of the Kondh as well as the Patrā from Jarasingha. Only a very abbreviated version is given here.

[27] My great thanks go to Rajkumar *thānāpati* (Ḍholo Kondh), priest from Pāṭkhaṇḍā temple in Jarasingha, and Buḍu Patharimali (medium of Birpānī and Jenābuḍhā) for their valuable information. They further provided all possible assistance during my documentation of the Pāṭkhaṇḍā festival in October 1999.

(*vana*) towards the settled civilized region (*kṣetra*) and fights for their rights in winning a new area of settlement for them through her brave and dedicated help during a war.[28] This movement from the forest to the plains is the central topic of the annual Pāṭkhaṇḍā *yātrā* in Jarasingha, a grand commemorative ritual lasting several days portraying the history of the Muṭkīā Kondh.

The priest's text can be divided into two episodes: EI and EII. The legend in EI tells why Pāṭkhaṇḍā leaves her place of origin in Mahasinghi together with her brothers. The second legend in EII narrates her great deeds in the war of the Chauhan ruler Vatsarājadeva against the king of Bastar.[29]

According to EI, Pāṭkhaṇḍā stayed in the house of a Kondh in the form of a powerful and magical *paniki*, a vegetable chopper which cuts things placed on it automatically. Once this Kondh took a loan from a Brahmin. As he could not pay it back, the Brahmin stole the magic *paniki*. Immediately the deity showed her presence and anger by breaking it into three pieces. He tried everything to keep the deity with him, including building a temple for her, but she disappeared. He tried to hide her in the deep river, but again she escaped. Pāṭkhaṇḍā vehemently refused to stay with the Brahmin. Being threatened in this way, she decided to leave her place of origin together with her brother Birpānī and her adopted brother Jenābuḍhā. They went north-west from Mahasinghi, via Kotgad, Balliguda and Bhuanpada, and finally to Jarasingha,[30] where Pāṭkhaṇḍā first asked the local hill god Buḍhādaṅgar for permission to stay. But he advised her to ask Pāṭaṇeśvarī and Samleśvarī, the

---

[28] According to Sontheimer 1994, 128-29, the dichotomy between *vana* and *kṣetra* is not mutually exclusive, but rather complementary or a continuum, like the continuum between tribe and caste. *Vana* was the realm of the tribals: the more the *kṣetra* spread into the *vana,* the more the tribal cults were integrated. The assimilation of the tribal cults into the *kṣetra* only meant their transformation, not their abolition.

[29] On Bastar cf. Sinha 1997, 331-3.

[30] One can find shrines or temples for Pāṭkhaṇḍā at all these places. In 1990 a large new temple was build at the place of the former open shrine under a tree in Balliguda financed mainly by business people. Another important centre of Pāṭkhaṇḍā worship is at Buanpada (present-day Bolangir District), where a yearly *yātrā*, very similar to Jarasingha, is also performed.

family deities of the Patnagarh Chauhan kings, to grant this favour. Episode I ends at this point.

Episode II tells that Vatsarājadeva, the King of Patnagarh, had simultaneously started a war against the king of Bastar to expand his territory.[31] So far, he had lost all his battles. Pāṭkhaṇḍā promised him her help in winning the war provided she was given a permanent place to stay. Pāṭkhaṇḍā went to the battlefield together with Birpānī and Jenābuḍhā. Being a Kondh goddess, she was bestowed with magical insight.[32] The reason that the king of Patnagarh had lost all his wars was the fact that Bastaren, the family deity of the king of Bastar, would rather protect the family that worshipped her than the enemy of that family. She was able to assume different forms. She appeared as a fruit-seller or curd-seller and sold poisoned food to the soldiers to weaken the Chauhan king's army.[33] Pāṭkhaṇḍā realized the true nature of Bastaren. Her brothers Jenābuḍhā and Birpānī seized Bastaren, burnt her body with hot iron rods and thus disfigured her. Bastaren surrendered, and the Chauhan king won the war. In return for her decisive help in the war, Pāṭkhaṇḍā obtained the area of Jarasingha from the king as her new region to rule. Bastaren, defeated by Pāṭkhaṇḍā, acknowledged the latter's supreme power and followed her to Jarasingha, but to hide her disfigured body she went under the earth. Bastaren appeared in the form of an anthill near the king's palace. To honour the defeated tutelary deity of the king of Bastar,

---

[31] On Vatsarājadeva, cf. N.K. Sahu, P.K. Mishra, J.K. Sahu, 1998, 245-68. According to these authorities, he began a war in order to expand the Chauhan kingdom. He defeated the ruler of Banai, Baudh, Khimadi, Nandapur and Bastar and invaded Dhenkanal and plundered the state. He also challenged the authority of the Gaṅgā king, who most probably was Nārāsimha IV (1378-1414). It is said that the Gaṅgā king defeated and killed the Chauhan king. Vatsarājadeva is said to be the grandson of Ramāīdeva, the founder of the Chauhan dynasty.

[32] It is a common idea that tribes are skilled in magic and are therefore to befeared.

[33] The motif of a disguised goddess selling poisoned food to soldiers is common in Orissa; for other examples, cf. Schnepel 1997 (b), 465 (the goddess Markama of Bissamcuttack) Kulke 1992, 61-62 (the goddess Bhaṭṭārikā from near Baramba).

Pāṭkhaṇḍā granted her the right to be worshipped as a village deity in all the villages of the area and gave her the new name Buḍhīāī ('old grandmother'). Episode II ends at this point.[34] Then she announced that Bastaren should always be worshipped before her.

The clan deity, represented by a vegetable chopper (*paniki*), plays an important role in EI. The clan members of the Muṭkīā Kondh are still not allowed to touch the *paniki* with their feet, so they use a special type of *paniki* with a wooden stand. It is said that the three pieces of iron, about 10 cm in length, which play a prominent role as a 'visual code' in the present-day Pāṭkhaṇḍā *yātrā* , are the three parts of the original *paniki*. The story of Pāṭkhaṇḍā's journey from Mahasinghi to Jarasingha mirrors the movement of the Muṭkīā Kondh to the plains. The latter are only one clan among many who settled in the foothills of the Guduvella and Tusra area.[35] The other Kondh clans still worship their own, very powerful clan deities, among the most important being Śūliā and Śikerpāṭ.[36] Today the Kondhs in this area no longer speak their original Kui language, and they have adopted the Hindu way of life. According to Kondh informants their ancestors came to the plains to clear the forest,

---

[34] The other name for Bastaren is Danteśvarī. The latter is the tutelary deity of the former *rāja* of Bastar at Jagdalpur and a very prominent deity in the present Chattisgarh District. She is also considered a village deity. Her main temple is at Dantewara, and her *daśaharā* festival is celebrated in grand style at Jagdalpur (on this festival cf. Mallebrein 1993 and 1996).

[35] The main Kondh groups and their clan deities in the Guduvella and Tusra area are: Māuñsia (clan deity Śūliā), Turkiā (clan deity Ḍelāguru Pinjerpāt), Kudrukiā (clan deity Bhima Bauri), Khadaṅgiā (clan deity Śikerpāṭ), Sekā (clan deity Bārabhāi Barni), Betka (clan deity Sunāmuin), Pradhani (clan deity Bhimā or Bhimā boiri). They are related to each other as friends (*bandhu*) in a relationship of marriage or as brothers (no marriage).

[36] The main site of the worship of Śikerpāṭ, the clan deity of the Khadaṅgiā Kondh, is at Ghuna, a village thought to contain his mother's house (*mā ghar*). Every year two large festivals take place in his honour, at *pauṣa duitiyā* and at *āsādha duitiyā*. His wife is called Pāhājīren. Śūliā is the clan deity of the Māuñsia Kondh, and his place of worship is at Khoirguda. The annual festival takes place at *pauṣa śukla pakṣa*. A paper analysing the legends and festivals linked with these two deities is under preparation.

whereas the Gond migrated to the area to rule over it.[37] Their movement to the plains may have been at the time when the Chauhan dynasty of Patnagarh was extending its power.[38] There is no concrete data on the foundation of the Chauhan dynasty in Patnagarh, which only gains prominence in history in the fourteenth century.[39] The story narrates that at this time the territory was administered by an oligarchy of eight chieftains (*aṣṭamallik*), the lords of eight forts, including Patnagarh and Jarasinghagarh. Rāmāīdeva managed to kill all the seven *mallik* and usurp the throne of Patnagarh. He is described as a very ambitious ruler who extended his territory as far as the border with Baudh. He fortified Patnagarh and constructed the temples to Pāṭaṇeśvarī and Jagannātha. His son Mahāliṅgadeva ruled only for six years (*c.*1380-85).

The second episode, EII, describes the struggle between the Chauhan ruler Vatsarājdeo and the king of Bastar.[40] This legend

---

[37] In about the fourteenth and fifteenth centuries, the Gonds created kingdoms of considerable size covering a vast area of central India, including famous kingdoms such as Garha-Mandla, Deogarh, Chanda and Kherla (cf. Chatterton 1916, Fuchs 1960, Mehta 1984).

[38] According to Berkemer 1993,7, the cutting of the jungle, foundation of temples, villages and towns, providing land for cultivation and tanks for irrigation and patronizing local cults were major tasks for the kings. In this way, the „frontier" Hindu civilization moved into the hilly tracts.

[39] For a critical discussion of the myths of migration, which were mostly created in the nineteenth to twentieth centuries as a suitable „ideological model of descent", cf. Berkemer 1993, 25-26, Sinha 1997, Kulke 1993, fn.20, Banerji 1928 and Pasayat 1998, 84. In what follows, I refer to published data on the history of Orissa. Different traditions speak of Rāmāīdeva as founder of the dynasty. They trace his origin back to the family of Prithviraj Chauhan, the last Hindu ruler of Delhi. After his defeat and death by Muḥammad Ghorī in A.D. 1192 a family member escaped to Mainpur (Uttar Pradesh) and established a small kingdom there. It is said that Rāmāīdeva's mother was Queen Asāvatī, who fled to western Orissa after her husband Hamirdeva was killed by the Muslims in the fourteenth century. She gave birth to Rāmāī in the house of Chakradhār Panigrahi, a Brahmin of Patnagarh. This took place around the middle of the fourteenth century.

[40] Vatsarājadeva (c.1385-1410), son of Mahāliṅgadeva, started a war with the chief of Bastar to expand his territory. Bastar was defeated and acknowledged

mirrors the Kondhs' history of settlement in this region. The war-like Kondh were feared and, for the ambitious and rising new rulers, indispensable and loyal soldiers. Dressed up in their characteristic and frightening warrior costumes, with their mighty headgear made out of huge buffalo horns, they intimidated the enemy and expressed their willingness to fight to the death.[41] It was only thanks to their help that Vatsarājdeo was able to win the war against the ruler of Bastar. It can be concluded from this that, in return for their help, the Kondh obtained the region around Jarasingha. For the king, this had a double advantage: in peacetime they cultivated the land and thus provided him with tax revenues, while in wartime they gave him the help he needed as soldiers. It was the clan deity who won the right to this land. Thanks to her magical insight, she recognized the treacherous and deadly power of Bastaren. The family deities of the Chauhan king did not have the power to win the war. The negotiations with the Chauhan ruler over a region for the permanent settlement of the Muṭkīā Kondh was not conducted on a worldly level. In the legend represented by the hill god, Buḍhādaṅgar, the local ruler of Jarasingha did not have the authority to grant permanent settlement but referred to the Chauhan ruler represented through his family deities.[42] Thus, Pāṭkhaṇḍā offers help to the king in return for land. In memory of her dedication in this war, the tribal deity – her original name is no longer remembered – obtains the honorific title of Pāṭkhaṇḍā, the 'topmost sword', recalling the mighty sword she used in the war. But this over-worldly contract needs a yearly confirmation visible to everyone in this world. Therefore, an earthen pot filled with

---

his supremacy. He tore the fort of Dantewada down, and the daughter of the chief of Bastar was given in marriage to the son of Vatsarājadeva. He brought the goddess Bastaren to Patnagarh as a trophy.

[41] For a depiction of „Khonds dressed for Battle" by W. Macpherson, published in 1865, cf. Hacker 1999, ill. 3.

[42] According to P. Siṅgh Deo at first a Gond *rāja* ruled the area of Jarasingha. Then Yuvrāj Singhdeo, an ancestor of P. Siṅgh Deo, took over the power in 1820. A spot near the present stadium called Uchguḍī marks the area of the former fort (Jarāgaḍa). In this fort was the first shrine of Pāṭkhaṇḍā and till today the earthen pot from Patnagarh is brought to this spot. There the first rituals of the *yātrā* are performed.

various presents (*pāṭsindūr*) is still sent to Jarasingha from Patnagarh today as a testimony to this agreement. It is said to be a present from the goddesses Pāṭaṇeśvarī and Samleśvarī, the other-worldly representatives of the Chauhan rulers. This precious pot is an expression of thanks for the great active help provided by Pāṭkhaṇḍā in the war. Only after the arrival of this earthen pot can the festival in Jarasingha start.

But the ritual objects in the Pāṭkhaṇḍā temple also recall the struggle and the final victory. Pāṭkhaṇḍā has no anthropomorphic image in the temple but is represented by a sword and a shield, her weapons of war. Another sword, representing the hill god Buḍhādaṅgar, is worshipped along with these weapons. Together with Pāṭkhaṇḍā, they share power over the land. The area beyond the settled sphere of Jarasingha is under his rule. These swords (three altogether), along with the three parts of the 'original' *paniki*, form the visual codes of memory. As movable images (*calanti pratimā*), they attain the highest attention and honour during the Pāṭkhaṇḍā *yātrā*.

2.3 Paraśurām Siṅgh Deo, Former Zamindar of Jarasingha

Whereas in the text of the two episodes told by the *thānāpati* the main stress is on Pāṭkhaṇḍā's role as a pathfinder and brave fighter, Paraśurām Siṅgh Deo, a descendant of the Chauhan family from Patnagarh and until 1948 Zamindar of Jarasingha, favours other aspects of the deity.

With the arrival of his family in Jarasingha, we enter on to historical ground for the first time. Concrete data concerning the history of Jarasingha starts in the eighteenth century. The Chauhan ruler Rāmacāndradeva of Patnagarh (1765-1820) gave the zamindari of Jarasingha to his son Jugarāj Singh (1820-48), whose heirs still continue the line. The grandfather of the present Zamindar, Paraśurām Siṅgh Deo, constructed the new palace, the temple of Pāṭkhaṇḍā and the Jagannātha temple.[43] The nineteenth century, the period of the Pax Britannica, was marked by a wave of planning new towns, since the constant armed conflicts with neighbouring rulers came to an end, the surplus money being invested in the construction of representative palaces and temples.[44] The new Chauhan rulers at Jarasingha also started to construct a royal complex south of the old village as a visible sign of their era of power. Along with the new temple for the tutelary deity, Pāṭkhaṇḍā, a great temple to Jagannātha was constructed.[45] This whole palace complex no longer exists, and only a richly decorated entrance of plaster recalls the glorious past. The ritual programme within the worship of Pāṭkhaṇḍā also changed. The Pāṭkhaṇḍā *yātrā* was included in the context of the *daśaharā* festival, and this means the victorious deity entered the realm of Durgā, the great goddess of victory. It was in the nineteenth century that the performance of the *daśaharā* festival developed in grand style. For the local ruler it became a visible symbol of royal power and legitimation. The *daśaharā* festival became the central festival of the year, patronized and financed by the ruler.[46] At the end of the festival, the goddess

---

[43] I would like to thank Paraśurām Siṅgh Deo, the former Zamindar of Jarasingha, for his great help, kind assistance and unparalleled co-operation during my field work in Jarasingha. According to him, the area was ruled by a Gond dynasty till the adopted son of Rāmacandra Deo (1765-1820) took over the control of this area after his death. This Gond family traces his origin back to Damāī Gond, a great heroic fighter. It was his sword which Rāmāī Deo, the founder of the Chauhan dynasty, took into his possession. This was the powerful sword of Pāṭkhaṇḍā.

[44] According to Kulke 1993, 87, most of the Jagannātha temples, symbols of Hindu kingship and royal authority, were constructed during the second part of the nineteenth century. Together with an impressive palace at the centre, they marked the new „royal centres".

[45] After the downfall of the Sūryavaṃśī, the central dynasty of Orissa, after 1568, the cult of Jagannātha spread to the capitals of the Garjhat states. The temples must be regarded as a symbolic declaration of independence; cf. Kulke 1993 (b), 87.

[46] At the centre of the *daśaharā* festival was the *rāja* and his tutelary deity, who granted him the right to rule. According to Schnepel 1997 the king was the main actor in the spectacle, the patron of the ritual events, the centre of the kingdom and even the cosmos. For further information on the *daśaharā* festival

granted the king her help in his war campaigns and bestowed on him the right to rule her country and people for the coming year.[47] The kings tried to widen their own secular authority by 'universalizing' their tutelary deities as much as possible.[48] Even today, after the abolition of the zamindari system, Paraśurām Siṅgh Deo still presides over the festival in his function as the rāja. For him the most crucial moment of the festival comes on the last day, when Pāṭkhaṇḍā, embodied by her priest, transfers the right to rule her country to him. Then she speaks to him: '*rāutt*, I am the forest god (*vanaspati*); I eat bitter fruits and I stay only in the forest. I am Banakhaṇḍī, *rāutt*, I am the *buḍelphul*.[49] I never stay for ever.... *Rāutt*, you will stay well as long as you worship me. *Rāutt*, call me when you are in danger.... I am going back to my place. Look after my country and my people with my elder sister (Buḍhīāī, the village deity)'.[50]

2.4 Pāṭkhaṇḍā in the Mālāśrī of the Sāhāṇi, the *Rajpurohit*

Her final association with Durgā and her links with other famous Hindu gods and goddesses are expressed by the present *rājpurohit* of the royal family of Jarasingha, Nārāyaṇa Siṅgh Sāhāṇi. His family traces their origins back to the first Chauhan rulers. Like the

in Jeypore, Orissa, cf. Schnepel 1978, 229-262; on Jagdalpur (Bastar), cf. Mallebrein 1996. For important literature on the *daśaharā* festivals in other regions of India, cf. Schnepel 1997, fn.16., Wilke 1996, Sontheimer 1981, Kane 1958.

[47] For a discussion of the king as the husband of the goddess, cf. Hara 1973.

[48] On this, cf. Preston 1992, 96. One obtains more merit as one travels further and further up within the network of Hindu sacred centres. The ultimate religious significance a goddess can obtain is a place among the Śakti *piṭha*s of India.

[49] A particular flower that comes out in the evening and closes up in the morning, and thus blosoms only for a short period.

[50] Pāṭkhaṇḍā adresses the *rāja* as Rāutt, a title which is also found in connection with the god Jagannātha as the state deity (*rāṣṭradevatā*). King Anaṅgabhima III (1211-1238) was praised as the *rāutta* („viceroy") who ruled Orissa under the *sāmrājya* (universal sovereignty) of Jagannātha; cf. Kulke 1993 (b), 86.

king the deity addresses him as *rāutt*, as he comes next to him in status.[51] During the *pūjā* performed for Pāṭkhaṇḍā, he recites the Mālāśrī, different verses composed in the style of a *māhātmya* and written down by his father. In this written text of the *māhātmya,* the deity is associated with Kālīsundarī, Rudrayānī, Kāmākṣī and Durgā.[52]

2.5 The Pāṭkhaṇḍā *yātrā*: Some Important Perspectives

Although the Pāṭkhaṇḍā *yātrā* was incorporated into the context of the *daśaharā* festival, it was able to retain its original character as a local tribal festival.[53] As it is not possible to deal in detail with the different phases of this fascinating festival within this paper, I shall provide a rough outline of some of its characteristic elements as a 'performative text'. Today the original tribal festival of fertility and healing is on the verge of losing its original character and merging with the Durgā festival.[54] In what follows, some points will be highlighted which mark the festival as a commemorative ritual. The 'text' of the five-day performance is divided into different scenes:

Scene 1: late afternoon and night from *āṣṭamī* to *navāmī*. A carrier bringing the pot (*pāṭsindūr*) from Patnagarh arrives at Jarasingha. He stops at Uchguḍī, the site of the former fort of Jharāgaḍa and the site of the original temple of Pāṭkhaṇḍā. It is believed that the *pāṭsindūr* pot contains not only several presents for Pāṭkhaṇḍā, but also 484 deities

[51] The *rājpurohit* is the royal priest of the king, who occupied the highest position in the list of state officials; cf. Padhy 1991, 72.

[52] I would like to thank Nārāyaṇa Siṅgh Sāhānī from Sahanisarasmal village for his valuable information and recitation of thc *Mālāṣrī māhātmya*.

[53] At present Paraśurām Siṅgh Deo makes an enormous effort to maintain the old style of the festival, but most probably his family members will not continue to carry this burden due to a lack of interest. The festival will then lose its original style and old tradition, and the *rāja*'s position may be taken over by the young *rājpurohit*.

[54] A detailed study of the Paṭkhaṇḍā festival is under preparation.

from the whole area who come to Jarasingha to attend the festival. After a ritual with tantric elements at Uchguḍī, the group proceeds to the new temple of Pāṭkhaṇḍā. There Pāṭkhaṇḍā's priest waits and, possessed by the deity, he dances out of happiness. He is guided by two men who hold his arms. These helpers belong to a group of 32 men (*dehuliā*) who are responsible for the smooth running of the festival. The *dehuliā* represent the various social groups of the village, clean castes as well as Scheduled Castes. What is the commemorative idea behind scene 1? The arrival of *pāṭsindūr* recalls the victorious Pāṭkhaṇḍā in the war of the Chauhan king and the promise of Pāṭaneśvarī and Samleśvarī to rule over the Jarasingha area. The 484 deities arrive in their function as witnesses. The fact that *pāṭsindūr*'s reception takes place at the historical site, associated with Jarāgāḍa, recalls the period of Gond rule and the original temple site. On this evening, the sword kept inside the cellar of the temple is taken out for a ritual bath and cleaned of all the impurities of the year. It symbolizes the end of the war and the victory over the Bastar king.

Scene 2: in the late afternoon of *navāmī.* Whereas scene 1 recalls the great deeds of Pāṭkhaṇḍā in the war of the Chauhan king, scene 2 places the emphasis on her origins in the forest (*vana*). Pāṭkhaṇḍā speaks of herself only as Banakhandi or Vanaspati. This event takes place in a holy forest grove called dejhār, about 4 km from Uchguḍī (scene 1). In this grove stands a Mahuā tree, in the roots of which the three parts of the 'original' *paniki* appear every year in a miraculous way. No one, except the priest of Pāṭkhaṇḍā, his brother Birpānī and a selected group of *dehuliā,* is allowed to go to this spot during the festival. As soon as the priest takes the three iron pieces in his hands, he becomes possessed by the deity's power. At the same time the medium of Birpānī also becomes possessed, and together the 'deities on earth' come out of the forest

> dancing. Their emergence from the forest grove recalls an important incident of her legend: her running away from the threatening Brahmin who had stolen her *paniki* from the house of a Kondh. The deity's power was kept within this *paniki*, her representation. By breaking into three parts, she signalled the withdrawal of her magical power. But now, within this ritual, the three parts are united again by the priest holding them in his hands in the trance. Thus, the magical power of Pāṭkhaṇḍā is restored and she regains the power to heal her devotees of all types of diseases, infertility as well as mental problems. Her happiness at having regained her original power is expressed by her emerging from the forest dancing.

In scene 2 the other-worldly and this-worldly realms merge. Pāṭkhaṇḍā and Birpānī are greeted first by the local gods, represented by the musical instruments of the village musicians. Only then do they proceed to the king, the worldly deputy of Pāṭkhaṇḍā, waiting just behind them. The iron drum (*niṣāṇ*) represents the village deity Buḍhiāī, the trumpet (*mohūrī*) Jenābuḍhā the younger brother of Pāṭkhaṇḍā. One musical instrument is especially important: the double membrane drum (*ḍhola*). This huge drum represents Hiṅjālrāṇī, the wife of Pāṭkhaṇḍā. For her devotees she is the daughter of a Harijan who, out of shame of her low origin, hides herself in a drum. The moment Pāṭkhaṇḍā arrives in front of the musicians, that is, the gods as the reception committee, he jumps on to the double membrane drum representing Hiṅjālrāṇī. This moment is eagerly awaited, as it is the visible sign of the consummation of the marriage, a symbol of fertility and prosperity. Then Pāṭkhaṇḍā proceeds with her entourage to the ritual site of Kuchguḍī to heal infertile couples waiting there from their affliction.

In this connection two points are remarkable: first Pāṭkhaṇḍā combines in herself male as well as female aspects: for *pātra* I and *pātra* II of Mahasinghi, she is considered to be a female goddess linked with the earth goddess Dharitrī, as she has the ability to withdraw her power of fertility and thus create a devastating drought. Conversely, in the Pāṭkhaṇḍā *yātrā* of Jarasingha, the closest attention is paid to her male aspect as a deity who has the power to heal infertility and mental disease. The way the priest holds and moves the iron pieces in his hands, while in trance, to heal infertile couples strongly recalls the male sexual act. For Paraśurām Siṅgh Deo, each phase of the *yātrā* emphasized either her male or female aspect.

It is interesting to note in this connection that the clan deities of other Kondh groups staying in this area are all male. One may conclude from this that Pāṭkhaṇḍā also goes back to a male clan deity. Throughout her period of worship at the different sites, her male character becomes increasingly lost through assimilation to ideas of local goddesses. It is the Pāṭkhaṇḍā *yātrā*, the old 'performative text', portraying the 'collective autobiography' of the Muṭkīā Kondh, which has the capacity to preserve the age-old, now nearly forgotten memories of her male origin. Due to her entry into the realm of Durgā, she is today worshipped as a goddess and lined up with Durgā, Chandī and Kālī.

The second significant point is the high status the Harijans are accorded in the Pāṭkhaṇḍā festival. According to Connerton (1978), rituals express social conflicts. Even today, there are many temples that Harijans do not enter. They are thus excluded from the direct worship of the deity. This is why certain deities are worshipped in the form of musical instruments. They are carried around from village to village by Harijans, who have traditionally been the local musicians.[55] But in the performance of the Pāṭkhaṇḍā *yātrā* , this traditional social and ritual exclusion of Harijans is turned on its head. The first group to be worshipped and blessed by Pāṭkhaṇḍā, much earlier than the king, are the Harijan musicians. Because of

---

[55] Old iron drums (*niṣāṇ*) can be seen outside the temple of Budhīāī, the village deity. They are worshipped by the Harijans, who do not enter the temple. The inhabitant of the Harijansahi in Balasgumpha keep three *niṣāṇ* and worship them as the goddess Barali. They carry them from village to village, perform rituals there and sing songs about her deeds. All over Orissa, one can see the bodies of old broken iron drums (*niṣāṇ*) in front of the temple, mostly near the entrance door, which represent the deity of the shrine but are worshipped by those who do not enter it.

the marriage of Pāṭkhaṇḍā to a Harijan girl, they attain the highest social status within the *yātrā* , but only at that time. Hiṅjālrāṇī is not given much attention in the daily life of the village, and her place of worship is an open shrine, not much looked after. The aim of the Pāṭkhaṇḍā *yātrā* is to place all social groups on an equal footing and thus merge the people of the village into one social unit. This is also expressed by certain ritual privileges. Thus the Harijans not only play music – creating the sounds, the voices of the gods – they also provide the undergarment for the priest of Pāṭkhaṇḍā and the material, the 'ritual dress', for the three metal pieces of the *paniki*.[56]

3. Concluding Remarks: Text, Context, Social Memory

The present paper analyses different forms of texts and their role within a given context. These texts reflect different phases in the historical development of the deity Pāṭkhaṇḍā, and they themselves refer to events the authors consider to be historically 'real'. These occurrences justify the transformation process within the history of the deity and her growth and assimilation into the context of Hinduism. The texts describe this development and legitimize it through legend and mythology, storing as a 'memory record' the different phases of change from tribal to Hindu deity.

The analysis revealed two facts:

1. Depending on the genre of text and context, the memory of Pāṭkhaṇḍā's tribal origin is more or less preserved or has an inherent capacity to be kept alive within the society. Texts illustrating a given situation of power and influence, such as those of the priestly families, are in greater danger of becoming lost in being transferred from one generation to the next. When the main function of a

[56] It was an old tradition in the tribal area that the Pano weave the dress. The Harijans do not do this themselves, but only provide the Pano with the spun material.

text becomes the legitimation of ritual supremacy, aspects of her tribal origin are begun to be lost.

2. Conversely, within a text with a performative character, such as the different parts of the Pāṭkhaṇḍā *yātrā* , her memory as a tribal deity is kept alive. It is by means of the commemorative ritual and its performance that social memory and thus identity as a tribal group are preserved. According to Connerton the images of the past commonly legitimate a present social order. Our experience depends upon the knowledge of the past. Past and recollected knowledge of the past is conveyed and sustained by (more or less) ritual performance. Thus, social memory can be found in commemorative ceremonies, they are commemorative as they are performative.[57] The ritual enactment of their history reflects the 'collective autobiography' of the tribes. The different performances are not only 'embodied culture' but also 'embodied theology'.[58] The human world becomes one with the divine space, and it is in this larger sphere that the re-enactment takes place. In oral tradition the perception of time is not linear but cyclical: every year the deity comes to her devotees, and thus the past is re-presented in the present.

An examination of the historical development of other deities of tribal origin reveals that the main tool for keeping alive the memory of tribal origin is ritual enactment presented within a commemoration ceremony. Social memory of the deities' tribal origin is preserved and kept alive through this synchronic representation of diachronic events. One meaning and function of rituals is that they stage a primary event and state. They transform this event through their ritual repetition into a timeless entity.[59]

---

[57] Cf. Connerton, 1989, 6-71.

[58] Cf. Waghorne, 1984, 49.

[59] Michaels, 1999, 44. He argues against the theory of the 'meaningless of rituals'.

The moment this 'performative text' changes or comes to an end, as might be the case with the Pāṭkhaṇḍā *yātrā* , the memory of her roots is lost. The analysis of commemorative ceremonies plays an important part in studying the process of the Hinduization of tribal deities, as they are of cardinal importance for keeping the deities' past alive in the present.

References

Assmann, A. 1999. *Erinnerungsräume: Formen und Wandlungen des Kulturellen Gedächtnisses*, München: C. H. Beck.

Assmann, J. 1999. *Das Kulturelle Gedächtnis. Schrift, Erinnerung und Politische Identität in Frühen Hochkulturen,* München: C. H. Beck.

Banerji, R.D. 1928. 'Rajput Origins of Western Orissa', in *Modern Review* 43, 285-329.

Berkemer, G. 1993. *Little Kingdoms in Kalinga: Ideologie, Legitimation und Politik Regionaler Eliten*, Stuttgart: Franz Steiner Verlag.

Carrin-Bouez, M. 1978. 'The Relevance of the Hinduization Model for the Understanding of Santal Society', in R. Moser and M.K. Gautam (eds.), *Aspects of Tribal Life in South Asia I: Strategy and Survival*, Bern: The University of Berne Institute of Ethnology, 83-92.

Chatterton, E. 1916. *The Story of Gondwana*, London.

Connerton, P. 1989. *How Societies Remember*, Cambridge: Cambridge University Press.

Das, A. 1967-8. 'A Study of the Socio-religious Life of Tribals in Guduvella area, Bolangir District', in *Adibasi* 4 (9), 3-30.

Das, H.C. 1999. *Sākta Pithas: A Study,* Bhubaneswar: Bharati Prakashan.

Eschmann, A. 1978 (a). 'Hinduization of Tribal Deities in Orissa: The śākta and śaiva Typology', in A. Eschmann, H. Kulke and G.C. Tripathi (eds.), *The Cult of Jagannath and the Regional Tradition of Orissa*, New Delhi: Manohar Publishers, 79-97.

Eschmann, A. 1978 (b). 'Prototypes of the Navakalevara Ritual and their Relation to the Jagannātha Cult', in A. Eschmann, H. Kulke and G.C. Tripathi (eds.), *The Cult of Jagannath and the Regional Tradition of Orissa*, New Delhi: Manohar, 265-83.

Eschmann, A. 1994. 'Sign and Icon: Symbolism in the Indian Folk Religion', in G.C. Tripathi and Hermann Kulke (eds.), *Religion and Society in Eastern India*, New Delhi: Manohar, 211-33.

Fröhlich, G. and I. Mörth. 1998. *Symbolische Anthropologie der Moderne*. Kulturanalysen nach Clifford Geertz, Frankfurt/New York: Campus Verlag.

Fuchs, S. 1960. *The Gond and Bhumia of Eastern Mandla* London: Asia Publishing House.

Gottowick V. 1997. *Konstruktion des Anderen. Clifford Geertz und die Krise der Ethnographischen Repräsentation*, Berlin: Dietrich Reimer Verlag.

Hacker, K.F. 1999. 'Displaying a Tribal Imaginary: Known and Unknown India', in *Museum Anthropology*, 23 (3), 5-25.

Hara, M. 1973. 'The King as a Husband of the Earth', in *Asiatische Studien* 27, 97-114.

Kane, P.V. 1958. 'Durgotsava', in *History of Dharmaśāstra* (Ancient and Mediaeval Religious and Civil Law in India), 5 (1), Poona: Bhandarkar Oriental Research Institute, 154 -85.

Kulke, H. 1978. 'Early State Formation and Royal Legitimation in Tribal Areas of Eastern India', in R. Moser and M.K. Gautam (eds.), *Aspects of Tribal Life in South Asia I: Strategy and Survival*, Studia Ethnologica Bernensia 1, Berne: The University of Berne Institute of Ethnology, 29-37.

Kulke, H. 1992. 'Tribal Deities at Princely Courts: The Feudatory Rajas of Central Orissa & their Tutelary Deities', in S. Mahapatra (ed.), *The Realm of the Sacred: Verbal Symbolism and Ritual Structures*, Calcutta: Oxford University Press, 56-78.

Kulke, H. 1993 (a). *Kings and Cults: State Formation and Legitimation in India and Southeast Asia*, Delhi: Manohar.

Kulke, H. 1993 (b). 'Kṣatriyaization and Social Change: A Study in the Orissa Setting', in idem, *Kings and Cults*, Delhi: Manohar, 82-92.

Kulke, H. 1995. 'The Early and the Imperial Kingdom: A Processural Model of Integrative State Formation in Early Medival India', in idem (ed.), *The State in India 1000-1700*, Oxford: Oxford University Press, 233-62.

Mallebrein, C. 1993. *Die Anderen Götter: Volks- und Stammesbronzen aus Indien*, Heidelberg: Edition Braus.

Mallebrein, C. 1996. 'Danteśvarī, the Family Goddess (kulsvāminī) of the Rājas of Bastar and the Daśaharā-Festival of Jagdalpur', in A. Michaels, C. Vogelsanger and A. Wilke (eds.), *Wild Goddesses in India and Nepal*, Berne: Peter Lang, 483-511.

Martin, R.C. 1984. 'Clifford Geertz Observed: Understanding Islam As Cultural Symbolism', in R.L. Moore and F.E. Reynolds (eds.), *Studies in Religion and Society*, Chicago: Center for the Scientific Study of Religion, 11-30.

Mehta, B.N. 1984. *Gond of the Central Indian Highland:. A Study of the Dynamics of Gond Society*, New Delhi: Concept Publishing Company.

Michaels, A. 1999. 'Le rituel pur le rituel' oder wie Sinnlos sind Rituale?', in C. Caduff, J. Pfaff-Czarnecka (eds.), *Theorien – Kontroversen – Entwürfe*, Berlin: Reimer, 23-47.

Mishra, P.K. 1983. 'Deities and State Formation in Ancient Orissa', in *The Journal of Orissan History* 4, 6-13.

Moore, R.L. and F.E. Reynolds (eds.). 1984. *Studies in Religion and Society*, Chicago: Center for the Scientific Study of Religion.

Ortner, S.B. 1999. *The Fate of 'Culture:' Geertz and Beyond*, Berkeley: University of California Press.

Padhy, A.K. 1991. 'Feudatory States of Orissa in 19th Century: A Study on Social Structure', in *The Journal of Orissan History* 11, 71-5.

Pasayat Ch. 1998. *Tribe, Caste and Folk Culture*, Jaipur and New Delhi: Rawat Publications.

Pasayat, Ch. 1997. 'Tribal-Non-Tribal Interaction in Orissa: A study of Samalei/Samaleswari Devi in Sambalpur', in G. Pfeffer and D.K. Behera (eds.), *Contemporary Society: Tribal Studies*, vol. II, New Delhi: Concept Publishing Company, 304-16.

Patnaik, N. 1989. *The Bondo,* Bhubaneswar: Tribal and Harijan Research-cum-Training Institute.

Pattnaik, U.N. 1969-70. 'Religious Ceremonies, Ordeals and a Legend about Oriya Infiltration in Kondh Hills', in *Adibasi* 4 (9), 81-4.

Preston, J.J. 1992. 'Sacred Centres and Symbolic Networks in India', in S. Mahapatra (ed.), *The Realm of the Sacred: Verbal Symbolism and Ritual Structures*, Calcutta: Oxford University Press, 79-112.

Sahu, N.K., P.K. Mishra and J.K. Sahu. 1998 (1st edn 1980). *History of Orissa (Pre-History to 1971)*, Cuttack: Nalanda.

Schnepel, B. 1993. 'Die Schutzgöttinnen: Tribale Gottheiten in Südorissa (Indien) und ihre Patronage durch hinduistische Kleinkönige', in *Anthropos* 88, 337-50.

Schnepel, B. 1997 (a). *Die Dschungelkönige. Ethnohistorische Aspekte von Politik und Ritual in Südorissa/Indien*, Stuttgart: Franz Steiner Verlag.

Schnepel, B. 1997 (b). 'Der Raub der Göttin. Rituelle Inszenierungen von Macht und Autorität in Orissa', in B.E. Schmidt and M. Münzel (eds.), *Ethnologie und Inszenierung: Ansätze zur Theaterethnologie*, Marburg: Reihe Curupira Band 5, 459-85.

Singer, M. 1972. 'Text and Context in the Study of Contemporary Hinduism', in idem, *When a Great Tradition Modernizes*, London: Vikas Publishing House, 39-54.

Sinha, S. 1997. 'State Formation and Rajput Myth in Tribal Central India', in H. Kulke (ed.), *The State in India 1000-1700*, Oxford: Oxford University Press, 304-42.

Sontheimer, G.D. 1981. 'Dasarā at Devaraguḍḍa: Ritual and Play in the Cult of Mailār/Khaṇḍobā', in L. Lutze (ed.), *Drama in Contemporary South Asia: Varieties and Setting, South Asian Digest of Regional Writing* 10, Heidelberg, 1-28.

Sontheimer, G.D. 1994. 'The *vana* and the *kṣetra*: The Tribal Origins of Some Famous Cults', in G.C. Tripathi and H. Kulke (eds.), *Religion and Society in Eastern India*, New Delhi: Manohar, 117-64.

Srinivas, M.N. 1955. 'A Note on the Sanskritization and Westernization', in *The Far Eastern Quarterly* 15, 481-96.

Staal, J.F. 1962. 'Sanskrit and Sanskritization', in *Journal of Asian Studies* 22, 261-75.

Urhahn, M. 1985. *Grenzen und Übergänge von Kasten- und Stammesgesellschaft in Indien*, Heidelberg: South Asia Institute (dissertation).

Waghorne J.P. 1984. 'From Geertz's Ethnography to an Ethnotheology?', in R.L. Moore and F.E. Reynolds (eds.), *Studies in Religion and Society*, Chicago: Center for the Scientific Study of Religion, 31-55.

Wilke, A. 1996. 'Mythos in Bewegung: Die Grosse Göttin in Symbolsystem, Kultus und Alltag', in *Zeitschrift für Missionswissenschaft und Religionswissenschaft* 80 (4), 265-83.

11

Imagining Orissa: Archaeology, Art History and Cultural Identity*

Kishor K. Basa

In the discourses concerning the construction of Oriya identity, emphasis has been given to legend,[1] literature,[2] literary history,[3] politics[4] and political economy.[5] An important theme in this has been the Jagannātha cult.[6] Except for its link with the Jagannātha cult, archaeology has played a very minor role in such construction in colonial Orissa. It is indeed surprising that such cultural splendours of Orissa as the temples, made much of by Fergusson,[7] and the antiquities, highlighted by R.L. Mitra[8] thanks to his advocacy of a nationalist discourse, were rarely emphasized by the proponents of Oriya identity. The primary objective of this paper, therefore, is to critically evaluate the use of art history and archaeology in constructing Oriya cultural identity in both the colonial and post-colonial periods. Although certain steps were taken in that direction in the colonial period, it is during the post-colonial period that archaeology has been playing an increasingly

---

* **Acknowledgement:** The first draft of this paper was written while I was a Commonwealth Post-Doctoral Fellow at the University of Cambridge. I convey my sincere thanks to the Association for Commonwealth Universities, London for this award. Thanks are also due to Himansu Mohapatra and Jatin Nayak for commenting on an earlier version and recommending improvements in style. However, I am responsible for any mistakes.

1 Mohapatra 1996.

2 Boulton 1979.

3 Dash 1978, Behera in this volume..

4 Patra 1979, Mohanty 1982, Mohapatra 1995.

5 Sengupta 1995.

6 Mishra 1971, Eschmann et al. 1978, Starza 1993.

7 Fergusson 1876.

8 Mitra 1875.

important role in defining and constructing Oriya identity. It will be shown that while the Jagannātha cult continues to remain an important marker from the pre-colonial to the post-colonial period, aspects such as Kalinga history (ancient Orissa), especially its maritime links, Odissi dance and the first historically known and powerful Kalinga King Kharavela (*c.* first century BC) have been emphasized by Orissan politicians and sometimes by the post-colonial state of Orissa.

Especially during the last two decades, the question of cultural identity has gained some contemporary relevance in the wake of the impact of globalization on society and economy. Mapping the cultural space of globalization is, indeed, difficult. However, while some assume that globalization would result in the homogenization of cultural forms, others believe that global capitalism would thrive through difference. Whatever the consequences, there seems to be an increasing concern for cultural identity either as a response to the threat of homogenization or as a means of celebrating difference. In this scenario, politicians in the Third World are put in a paradoxical situation. For example, in India, while on the one hand, most of them welcome globalization in the economy in the hope of multinational investments, they are sharply aware, on the other hand, that mere talk of globalization would not win them votes in the face of loss of jobs in various sectors. Hence, they sometimes fall back on cultural heritage for the sake of political survival and legitimacy. Besides, since the mid-1990s in the annual meetings of the two recently formed groups in Orissa – Vikalpa Sandhani Mancha (A Forum for Alternative Seekers) and Odisa Gabesana Chakra (The Orissa Research Circle) – various issues related to Orissan society and economy, including cultural identity, are being critically evaluated. For example, according to Birendra Nayak, one of the convenors of the former, 'We are convinced that the Oriyas, as a community, can never remain dignified just by raising the bogey of Oriya self-respect and behaving fanatically. The Oriyas can only remain dignified if they can make their community self-reliant both in application of knowledge and in managing its economy."[9]

Another post-colonial dimension of Oriya identity formation is its configuration in the diasporic imagination stemming from Britain and the United States, although in a limited manner, mainly in the form of a valorization of the Jagannātha cult and Odissi dance. While discussing various themes emphasis will also be given to the multiple nature of such identities. Before that some general remarks about Orissa, its history and its modern quest for identity are necessary.

Orissan History and Oriya Identity

The typical features of Orissa include firstly its location on the eastern coast of India with an area of 60,172 sq. m, as a bridge, like the Deccan, between north and south India, thus comprising a geographical unit with its distinct cultural and political history; secondly, it has three major outlets connecting it with the neighbouring regions – while the northern and southern influences met in Orissa via the sea coast, it had direct contact with central and northern India through the Mahanadi valley. Other features are an unbroken cultural development and the persistent existence of a strong tribal element in its history.[10]

In ancient times, the region of modern Orissa was known by various names – Kalinga, Utkala, Odra and Kosala. The great Mauryan King Asoka's war with Kalinga in 261 BC and his subsequent pacifist approach even after his victory is well known in Indian history. However, the first historically known Kalinga King was Kharavela (*c.* first century BC) who defeated the King of Magadhan, as can be concluded from the *Hathigumpha* inscription near Bhubaneswar, the modern capital city of Orissa. While the Bhaumakara dynasty (eigth-tenth centuries) is primarily known for the support of Buddhism, Orissa was ruled subsequently in medieval times by the Somavamsis, the Gangas, the Suryavamsis,

[9] Nayak 1995.

[10] Eschmann et al. 1978, xv.

the Bhois and the Chalukyas.[11] It was also under the Mughal and Maratha rule for some time. The British annexed Orissa in 1803 after defeating the Marathas. Besides the feudatory states, Oriya speaking people during the colonial period were found mainly in three areas – coastal Orissa in Bengal Presidency, the southern part in the Madras Presidency and the western part in the Central Provinces. After the Great Famine of 1866 in Orissa, nationalism was on the rise, based primarily on the majority Oriya language. Prior to that, the proclamation of Wood's Despatch in 1854, that led to an increase of the number of vernacular schools, had raised an important question relating to the medium of instruction. The dominant Bengali group advocated for Bengali, although some Bengalis based in Orissa strongly supported the cause of Oriya. But the retention of Oriya as the language of offices and schools meant more employment opportunities for Oriyas, particularly their middle class. For the Oriyas the language agitation was not 'a mere instrumental identification of their community with the language – (but rather) an assigning of authenticity to their language, as being experientially unique and, therefore, functional in a way that no other language, however close it may be to theirs, can match'.[12] In 1905 Sambalpur (modern west Orissa) was ceded from the Central Provinces to Orissa in Bengal Presidency. In 1912 Bihar and Orissa together were separated from Bengal. Orissa became the first state in India to be formed on a linguistic basis in 1936, but it is only after the merger of feudatory states in independent India in 1948-9 that the present state of Orissa came into being.

In the pre-modern period, a conception of a large speech-community existing outside the confines of small kingdoms in Orissa is known from the works of poets and priests as well as the pilgrimage to Puri (Jagannātha) from small kingdoms.[13] This acquired 'a historical consciousness' in the colonial period.[14] In

[11] Panigrahi 1981.

[12] Mohapatra 1995, 129.

[13] Mohapatra 1996, 206.

[14] Ibid.

another vein, Behera visualized the 'many-layered sense'[15] of a traditional pre-modern Oriya community which was a fuzzy and unenumerated one. It has been argued that the Oriya elite evolved a distinctive style of political bargaining in the British Raj in its 'rhetoric of deprivation' in which it divorced identity from any specific class context. 'The plight of immiserized Oriya peasants and labourers and the aspirations of a distraught regional elite were thus fashioned together into a collective, imagined community of "suffering Oriyas".'[16] Moreover, underlying the emergence of Oriya consciousness was the attempt on the part of the Oriya middle class to create a political community based on two principles – exclusion and inclusion – the former isolating the neighbouring ethnic groups, and the latter bringing other Oriyas into the political fold[17]. Moreover, 'regional' nationalism and Indian nationalism do not necessarily constitute a binary model, nor does the latter neatly follow from the former. Rather their relationship is complex and multilayered.[18]

Now we turn to various defining elements of Oriya cultural identity and the increasingly important role of art history and archaeology in it during the post-colonial period. Such role of archaeology arises primarily from the assumption that archaeology provides the most 'scientific' source of ancient history. This assumption has gained significance during the last few decades whose climax (or anti-climax) could be noticed in the Ramjanmabhumi-Babri Masjid debate. It is well known that while the proponents of the temple theory argued that there was a temple below the now demolished Babri mosque, its opponents rejected it for lack of proper contextual evidence. Despite their radically different interpretations, both the groups used archaeology to substantiate their arguments. This was crucial since legends and literature could be brushed aside, but not archaeological evidence where recovery involved 'scientific' evidence following the

---

[15] Behera in this volume.

[16] Sengupta 1995, 87.

[17] Mohapatra 1995, 141.

[18] Ibid., 140.

'scientific' methods of excavation and exploration. While discussing Europe, Diaz-Andreu and Champion emphasized the distinctive value of archaeology for nationalism,[19] since (a) archaeological evidence is very versatile, (b) it can be very old, (c) it is physical and visible, and (d) because archaeological sites and monuments have potentiality for being appropriated by nationalism. The following contains a brief discussion on various aspects of Oriya cultural identity and the role of art history and archaeology in it.

Jagannātha Cult: Oriya Identity and Political Legitimacy

Lord Jagannātha, the *daru devata* ('wooden deity') worshipped along with his brother Balarama and sister Subhadra, has played an important role in the regional tradition of Orissa.[20] The present temple at Puri on the Bay of Bengal was constructed in the twelfth century. Nothing is known from archaeological and epigraphical sources about the Jagannātha cult before the tenth century AD when it is mentioned as an important pilgrim centre in an inscription from central India.[21] The origin of Jagannātha is a 'fascinating field of speculation'[22] being associated with Buddhism, Jainism, Vaisnavism and tribalism. An important aspect of this cult is, according to Kulke, 'its mutual relationship with the political power in Orissa' in which 'kingship became part of the cult and the cult became part of Orissan kingship and its main source of legitimation' and 'this mutual osmotic penetration is closely linked with the formation of the first medieval empire by the Gangas in the early twelfth century which unified their southern homeland Kalinga with central and northern Orissa'.[23] The linking of the Jagannātha cult with political legitimacy, however, was first

---

[19] Diaz-Andreu and Champion 1996.

[20] Mishra 1971, Eschmann et al. 1978.

[21] Eschmann et al. 1978, xvi.

[22] Starza 1993, 53.

[23] Kulke 1978, 139.

emphasized by R.D. Banerji in 1931. He argued that the worship at an originally local holy place and shrine of Orissan aboriginals at Puri was taken over by the Gangas and that the sanctity of Puri (Jagannātha) was entirely due to the very active propaganda which seemed to have begun with their conquest of northern Orissa.[24] Kulke further refined this by arguing that construction of the Vaisnavite Jagannātha temple by the traditionally Saivite Gangas was 'primarily a political means to secure legitimation which culminated in the ritual dedication of the whole Orissan empire to Lord Jagannātha in the early thirteenth century by the Ganga King Anangabhima III (1211-38)'.[25]

While the medieval kings elevated Jagannātha from relative obscurity to state deity, the Oriya cultural nationalists made Jagannātha a symbol of unity and repository of their religions and cultural traditions; thus, the power of this symbol came primarily from its ability to lend meaning to political and cultural aspirations of the middle class.[26] According to Dash, in the late nineteenth century in particular, 'the contradiction between Hindu nationalism and Oriya nationalism was never apparent to the Oriyas, and this was perhaps indirectly responsible for retaining Lord Jagannātha in the centre of Oriya nationalism'.[27] The Puri Temple Case of 1886-7 at Cuttack, fought by M.S. Das (who later emerged as an important leader and who had embraced Christianity) on behalf of the Queen of Puri, challenging the alleged attempt by the Government of India to take away the hereditary rights of superintendence and management of the Jagannātha temple from the Raj family and to vest them in a committee, generated, according to Dash, 'national sentiment and not religious sentiment as Jagannātha had already become associated with the Oriya nationalism'[28] and 'drew the common people, the silent thousands, to the fold of Oriya

---

[24] Banerji 1931, 370.

[25] Kulke 1978, 139.

[26] Mohapatra 1996, 217.

[27] Dash 1978, 371.

[28] Ibid., 368.

nationalism'.[29] Thus by the twentieth century Jagannātha had begun to be constructed in a secular mould as the deity came to be seen as a metaphor for the Oriya unity and past glory.[30] Although in the twentieth century Oriya nationalism and Indian nationalism were found to be in competition with each other on some occasions,[31] the advocates of Indian nationalism in Orissa did not ignore or forget the historic tie existing between the Oriyas and Lord Jagannātha.[32]

The appeal of Puri as an important pilgrim centre[33] has continued from medieval times and hence implies an Indian dimension. However, the use of Lord Jagannātha and His temple for political ends has not ceased to continue in post-colonial Orissa.[34] For example, in the recent past, J.B. Pattnaik, a former Chief Minister of Orissa, was fond of presenting himself as an humble devotee of Lord Jagannātha, and the late Biju Pattnaik, another former Chief Minister, claimed a special relationship with *Kalia* (meaning Lord Jagannātha in popular parlance) and found in him a staunch ally of Oriya nationalists dreaming of regenerating Kalinga. Hence, during his Chief Ministership (1990-95), when a stone fell from the Jagannātha temple, Biju Pattnaik strongly took up the case with the Indian government for the temple's effective conservation by the Archaeological Survey of India. Taking advantage of this, the Hindu religious forces (comprising Bharatiya Janata Party, Visva Hindu Parishad, Rastriya Swayamsevak Sangh) formed a family – which had no substantial political presence in Orissa then – and sought to counter this by laying particular emphasis on the identity of Jagannātha as a Hindu God.[35] Thus, there emerged a struggle for the monopoly of cultural symbols. The importance of

---

[29] Ibid.

[30] Behera in this volume.

[31] Mohanty 1982.

[32] Dash 1978, 373.

[33] Acharya 1991.

[34] Nayak and Mishra 1994.

[35] Ibid.

Jagannātha in the diasporic imagination is known from the depiction of the eyes of Jagannātha as a typical feature in the paintings of Prafulla Mohanti, an Oriya painter settled in London.

Kalinga: Its Architectural Style and Maritime Heritage

Since the nineteenth century, the typical features of Orissan temples have been regarded as *Vimana, Jagamohana, Natamandir* and *Bhogamandapa*, the last two being considered later additions.[36] Fergusson considered the Mukteswar temple (Bhubaneswar) as 'the gem of Orissan architecture'[37] and the Lingaraj, the Siva temple at Bhubaneswar, as 'perhaps the finest example of a purely Hindu temple in India'.[38] For Ganguly, 'Orissa towers above all in solitary grandeur'[39] concerning its temple-building style. However, it was the 'Two Bachelors of Arts' who cited temples, among other proofs, in the Oriya nationalist cause (1919,155-60). According to them, 'the genius of the people ... expressed itself ... in ... devotional architecture ...'. Bhubaneswar was regarded as 'one of the greatest cities which India ever saw', and Konarak as the world's most magnificent temple. They also stressed the 'architectural unity throughout' Orissa with 'far more glorious ... history than Bengal'. They considered Orissa as 'the seat of Indo-Aryan style in its purest form'. Thus, this book – which was given to both the Secretary of State for India and Gandhi[40] – was a rare example for Orissan temples being used for the construction of Oriya identity.

It was R.D. Banerji who clearly pointed out that 'the Orissan style, though originally regarded as belonging to the *Nagara* class, is not *Nagara* at all'.[41] Rather he called the Orissan temple architecture the Kalinga style on the basis of a south Indian

---

[36] Fergusson 1876, 414-36, Mitra 1875.

[37] Fergusson 1876, 419.

[38] Ibid, 420.

[39] Ganguly 1912, 106-7.

[40] Mohanty 1982, 122.

[41] Banerji 1931, 375.

inscription which records that 'the sculptor Bammoja … had mastered the sixty-four kalas or arts and had invented (studied?) the four types of buildings, viz. *Nagara, Kalinga, Dravila (Dravida)* and *Vesara*'. This, Banerji pointed out, 'proves that long before the Muhammadan conquest of northern India the Architects of Kalinga had won for themselves separate recognitions among contemporary architects from all over India'.[42] For him, the Kalinga style could be recognized by the curvature of the *sikhara* (spire). However, Panigrahi[43] considered the Kalinga style as a sub-class of the Nagara style since both possess *sikharas* and *mukhasalas*, owing their origin probably to the same wooden models. After all, in their early developments the Nagara and Kalinga spires do not seem to differ greatly. The real distinction between the two types, for Panigrahi, 'is to be seen in their ground plan which is octagonal in the former but is square in the latter'.[44] However, Panigrahi accepted that 'all temples built between the sixth and sixteenth century AD in Orissa belonged to this Kalinga type'.[45]

It is interesting that Mitra's[46] emphasis on Orissan art and architecture as relatively pristine and unaffected by foreign elements has certainly aided in the construction of Indian nationalist historiography. But the typical aspects of Orissan architecture were very rarely emphasized for constructing Oriya identity during the colonial period. Second, Mitra became a good example of the 'colonized as the colonizer' by his contradictory approach of celebrating the art historic splendour of Orissan past on the one hand, and his disparaging attitude towards the Oriya language by denying its status as a separate language on the other. Third, Banerji – who emphasized the distinctiveness of the Kalinga style – belonged neither to the Indian nationalist school, nor was he a conscious exponent of Oriya identity; however, for his project *History of Orissa* he was helped financially by the Chief of

---

42 Ibid., 335.

43 Panigrahi 1981, 373.

44 Ibid.

45 Ibid.

46 Mitra 1875.

Mayurbhanj whose predecessors had contributed significantly to Oriya culture.

The maritime heritage of ancient Kalinga and some art historic aspects were emphasized by some Indian nationalist historians during the colonial period as a part of their discourse on the Indianization of South-East Asia.[47] However, it played hardly any role in Oriya identity construction then. In the post-colonial period, increasing emphasis is being given to studying Orissa's maritime heritage.[48] An Institute of Maritime and South-East Asian Studies has been set up by the Orissa government in Bhubaneswar. It has excavated an important port site at Manikapatana.[49] Excavations have shown that Orissa was participating in the Bay of Bengal trade network and, by extension, in the Indo-South-East Asian trade. But there is a problem in arguing the specificity of Orissan evidence archaeologically, because the two most well known items of Orissan trade as known from literary sources are textile and ivory, the former surviving archaeologically only under exceptional circumstances and the latter very rarely found at archaeological sites. Even when found it would be difficult to determine the provenance. Much more critical study is necessary in this regard. However, every year on the *Kartika Purnima* day (full-moon day in November) a festival is organized at the modern port of Paradeep, recalling the voyage of Oriya *sadhavas* (merchants) to South-East Asia. The best example of the political use of such heritage was observed during Biju Pattnaik's Chief Ministership (1990-5) when a voyage was organized from Paradeep in Orissa to Indonesia. Even a conference was organized in Indonesia involving not only scholars but also some important politicians from Orissa and Indonesia.

---

[47] Basa 1998.

[48] For a summary, cf. Basa and Behera 2000.

[49] Pradhan et al. 2000.

Odissi Dance

Although the revival of classical Indian dance was spearheaded during the 1930s-40s by the national elite for the retrieval of an authentic Indian past, representing India's national identity, and although the Sangit Natak Akademi was set up by the Government of India in 1953 as an official patron of dance and music,[50] it was not until the 1960s that Odissi as a classical dance form began to be popular.[51] Before that it was performed by *maharis* (female temple dancers) in the Jagannātha temple and by *gotipuas* (pre-pubertal boy dancers) who travelled in troupes performing dance dramas throughout Orissa. Incidentally both these groups are also associated with the Jagannātha cult. On the basis of dance scenes of Rani Gumpha and specific reference to dance and music in the *Hathigumpha* inscription of Kharavela in his third regnal year, which are believed to be traceable to a period even prior to the writing of the Indian classical dance treatise Bharata's *Natyashastra* (*c.* second century AD), Kothari and Pasricha argued that 'Odissi dance appears to be the earliest classical dance style of India'[52] and gave 'staggering sculptural evidence of dance in Orissan temples', implying 'that the sculptor certainly knew the art of dance and its codification as found in the *natyashastra* texts'.[53] Thus, they discussed different postures especially in terms of the descriptions of *natyashastra.*[54] At Konarak, there are graceful standing figures in different positions. Even in the famous wheel of Konarak – the symbol of Orissa tourism – there are *nayikas* in sitting positions in the round medallions in the spokes. Apart from epigraphic and sculptural evidence, other important sources for Odissi dance are the palm leaf manuscripts and the *sangita* texts –some of them even dating to the seventeenth century – throwing light on the technique of Odissi dance. The most typical pose for Odissi is the *tribhanga*

---

[50] Chakravorty 1998.

[51] Vatsyayan 1968, Devi 1972, Chapters 16-17.

[52] Kothari and Pasricha 1990, 13.

[53] Ibid., 1990, 13.

[54] Also cf. Vatsyayan 1968, 354-5.

where the body is divided into three bends by which the torso is moved in the direction opposite to the head and hip.[55] In order to reach a certain degree of clarity, authenticity and acceptability, a collaborative effort was made between theoreticians on the one side and practitioners on the other. Thus, 'the repertoire of the Odissi dance started to take shape in the image of a tree, beginning with the seed or *mangalacharan*, to the trunk or *batu nrutya*, the efflorescence of the *pallavi*, the fruitfulness of the *abhinaya*, and the falling of the leaves or *mokshia* at the end'.[56] In order to make Odissi appear authentic, equal importance was given to the elaboration of *swara* (melody) and *vadya* (rhythm) and the definition of *pallavi* was made following the text *Abhinaya Chandrika*. Besides discussions on hand gestures and their uses were based on the indications contained in the *Abhinaya Darpana Prakash*, a seventeenth century text.[57]

Emphasizing the Indian character and common features of various classical dances, Vatsyayan made two points – firstly, that the classical dance forms were broadly following the tradition of *natyashastra*, and secondly, that the evolution of the stylization of movement which had begun from the eigth to the ninth centuries resulted in the distinctive character of regional schools of both sculpture and dancing.[58] In this view, Odissi as the classical dance of a region and the concept of classical Indian dance were complementary. Hence, such dance styles, including Odissi, are projected as important markers of Indian identity in various Festivals of India organized abroad, as for example in London in 1982.[59] While the first generation of professional Odissi dancers had to transcend the conservatism of the Oriya middle class, of late it has become a symbol of status and sophistication not only for Oriya middle class women, but also for some women in Indian metropolises. The importance of Odissi is increasingly felt in the

[55] Vatsyayan 1968, 354.

[56] Citaristi 2001, 99.

[57] Ibid., 100.

[58] Vatsyayan 1968, 325.

[59] Vatsyayan 1982.

diasporic imagination in the form of Oriyas in Britain and the United States sponsoring Odissi dance sometimes in their countries of residence, and even a few learning it in Orissa. Odissi receives patronage from the state government in the form of an Odissi Research Centre at Bhubaneswar, and is sponsored at different festivals as well. Awards by various organizations have also been instituted.

Chakravorty recently has argued that the discursive formation of classical dance is a legacy of colonialism and subsequently of decolonization and nationalism; that such formation is hegemonic if its ideological map was constructed by the intellectual and moral leadership of the nationalist discourse and was forged by the dominant class in India to serve its national ideology.[60] For her, the establishment of the legitimacy of classical dance through revivalism and history, and clothing it in the spiritual essentialism of a Hindu identity, cannot be dissociated from the revivalism of a Hindu national identity. The applicability of such views of Odissi dance is yet to be formulated in a comprehensive manner.

Sacred Space, Heritage Site and Multiple Identities

Talking primarily about tourism, N. James[61] has discussed the Golden Triangle comprising the temples of Puri, Konarak and Bhubaneswar as representing the double identity of Orissa as well as India. If one takes the case of Konarak as a UNESCO declared World Heritage Site acknowledging its international importance,[62] one could even talk of a triple identity. Besides, the Jagannātha temple at Puri is an important centre of pilgrimage for the whole of India.[63] It also attracts international crowds during the Car Festival, particularly the devotees of the International Society for

---

[60] Chakravorty 1998.

[61] James 2000.

[62] Behera 1996.

[63] Acharya 1991.

Krishna Consciousness. Although apparently complementary, such identities are at times conflictual, as we have seen in the case of Puri.

Use of Kharavela for Political Legitimacy

The military, political and cultural achievements of the first historically known Orissan King Kharavela are delineated on the basis of the *Hathigumpha* inscription at Udayagiri near Bhubaneswar. It is during the post-colonial period that the name of Kharavela has been increasingly used as a symbol of Orissa's past glory. Biju Pattnaik, a former Chief Minister, often invoked Kharavela's name in his address to the Orissan people in order to make a contrast to Orissa's contemporary backwardness and, thus, to incite them to try and revive the glory of Orissa.

A very recent attempt at appropriating the past for political legitimacy was made by J.B. Pattnaik in 1999. When his leadership as Chief Minister was challenged by some of the members of his own Congress party as well as the opposition after some gruesome atrocities against women and minorities, J.B. Pattnaik called for the observance of the year as the year of Kharavela. This was done probably to deflect the public opinion. However, he had to resign ultimately.

Some Potential Markers of Oriya Identity: Construction and their Rupture

Important markers identified by archaeologists during the colonial period but not emphasized by others are the Puri-Kushana coins. The term Puri-Kushana coin was first used by Hoernle in 1895 to refer to some copper coins discovered near the Gurbai Salt Factory at Manikpatna in the Puri district which were regarded as copies of Imperial Kushana coins. These acted as 'coined money during the period when the Kushana originals became scarce after the decline of the Imperial Kushana rule in northern India'.[64] Such coins were

[64] Tripathy 1986, 40.

reported for the first time in 1858 by Walter Elliot from the Ganjam district. Subsequently, more were discovered not only in the Balasore, Mayurbhanj and Keonjhar districts of northern Orissa, but also in the adjoining areas of Rakha hills, Saraikela-Kharsuan, Mahulia and Barbhum in the Singbhum district of Jharkhand, Purulia and the Manbhum district of West Bengal and Bhilingi in the Srikakulam district of northern Andhra Pradesh.[65] These are generally said to date from the third or the fourth century AD.[66] Acharya argued that there was a mint at Khiching in northern Orissa.[67] It was R. P. Chanda who designated the Puri-Kushana coins as 'Oriya-Kushana' coins, who was supported even by the doyen of Indian nationalist historians, R.C. Majumdar.[68] Soon after the formation of the state of Orissa, P. Acharya, a leading Oriya archaeologist based in the feudatory state of Mayurbhanj, termed them 'early Orissan coins' which were all practically found in Orissa and adjacent areas containing enough relics of Orissan culture.[69] However, Tripathy preferred the term 'imitation Kushana type' since these imitated the Imperial Kushana coinage and were also found beyond Orissa in the neighbouring regions.[70] It is not certain who issued these coins, but Tripathy assumed that 'traders who came to trade in Orissa brought the struck coins with them, and when the supply was short, the Orissan traders who were used to these coins started minting, imitating these original pieces by casting method'.[71] However, since the political geography of early historic Orissa was fluid and the distribution of the punch-marked coins is in modern Orissa and its adjoining regions, the Puri-Kushana coin is a potential marker for Oriya identity.

---

[65] Ibid., 40-4.
[66] Ibid., 41.
[67] Acharya 1940, 124.
[68] Tripathy 1986, 40.
[69] Acharya 1940, 126.
[70] Tripathy 1986, 40.
[71] Ibid., 57.

Another potential identity marker is the rock art[72] which has emerged as an important area of research in post-colonial Orissan archaeology. The rock art sites are primarily distributed in western Orissa. In this regard, Behera (1991-2) related the female genital organ to a fertility cult and traced the earliest phase of rock art to the Mesolithic period. According to Pradhan, the unique character of Orissan rock art is 'the complete absence of hunting or chasing scene, so common in central Indian rock art, restricted depiction of animal and human forms, and the popular depiction of certain patterns like the harpoon and broom, so far never encountered elsewhere in India'.[73]

However, the 'scientific' evidence of archaeology and its increasing use in Oriya identity construction during the post-colonial period has also the potential effect of rupturing a monolithic and homogenous Oriya identity. For example, the very evidence of a typical rock art tradition which is a potential marker of Oriya identity can also be used as a marker of a sub-region, i.e. western Orissa because the rock art sites are primarily distributed in western Orissa and the specificity of this tradition has been emphasized primarily by archaeologists from western Orissa. Likewise, the Puri-Kushana coins, primarily distributed in northern and coastal Orissa, have the potential of being used and appropriated for identity construction in these sub-regions.

Two other archaeological features typical of two sub-regions of Orissa may be mentioned. For example, on the basis of archaeological evidence at the early historic urban centres of Sisupalgarh[74] and Jaugada,[75] one could argue for a roughly square shaped fortification for the early historic coastal Orissa which is rather rare in early India. Another example is related to southern Orissa that has been said to be potentially an important area for the emergence of rice agriculture, even if a secondary one. There are three important features of the south Orissan Koraput region. First,

---

[72] Singh Deo 1976, Behera 1991-2, Erwin 1992, Pradhan 1997.

[73] Pradhan 1997, 51.

[74] Lal 1949.

[75] Chakrabarti 1995, 240.

it is perhaps the richest zone of wild rice distribution in India. Second, this is the terminal point of the distribution of Austro-Asiatic linguistic groups with swidden cultivation. Third, evidence of a Mesolithic culture has already been reported. All these provide a good case for the emergence of rice agriculture. Thus, archaeological features typical of a sub-region have the potential of being used and appropriated as identity markers of those areas when there would be aspiration for construction of a separate identity distinct from a homogeneous and fictitious Oriya identity.

To conclude, this paper is a humble beginning to the complex and problematic exercise of reinventing Orissa on the basis of art history and archaeology. The increasing emphasis on (or the potentiality of the use of) archaeology in the identity construction of Orissa in the post-colonial period is mostly due to the assumption that archaeology is the 'most scientific' source of ancient history. Oriya cultural identity, like any other identity, does not comprise an unchanging and timeless essence and hence, various markers of identity – in this case art history and archaeology – are historically situated. Attention was also focussed on how various aspects of archaeology and art history have been in reality (or the potentiality for being) consumed, appropriated, even manipulated for constructing and contesting cultural identity. For example, the Jagannātha cult has been used for political legitimacy from medieval to post-colonial times. This has also become a contested site of struggle for symbols between Oriya nationalist identity and Hindu religious identity recently. Likewise Odissi dance has emerged as an important marker for the middle class and the Indian and Orissa governments. Both the Jagannātha cult and Odissi dance have become the central features of the Oriya diasporic imagination. Contest could also occur in the multiple identities of heritage and sacred sites. Some potential archaeological markers of Oriya cultural identity are identified in the form of the Puri-Kushana coins and rock art sites. An important issue discussed in this paper is the potential use of archaeology for constructing sub-regional identity leading to the rupture of a monolithic Oriya cultural identity. For example, features like square-forts are applicable to coastal Orissa, Puri-Kushana coins to coastal and northern Orissa, rock art to western Orissa and the possibility of rice origin to the tribal dominated Koraput of southern Orissa. Thus, the very archaeological features used in the construction of a distinct cultural identity contain the disruptive logic by which a monolithic and homogeneous Oriya cultural identity could splinter or fragment in to various regional and sub-regional identities.

References

Acharya, Paramananda. 1940. 'Ancient Coins from Mayurbhanj', in *Journal of the Numismatic Society of India* 2, 123-6.

Acharya, S. 1991. 'Puri: A Centre of Pilgrimage of an Eclectic Shrine', in M. Jha (ed.) *Social Anthropology of Pilgrimage,* New Delhi: Inter-India, 217-25.

Banerji, R.D. 1931. *History of Orissa*, vol. 2, Calcutta: R. Chatterjee.

Basa, Kishor K. 1998. 'Indian Writings on Early History and Archaeology of South-East Asia: A Historiographical Analysis', in *Journal of Royal Asiatic Society* 8(3), 395-410.

Basa, Kishor K. and K.S. Behera. 2000. 'Maritime Archaeology of Orissa', in Basa and Mohanty (eds.), 566-600.

Basa Kishor K. and P. Mohanty (eds.). 2000. *Archaeology of Orissa,* Delhi: Pratibha.

Behera, Karuna Sagar. 1996. *Konarak*, New Delhi: Aryan Book International.

Behera, P.K. 1991-92. 'Prehistoric Rock Art Pertaining to Fertility Cult and Other Subjects of Orissa', in *Pragdhara* 2, 7-17.

Behera, S.K. In this volume. 'Appropriating Jagannātha: Texts and Their Contexts' in this volume.

Boulton, J. 1979. 'Nationalism and Tradition in Orissa, with Special Reference to the Works of Phakirmohana Senapati', in R.J. Moore (ed.) *Tradition and Politics in South Asia,* New Delhi: Vikas, 228-60.

Chakrabarti, D.K. 1995. *The Archaeology of Ancient Indian Cities*, Delhi: Oxford.

Chakravorty, P. 1998. 'Hegemony, Dance and Nation: the Construction of Classical Dance in India', in *South Asia* 21(2),107-20.

Citaristi, I. 2001. *The Making of a Guru: Kelucharan Mohapatra. His Life and Times*, Delhi: Manohar.

Dash, G.N. 1978. 'Jagannatha and Oriya Nationalism', in Eschmann et al. (eds.), 359-74.

Devi, R. 1972. *Dance Dialects of India,* Delhi: Vikas.

Diaz-Andreu, M. and T. Champion. 1996. 'Nationalism and Archaeology in Europe: an Introduction', in M. Diaz-Andreu and T. Champion (eds.). *Nationalism and Archaeology in Europe,* London: UCL Press, 1-23.

Erwin, N. 1992. 'Rock Pictures in Orissa', in *Puratattva* 22, 13-24.

Eschmann, A., H. Kulke and G.C.Tripathi (eds.). 1978. *The Cult of Jagannath and the Regional Tradition of Orissa*, New Delhi: Manohar.

Fergusson, J. 1876. *History of Indian and Eastern Architecture*, London: John Murray.

Ganguly, M.M. 1912. *Orissa and Her Remains*, Calcutta: Thocker Spink.

James, N. 2000. 'Double Identity in Orissa's Golden Triangle', in *Antiquity* 74, 682-7.

Kothari, S. and A. Pasricha. 1990. *Odissi: Indian Classical Dance Art*, Bombay: Marg.

Kulke, H. 1978. 'Early Royal Patronage of the Jagannatha Cult', in Eschmann et al. (eds.), 139-55.

Lal, B.B. 1949. 'Sisupalgarh 1948: Early Historic Fort in Eastern India', in *Ancient India* 5, 62-105.

Mishra, K.C. 1971. *The Cult of Jagannatha*, Calcutta.

Mitra, R.L. 1875. *Antiquities of Orissa*, Calcutta: Wyman and Newman.

Mohanty, N. 1982. *Oriya Nationalism: Quest for a United Orissa, 1866-1936,* New Delhi: Manohar.

Mohapatra, B.N. 1995. 'Anticolonial Politics in Orissa 1920-1936: the Power and Limits of Oriya Nationalism', in *Calcutta Historical Journal* 17(2), 139-75.

Mohapatra, B.N. 1996. 'Ways of Belonging: the Kanchi Kaveri Legend and the Construction of Oriya Identity', in *Studies in History* 12(2), 203-21.

Nayak, B.K. 1995. 'In Search of an Alternative Discourse: Rediscovering Oriya and Orissa', in *Odia O Odisa: Samikshya 1994*.

Nayak, J. and D. Mishra. 1994. 'Homeless Deities and Temple Politics in Orissa', in *New Quest* 106, 227-9.

Panigrahi, K.C. 1981. *History of Orissa,* Cuttack: Kitab Mahal.

Patra, S.C. 1979. *Formation of the Province of Orissa,* Calcutta: Punthi Pustak.

Pradhan, D., P. Mohanty and J. Mishra. 2000. 'Manikapatana: An Ancient and Medieval Port on the Coast of Orissa', in Basa and Mohanty (eds.), 473-94.

Pradhan, S. 1997. 'Rock Art of Orissa', in P. K. Mishra (ed.), *Comprehensive History and Culture of Orissa* vol. 1, New Delhi: Kaveri, 46-53.

Sengupta, J. 1995. 'The Political Economy of Oriya Nationalism, 1900-1936', in *Calcutta Historical Journal* 17(2), 85-138.

Singh Deo, J.P. 1976. 'Prehistoric Rock Paintings of Jogimath Dongar', in *Orissa Historical Research Journal* 22(2), 21-2.

Starza, O.M. 1993. *The Jagannatha Temple at Puri: Its Architecture, Art and Cult,* Leiden: E.J. Brill.

Tripathy, S. 1986. *Early and Medieval Coins and Currency System in Orissa,* Calcutta: Punthi Pustak.

Two Bachelors of Arts. 1919. *The Oriya Movement: Being a Demand for a United Orissa*, Aska: H.H. Panda.

Vatsyayan, K. 1968. *Classical Indian Dance in Literature and the Arts,* New Delhi: Sangeet Natak Akademi.

Vatsyayan, K. 1982. 'Guru-Shishya Parampara', in K. Vatsyayan, N. Menon and A. Mithal *Guru-Shishya Parampara: the Master-Disciple Tradition in Classical Indian Dance and Music,* London: Arts Council of Great Britain.

12

Gita-Govinda Traditions: A Medieval Debate and Its Impact on Modern Oriya Identity[1]

Gaganendra Nath Dash

In this paper I will try to argue that some traditional accounts– which are accepted as texts in this paper – bear the direct reflection of contemporary events. Other traditional accounts emerge out of the context in order to participate in, or even to directly influence, the interplay of forces and counter-forces. The traditional accounts transmit specific messages when they emerge, but these messages may change if and when the context is altered in the course of time. In order to explain the above hypothesis I have chosen some traditional accounts centring round the famous twelfth century Sanskrit text, *Gita-Govinda*, its author Jayadeva and his wife Padmavati. At the same time, I will also make an endeavour to show how a medieval and primarily religious debate over two literary texts, (the *Gita-Govinda* of Jayadeva being one of them), helped to shape and strengthen the Oriya identity in modern times.

---

[1] This paper is an extension of my earlier paper on a *Gita-Govinda* tradition, written a quarter-century ago, which has not attracted much scholarly attention, as it was published in a lesser known journal, *Visva-Bharati Quarterly*. The opinion expressed in my earlier paper has been dealt with rather extensively in the present paper. 'Because of this controversy several other traditions were created to prove that Jayadeva's *Gita-Govinda* was dear to Lord Jagannātha.... The priests of the Jagannātha temple must have contributed and actively participated in the creation of these traditions. (Dash 1976, 239). Hermann Kulke went through the original draft of this paper after it was presented at the Salzau conference, raised a few questions and offered suggestions for improvement on the basis of which some additions and modifications were made. I am grateful to him for his suggestions.

I

The *Gita-Govinda* of Jayadeva originated as a literary text, a narrative poem (*kavya*) and an erotic literary text, depicting forbidden love and sensuous pleasure[2] of its main characters, the hero and heroine being Lord Krishna and his beloved Radha. Perhaps, unknown to its author, it provided a scope for an interpretation as a quasi-religious text on theological grounds by religious sects such as the Vaisnava Sahajiyas of Bengal and the Vaisnavas belonging to the Caytanya sect.[3] These developments resulted in the assignment of a religious status to the *Gita-Govinda*. The very first step in that direction was taken when it was introduced into the temple of Jagannātha in Puri to be sung by the Maharis,[4] the dancing girls attached to the temple.

Although it is difficult to say with any certainty when the performance of the *Gita-Govinda* was introduced in the Jagannātha temple at Puri, it appears almost certain that it was prevalent even before the rule of Gajapati Purusottama Deva (1468-97) of Orissa. This is probably the case because the singing of a new or *Abhinava Gita-Govinda* was introduced and even made compulsory. At the same time, the singing of any other song – by implication the *Gita-Govinda* by Jayadeva in particular – was banned in the Jagannātha temple by a royal order of Gajapati Purusottama Deva's son and

---

[2] A.K. Majumdar, S.K. Chatterji and Siegfried Lienhard, etc., are of this opinion. Cf. also Majumdar 1955, 240-1; Chatterji 1981, 13, 15, 27; and Lienhard 1984, 205, 206-7.

[3] For more information cf. Majumdar 1955, especially 251-7; De, S.K. 1961, 93-4, 453, 573; Dimock Jr. 1966, 55-7; Das Gupta 1969, 114-5 and Siegel 1978, Introduction IX-XII, 193 ff., 227-32.

[4] In Puri the women singers-and-dancers attached to the temple of Jagannātha are traditionally known as Maharis. The derivation of the term 'Mahari' is not known. Pt. Nilakantha Das says that the term is closely related to and derived from the Sanskrit words *maharaja* and *maharani*. Cf. (Pt.) Nilakantha Das 1953, 88-93, also reproduced in 1967, 193-5. Later Marglin has tried to substantiate this hypothesis. Cf. F.A. Marglin 1985, 77-8. According to others, the term is derived from the compound word *Maha-Nari* meaning 'great women'.

successor Gajapati Prataparudra Deva (1497-1533/4) in July 1499.[5] Further, it appears that this new *Abhinava Gita-Govinda*, the authorship of which has been ascribed to Prataparudra's father, was specifically prepared for the purpose of replacing the performance of the *Gita-Govinda* of Jayadeva in the Jagannātha temple. Therefore, it may be safely assumed that the *Gita-Govinda* of Jayadeva was sung in the temple even before the time of Gajapati Purusottama Deva. The Rajabhoga section of the *Madala Panji*, the Jagannātha temple records, mentions that the singing of the *Gita-Govinda* of Jayadeva was introduced in the Jagannātha temple by Kavi Narasimha Deva of the Ganga dynasty of Orissa,[6] who may be identified with one of the four Narasimha Devas of the dynasty who reigned, at different times, between the mid-thirteenth and early fifteenth centuries. Therefore, this reference in the Rajabhoga may have been made on the basis of the then prevalent tradition of the sixteenth or early seventeenth centuries. Alternatively, it may have been created by the supporters of the *Gita-Govinda* in order to provide legitimacy to its singing in the Jagannātha temple and thus to resist the replacement of the *Gita-Govinda* by the *Abhinava Gita-Govinda*.

It appears that this practice of singing the *Gita-Govinda* in the Jagannātha temple was introduced because of its excellence, and because it deals with Krishna's amorous sport with Radha, their separation and their reunion. It may be remembered that during this time, Purusottama-Jagannātha was identified and equated with Krishna also known as Govinda. The singing of the verses of the *Gita-Govinda* in the Jagannātha temple is not an uncommon act or a unique tradition. Such tradition was either prevalent in the temple or once existed elsewhere as well. 'From all accounts, it would appear that the singing of *Gita-Govinda* was well established in the Vaisnava centres of Patan by the end of the thirteenth century, and

---

[5] Tripathy 1962, 300-1.

[6] *Madala Panji* 1940, 36. But S.N. Rajaguru, without any supporting evidence, believes that Chodaganga Deva (1077-1147), the founder of the Ganga dynasty, introduced the singing of the *Gita-Govinda* in the Jagannātha temple. Cf. Rajaguru 1996, 178-9.

must have continued all through the fourteenth....'[7] It was also sung in 'Guruvayoor temple, Kerala ... Nabadvipa temple and a few temples of Mathura.'[8] Further, most probably the *Gita-Govinda* was performed as a play on a stage inside the Anavada temple in Gujarat at the end of the thirteenth century.[9]

But after some time the performance of the *Gita-Govinda* in the temple of Jagannātha raised a controversy. Probably it started at the end of the fifteenth century and continued into the sixteenth century. The aforesaid royal order of the Suryavamsi Gajapati Prataparudra Deva of Orissa, issued in the fourth Anka year of the king (1499), found in an inscription installed at the Jaya-Vijaya doorway of the Jagannātha temple, commanded the singing of only the songs of the *Abhinava Gita-Govinda* and at the same time, by implication, banned the singing of the *Gita-Govinda* in the Jagannātha temple. This order is connected with the controversy, although it cannot be said for certain whether it either started the controversy, which seems more likely, or whether it arose out of it.[10]

The real reason for taking such a controversial step and issuing this order might have been Prataparudra's desire to perpetuate the memory of his deceased father, Purusottama Deva, who is supposed to have authored the *Abhinava Gita-Govinda*.[11] But there were perhaps other reasons as well, which might have

---

[7] Vatsyayan 1986, 3.

[8] Ibid., 11-2.

[9] Majumdar 1955, 242.

[10] For more information on this controversy on the *Abhinava Gita-Govinda* and the royal order issued by Gajapati Prataparudra and its correct interpretation, cf. Dash 1976. But even after the publication of this paper and its new interpretation of the text of the royal order, scholars like Barbara Stoler Miller, Lee Siegel, F.A. Marglin and T.E. Donaldson as well as Rath, Rajaguru and others continue to accept the interpretation of this royal order provided by M. M. Chakravarti in 1893, more than a century ago. Cf. Stoler Miller 1984, 6; Siegel 1978, 229; Marglin 1985, 325 Donaldson 1987, 371. Rath 1986, 18 and Rajaguru 1996, 106-7, 207. Cf. also footnote 5.

[11] However, the real author of the *Abhinava Gita-Govinda* is one Kavichandra Ray Divakar Misra. Cf. 'Abhinavagitagovinda-Mahakavyam', 1977, Introduction 2-11, and Mahapatra, 1961.

prompted such a step. It appears likely that the *Gita-Govinda* had already come under severe criticism from orthodox Vaisnavas[12] because of its eroticism, its extreme sensuousness and amorous excesses. Especially objectionable were the lines

> Place your foot on my head –
> A sublime flower destroying poison of love!
> Let your foot quell the harsh sun
> Burning its fiery form in me to torment Love.[13]

Krishna utters these words while he supplicates the sulking Radha. It certainly hurt the feelings and sentiments of the orthodox Vaisnavas as, in the words of S.K. Chatterji, 'to make Krishna, who was the Supreme Divinity Vishnu incarnate and was the Lord of the Universe, speak to Radha in this strain and request her to place her foot on his head'[14] was not at all acceptable to them. After all it was a male-dominated society that the Vaisnavas lived in. Also, as Carstairs has pointed out, in the Hindu conceptualization – which is related to purity and defilement – the head is the purest and most important part of the human body whereas the feet are the lowliest.[15] Moreover, it may have been observed that the Lord of

[12] Here the term 'orthodox' is not used as a technical term with some specific meaning, but rather loosely to denote those Vaisnavas who hold rigidly to tradition and are not in favour of any change or innovation.

[13] Translation: Barbara Stoler Miller 1984, 113. The original is:
smara garala khandanam mama sirasi mandanam
dehi pada pallavamudaram
jvalati mayi daruno madanakadanaruno
haratu tadupahitavikaram (10/8).

[14] Chatterji 1981, 45.

[15] Carstairs 1957, 77-9. Carstairs states, 'It was not the fact of this discrimination between the head and the feet which was unfamiliar: to some extent Westerners share in this evaluation. The difference lies in the intensity of feeling which Hindus invest in this subject' (Carstairs 1957, 79). Later Freeman, referring to Carstairs and supplying corroborative evidence from his field study in Orissa also observes: 'According to Hindu belief, the head is the highest and purest part of the body, the feet the lowest and most defiling. To place a person's foot on another's head or to hit a person with a shoe are great insults' (Freeman

Blue Hill in Puri (Nilgiripati), Jagannātha, is completely ignored in the *Gita-Govinda*, as the name Jagannātha is not mentioned even once, while several other names of Vishnu occur quite frequently. Therefore, it may have been felt in some quarters that the *Gita-Govinda* was unsuitable to be sung in the Jagannātha temple.

It appears that all these reasons were responsible for Prataparudra's order to ban the singing of the *Gita-Govinda* and to make only the singing of the *Abhinava Gita-Govinda* obligatory in the Jagannātha temple. The objections levelled and raised against the *Gita-Govinda* could not be applied to the *Abhinava Gita-Govinda* which seems to have been specifically composed keeping these criticisms and objections in mind. Frequent use of the epithets Nilagiripati and Nilachalapati (Lord of the Blue Hill) for Lord Jagannātha and particularly viewing him as the source of all incarnations (avatari), including Krishna, in the *Abhinava Gita-Govinda* are quite significant.

The orthodox Vaisnavas and other devotees of Lord Jagannātha may have supported the king or, at least, may not have raised objections against his order. But the priests of the temple resented and opposed it because it appeared to them as an unwarranted royal interference in the affairs of their temple, which they were not prepared to tolerate. The temple priests, who were known for their opposition to the interference of the kings in their affairs, had emerged even more powerful after successfully intervening and playing crucial roles in the usurpation of Kapilendra and Purusottama, grandfather and father respectively of Prataparudra.[16] Therefore, it is not surprising that they challenged Prataparudra's order and the superiority of the *Abhinava Gita-*

1993, 85, footnote). In this connection the Vedic reference to the Primeval Man from the body of whom the four *varnas* came into being may also be mentioned. According to *Rig Veda* the Brahmans, the highest, and the Sudras, the lowliest in the social hierarchy of the four *varnas* were born out of the mouth and the feet respectively of the Primeval Man (cf. Basham 1981, 242-3). This belief of the origin of the four *varnas* of Hindu society is also repeated in later Hindu scriptures like *Manusmriti* (1/31, 1/87 and 1/93), etc. Therefore, it is not at all surprising that the mention of a suppliant Krishna entreating a sulking Radha to place her foot on his head hurt the feelings of the orthodox Vaisnavas.

[16] Cf. Dash 1978a and 1978b.

Govinda over the *Gita-Govinda.* It appears that they were successful in getting the royal order countermanded in quick time.[17]

This controversy centring on the superiority and also the suitability of the *Gita-Govinda* to be sung in the Jagannātha temple is reflected in a traditional account, the variations of which have been recorded in several medieval texts.[18] According to this traditional account, a test was conducted in order to find out which of the two songs was superior, and to ascertain which was dearer to Lord Jagannātha. Accordingly, both the texts were placed before Lord Jagannātha inside the sanctum sanctorum of the temple. Then everybody went out and the door was closed for a moment. When the door was reopened, it was found that the *Gita-Govinda* had been placed on top of the *Abhinava Gita-Govinda*, indicating that the *Gita-Govinda* was not only superior but also dearer to Lord Jagannātha.[19] Although the historicity of this supernatural phenomenon may be rejected, the historicity of the controversy could have to be accepted, especially in view of Prataparudra's aforesaid order and the existence of the *Abhinava Gita-Govinda.* Further, it appears that the supernatural elements in this traditional account were purposefully added in order to legitimize the singing

---

[17] Dash 1976, 241-2. Among the high officials of Prataparudra, Ray Ramananda, the governor of the southern provinces, may have opposed the singing of the *Abhinava Gita-Govinda* and supported the singing of the *Gita-Govinda* in the temple of Jagannātha, as he had great reverence for the *Gita-Govinda*, and had later assigned scriptural status to the *Gita-Govinda* (*Caitanya Caritamrta*, Madhya Lila, Chapter 8). But it appears that his intellectual standing was not very high in Prataparudra's court prior to the arrival of Caytanya in Orissa before 1510, a point corroberated by Vasudeva Sarvabhauma (Bhattacharya), a highly honoured pandit of Prataparudra's court (*Caitanya Caritamrta* 2/7/60 – 2/7/68).

[18] (a) *Bhaktamala* (in Sanskrit) by Chandradatta.
(b) *Bhaktamala Tika* (in Hindi) by Priya Das.
(c) *Bhaktamala* (in Bengali) by Sri Krishna Das.
(d) *Bhakta Vijaya* (in Marathi) by Mahipati.
(e) *Dardhyata Bhakti* (in Oriya) by Rama Das.
Except *Bhaktamala* (in Sanskrit) by Chandradatta, which was most probably written in the seventeenth century, the other texts were written in the eighteenth century. For more information cf. Mahapatra 1973, 52-68, Siegel 1978, 227-8.

[19] Cf. Dash 1976.

of the *Gita-Govinda* in the temple. Therefore, this traditional account as a text not only bears the direct reflection of the controversy, the context of its origin, but at least partly arose out of it.

Because of this controversy involving, on the one hand, the emperor of Orissa and, on the other, the priests of the Jagannātha temple, it was assumed that Jayadeva was an inhabitant of Orissa, and that the place of his birth, Kendubilva, mentioned in the *Gita-Govinda* (3/10), was also situated somewhere in Orissa, most likely near Puri. This assumption was reinforced by some other traditional accounts which arose out of this controversy. They did not directly bear the reflection of the controversy like a mirror but in fact originated out of it in order to actively participate in it. This point will become obvious if we examine these traditional accounts closely.

It may be noted here that these traditional accounts were recorded in several texts (in Sanskrit, Hindi, Bengali, Marathi and Oriya)[20] none of which, however, is dated earlier than the seventeenth century. Therefore, it may be safely assumed that these traditional accounts originated not earlier than the sixteenth century, the time of the controversy, almost four hundred years after the *Gita-Govinda* was written and at a time when Jayadeva was alive. But it may also be remembered, at this juncture, that the primary purpose of these traditional accounts was to silence the criticism against the *Gita-Govinda*, to establish its holiness and its superiority over the *Abhinava Gita-Govinda* and legitimize its singing in the Jagannātha temple. Once this was taken care of, the order of King Prataparudra could successfully be challenged.

The traditional accounts which emerged out of this controversy can be classified into three major groups:

1. The first group depicts Jayadeva not merely as a poet, but primarily as a saint, who dedicated his work *Gita-Govinda* to Lord Jagannātha as his devotee. Therefore the *Gita-Govinda*,

---

[20] Cf. footnote 18. Cf. also Siegel 1978, 213-32, Stoler Miller 1984, 3-5 and Mahapatra 1973, 52-68.

written by a saint and a devotee, must be treated as a sacred text, and not be ignored in favour of a text written by a mere king. Moreover, for obvious reasons these traditional accounts claim that Jayadeva was an inhabitant of Puri. Kendubilva, his place of birth, was not very far from Puri. In addition, the traditional accounts of the first group also narrate that Jayadeva's wife Padmavati was of divine origin, born out of the wish of Lord Jagannātha. For the same reason – according to these traditional accounts – she was dedicated to the service of Lord Jagannātha, i.e. to serve him as a Mahari even before her birth. This image of Padmavati as a Mahari, a singer-and-dancer attached to the temple, was created in view of the controversy centring on the singing of the *Gita-Govinda* in the Jagannātha temple which was banned by the king. Corroboration of this could be obtained from 'Jayadeva, wandering king of bards, Who sing at Padmavati's lotus feet ...' a line occurring in the *Gita-Govinda*[21] which was interpreted accordingly.

2. The second type of these traditional accounts seeks to establish that Lord Jagannātha is very fond of listening to the songs of the *Gita-Govinda*. To illustrate this point, one traditional account narrates that once on a moonlit night a woman was plucking egg-plant fruits in her garden while singing the *Gita-Govinda*. Lord Jagannātha, who came there attracted by the song, followed her to the garden secretly. But his dress got caught in the thorns of the plant and was torn. Some of the thorns even got stuck to his dress. When the woman stopped singing and went home, the Lord also returned to the temple. But the next morning the priests as well as the king discovered that the Lord's dress had been torn by the thorns of the egg-plant bush. They were perplexed by their discovery. But that night in a dream the Lord explained to them how his dress had been torn. Then the king sent for that woman and ordered her to sing the *Gita-Govinda* every

---

[21] Translation: Stoler Miller 1984, 69. The original is *Padmavaticarana-caranacakravarti* (1/2).

day in the temple. The traditional accounts of this group stress the divine origin of the practice of singing the *Gita-Govinda* in the temple and suggest that to stop it would really mean to go against the wishes of Lord Jagannātha. The traditional account earlier referred to,[22] which partly bears the direct reflection of the controversy but partly arose out of it, may also be included in this category.

3. The only traditional account of the third category seeks to legitimize the lines of the *Gita-Govinda* quoted earlier,[23] which appeared to be the most objectionable. It tells us that while writing the *Gita-Govinda* Jayadeva came to a point where he was unable to express his ideas and his feelings out of deference and devotion to Krishna despite his best efforts. He had conceived the idea that Krishna, while supplicating a sulking Radha, would go to the extreme and even ask her to put her foot on his head. But Jayadeva was unable to equate Krishna with ordinary mortals and give expression to his thought in words that would be most objectionable. He was in a dilemma. After he left his hut in order to take his bath in the nearby river, Krishna, in order to help Jayadeva out of his dilemma, came to Jayadeva's hut in his (Jayadeva's) guise and requested Jayadeva's wife Padmavati, who did not suspect anything, to bring the *Gita-Govinda* manuscript to him, pretending that he had suddenly thought of a few lines. He then composed the above quoted lines '*smara garala* ...', etc., (10/8) and left. After Jayadeva returned from his bath he and his wife Padmavati realized that Krishna himself had come to Jayadeva's rescue. Later, Krishna explained to Jayadeva in a dream what had really happened. Thus, this traditional account not only legitimizes the most objectionable lines of the *Gita-Govinda*, but also raises its status to that of a sacred book, as Krishna himself wrote a few lines of it, thereby overruling any objections. This version may be regarded as the final act of legitimization of the *Gita-Govinda*

[22] Cf. footnotes 18 and 19.

[23] Cf. footnote 13.

and its singing in the temple of Jagannātha in the context of the controversy.

Looking at all these traditional accounts closely and in their totality makes it quite clear that the controversy over the singing of the *Gita-Govinda*/*Abhinava Gita-Govinda* in the Jagannātha temple was the real context out of which these traditional accounts emerged. They were created in order to serve a certain specific purpose and thereby to participate in the controversy which constituted the context. The purpose was to establish the sacredness of the *Gita-Govinda*, and also to legitimize its performance in the Jagannātha temple. It may be mentioned in this connection that although this controversy remained confined to the temple of Jagannātha and to Puri, the traditional accounts and the message they convey went far beyond the borders of Orissa, transmitted through the temple priests and the pilgrims.[24] The literary and political issues of this controversy were overshadowed by and subsumed under the religious issues. They were interpreted in terms of religion. In the medieval period religion did influence both literature and politics. In this very process, the *Gita-Govinda*, although it originated as a literary text, was transformed into a religious text, a sacred book, a symbol of religion.[25]

---

[24] This is proved by the fact that some of these traditions are recorded in medieval texts authored by persons belonging to different regions of India and written in Hindi, Marathi and Bengali languages. Cf. footnote 18.

[25] Lee Siegel comments, 'As the work became accepted as a sacred text of the Vaisnava devotional schools, hagiographic legends about Jayadeva proliferated in vernacular languages', Siegel 1978, Introduction XII-XIII. However, in the case of some of the traditional accounts the truth seems to be the opposite, i.e. the traditional accounts were created in order to establish the sacredness of the text and thus to reject any criticism against it.

II

In modern times, the very same traditional accounts, which were created in order to legitimize the singing of the *Gita-Govinda* in the Jagannātha temple, were manipulated to convey a totally different message in the context of the evolution of an Oriya identity of the 'imagined community' of Oriya speakers. As far as it is known, the very first step in this direction was taken in 1917 by one Jagabandhu Singh, a champion of the Oriya movement, when he put forward a claim that Jayadeva was born in Orissa, and was an Oriya.[26] In order to understand the implication and nature of this development, and also to gain an insight into the immensely complex context, a short overview of this development may not be out of place.

Although the interaction of certain forces and counter forces led to the blossoming of another 'imagined community' (to use Benedict Anderson's famous expression) of Oriya speakers only in the latter half of the nineteenth century, its origin can be traced back to the end of the sixteenth century.[27] But in the nineteenth century, under British imperialism, and to a large extent because of the colonial rule, it took an easily definable concrete shape. The Orissa famine of 1866 and the attempt by some Bengali (and British) officials and intellectuals in the 1870s to replace the Oriya language with Bengali in the educational curriculum of Orissa gave a distinctive shape to the 'imagined community' of Oriya-speaking people of eastern India.[28] These two events exposed the inherent weakness of the administrative arrangement in which the Oriya-speaking tracts remained divided into, and appended to, three different administrative units. As never before, these events demonstrated that Orissa (comprising the Cuttack, Puri and

---

[26] Cf. Mahapatra 1973, Preface 1. Singh later elaborated his arguments to prove the Orissan origin of Jayadeva in his book *Prachin Utkala*, published for the first time in 1929 which was later reissued in 1964 and 1982. Cf. Singh 1982, 42-52.

[27] Cf. Dash 1978c, 359-63.

[28] Compare the article by Lotz in this volume.

Balasore districts) was a colony within a colony: the middle rank officials working in Orissa were non-Oriyas (mostly Bengalis) while the higher rank officials were all British. The Oriya speakers would continue to suffer in such an administrative arrangement as long as the Oriya-speaking tracts were not united. With this comprehension, demands were made increasingly for the unification of the Oriya-speaking tracts under one administration and, at a later stage, for a separate administrative unit.[29] This realization was brought home to the speakers of the Oriya language mainly through *Utkal Dipika*, an Oriya weekly, and its editor Gouri Sankar Ray. This was possible because of the advent of the printing press, which facilitated the emergence of what Benedict Anderson calls the national print-language, which played an important role in the consolidation of an Oriya identity. With this emerging awareness, an Oriya identity came into being, primarily in the form of the language agitation in the 1870s. The establishment of the Utkal Union Conference in 1903 by Madhusudan Das greatly reinforced the movement, hastening its pace. Another major step was the establishment of the Satyavadi School in 1909 by Gopabandhu Das, which provided a great impetus to the Oriya movement.[30]

The process of further consolidation of the still emerging community of Oriya speakers took different forms. The search for a history was one of them. The quest for a glorious heritage – not only military and material, but also cultural and literary – of this emerging community of Oriya speakers was pursued in earnest and with great vigour. An emotional claim on history was made. The Oriya intellectuals who played a leading role in the creation of an Oriya identity tended to imagine and conceive a glorious past of the Oriya-speaking people even when the evidence to this effect was either lacking or insufficient. Therefore, the dynastic kingdoms and empires which once flourished in or about the present day Oriya-speaking territories in ancient and medieval times were interpreted and quite successfully 'reconstructed' as modern Oriya nation

---

[29] Mohanty 1982, 173-83.

[30] For more information cf. Dash, 1978c and also Mohanty 1982. For details about the language agitation cf. Dash 1993.

states. This was possible because, at least from the first half of the twelfth century till the second-half of the sixteenth century, almost the entire Oriya-speaking territories were under one government (with centralized administration). The medieval Orissan empire thus satisfied what E.J. Hobsbawm calls 'the most decisive criterion of proto-nationalism, the consciousness of belonging or having belonged to a lasting political entity'.[31] As a result the continuous existence of a community of Oriyas from ancient times was imagined and projected into the present. The anomalous nature of such a conception was not at all perceived.

It was further imagined these dynastic kingdoms, which once flourished in the present-day Oriya speaking territories, were vast empires in ancient and medieval times. The Oriya intellectuals – in their imagination when historical evidence was not yet available – sought to extend and push the boundaries of these kingdoms or empires far beyond the Oriya speaking areas. Any aggression against, or forcible annexations of, the territories of other kingdoms and empires in those glorious days – either in reality or in their imagination – were not only justified but considered to be something to be proud of; indeed, they were considered to be evidence of the prowess of the Oriya might.[32] A national legend with such a motif – *Kanchi-Kaveri* – was created out of a primarily mythical tradition.[33] Its central figure, the Hindu deity Lord Jagannātha, was transformed into a secular symbol. Similarly, the dates of medieval literary and religious texts, in Oriya as well as Sanskrit, as well as monuments and archaeological remains were dated back to the 'hoary past' in order to establish a very long and glorious history of the Oriyas. Likewise many eminent Indians of the past such as Buddha, Kalidas, Bana Bhatta, Bishnu Sharma, Sri Harsha and Caytanya were claimed to be Oriyas or at least of Oriya origin. So also was Jayadeva, the celebrated author of the *Gita-Govinda*. As has already been pointed out, this claim was made for

---

[31] Hobsbawm 1995, 73.

[32] *Utkal Itihasa* (1926) by Krupasindhu Mishra and *Prachin Utkala* (1929) by Jagabandhu Singh are examples of such historiography.

[33] Cf. Dash 1978c, 368-9 and 1979 and Mohapatra 1996.

the first time in 1917 by the Oriya historian, Jagabandhu Singh. He was followed by many historians and authors. In this context the already mentioned traditional accounts, which were once created to legitimize the performance of the *Gita-Govinda* in the Jagannātha temple came in handy as proofs of Jayadeva's Orissan origin. As they were already recorded in several medieval texts, there was not much scope for additions and alterations by modern poets. But that was not necessary as they contain enough material for new interpretations to suit the purpose. What was needed was corroborative evidence, which was obtained from different sources as will be shown in the paragraphs that follow.

As has already been pointed out, many traditional accounts which emerged out of the controversy over the singing of the *Gita-Govinda/Abhinava Gita-Govinda* in the Jagannātha temple mention that Kendubilva, the birth place of Jayadeva, was situated near Puri in Orissa, and not in Bengal, as usually postulated by non-Oriya scholars. Moreover, these traditional accounts also associate Jayadeva and his wife Padmavati with Lord Jagannātha and Puri. Other traditional accounts, which associate Jayadeva and his wife with the court of King Lakshman Sen (1179-1205) of Bengal,[34] were rejected outright by Oriya intellectuals and scholars who were determined to prove Jayadeva's Oriya origin and his association with Lord Jagannātha.

Before proceeding any further with our discussion of these traditional accounts, it will be worthwhile to shift our focus briefly to another related issue. From its inception, an anti-Bengali feeling had been associated with the emerging Oriya identity. Notwithstanding the fact that some Bengalis of Orissan origin such as Gouri Sankar Ray and poet Radhanath Ray played very prominent roles in the emergence of Oriya identity, and in spite of the active support rendered by Calcutta-based Bengalis like Bhudeb Mukherji and Rangalal Bandyopadhyay to the Oriya language in the course of the language agitation (and especially the latter's role in the transformation of *Kanchi-Kaveri* tradition into the national

[34] Cf. Chatterji 1981, Mukhopadhyay 1407, 27-48, and Mahapatra 1973, 30-8, 213-48. Cf. also Stoler Miller 1984, 4-5.

legend of Oriyas), the ill-feeling against the Bengalis persisted. Several reasons were responsible for such a complex phenomenon. Perhaps one of the 'pre-colonial' reasons was the rivalry between the two Vaisnava sects, viz., the Gaudiya, the followers of Caytanya with their base in Gauda or Bengal, and the Utkali or Odisi, the followers of the Panchasakhas with their base in Orissa. Tension between these two groups existed since medieval times.[35] Further, in the nineteenth century the behaviour of some of the petty Bengali officials working in Orissa, and their exploitation of Oriyas, usurping most of the government jobs and also *zamindaris* in Orissa by questionable means (as exemplified by the case of Buxi Jagabandhu Bidyadhar of Khurda Paik Rebellion fame), generated intense anti-Bengali feelings among the Oriyas.[36] This was aggravated by the attempt of some Bengali officials and intellectuals to replace Oriya by Bengali in the schools of Orissa. In answer to this Jayadeva, the great medieval poet, was in turn claimed as an Oriya with an added vigour. As he was already claimed as a Bengali by the Bengalis, the authenticity of their traditional accounts associating him with the court of King Lakshmana Sena of Bengal was rejected outright.[37] For similar reasons some Bengali scholars also tried to put forward corroborative evidences to authenticate their traditions. On the whole, all these traditions which had emerged in the medieval period were instrumentalized in the web of the two contesting modern identities: Oriya and Bengal.

In order to authenticate the traditional accounts, which associate Jayadeva and his wife Padmavati with Lord Jagannātha, Puri and

---

[35] Cf. Dash 1978c, 361 and *Jagannatha Caritamrta* by Dibakar Das, Adhyayas 1, 2 and 3. Cf. also Mukherji 1940, 135-50.

[36] For detailed information on the exploitation of the petty Bengali officials serving in Orissa cf. Banerji 1931, 279-88, 329-32, and on Khurda Paik Rebellion cf. De 1957, 119-57 and Ray 1960, 257-89.

[37] However, only a few among the Oriya authors and intellectuals such as Mrutyunjaya Rath, Pt. Nilakantha Das and Sachidananda Routray concede that Jayadeva might have been associated with the court of King Lakshman Sen of Bengal. For M. Rath cf. Mahapatra 1973, Preface 1. Cf. also (Pt.) Nilakantha Das 1953, 91, 414 and Routray 1960a and 1960b.

Orissa, further corroborative evidence was necessary. Apart from the identification of Kendubilva, the birth place of Jayadeva, with a village named Kenduli near Bhubaneswar, the Madhava worship, prevalent in the Prachi valley and other places in Orissa, was sought to be linked with the frequent use of Krishna's name Madhava and the prominence attached to it in the *Gita-Govinda*.[38] But in their zeal these Oriya intellectuals and scholars overlooked the fact that the Madhava images worshipped in medieval Orissa, and especially in the area near Kenduli, were four-armed Vishnu images whereas the *Gita-Govinda* refers only to a two-armed, flute-playing Krishna.

Similarly, efforts were made to provide corroboration for Jayadeva's and his wife's association with Lord Jagannātha and Puri. It may be pointed out in this connection that by this time, Lord Jagannātha had already been appropriated by the champions of the newly imagined community of Oriya speakers as a symbol of their identity. In this context, the traditional accounts which associate Jayadeva with Lord Jagannātha and Puri gained great importance as they narrate that Jayadeva lived in Puri and was a devotee of Lord Jagannātha; his wife Padmavati was born out of the wish of Lord Jagannātha and was originally dedicated to the service Lord Jagannātha as a Mahari; she was married to Jayadeva as Lord Jagannātha so desired; she used to dance when Jayadeva used to sing the *Gita-Govinda* and finally Jayadeva dedicated the *Gita-Govinda* to Lord Jagannātha after it was completed, etc.[39]

The Oriya intellectuals not only accepted these narratives and highlighted the same, but even went a step further in their effort to claim that Jayadeva was an Oriya: they claimed that Jayadeva had written the *Gita-Govinda* sitting inside the compound of the Jagannātha temple.[40] This recent addition by Oriya 'historians' to the text of earlier traditional accounts, however, is contradicted by the text of another traditional account. As mentioned earlier, the

---

[38] Cf. Mahapatra 1973, 111-27 and Rath 1977, 5 who sought to link the Madhava worship in medieval Orissa with the name Madhava frequently occurring in the *Gita-Govinda*. The name Madhava occurs in I,1; III,2; IV,1,2,7; V,7; VII,12, 39; VIII,2; IX,2; XI,14 of the *Gita-Govinda*.

[39] Cf. footnotes 18 and 20.

[40] Mahapatra 1973, 69-80.

latter relates that Jayadeva was an inhabitant not of Puri but of a place near a river, and that he wrote his work, the *Gita-Govinda*, in his own hut, and not inside the compound of the Jagannātha temple. But this contradiction obviously escaped the notice of the Oriya intellectuals. Again, in order to provide corroborative evidence for Jayadeva's association with Lord Jagannātha, and especially for the claim that his wife Padmavati was originally dedicated to serve Lord Jagannātha as a Mahari, an allusion was made to the already mentioned lines of the *Gita-Govinda*:

> Jayadeva, wandering king of bards
> Who sing at Padmavati's lotus feet,...[41]

While Padmavati may have been an accomplished dancer, there is no reason to assume that originally she was also dedicated to the service of Lord Jagannātha as a Mahari. At least this line of the *Gita-Govinda* does not prove it. On the contrary, the tradition that Padmavati was originally meant to serve Lord Jagannātha as a Mahari, and married to Jayadeva only because Lord Jagannātha so desired, may have been created in order to legitimize the performance of the *Gita-Govinda* in the Jagannātha temple.

In order to provide yet another corroborative evidence for Jayadeva's close association with Lord Jagannātha and Puri, the use of the epithet Jagadisa ('Lord of the World') for Krishna in the very first song of the *Gita-Govinda* was identified with the name Jagannātha.[42] Apart from the similarity between the epithet Jagadisa and the name Jagannātha, there is no reason to believe that by using the epithet Jagadisa, Jayadeva really meant Lord Jagannātha of Puri. Nevertheless, even a scholar like Barbara Stoler Miller seems to accept this interpretation when she comments: 'recurrent reference to Sri Jayadeva's use of the epithet Jagadisa, 'Lord of the World' for Krishna in the first song is too similar to Jagannātha to be accidental...'.[43] But then one may justifiably ask: why is it that

[41] Cf. footnote 21.

[42] Mahapatra, 1973, 72-5; Rath 1977, 6.

[43] Stoler Miller 1984, 5- 6 and also 20.

Jayadeva not once used the term Jagannātha explicitly in the *Gita-Govinda*, although he used several other names of Vishnu quite frequently? One has to emphasize in this context that, in all probability, the Puri deity was known and referred to as Purusottama, and not yet as Jagannātha, at the time Jayadeva wrote his *Gita-Govinda*.[44] Therefore, it is highly improbable that Jayadeva used the epithet Jagadisa for Jagannātha because of the similarity between the two terms. Furthermore, Jayadeva never used other well-known names and epithets of the Puri deity like Purusottama,[45] Nilagiripati, Niladrinatha, etc., in the *Gita-Govinda*. Jayadeva's silence about these names and epithets (and also the lack of any reference to Puri) is a strong argument against the assumption that he was associated with Lord Jagannātha of Puri.

So far the most important exercise that has been undertaken to obtain corroboration for Jayadeva's sainthood and also for his Oriya identity is the discovery of an inscription on the wall of the Lingaraja temple in Bhubaneswar.[46] According to this inscription, issued during the reign of the Ganga monarch Raghava Deva (1156-70/1), a lady named Madama Devi donated a perpetual lamp to the temple of Kirttibasa (i.ẹ. Lingaraja). To meet the expenses of the perpetual lamp, she purchased a piece of land at Devadharagrama from a merchant either in the presence of, or jointly with, one Sadhupradhana Jayadeva of Kurma Pataka.[47] S.N. Rajaguru identifies this Jayadeva with the author of the *Gita-Govinda* and interprets the epithet *sadhupradhana* to mean 'the best among the

---

[44] 'The application of the term Jagannātha to Visnu in his particular manifestation in Puri occurs for the first time in the inscriptions of Bhanudeva II in the early 14th century,' Stietencron 1978, 62. Cf. also Rajaguru 1996, 72, 80-2, 100.

[45] The name 'Purusottama' occurs only once (in the *Gita-Govinda*) in a verse at the very end of the text of the Rasika Priya commentary of Maharana Kumbhakarna (1433-68) of Mewar. As this verse is not found in any other version either of the Longer Recension or the Shorter Recension it is considered as a later interpolation. Cf. Mahapatra 1973. Barbara Stoler Miller also considers this verse as an interpolation and has not included it in her critical edition. Cf. Stoler Miller 1984, particularly 206.

[46] Rajaguru 1956-7, 179-82.

[47] Rajaguru 1968, 3-7 and 1986, 22-8.

saints'. According to Rajaguru, he accompanied Madama Devi from Kurma Pataka (i.e. Sri Kurmam in northern Andhra Pradesh) where he was living when she came to Bhubaneswar on a pilgrimage.[48] If both the identification and interpretation are accepted, then the inscriptional evidence would indeed corroborate the narrative of the traditional accounts, that is, that Jayadeva was a saint (and not merely a poet) who was associated with Orissa.

D.C. Sircar, however, offers a completely different interpretation. According to him *sadhupradhana* means a 'leading merchant' (*sahu* or *sahukara* in Oriya).[49] As the purpose was to purchase a plot of land from a merchant it seems much more plausible that Madama Devi did that either in the presence of or jointly with another 'leading merchant' named Jayadeva. Therefore, D.C. Sircar's interpretation appears to be nearer the truth, particularly as we have no further evidence that Jayadeva was really a saint besides being a poet. In that case the Sadhupradhana Jayadeva cannot possibly be identified with the author of the *Gita-Govinda*, although both Jayadevas may have been contemporaries.

The most recent exercise to establish Jayadeva's Oriyaness as well as to authenticate the traditional accounts is to present *Vaisnava Lilamrta*, a recently discovered, supposedly medieval Oriya text of the sixteenth century, as evidence.[50] According to this text Jayadeva was born in the village named Kenduli Sasana near the Madhava temple in Niali and the river Prachi in Orissa. He came to Puri and wrote the *Gita-Govinda* inside the compound of the Jagannātha temple there. When he used to sing the *Gita-Govinda* (inside the temple) his wife Padmavati danced to the tune of the music. A king named Bhima Deva (Anangabhima Deva) introduced the singing of the *Gita-Govinda* in the Jagannātha temple (Chapter 2/55-74). Later a Brahman, Kavichandra Divakara,

[48] Ibid. Cf. also Dash 1993.

[49] *Epigraphia Indica*, vol. XXX (1958), 158-61. It may also be mentioned here that in 1956-7 Rajaguru did not identify the Sadhupradhana Jayadeva of this inscription with the poet Jayadeva and said, 'We are unable to identify Jayadeva Sadhu Pradhana for want of any corroborative evidence,' Rajaguru 1956-7, 179. He did that later. K.C. Panigrahi agrees with Sircar. Cf. Panigrahi 1994, 150.

[50] Vaisnava Lilamrta, eds. G. Rath and B.C. Acharya 1986.

wrote a new *Gita-Govinda* or the *Abhinava Gita-Govinda* but ascribed its authorship to the King Gajapati Purusottama Deva. Then, by the order of Purusottama Deva, the singing of the *Gita-Govinda* was banned and the *Abhinava Gita-Govinda* was introduced in the Jagannātha temple instead. After the death of that king, a Brahman named Jivadeva challenged and opposed the singing of the *Abhinava Gita-Govinda* in the temple. In order to find out which of the two texts was more suitable to be sung in the temple, a test was arranged. Placing palm-leaf manuscripts of both the texts the *sevakas* (temple-servants) closed the door of the temple. When the door was opened the next morning it was found that the *Gita-Govinda* had been placed on top of the *Abhinava Gita-Govinda*. After he was informed about it by the temple servants, Rudra Deva (Prataparudra Deva, the King) ordered that both the texts, the *Gita-Govinda* and the *Abhinava Gita-Govinda*, were to be sung and performed in the temple. He also specified the time when the *Gita-Govinda* and when the *Abhinava Gita-Govinda* should be performed, and by whom. Other songs were banned from the temple. This royal order was inscribed at the Jaya-Vijaya door of the temple in the 4th Anka year by the king:[51] Kavichandra Divakara then complained to the king that the temple servants disobeyed his (the king's) order; the king, knowing this, became silent (i.e. did not act). Kavichandra Divakar felt humiliated and left the kingdom (Orissa) and went abroad. Thereafter Jivadeva and the temple servants were happy because the *Abhinava Gita-Govinda* was abandoned, and only the *Gita-Govinda* was performed in the temple by all the Vaisnavas (Chapter 3/1-46). This text further mentions that the Panchasakha poets and saints of Orissa knew that Jayadeva was born in the village of Kenduli in Orissa. They used to visit it on a specific day of the year in course of their *kirtan* tour in the company of Caytanya to propagate their sectarian religion (Chapter 8/52-3).

---

[51] This is a clear reference to an inscription found at the Jaya-Vijaya door of the Jagannātha temple containing Gajapati Prataparudra's royal order. Cf. footnotes 5 and 10.

Some Oriya scholars accept the authenticity as well as the authority of this text and present it as a strong evidence of Jayadeva's Oriyaness.[52] However the text is extremely doubtful and its authenticity has been seriously questioned and challenged.[53] All the incidents just recounted show very clearly the motivation of certain Oriya intellectuals and scholars, and their strategies to prove Jayadeva's Oriya origin.

In Orissan historiography the quest for the creation of an Oriya identity continued unabated throughout the twentieth century – even after Orissa became a separate province in 1936 and later became an independent state. But Oriya historians were only partially successful in their mission. Although they were able to communicate their ideas to the educated Oriyas, and also to convince most of them of the Oriya identity of Jayadeva, beyond the border of the Oriya-speaking tracts their message remains virtually unknown.

III

The emergence and subsequent re-interpretation of the traditional accounts, centring on the *Gita-Govinda* and its author Jayadeva, were closely examined against the background of two controversies. The medieval controversy was primarily political and religious in nature, while the modern one was purely political. These controversies determined the nature of the traditional accounts, their medieval emergence and their modern re-interpretation. The traditional accounts which originated in the medieval period in order to legitimize the singing of the *Gita-Govinda* in the Jagannātha temple in the context of a temporary royal ban imposed on its singing were manipulated in modern times by the champions of a newly imagined community of Oriya-speakers for the consolidation of its identity. In other words, the traditional accounts

[52] Acharya 1986, 29-36, Tripathy, A.K. 1993, 33-5.

[53] Cf. Das 1992, Dash 1992, who dealt extensively with the issue, and Mishra 2000.

which arose in a specific medieval context were made to participate in the interplay of another set of forces and counter-forces in the completely changed context of modern Orissa.

References

Acharya, B.C. 1986. 'Kavi Jayadevanka Janmasthana O Samaya: Eka Nutana Alokapata', in K.C. Misra, N. Misra and B. Panda (eds.), *Odisara Kavi Jayadeva*, Bhubaneswar: Institute of Orissan Culture (in Oriya).

Anderson, Benedict. 1991. *Imagined Communities. Reflections on the Origin and Spread of Nationalism*, London and New York: Verso.

Banerji, R.C. 1931. *History of Orissa*, vol. II, Calcutta: R. Chatterji.

Basham, A.L. 1987. *The Wonder that was India*, Calcutta: Rupa (1st edn 1954).

Carstairs, G. Morris. 1957. *The Twice-Born: A Study of a Community of High-Caste Hindus*, London: Hogarth Press.

Chatterji, S.K. 1981. *Jayadeva*, New Delhi: Sahitya Akademi (1st edn 1973).

Das Gupta, S.B. 1969. *Obscure Religious Cults,* Calcutta: Firma K.L. Mukahopadyay (1st edn 1946).

Das, (Pt.) Nilakantha. 1953. *Odisa Sahityara Kramaparinama, Dvitiya Bhaga*, Cuttack: Nababharata Granthalaya (in Oriya).

Das, (Pt.) Nilakantha. 1967. *Nilakantha Granthabali, Trutiya Khand,* Cuttack: Cuttack Students' Store (in Oriya).

Das, Dasarathi. 1992. 'Prasanga: Caitanya Bilasa', in *The Jhankar* 44 (1), 5-12 (in Oriya).

Dash, G.N. 1976. 'The King and the Priests: An Analysis of a Gita-Govinda Tradition', in *Visva Bharati Quarterly* 40 (3) 227-46.

Dash, G.N. 1978a. 'The Evolution of Priestly Power: The Ganga Vamsa Period', in A. Eschmann, H. Kulke and G.C. Tripathi (eds.), 157-68.

Dash, G.N. 1978b. 'The Evolution of Priestly Power: The Surya Vamsa Period', in A. Eschmann, H. Kulke and G.C. Tripathi (eds.), 209-21.

Dash, G.N. 1978c. 'Jagannatha and Oriya Nationalism', in A. Eschmann, H. Kulke and G.C. Tripathi (eds.), 359-74.

Dash, G.N. 1979. *Janasruti Kanci-Kaveri,* Berhampur: Pustak Bhandar (in Oriya).

Dash, G.N. 1993. *Oriya Bhasa-Surakhya Andolana*, Cuttack: Cuttack Students' Store (in Oriya).

Dash, K.C. 1992. 'Vaisnava Lilamrta: Eka Drustipata', in *The Jhankar* 44 (9) 815-25 (in Oriya).

Dash, R. 1993. 'Sadhupradhan Jayadeva', *Orissa Review* 49 (10) 41-43.

De, S.C. 1957. *History of the Freedom Movement in Orissa,* vol. I (chief ed. H. Mahtab).

De, S.K. 1961. *The Early History of Vaisnava Faith and Movement in Bengal*, Calcutta: Firma K.L. Mukahopadyay.

Deva, Gajapati Sri Purusottama, *Abhinavagitagovinda-Mahakavyam*, ed. B. Panda, Bhubaneswar, 1977.

Dimock, Edward C. 1989. *The Place of the Hidden Moon: Erotic Mysticism in Vaisnava Sahajiya Cult of Bengal,* Chicago and London: University of Chicago Press (1st edn 1966).

Donaldson, Thomas E. 1987. *Kamadeva's Pleasure Garden: Orissa*, Delhi: B.R. Publishing Corp.

Eschmann, A., H. Kulke and G.C. Tripathi (eds.). 1978. *The Cult of Jagannath and the Regional Tradition of Orissa*, New Delhi: Manohar.

Freeman, James M. 1993. *Untouchable: An Indian Life History*, London: Indus (1st edn 1979)

Hobsbawm, E.J. 1995. *Nations and Nationalism since 1780*, Cambridge (1st edn 1990).

Kaviraj, Krishnadas. *Caitanya Charitamrta,* edited with Gaurakripa-tarangini commentary by Radhagobinda Nath, 6 vols, Calcutta: Sadhana Prakashani, 1947-53.

Lienhard, Siegfried. 1984. *A History of Classical Poetry: Sanskrit-Pali-Prakrit*, Wiesbaden: Harrasowitz.

Madala Panji, ed. A.B. Mohanty, Cuttack: Prachi Samiti, 1940.

Mahapatra, K.N. 1961. '*Abhinava Gita-Govinda* by Gajapati Purusottama Deva (1466-1497 A.D.)' in *Orissa Historical Research Journal* 9 (3-4), 51-68.

Mahapatra, K.N. 1973. *Sri Jayadeva O' Sri Gitagovinda*, Bhubaneswar (in Oriya).

Majumdar, A.K. 1955. 'A Note on the Development of Radha Cult', in *Annals of the Bhandarkar Oriental Research Institute* 36, 231-57.

Manusmrti, ed. B.K. Swain, Puri: Sad Grantha Niketan, 1997.

Marglin, Frédérique Apffel. 1985. *Wives of the God-King,* Oxford: Oxford University Press.

Mishra, K. 1926. *Utkala Itihasa,* Cuttack: Cuttack Trading Co. (in Oriya).

Mishra, K.C., N. Mishra and B. Panda (eds.). 1986. *Odisara Kavi Jayadeva,* Bhubaneswar: Institute of Orissan Culture (in Oriya).

Mishra, S. 2000. 'Vaishava Lilamrta: Aitihasika Mulya Nirddharana', in D. Nayak, S.N. Dash, B. Kar and S. Mohanty (eds.), *Prajnaloka (Professor Basudev Sahoo Felicitation Volume),* Cuttack: Vidya Prakashan, 168-74 (in Oriya).

Mohanty, Nivedita. 1982. *Oriya Nationalism: Quest for a United Orissa*. New Delhi: Manohar.

Mohapatra, Bishnu N. 1996. 'Ways of Belonging: The Kanchi-Kaveri Legend and the Construction of Oriya Identity', in *Studies in History* 12 (2) n.s. 203-21.

Mukhopadhyay, H. 1907. *Kavi Jayadeva O' Sri Gitagovinda,* Calcutta: Dey's Publishing (in Bengali).

Panigrahi, K.C. 1994. *Sahitya O Sanskruti*, Cuttack: Prajatantra Prachar Samity (in Oriya).

Pattanayak, Madhava. 1986. *Vaisnava Lilamrta,* ed. G. Rath and B.C.Acharya, Sambalpur: Pradip Publication.

Rajaguru, S.N. 1956-7. 'Two Lingaraja Temple Inscriptions of the Time of Sri Raghava Deva', in *Orissa Historical Research Journal* 5 (3&4), 179-82.

Rajaguru, S.N. 1968. 'Jayadeva, the Author of the Gitagovinda', in N.K. Sahu (ed.), *Souvenir on Sri Jayadeva*, Bhubaneswar: The Jayadeva Sanskrutika Parishad, 1-8.

Rajaguru, S.N. 1996. *Sri Purusottama O' Sri Mandira,* Bhubaneswar: Orissa Sahitya Akademi (in Oriya).

Rajaguu, S.N. 1986. 'Mahakavi Jayadevanka Janmasthana', in K.C. Mishra, N. Mishra and B. Panda (eds.), *Odisara Kavi Jayadeva,* Bhubaneswar: Institute of Orissan Culture (in Oriya), 22-8.

Rath, B. 1976. 'Orissa, The Homeland of Jayadeva', in *The Mysore Orientalist* 9, 1-4.

Rath, B. 1977. 'Orissa, The Homeland of Jayadeva', in *The Mysore Orientalist* 10, 1-12.

Rath, B. 1986. 'Odisara Kavi Jayadeva', in K.C. Mishra, N. Mishra and B. Panda (eds.), *Odisara Kavi Jayadeva*, Bhubaneswar: Institute of Orissan Culture (in Oriya), 1-21.

Ray, B.C. 1960. *Foundations of British Orissa*, Cuttack: New Students' Store.

Routray, S. 1960a. 'Jayadeva', in *The Jhankar* 12 (6) 430-4 (in Oriya).

Routray, S. 1960b. 'Jayadeva (2)', in *The Jhankar* 12 (8) 733-45 (in Oriya).

Siegel, Lee. 1978. *Sacred and Profane Dimensions of Love in Indian Traditions as Exemplified in the Gitagovinda of Jayadeva*, London and New York: Oxford University Press.

Singh, J. 1982. *Prachina Utkala*, Bhubaneswar: Orissa Sahitya Akademi (in Oriya).

Stietencron, H. von. 1978. 'Early Temples of Jagannatha in Orissa: The Formative Phase', in A. Eschmann, H. Kulke and G.C. Tripathy (eds.), 61-78.

Stoler Miller, Barbara. 1984. *The Gitagovinda of Jayadeva: Love Song of the Dark Lord*, Delhi: Motilal Banarsidass (1st edn 1977).

Tripathy, A.K. 1993. 'Vaisnava Lilamrita and Jayadeva', *Orissa Review* 49 (10) 33-5.

Tripathy, K.B. 1962. *The Evolution of Oriya Language and Script*, Bhubaneswar: Utkal University.

Vatsyayan, Kapila. 1986. *Gita-Govinda: Its Influence on Indian Painting, Music, Dance and Drama* (Dr. Arttaballabha Mahanti Memorial Lecture), Bhubaneswar: Orissa Sahitya Akademi.

13

Appropriating Jagannātha: Texts and their Contexts

Subhakanta Behera

The relation between text and context, between representation and reality, becomes an important area of inquiry when identity is treated as a cultural construct, or collective consciousness is construed as a discursive phenomenon. In either case, the relation between textual contents and their contexts needs to be explored because it is an essential precondition for a 'constructionist' perspective on any identity/consciousness discourse. Without delving into the essentialist-constructionist debate, this article intends to deal with the constructionist perspective on identity focusing on Oriya and Jagannātha. However, it should be clarified at the very outset that in pre-modern times, that is, before the later part of the nineteenth century, the conceptualization of Oriya identity did not exist due to obvious historical reasons. But one cannot ignore the existence of what Sudipta Kaviraj would call 'many-layered sense' or 'multiple layers of selfhood' of a traditional pre-modern Oriya community which, like any other community, was fuzzy.[1] Because of the complex sum of these layers, the community in question becomes trapped in fuzziness, and hence the assertion of a singular identity of 'self' in a modern sense is not possible. This is why, in pre-modern times, the concepts of 'Oriya' and 'Orissa', which are now charged with identity-connotations, had not assumed their standard meanings. However, in the absence of identity-conceptualization, there was a common religious consciousness based on Jagannātha which gradually graduated to a religious identity of Oriyas and the region.

This article studies the ways in which the Jagannātha-based collective religious consciousness, which to me was a prominent

---

[1] Kaviraj 1997, 147-8.

and pronounced 'layered sense' of Oriyas' selfhood in pre-modern times and which later on assumed a form of religious identity, has been articulated and treated in Oriya texts and literary narratives, in a reified form. However, the link between the reality, the context and these texts was extremely important. The core meaning of textual contents remains unexplained, or at best superficially deciphered, unless context of both production and interpretation is historicized. This text-context analysis becomes more important when the questions of collective consciousness or identity are addressed.

This study is primarily based on original writings of the authors and some secondary works done on them. For the Panchasakha devotional poets, extra caution has been exercised to use the most authentic, available version of their writings. As one can see, all the primary sources used here are in Oriya, since the study pertains to Orissa and its religious tradition. As to the structure of the study, it starts with a discussion of the Panchasakha literature and its relation with the context in which it arose. It is followed by a study of two more Oriya texts of a relatively modern period, both dealing with the Jagannātha cult, i.e., the origin legend. I have shown the changes in the evolution of this legend in the two texts in two different time-frames under the impact of different historical contexts.

The Panchasakha literature of Orissa in the fifteenth and sixteenth centuries has bearings on the evolution of Oriya religious traditions. The mighty Gajapati Empire really presented two contradictory trends in quick succession during its existence of almost a century. One was the empire-building activity encompassing growth of culture, literature, religion, etc., as evidenced in territorial conquest, literary activities and elevation of the Jagannātha cult. The other one was almost a state of nemesis, epitomized by defeat, political humiliation, rejection and religious intolerance. Both these trends ultimately resulted in a religious 'hegemony' which provided the immediate context for the Panchasakha poets to work on the vast socio-religious canvass of the time. The Panchasakha refers to five devotional poets, Balarama Dasa, Jagannatha Dasa, Achyutananda Dasa, Yasobanta Dasa and

Ananta Dasa who belonged to the late fifteenth and early sixteenth centuries, thus broadly corresponding to the period of two Suryavamsi Gajapatis, Purushottamadeva (1467-97) and Prataparudradeva (1497-1540), but at the same time inheriting the great legacy of Kapilendradeva (1435-67). Although there is some dispute over the contemporariness of the Panchasakha poets, the term *Panchasakha* can be used to denote them collectively because of their similar poetic genre and socio-religious vision and perception.[2]

It has been suggested that the Panchasakha poets acted under a religious hegemony that was exercised by and embodied in the Jagannātha cult. The pre- and post-writing context of their texts had important bearings on the Oriya appropriation of Jagannātha and subsequent construction of religious identity. During the pre-Panchasakha period, Vaishnavism had made rapid headway in the Orissa region, thanks to the impact of great Vaishnavite teachers like Ramanuja, Narasimha Muni and Narasimha Tirtha and the great poet Jayadeva. All the developments in the Vaishnavite fold in Orissa came to revolve round Jagannātha who had started receiving royal and state patronage right from the days of the Imperial Gangas. By the Panchasakha period, two important developments were almost complete. The first was the Vaishnavization of the Jagannātha cult and the second was the transformation of Jagannātha to the State deity of the land with its political accretions. Both these events established the inescapable hegemony of the Jagannātha cult.

How do Panchasakha texts relate to such a context? Under the hegemony of the Jagannātha cult, these poets could not help but become its intellectual preceptors. I am using this phrase 'could not help' to bring out the element of compulsion in their Vaishnavite orientation, which is also very well evidenced in their writings. This compulsion arose out of the state of religious affairs of the time that may be characterized as a stage of religious re-orientation. It was marked by a conscious attempt by diverse religious faiths such as Buddhism, Jainism, Shaivism and Tantrism to adopt the presiding

[2] Behera 1999.

deity, Jagannātha. In this exercise, Buddhism could come much closer to success. Though by the Panchasakha period Buddhism had declined in the Orissa region, it was still very much alive in the intellectual and religious consciousness of Oriyas. Indrabhauti (*c.* ninth century AD), a celebrated preceptor of Vajrayana and the King of Sambalpur, in his book *Jnanasiddhi* first mentions Lord Jagannātha as a manifestation of the Buddha.[3] This conceptualization may be seen as an anticipation of Jagannātha/Purushottam of Puri as a Buddhist incarnation. The great Vaishnavite poet Jayadeva (*c.* twelfth century) also imagined the Buddha as the ninth incarnation of Vishnu. In the thirteenth century, the conception of the Puri deity as the Buddha gradually became popular. The 'Dharma Cult' preached by Ramai Pandit in the Midnapore district, then a part of the Orissa region, popularized this conception. Ramai Pandit in his work *Dharma Puja Vidhana* described the deity on the seacoast as the Buddha, the ninth incarnation of Hari.[4] But Sarala Dasa is the first Oriya poet to describe Jagannātha of Puri-Sri Kshetra as the Buddha. In his imagination, Krishna of *Dwaparayuga* informed Jara Savara in a dream sequence that He would take the form of Jagannātha in His Buddha incarnation and punish the wicked and redeem the good.[5]

Apart from this religious-intellectual tradition, we have historical evidence of a general antagonism between Buddhism and the Oriya Hindu royalty from the Imperial Ganga days. The Panchasakha poets themselves were persecuted and subjected to harassment by Prataparudradeva because of their interpretation of Jagannātha as the Buddha and the adoption of rituals of Tantric Buddhism. They were even taunted as Prachhana Buddhas or Buddhists in disguise.[6] Prataparudradeva received Sri Caytanya in Orissa in order to counter the spread of Buddhism. Paritosh Das has shown that during the sixteenth, seventeenth and even eighteenth centuries, many of these Buddhists, residing in different parts of the

---

[3] Behera 1983, 33-5.

[4] Mukherjee 1976, 29.

[5] *Sarala Dasa's Mahabharata* 1970, 109.

[6] Mohanty 1982, 21.

Orissa region, cherished the loving memory of their religion and made no secret of it amongst themselves, although they passed for devout Vaishnavas in society.[7] I think that this really explains a unique 'sublimation process' in the cultural history of Orissa, whereby the repressed force of Buddhist culture was transformed into a new, vigorous Vaishnavite movement centring round Jagannātha. But from time to time they have invoked the Buddha and hailed various Buddhist principles and philosophies, in conformity as much with their subconscious religious past as with the religious traditions of the land. The study of Panchasakha literature may be undertaken in this context.

The Panchasakhas further helped in the Vaishnavization of Jagannātha. They identified Vishnu and Krishna with Jagannātha. For them Jagannātha became *Avatari*, the Incarnator from whom emanated ten incarnations and even Krishna, who were again absorbed in Jagannātha.[8] This is in contrast to the belief of the Gaudiya Vaishnavism that Krishna was the Incarnator. In conformity with the Vaishnavite tradition, the Panchasakhas glorified Jagannātha's abode – Sri Kshetra Puri which came to be seen as the *Nitya Kshetra* or Eternal Holy Place from which were born other *Kshetras*. They also identified different places in Puri with different sites of Mathura-Brindaban, supposedly originally associated with Krishna. Thus, the Bhargavi River became the Yamuna River; the Gundicha Mandap became the Govardhan Hill; the Markandeswar pond became the Kalindi Lake and Atharanalaghata became Kadambaghata of Gopapura.[9] Ultimately, Puri became the *Nitya Golaka* (Eternal Paradise) where Jagannātha has His *Nitya Leela* (Eternal Dalliance). This sort of Jagannātha-centric construction of Vaishnavism was in opposition to the philosophy of the Gaudiya Vaishnavism. According to this latter tradition, Krishna is the centre of the universe and the places like Mathura and Brindavan are the *Nitya Sthalis* (Eternal Places) and His *Raasa Leela* (Youthful frolic) is the *Nitya Leela*.

---

[7] Das 1988, 183.

[8] Dasa n.d. a, 13.

[9] Mishra 1961, 56-7.

Similarly, in tune with the dominance of Vaishnavism and the continuing tradition of Buddhism, the Panchasakhas constructed a new religious philosophy, particularly a new cosmology and theology. But the most important consideration is how their philosophy was epitomized in Jagannātha, who was also made the centre of the universe. Borrowing from the Buddhist concept of *Shunyavada* (voidism), the Panchasakhas imagined a *Shunyarupa* (void shape) of the Supreme Being before the creation. Achyutananda Dasa in his *Chhayalisha Patala* describes the period of the *Shunyarupa* as without world, day, night, land, water, sky, man, god or demon.[10] In his imagination, Jagannātha ultimately embodied the *Shunyarupa* and became *Shunyapurusa*, the Void Personified. The whole world was created from *Shunya*, which was the original shape of the god Jagannātha. Achyutananda in his *Shunya Samhita* sings the glory of *Shunyapurusa* and characterizes Him as both *Saguna*, with attributes, and *Nirguna*, without attributes. *Shunyapurusa* or Jagannātha is imagined as residing in everybody and guarded by truth, peace, compassion, desire, anger, etc.[11] But at the same time, He is *Nirakara* (Formless) and expresses Himself as *Alekha* (Indescribable). For Achyutananda Dasa, *Saguna* and *Nirguna* are as inseparable as the two wings of birds and *Nirguna* becomes *Saguna* when one wishes to realize *Shunyapurusa* or Jagannātha by worship and meditation.[12]

It is interesting to see how the *Pinda-brahmanda* or macrocosm-in-microcosm theory as propounded by the Panchasakhas was adapted to Jagannātha. Applying this theory to Jagannātha and the holy Triad was necessary not only for the *sadhana* or spiritual practice of god-realization. I also provided an alternative to the Bengali Caytanya practice of god-realization. According to this theory, the cosmic universe (*Brahmanda*) is epitomized in the individual body (*Pinda*). Different aspects of the universe such as sun, moon, stars, mountains, rivers and even the Supreme Being can be realized in the body. Balarama Dasa has

---

[10] Cf. Dasa 1966.

[11] Dasa n.d. a, 51-2.

[12] Dasa 1970, vol. II, 44.

expressed the mystic idea of realization of the Supreme Being inside the body in an allegorical form such as the vessel containing water in the midst of water.[13] Balarama Dasa's *Brahmanda Bhugola* expounds the theory of *Pinda-brahmanda* and traces the spread of the universe in the individual body.[14] He has also located the entire complex of the Jagannātha temple in the same body – the twenty-two steps leading to the entrance as well as the *sanctum sanctorum* where the Jagannātha Triad is seated.[15] Symbolically, the body thus contains the Puri temple, the universe itself whose Master is Jagannātha Himself. The Panchasakhas have even imagined each part of the human body, from nail to hair, as different holy places of the universe. According to Balarama Dasa, our body contains the earth, the heaven and the underworld. In the Panchasakha scheme, the *Pinda-brahmanda* theory reaches its acme in the image of Jagannātha. According to Achyutananda Dasa, the whole cosmic process of creation by Lord Brahma, known as *sthula* or integrated existence, is in Jagannātha.[16] The Puri temple is also considered as the *kaya* or the body where Jagannātha is the presiding deity.[17] The Jagannātha Triad has been symbolized by different parts of the body. The poet Ananta Dasa imagines the very existence of the entire universe in the embodied form of Jagannātha, inside the human body which is compared with Shri-Kshetra Puri.[18]

We have discussed the overarching hegemony of the Jagannātha cult under which the Panchasakhas could not help but locate Jagannātha in the centre of their theological constructions. At the same time they also echoed the reality of their repressed Buddhist leanings, but all within the confines of the theology and religion of Jagannātha. But the 'context' study of the Panchasakha texts would remain incomplete without a reference to the Caytanya movement and particularly Gaudiya/Bengali Vaishnavism that has

[13] Dei 1988, 27.

[14] Cf. for details Sahu 1985.

[15] Das 1982, 78-9.

[16] B.Mohanty 1995, 113.

[17] Dasa 1959, 10.

[18] Cf. for details Dasa n.d. b.

been constructed as the oppositional 'Other'. Going by the contents of the Panchasakha writings, we may conclude that, intellectually and philosophically, the relation between the Panchasakhas and Caytanya was very loose. One may not forget that Caytanya came to Puri from Bengal only in AD 1510, by which time the Panchasakhas, particularly Balarama Dasa and Jagannātha Dasa, had already finished writing their major works.[19] So in the practical sense, it was not possible for the Caytanya philosophy to impinge on their formulation of ideas and philosophy. Even in their later writings, except for Caytanya being invoked here and there as a great soul, *Mahatma*, he had no great influence. By this, the possibility that the Panchasakhas were aware of the Caytanya philosophy or the Bengali Vaishnavite tradition is not denied. But this awareness did not make them walk out of the hegemony of Jagannātha. On the contrary, I would like to argue that Panchasakhas managed to develop a separate identity of their Jagannātha-centric ideas and philosophy. Their differences and points of disagreement with Caytanya helped them in this exercise. One of the major differences lies in the approach to the god-realization. The Panchasakhas had *Jnana-Misra Bhakti* or knowledge-based devotion whereas Caytanya and his followers followed *Suddha Bhakti* or pure love-based devotion. But for both, there was a personal godhead to reach and realize. For the Panchasakhas, it was Jagannātha and for Caytanya, it was Krishna. The totalizing influence of love in Caytanya's approach is evidenced by the fact that he used to be in spiritual trances-sometimes in rapturous joy of union with Krishna, but often in excruciating pangs of separation from Him – always identifying himself with Sri Radha, the most beloved of Krishna. For Caytanya and his followers, Krishna has to be approached through a 'divine' love that starts with *rati* or *premankura* that ultimately ripens to *mahabhava* or supreme love through successive stages.[20]

But while maintaining their way of appropriating Jagannātha, the Panchasakhas positively influenced Caytanya in his worship of

[19] Mansinha 1962, 144.

[20] Nath 1993, 192-7.

Jagannātha who for him became Krishna in Puri. At the very sight of Jagannātha, he had the same feeling and emotion that he had for Krishna. It justifies what Boulton had observed, Caytanya came to Orissa not to teach, but to be taught.[21] In reality, Caytanya's Krishna cult was not new to Orissa. Jayadeva's *Gita Govinda*, Sarala Dasa's *Mahabharata* and Sanskrit dramas on the Radha-Krishna themes had already popularized the Krishna cult in Orissa. All this leads to the argument that Caytanya was co-opted by the Odissi Vaishnavite fraternity led by the Panchasakhas.

It is through the construction of a corpus of ideas and philosophies based on Jagannātha that the Panchasakhas could develop what I refer to as Jagannātha Dharma, the so-called Odissi Vaishnavism. Making Jagannātha the pivot in its theological understanding, it remained distinct and retained a separate identity from the Gaudiya/Bengali Vaishnavism or, for that matter, from any variant of Vaishnavite movement elsewhere in India. At the same time, Jagannātha Dharma could not separate itself from Buddhism because of the historical context, as mentioned earlier. Achyutananda Dasa in his *Sunya Samhita* explains his encounter with the Buddha in Dandaka on the bank of the river Prachi. The Buddha tells him, 'In the *Kaliyuga*, I have made myself manifest again as the Buddha. It is desirable, however for you in the *Kaliyuga* to hide your Buddhist frames of mind away from public view...know that the Buddha is none else but Brahma Himself.'[22] This explains, of course symbolically, the logic of the context and representation of the Panchasakha literature. The question of the Panchasakhas' relation with Caytanya on the one hand and Buddhism on the other could not be settled in textual debates unless addressed from the vantage point of their 'context' that we have just discussed. But undoubtedly, it is the 'hegemony' of Jagannātha that was the overarching factor in that context for any textual representation by the Panchasakhas.

The dividing line between the Jagannātha-centric medieval Vaishnavism and Bengali Vaishnavism in modern times,

---

[21] Boulton 1984, 4.

[22] Cf. Dasa n.d. b, 87.

particularly during the 1920s and 1930s, has been more of ethnic-linguistic construction than of any substantial consequence to the overall pan-Vaishnavism. The construction itself demonstrates how context gives meaning to contents. The Oriya literary-cultural organization, the Prachi Samiti's (established in the 1920s) advocacy for a distinct brand of Utkaliya Vaishnavism in opposition to Gaudiya Vaishnavism triggered a more parochial treatment of medieval Vaishnavism of Orissa, forgetting the ultimate identification of Krishna with Jagannātha on the one hand and exaggerating the difference between *Jnana-Misra Bhakti* and *Suddha Bhakti* on the other. In the Prachi Samiti-edited old Oriya texts like Dinakrushna Das' *Rasakallola* and Abhimanyu Samantasinhara's *Bidagdha Chintamani* the distinction in the realization of god in these two variants of Vaishnavism was exaggerated. They also tried to prove the intellectual-theological superiority of Oriya Vaishnavas' dual methodology of *Sakara/Nirakara*, *Saguna/Nirguna* and *Sabishesha/Nirbishesha* in god-realization over that of Bengalis' in which only *Sakara*, *Saguna* and *Sabishesha* are accepted without their respective opposites. Even such modern Oriya scholars like Binayak Mishra and Nilakantha Das tried to promote and circulate the idea of two totally different Vaishnavite variants and downgraded Gaudiya Vaishnavism.[23] All resulted in a growing consciousness of Oriya cultural identity. The Panchasakha literature was reinvented and the medieval past of Orissa came to be projected as having a unique cultural tradition, particularly vis-à-vis the more advanced Bengalis in colonial India.

Our text-context analysis of the Panchasakha literature demonstrates how in the textual construction and its representation of the Jagannātha cult, the meaning of textual contents can be located and specified. I want to demonstrate the same with the help of the development of the origin legend of Jagannātha, as constructed in some of the well-known Oriya texts. The Sanskrit versions of the legend as it appears in the *Skanda Purana, Brahma Purana, Narada Purana* and *Niladrimahodaya* have been left out.

---

[23] Cf. Mishra 1928, 30-40 and Das 1948, chapters 5 and 6.

Only Oriya texts have been studied because of the implication of the nature of the language in the identity-question and the contextual delimiting. I also refrain from discussing the version of Sarala Dasa's *Mahabharata* because it is not a self-contained text or theme, but it will be referred to when required.

Let us first take the *Deulatola* version of the origin legend which has been rendered textual form by different poets; the most important texts are those by Krishna Das and Bipra Nilambar. All these versions do not differ in content, but only in details and language. The main outline of the legend as one finds it in the Sanskrit Puranas is almost maintained in the seventeenth century poet Krishna Das' *Deulatola* which I have taken here for what Clifford Geertz would call 'thick' rather than 'thin' description.[24] *Deulatola* also owes to the *Sarala Mahabharata*, particularly in maintaining the ancestry of Jagannātha's original custodian Viswabasu and the building of the Jagannātha Triad and Sudarshan chakra.

Here is a brief account of Krishna Das' *Deulatola*.[25] The Vishnu devotee, King Indradyumna, had sent emissaries in four directions to search for Vishnu. One of his emissaries, the Brahmin Vidyapati in the east, came across a Savara village where he accepted the hospitality of a Savara called Viswabasu. Vidyapati was then *forced* to get married to Viswabasu's daughter Lalita or otherwise he would face death. After marrying Lalita, Vidyapati was able to go with his father-in-law to Nilgiri and have a glimpse of Nilamadhava/Vishnu. Upon his request, he was taken to Nilamadhava. He was blind-folded, but Lalita tied some mustard seeds to his cloth which were to be sown on the way. The purpose was that when it would rain, the seeds would grow into seedlings leading the path to Nilamadhava. After visiting the place, Vidyapati came back to the court of Indradyumna and narrated the whole story. On hearing it, Indradyumna immediately started for Nilgiri. But upon his arrival, he did not find the deity, as the latter had already disappeared. The King was thus punished for his pride that

[24] Geertz 1975, 7,14.

[25] Cf. for details Das n.d.

since he would get Nilamadhava, he would be the greatest in the universe. But without realizing his mistake, he thought that the Savara Viswabasu had stolen the god's idol, so he arrested Viswabasu. At this point, the King heard an oracle and was instructed to free Viswabasu. He was also asked to build a temple where the god would reappear. Accordingly, he constructed a temple and then went to the abode of Lord Brahma, *Brahmalok,* to invite Lord Brahma to consecrate the temple. During his absence, many ages had passed away on earth and, as a result, the temple got buried in the sand. Although it was discovered by another king, Galamadhava, he had to renounce his claim to the temple when Indradyumna came back and asked for its custody. But Indradyumna had no idols to install. So he was struck with grief and refused food and water. But ultimately, as revealed in a dream, Indradyumna found a log floating in a place called Banki Muhana in coastal Orissa. It was impressed with Vishnu's insignia. No carpenter, however, could carve out the images from the log. At last, the god appeared disguised as Ananta Maharana and carved out the image in the closed sanctum. But as he could make only the incomplete images, the King was full of remorse. The god consoled him again in a dream that He would reappear, reincarnated as Buddha in the *Kaliyuga*.

Before contextualizing the contents of *Deulatola*, let me make it clear that it became easily comprehensible and acceptable to the Oriya people across Orissa. It was, and still is, sung by the wandering Sannyasins and beggars of Orissa and enacted as *Suanga* in villages, bringing the lore and miracle of Jagannātha to the religious psyche of the Oriya mind. Apart from the language factor, the communicability of *Deulatola* was increased by its popular elements like the Vidyapati-Lalita episode, the dramatic appearance of the god himself as a carpenter, the strange way the Triad was carved, etc., which are couched in very plain and colloquial Oriya language. But more important than anything else, it was the context-sensitive nature of its contents which, as I believe, were added under the compulsion of the time. First, the *Deulatola* version of the origin legend is less biased than the *Sarala Mahabharata* towards the original, autochthonous Savara socio-cultural base on which the

Jagannātha cult originated. This is evidenced by maintaining the Puranic Sanskrit tradition of calling the first Savara worshipper of Nilamadhava 'Viswabasu' and the Brahmin discoverer of Nilamadhava/Jagannātha 'Vidyapati' as opposed to Jara and Basu respectively in the *Mahabharata*. Again, *Deulatola* is not prejudicial in terms of lifting capacity, either to Viswabasu or Vidyapati while they were lifting *Darubrahma*, the divine log, but in the *Musali Parva* of the *Sarala Mahabharata*, it was easier for Jara Savara to lift his portion. Then comes the inclusion of a category of *sevakas* or servitors, called *Suddha Suaras* in *Deulatola* in addition to Brahmin or *Prakruta* and *Daita sevakas* who are mentioned in the *Mahabharata* and Puranic versions. To me, this sort of textual marginalization of Savaras in *Deulatola* directly relates to the seventeenth century socio-religious context of the Orissa region. By the seventeenth century, the unique *Jagannatha Dharma* was a reality within the broad framework of Vaishnavism. So it was more appropriate to follow the Sanskrit, Puranic line and to gradually reduce Savara dominance in the origin legend. Regarding the inclusion of the *Suddha Sauras* as a new category of *sevakas*, though I broadly agree with G.N. Dash's contention that the Vidyapati-Lalita episode had the important function of recognizing the Brahmin identity of the *Suddha Suaras* by way of biologically linking Brahmins and Suaras, I have reservations on some assumptive conclusions of Dash.[26] To me, the inclusion of *Suddha Suaras* in *Deulatola* reflects the social context of the time, as far as *Deulatola* is an undeclared document of triumphant Hinduization of Orissa, in the form of hegemony of the *Jagannatha Dharma*.

During this period, Hinduization or any upward social mobility within the Hindu social framework was not without accompanying tensions. In *Deulatola*, the matrimony between Brahmin Vidyapati and the Savara girl Lalita did *not* spring from any romantic love, but was a forced union imposed on Vidyapati by pain of death. But after their marriage, Lalita was identified with Vidyapati, which means that, in a sense, she was Hinduized, as per

---

[26] For Dash's views cf. Dash 1982, 337-46.

Hindu social norm. So the question is: if, in a hypergamous marriage (*anuloma*) like this, the husband's status was higher than that of the wife, how and why did the descendants of such a marriage claim a separate identity for themselves? In the Hindu system, the *anuloma* marriage is allowed and by no means disapproved of because it is 'in accordance with the direction of the hair', smooth and natural.[27] So it is natural that after her marriage, Lalita would be absorbed into her husband's caste, clan and lineage, and logically so too would be the descendants of such a wedlock. Then, where was the necessity for *Deulatola* to make a plea for the Brahmin identity of these descendants, the *Suddha Suaras,* when it was already socially and customarily approved? In this sense, describing the *Suddha Suaras* as the descendants of Vidyapati and Lalita is again to marginalize the Savara dominance in the origin legend.

At the same time, *Deulatola* constructs the Vidyapati-Lalita episode more to appropriate one more category of *sevakas* of Jagannātha to the Savara ancestry, thereby pushing their position low in the Hinduized Oriya society. If carefully observed, one could find how the duties of the *Suddha Suara* are more those of an assistant or facilitator for the main *puja* and rituals in the Jagannātha temple.[28] So they needed to be assigned a lowly position and at the same time be distinguished from *Daitas*. This could be achieved by a forced *anuloma* marriage between Vidyapati and Lalita, which is again symbolic of tensions of the Hinduization/Aryanization of the society. The Vidyapati-Lalita episode might recognize the *Suddha Suaras*' Brahmin identity, which is its secondary function, but its primary function is to give an identity to this class appropriate to its functions and to resolve the tension caused by the Hinduization of the society.

A pertinent point is that the *Suddha Suaras* as a category of temple *sevakas* was a comparatively new addition to the temple *sevaka* community as this found its mention only from the

---

[27] Basham 1988, 146-7.

[28] No. 37. Record-of-Rights prepared under the Puri Shri Jagannātha Temple (Administration) Act (Orissa Act XIV of 1952), part II.

Deulatola versions. Most probably, a particular section of non-Brahmin *sevakas* was traditionally doing this job of assistants, but gradually they must have felt the need for a separate identity vis-à-vis *Daitas* and Brahmin *sevakas*. They may be descendants of the tribe called *Suddha Sauras* or Savaras, as Dash has shown. They could claim a separate identity by creating a new origin myth of the Vidyapati-Lalita episode. But to me, this origin myth is again a design of the triumphant Hinduization in the Orissa region as it succumbs to the influence of the hegemony of Jagannātha/Hinduism. We have evidence of social tensions and conflicts between Brahmins or so-called high-castes and non-Brahmins or tribals. Sarala Dasa in the fifteenth century mentions in the *Adi Parva* of the *Mahabharata* a fight between the Brahmin-Kshatriya combine and *Chandalas* who were savage and barbaric. The latter were ultimately defeated and subjugated. We have anthropological evidence of how Savaras have been co-opted into the high Hindu fold. The famous Tena Sauri Khandayats or Kshatriyas are supposed to be the descendants of the wedlock between a king and a Savara lady of the Padmini class.[29] Moreover we have seen social tension in the Panchasakha period. The *Deulatola* origin legend, as found in the versions of Krishna Das, Nilambara Das and Maguni Jyotisha and hopefully in other versions too, categorically designates Brahmins as the *Prakruta* or real *sevakas* whereas it assigns *Daitas* and *Suddha Suaras* to the status of peripheral *sevakas*. This real or central/peripheral dichotomy itself symbolizes the triumph and dominance of Hinduism in the particular context and the co-option of other low castes and tribes as junior partners in the Jagannātha cult. But logically this also suited the *Suddha Suaras* who clamoured for a separate identity.

Thus, *Deulatola* relates to a context in which subalterns were demographically predominant. Perhaps that is why this region was once known as Bratyabhumi, the land of the fallen. If Jagannātha had to be the presiding deity of the land, the subalterns – tribals, autochthons and lower classes had to be ritually associated with the

---

[29] Panda 1991, 88.

Jagannātha cult. But for pride's sake, as the *Daitas* have done, the *Suddha Suaras* had to reinvent an exotic ancestry of their own in *Deulatola*.

Now the development of this origin legend in twentieth century Orissa can be shown from the play *Sri Mandir* written by the great Oriya playwright Aswini Kumar Ghosh. Written in 1934, *Sri Mandir's* immediate context was provided by the rising tide of the Oriya consciousness which was already being articulated in the form of Oriya identity. At the same time, the anti-colonial nationalism and struggle against the British rule had stirred Oriyas. Thus, there were two parallel strands, articulated and practised in Orissa during the time but without any mutual opposition. Here, an attempt would be made to decipher and locate the meaningful content of *Sri Mandir* in early twentieth-century Orissa. Before this, its story may be briefly recapitulated in order to show how the origin legend has been recreated and recast in a different mood.[30] Vidyapati, the commander and minister of King Indradyumna of Avanti, came to Utkal in search of Nilamadhav, the sapphire form of Vishnu. During his search, he came to a Savara village where by accident he touched the village Chief Viswabasu's daughter Lalita. According to the Savara tradition, he had to marry Lalita as he had touched her. In due course, Lalita came to know about her husband's real intention, but as a devoted wife, she helped him to visit Nilamadhav who was being secretly worshipped by her father. Lalita also stole her father's ring that gives strength and gave it to her husband. She herself guided Vidyapati to Nilamadhav. Then, one day, Vidyapati stole the idol of Nilamadhav and sent it to Avanti.[31] After the disappearance of the idol, Viswabasu broke down and finally died. Vidyapati and Lalita also separated over this issue. Lalita asked Vidyapati to return the idol, but the latter refused to do so. Meanwhile, Nilamadhav was installed in Avanti. King Galamadhav of Utkal also cleared the forest where the Savara village was originally situated and established a city there. He also unearthed a temple from the sand, restored it and named it Sri

[30] Ghosh 1963, 333-67.

[31] Ibid., 352-3.

Mandir. But the right of Galamadhav over the temple was contested by Indradyuman and a battle was fought. Lalita was entrusted the task of protecting the temple by Galamadhav. Vidyapati was the commander of Indradyumna's army. In the battle, Vidyapati was killed and this changed the whole course of events. Lalita broke down because of the death of her husband and committed suicide. Everybody was shocked. The battle came to an end and King Indradyumna returned the idol of Nilamadhav, which was thereafter installed in the temple restored by Galamadhav.

Sri Mandir is more of a discourse on power and recognition of the Oriya *jati*[32] than a narrative on how Jagannātha was established. The religious or Bhakti element is not a predominant force in the text as it highlights power and military might. In this sense, Jagannātha has been relocated in a secular matrix. Unlike the Sanskrit Puranic and even *Deulatola* versions, *Sri Mandir* does not have such teleological elements like Vishnu's desire to manifest Himself as Jagannātha, His disappearance from the Nilgiri hill, reappearance in the form of a wooden log and carving of the Jagannātha Triad. Instead, the emergence and installation of Jagannātha was the result of a power play, the struggle between Utkal and Avanti. Another important dimension of the text is the playing down of the ethnic tone so far as there was no animosity or tension between the Hindu/Aryan royalty and Savaras. All these have meaningful bearing on contemporary Orissa.

By the twentieth century, Jagannātha had started to be constructed in a secular mould as He came to be seen as a metaphor for the Oriya unity and past glory. Reification of the Oriya identity in terms of demand for politico-cultural recognition and unity came to borrow heavily from Jagannātha. In *Sri Mandir*, Ghosh has precisely done this by positing Jagannātha in a dialogue between the 'Oriya' and the 'Other'. Jagannātha has been established in the

---

[32] *Jati* in Oriya connotes race, clan, nationality, community, caste and a host of other meanings. Hence, in Oriya, *jati* has context-specific usages. The Oriya translation of 'national' is *jatiya* which implies Oriya consciousness. But Oriya *jatiyata* should not be used in the same sense as Indian nationalism is used. So it is safe to translate Oriya *jatiyata* as Oriya consciousness or identity rather than Oriya nationalism.

Orissa region not by any mystic divine intervention, but by the prowess and sacrifice of the Oriya *jati*, which is again composed of both Aryans and non-Aryans. The association of Jagannātha with Utkal is so sacred and sacrosanct that Lalita, the Savara wife of Vidyapati, had to fight against her husband, a battle in which Vidyapati was ultimately killed. But the traditional wife in Lalita had not died out; she committed suicide after Vidyapati's death. This changed the course of events and Indradyumna returned the idol of Nilamadhav to the Orissan King Galamadhav. So from the vantage point of recognition, the Oriya prowess and sacrifice was recognized and the idol of Nilamadhav was returned. I would like to argue here that it is a symbolic recognition of and inspiration to the Oriya movement in its efforts for a separate, united Orissa in the face of British colonialism and Bengali-Telugu dominance. Jagannātha was the metaphor for Oriya unity and exclusiveness, which must be won at any cost, maybe by power or sacrifice. This symbolism of Jagannātha in the 1930s was further heightened because of the decline of the Utkal Union Conference-led Oriya movement and the adoption of the Oriya cause by the Congress leaders of Orissa. Invoking Jagannātha in *Sri Mandir*, particularly the decision of the two kings, Indradyumna and Galamadhav to maintain equality in the Jagannātha temple by allowing everybody to partake in the *Mahaprasad* (the offering to the Jagannātha Triad), was symbolic of presenting a united front of Oriyas even if the Congress appropriated the Oriya cause.

My discussion of Ghosh's *Sri Mandir* may be concluded with some observations on the character of Lalita. If in *Deulatola*, she was a tradition-bound, devoted wife, in *Sri Mandir* she is a great balancer, in the sense that she is equally committed to her duty and obligation and devoted to her husband/family. By implication, Lalita ideally combines the concern and devotion for her ancestral faith with the truthfulness of a wife. This role model was not hard to find in contemporary Orissa. Mention may be made of Ramadevi, Kuntala Kumari Sabat, Sarala Devi, Malati Chaudhury and a host of others who were prominent Oriya woman leaders and social activists in the twentieth century. Ramadevi's (1899-1985) success as a great nationalist woman leader and reformer, coupled with her exemplary role as a wife, might have unconsciously inspired Ghosh to reinvent the Lalita character. Seen from this perspective, could the representation of the Lalita character be removed from the context or be proved wrong?

What we have seen in this study of some select Oriya texts on Jagannātha is that a network of meanings implicated in the textual contents can be located in their context only. Similarly, a particular context can also determine the interpretation of a text. One may say that the relation between text and context, between representation and reality, is a symbiotic one so far as text and context lend meaning to each other.

References

Basham, A.L. 1988. *The Wonder that was India* (3rd rev. edn), London.

Behera, P.K. 1983. 'The Influence of Buddhism on the Cult of Jagannatha' in *Journal of Indian History*, vol. 61.

Behera, Subhakanta. 2002. *Construction of an Identity Discourse: Oriya Literature and the Jagannatha Cult (1866-1936)*, New Delhi: Munshiram Manoharlal Publishers Pvt. Ltd.

Boulton, J.V. 1984, 'Phakirmohun Senapati and his Times', in B.K. Satpathy and B. Rath (eds.), *Phakirmohun: His Life and Literature*, Balasore.

Das, Chittaranjan. 1982. *A Glimpse into Oriya Literature*, Bhubaneswar.

Das, Krishna. n.d. *Deulatola*, new edn., Cuttack.

Das, Nilakantha. 1948. *Odia Sahityara Krama Parinama*, part I, Cuttack.

Das, Paritosh. 1988. *Sahajiya Cult of Bengal and Panchasakha Cult of Orissa*, Calcutta.

Dasa, Achyutananda 1966. *Chhayalisa Patala*, Cuttack.

Dasa, Achyutananda. 1970. *Gurubhakti Gita*, Cuttack: Prachi Publishers.

Dasa, Achyutananda. n.d. *Shunya Samhita* (new edn.), Cuttack.

Dasa, Balarama. 1959, *Birata Gita* (3rd edn), Cuttack.

Dasa, Sisu Ananta. n.d. *Hetu Udaya Bhagavata*, Jagatsinghpur.

Dash, G.N. 1982. 'Janasruti o' Samajika Itihasa', in *Jhankara,* July 1982, 34 (4).

Dei, Shantilata. 1988. *Vaisnavism in Orissa,* Calcutta.

Geertz, C. 1975. *The Interpretation of Cultures,* London.

Ghosh, Aswini Kumar. 1963. *Aswini Kumar Granthavali*, Cuttack.

Kaviraj, Sudipta. 1997. 'On the Construction of the Colonial: Structure, Discourse and Hegemony', in S. Kaviraj (ed.), *Politics in India,* Delhi.

Mansinha, Mayadhar. 1962. *Odiya Sahityar Itihasa,* Cuttack.

Mishra, Binayak. 1928. *Odia Sahityara Itihasa,* Cuttack.

Mishra, K.C. 1961. *Odissi Vaishnava Dhara,* Bhubaneswar.

Mohanty, B. (ed.) 1995. *Bhaktakavi Achyutananda,* Cuttack.

Mohanty, Surendra. 1982. *Lord Jagannatha,* Bhubaneswar.

Mukherjee, Prabhat. 1976. *'Buddha and Jagannatha', Souvenir of International Seminar on Buddhism and Jainism,* Cuttack.

Nath, R.G. 1993. 'A Survey of Caitanya Movement', in H. Bhattacharya (ed.), *The Cultural Heritage of India*, vol. IV (2nd edn), Calcutta.

No. 37. Record-of-Rights prepared under the Puri Shri Jagannatha Temple (Administration) Act (Orissa Act XIV of 1952), part II.

Panda, S.K. 1991. *Medieval Orissa. A Socio-Economic Study,* New Delhi.

Sahu, K.C. (ed.). 1985. *Balarama Dasa's Brahmanda Bhugola*, Cuttack.

Sarala Dasa's Mahabharata (*Musali Parva*), ed. A. Mohanty, Bhubaneswar, 1970.

14

Autobiographies of Oriya Leaders: Contributions to a Cause

Barbara Lotz

Autobiographies of influential time witnesses certainly invite special consideration when studying consolidative processes of a regional collective. Their role as documents of crucial periods of change makes them an important communicator of a commonly experienced past, and the complex modes of remembering to be found in and activated by autobiographies work in different ways than a supposedly linear, factual and objective historical account[1]. They appeal to an internal memory that is not necessarily related to events. Perspectives are biased, unbalanced and selective. Statements are full of contradictions, omissions or even lies, and by their very nature they are bound to be subjective. By preserving a cultural knowledge that history books fail to grasp and convey, they are contributing to the 'timeless' fabric of public memory.

The frequent use of autobiographies as sources of historical information reveals the somewhat fuzzy relation between autobiographical and historical writing, which is also evident in the presently selected autobiographical texts of Fakirmohan Senapati: *Ātmajīvancarita* ('Autobiography'), Godavarish Misra: *Arddha Śatābdīrā Oṛiśā o tahire mo sthān* ('Half a Century of Orissa and my · Place in it') and Gopabandhu Das: *Bandira Ātmakathā* ('Autobiography of a Prisoner').[2] The history of the language movement, the history of the Satyavadi School, the history of the beginning non-cooperation movement in Orissa – all these are opics

---

[1] Assmann 1999, 42. It seems however problematic to juxtapose cultural memory and history as completely separate entities of remembrance. Cultural memory can not remain an autonomous, monolithic stock unaffected by change, nor should history be considered a realm of 'truths' and facts.

[2] Henceforth referred to as Fakirmohan, Godavarish, Gopabandhu.

of national interest, which we find presented closely linked to individual life-stories providing the narrative frame. In fact, at least in the first two texts, the historical content seems to serve as a major legitimization for the narration of one's life-events, as the authors express their responsibility to document a historic process they themselves initiated and pursued. They receive further authorization by their status of a historic personality at the end of their lives, and a high degree of authenticity is ascribed to their statements due to their participation in certain processes.

Thus, the reception of these texts as historical writing seems to a certain extent justified by the often explicitly expressed desire of the authors themselves to create historicity, formally demonstrated by a profusion of dates, facts, events, prominent titles, institutions and locations, that serve as a framework wherein family details, personal thoughts, essayistic reflections or explanatory technical paragraphs are inserted. The gap in time between the writing of the text and the actual events described allows the author to convey a cohesion to otherwise incoherent and isolated elements. By assigning a 'meaning' to historical events, he also achieves a meaning for his own life. In this comprehensive way of remembrance, history functions as a context for the individual memory, reciprocally rendering the autobiography a text in the service of history. A chronological narration, as well as the often thematized concern for 'truth' and 'relevance' of the narrated matter, further point to a consciousness of the authors as contributors to and preservers of a stock of historical writings according to Western standards and expectations. When Kaviraj observes: 'In the Bengali discourse of the nineteenth century, 'history' breaks out everywhere',[3] we can assume the validity of that statement for the then culturally and administratively closely connected province of Orissa, too.

Well in the hagiographic tradition of the biographies of Vaishnava saints, the promotion of model-characters and model-lives can be traced as a prominent motive in the beginning of biographical and autobiographical writings in Bengal. A modern

[3] Kaviraj 1995, 107.

orientation was however emerging in the circles of the Brahmo-Samaj with its propagation of individualism and its concentration on the mundane. Paired with a contempt for corrupt and decadent religious structures, it popularized a trend in biographies and autobiographies to enlighten the readership concerning social reforms and spiritual reorientation. One step further, the patriotic and national fervour at the beginning of the twentieth century led to a host of political biographies and autobiographies such as reminiscences of freedom fighters.[4] The pronounced goal of instructing the readership appears thus to be an important aspect of self-legitimization in a writing tradition, where the authorship was of less importance than the text, and individual authority preferably submitted itself to a greater poetic or religious context. The author's commitment to share his experiences in a spiritual or historic process with his fellow-countrymen relieves him from the suspicion of attempted self-projection. By subordinating his life and work to a common cause, the author's autobiographical account, however self-centred, could no longer be accused of being selfish.[5] Consequently, the unifying concept of these autobiographical texts

---

[4] The first autobiography in Bengali *Āmār jīban* was written by a Vaishnava housewife, Rashasundari Dasi in 1876. She secretly learned to read in the desire to read the *Chaitanya Bhāgabat*, the first Bengali biography of the saint Caitanya which was completed around 1548 (Sarkar 1999, 3). Debendranath Tagore, one of the leading figures of the Brahmo Samaj, wrote an autobiographical account of his religious development in his *Ātmajīvanī* published in 1898. A grand precursor of revolutionary autobiographies was Upendranath Bandyopadhyay's *Nirbāsiter Ātmakathā* ('Autobiography of a Transportee') of 1908, which seems to have inspired Gopabandhu's title 'Autobiography of a Prisoner' (Bhattacharya and Chakravorty 1976, 28).

[5] Fakirmohan and Godavarish both mention in the preface or introduction that it was only on the request of colleagues and friends that they decided to write down their life stories. These opening remarks are to be found in Gandhi's autobiography, too: 'Four or five years ago, on the insistence of my co-workers, I decided to write down my autobiography.' For further legitimization, Godavarish wishes to leave a 'useful contribution to the storehouse of literature', Fakirmohan wants 'to inaugurate the tradition of autobiographical writing in Oriya literature to inspire many followers'. Gopabandhu's whole text is presented as result of deep concern and a feeling of duty towards his countrymen in order to console and reassure them.

can be visualized to a large extent beyond the 'story of the self' in pursuit of a larger and more complex goal.

Almost eighty years of Oriya history are reflected in the writings of the three authors that will be dealt with here, covering a period from the beginnings of an independent Oriya consciousness in the 1860s up to the formation of a separate state in 1936. Written between 1917 and the 1950s, these autobiographies had not only become extremely popular during their own times, but have exerted a lasting influence. Certainly their literary qualities play an important role in the fact that they are still read and remembered, as all three authors were renowned prose and poetry writers. Another important factor is the role in public life which the authors occupied as administrators, teachers, educationists, politicians, journalists, publicists – and significantly in a personal union of all these activities. To a certain extent their biographies resemble each other: a lower middle class background with little economic resources, the struggle for education and financial improvement, the early break with traditional religious upbringing,[6] the exposure to Western ideals and philosophies and lastly the close contact with the British. All of them earned a certain fame, and their lives remained intimately intermeshed with the political and social life of their times, making their texts sources of extremely valuable first hand information, perhaps not so much at the level of historical facts and figures, but certainly by their world views, attitudes and concerns.

The features of Oriya identity are seldom clearly outlined by the authors in concrete political, religious, ethnic or geographical terms. The Oriya Self, though recreated in myriad details of a culturally and historically shared past, gears up as a distinct force mainly in opposition to the dominating 'Other', be it the Bengalis in

[6] Fakirmohan describes the advent of the first Brahmo-teachers in Orissa, and the foundation of a Brahmo-society at Balasore around 1867. He recalls in this chapter the various disappointments he had with saints, miracles and rituals, and that he was on the verge of embracing Christianity before he joined the Brahmo-movement (Fakirmohan, 65-8). Already in the 1850's, Maharishi Debendranath Tagore came to Orissa and soon after efforts were made to establish a Brahmo Samaj after the Adi Brahma Samaj model, which was called Cuttack Samaj (Patra and Devi 1983, 179).

Fakirmohan's case or the British in Gopabandhu's. The salient features of identity remain almost exclusively related to the linguistic factor, the realm of 'Oriyaness' being largely visualized as within the predominantly Oriya-speaking areas. The specific lingual situation in border areas or of the tribal population in Oriya speaking areas is rarely a matter of concern, and these parts of the population find themselves as tacitly included into the conglomerate image of the Oriya Self,[7] as are other members of different beliefs or origin. Apart from the spoken language, it is the literary heritage of traditional religious texts, mythological or historical legends that provide a common cultural stronghold for these authors, who otherwise had developed a critical distance to matters of religion and belief, as all three were strongly influenced by the reformist teachings of the Brahmo-faith.[8] Being middle class intellectuals of the coastal belt, belonging to a rather limited section of society, they feel amazingly confident to speak for the whole population of Utkal,[9] the peasants, the feudals, the illiterate and the educated, and

---

[7] Godavarish Mishra, while on his Oriya-campaign in Podahat/Singhbhum, refers mainly to the 'Aryan' population. The 'non-Aryan' population is, however, credited with a rebellious past against the British rule, who subdued Podahat as the last tract of Singhbhum in 1858 (Godavarish, 145). In the disputed border areas, the tribal population sometimes played a significant role in regard to which 'regional' language they would call their own when asked by border or census commissions. In 1916, Gopabandhu toured various interior places to convince the tribal population, amongst them the Ho leader Dolmanki, to study in Oriya, in view of an eventual amalgamation of Singhbhum with Orissa. Yet, under the influence of powerful counter movements, an anti-Oriya feeling began to spread among the Hos and other parts of the population, but still the Oriyas took the support of the tribals, who constituted a major force for their cause, for granted. In 1936, Singhbhum was not included by the Boundary Commission in the proposed province of Orissa and was finally lost to Bihar (Mohanty 1982, 163-71).

[8] Cf., for example, the long list of religious texts such as parts of the *Rāmāyaṇa* or the *Mahābhārata* translated into Oriya by Fakirmohan, the historical dramas and poems written by Godavarish or the references to the *Bhāgabata-Purāṇa* and the *Bhagavadgītā* by Gopabandhu.

[9] The frequent use of 'Utkal' by Fakirmohan or Gopabandhu instead of 'Orissa' (which is preferred by Godavarish) represents a more ancient, geographically rather vague and somewhat 'internal' concept as opposed to the more

the high degree of popularity seems to prove them right. As their own identities are already multi-layered and problematic, and they can be observed struggling with both tradition and progress, these authors offer a wide and convincing basis for identification, enabling the readership to appropriate history as a very 'own' experience. In their individual remembrance, both the outer context of history and the internal cultural memory is transformed into a public memory; the text mirrors public memory and constructs it at the same time in the reception of the readership.

More than formal qualities or historical information, the immense appeal and lasting impact on their target group decided over my selection of the texts, which are quite heterogeneous in style, format and structure. Whereas the books of Fakirmohan and Godavarish comply with the prescriptions for 'real' autobiographies regarding a chronological narration pattern in prose that covers the span of a lifetime or at least a substantial portion of it, the text by Gopabandhu is a lyrical and comparatively short piece, presenting and connecting memories that surface during a train journey through Orissa. True, there is a first person narrator who is undoubtedly the voice of the author, and the events described are experienced by him; but apart from the title proclaiming this text as an autobiography, there is little in it to be compared with the host of insider information and entertaining anecdotes the other two texts have to offer. If we, however, consider the effect of evoking a collective consciousness within the readership, Gopabandhu's text certainly surpasses the other two in its capacity to communicate an immediate concern and to mobilize the residents of Utkal in their fight for one common goal. We find an imminent and yet unfulfilled cause to be the reason for actually composing the piece, whereas Fakirmohan and Godavarish write in retrospective about causes that had been achieved to a large extent. The latter two (re-)create a common past by selecting important events and sharing the historic steps on the way to an independent Oriya identity that is presented

---

bureaucratic and political dimensions of 'Orissa' within the colonial nomenclature from 'outside'. Fakirmohan and his contemporaries are said to have reintroduced the use of Utkal as a symbol of unity against the neighbouring influences.

as an outcome of their and their contemporaries' endeavours. In the analysis of the first two texts I will therefore rather concentrate on the way the historic context is recalled and how the authors position themselves in it; the third text then shall be analysed more in view of its literary aspects and its capacity of bonding with the reader.

While all authors contribute to the common cause of promoting an image of Oriya identity, and their concerns are overlapping to a large extent, for the present paper one particularly significant cause was singled out of each author's text, on the basis of a central concern or activity the authors are remembered for until the present day. Generationwise, Fakirmohan could figure as the 'father' of Godavarish and Gopabandhu, who were only ten years apart. Thus their autobiographies could be viewed in the context of different historical phases within the struggle for Orissa's independence. The first phase entails the initial attempts to counter the dominance of Bengali by creating a stock of Oriya textbooks, literature and journals, in order to lay the foundations for a proud awareness for one's language, literature and history. The second phase can be seen as a period of consolidation and expansion, where a major stress was put on the spread of education and educational reforms, combined with Oriya campaigns in the outlying tracts aiming at their eventual amalgamation to an independent province. The third phase includes the gradual absorption of the regional movement into nation-wide political activities within the Congress network, the concentration on basic relief work and the struggle against colonial domination. In Fakirmohan's autobiographical account therefore, I will concentrate on his involvement in the Oriya language agitation; the concern for (higher) education will be discussed in the context of Godavarish's writing, and the excitement of the non-cooperation movement figures as a background of Gopabandhu's text. Finally, if viewed in succession, these different causes may represent a distinct change of concerns that becomes visible between the 1860s and the 1920s, as will be pointed out in the conclusion.

1. The Emancipation of Language and Literature: Fakirmohan Senapati

The first autobiography in Oriya was written by Fakirmohan Senapati (1843-1918).[10] The text starts with a short genealogy reaching back several generations and moves chronologically from childhood memories and the start of his education to early jobs as labourer, followed by first teaching assignments. The midsection deals with his first contacts with the British, a certain consolidation of his official and financial position and the initial steps of the Oriya language movement. More than the remaining half of the book is dedicated to his experiences posted as a Manager in several kingdoms under British sovereignty. The book ends in the last year before the author's death in 1918. An early orphaned, largely self-educated man with little family support, Fakirmohan's position as one of the major spirits behind the emergence of a public sphere in Orissa was based on the promotion of his mother tongue Oriya in all fields of education, press, translation and, comparatively late in life, his own creative writing.[11] His 'career', as described in his autobiography, can be viewed in many respects as typical of a self-made man of modern times, who makes it big in spite of all odds, and it is obvious that he was not in the least objecting to that image he had earned already during his life-time. It is a matter of pride for him to narrate that, although his own education started late and remained fragmentary, he was very early entrusted with teaching assignments. His perspective on the British administrators gives

[10] The text was commenced in 1916 under severe physical pain, and was serially published in *Utkal Sāhitya* from July 1918. In the late 1960s, the full length version appeared in book form. Apart from Biswanath Kar who edited the text for *Utkal Sāhitya*, Fakirmohan's son, Mohini Mohan Senapati, later on edited his autobiography and, as he was on adverse terms with his father, is supposed to have added or deleted events quite deliberately.

[11] He was nearly fifty when he produced his first work *Utkaḷ Brahmanam* ('Orissa Tour') in 1892, a satirical treatment of the contemporary literary scene. His first novel *Cha māṇa āṭha gunṭha*, which gradually grew from a story to a novel, was a huge success with the readership when it first appeared in 1897. From 1897 till 1918 followed a continuous output of novels and short stories.

evidence how large their support and appraisal figured in the emerging Oriya 'society' especially as regards education and publication.[12] His contact with the British started when he was offered the post of headmaster by the Secretary of the Christian Mission School at Balasore, Rev. E. C. B. Hallam,[13] who also later introduced him to his friend, Collector John Beames. Beames, while at Balasore, was completing his *Comparative Grammar of the Indian Languages*[14] and asked Fakirmohan from then on for weekly meetings to discuss linguistic problems with him. Fakirmohan at this point narrates how the respect he enjoyed from the British gave him enormous official advantage, as the Bengali officers, high and low, were now addressing him with deference and distance. In all his efforts so far to spread education, also among girls, and to improve the status of his own language, he could suddenly count on the support of government representatives from the highest reaches. In retrospect, he adds gratefully, how important the support of Beames had been for his career, and had helped him out of serious difficulties many times.

In the context of enhancing the status of Oriya among the Oriya population, the writing of textbooks which Fakirmohan had started earlier gained an increasing importance, as we can see from

---

[12] The perception of 'society' as documented by the British, however, remained largely eurocentric. Beames does not mention Fakirmohan even once in his autobiography (written in 1896), let alone other 'natives' of Balasore, its press, literary circles or schools. Even Beames' own substantial involvement in the Oriya language agitation (with his linguistic statement on the independent status of Oriya of 1870, cf. fn 29) is not mentioned. He just remarks: 'I quickly learnt Oriya, the language of Orissa, and assisted E.B. Hallam, one of the American Baptist Missionaries, in writing an Oriya grammar.... Our small society consisted of a Joint Magistrate, a doctor, a Superintendent, an Engineer, a Harbour-master, and an Inspector of Telegraphs' (Beames 1984, 193). Ravenshaw at least mentions Fakirmohan in his annual report of 1873: 'The mission school (at Balasore) was conducted by one of the finest specimens of an Ooriah, I have ever seen, Baboo Fakeer Mohun Senapaty' (Mansinha 1976, 25).

[13] Hallam published his *Oriya Grammar* in 1874 in Calcutta.

[14] Beames wrote this three volume book, which won him considerable fame, during his collectorship from 1872-9, the first volume appeared in 1873 when he was at Balasore (1869-73).

his description of the desolate situation concerning not only the teaching material, but also printed matter in Oriya in general in the middle of the nineteenth century.[15] A profusion of qualified textbooks, translations of English literature, modern journals and by-weeklies came in from Bengal after 1857, whereas practically nothing new was produced in Oriya. Fakirmohan used to read whatever Bengali texts were available through friends or other people who held subscriptions, and gradually the wish grew to produce similar material in his own language. Although in 1836 the use of Persian in administration had been discontinued, files and records and even household accounts were still kept in Persian, and upper class people conversed in a mixture of Persian, English and Bengali. The Zilla School at Balasore of course had Oriya as a subject, but it was taught with contempt by a Sanskrit teacher, who was a Bengali, like all the rest of the staff. Parents too were not interested in improving the Oriya studies of their sons 'in English schools'. Due to continuous neglect, even the stock of old books or manuscripts of traditional Oriya literature was lost or damaged. Because of a complete lack of teaching material in Oriya, demands to replace this language in schools by the far better equipped Bengali seemed justified. To counter these claims, the creation of a stock of textbooks thus emerged as an immediate need. The great educationist-reformer Ishvarchandra Vidyasagar suggested that Fakirmohan should translate his *Jībana carita* into Oriya, which then came to replace the *Hitopadeśa* as a textbook.[16] The British honoured his attempts by awarding him prizes for his two-volume

---

[15] During his schooldays, the only printed Oriya book available was the Bible, printed by the Cuttack Mission Press (Fakirmohan, 8). The first block of Oriya letters was engraved on wood in 1804 thanks to the efforts of Christian missionaries. The first Oriya printed book *New Oriya Rules* came out in 1809. The Bible in Oriya was published in 1814. The first *Oriya-English Vocabulary* was printed in 1811 (Swain 1999, 300).

[16] *Jībana carita* is a compendium of biographies of leading men from the East and West. The Oriya version by Fakirmohan was published in 1866 by the Baptist Mission Press at Calcutta. A translation of Vidyasagar's *History of India* followed, as well as Fakirmohan's own textbooks on grammar and arithmetic, all of them to be used as prescribed textbooks for many years.

history book[17] in Oriya and he received Rs 300 from Ravenshaw and Rs 700 from the School Inspector, as he proudly mentions. Fakirmohan cannot help to remark gleefully how unhappy the Bengali Babus were about this incident, especially as it occurred during an ongoing Bengali-Oriya rivalry in the Barabati school committee of which he was the only Oriya member.[18] The frequent narration of episodes like these, where the Bengalis are projected as larger-than-life images of malicious intrigants, manages to create a strong divide between 'us' and 'them' in front of the readership, the author connecting with his countrymen by recalling his heroic efforts to save his country's identity from sure extinction.

The production of textbooks alone, however, could not do much to enhance the prestige of the language in the literary field, as there were hardly any aspiring writers.[19] The public taste was still very much oriented towards traditional forms of poetry, and prose writing was virtually non existent.[20] Initiated by Fakirmohan and a few other concerned and educated people, a literary circle emerged in which also the famous poet Radhanath Ray, then a student, participated.[21] In view of the prevailing preference for poetry it was decided to start with reprints or new editions of popular texts[22], and use the profit from their sale for the production of more modern literature. Finally, a Press Company was founded at Balasore along

---

[17] *Bhāratbarṣara Ithihāsa*, published in 1869/70. In 1873, Madhusudan Rao was posted by Beames to Balasore Zilla School. M. Rao and Radananath Ray (Rao of Maratha and Ray of Bengali origin) were also substantially involved in producing poetry and prose collections. They also published a literary magazine, *Utkala Darpaṇa* (Mohanty 1996, 15).

[18] Fakirmohan, 61.

[19] Fakirmohan writes that his first prose piece could not appear due to horrendous printing costs demanded by the Cuttack Mission Press (ibid., 46).

[20] Fakirmohan remembers amusedly how even dry instructional texts used to be intoned as '*Raga-raginis*' (ibid., 47).

[21] Radhanath, who was of Bengali origin and also wrote Bengali poems then, was not allowed by his father to participate in this Oriya circle and had to join secretly.

[22] The first text chosen was *Rasakallola*, which was to be presented in a new edition with an elaborate commentary. Fakirmohan describes how they discussed it word by word with the help of dictionaries in endless sessions.

the lines of the Cuttack Printing Company established some years before, but, as Fakirmohan remembers, all of its members were fairly ignorant about what such a machine actually looked like, 'whether it was of wood or mud', and therefore it took quite some time until the press actually started working.[23] Funds were collected from landlords, officers and rich people, who had to be convinced in the manner of door-to-door salesmen of the good that such a machine would eventually bring to them. After the first discouraging attempts with a discarded, faulty machine sent to them by the Medinipur missionaries, a loan had to be obtained by Fakirmohan in order to obtain a proper machine from Calcutta, which arrived finally at Balasore by bullock cart. The long awaited printing miracle could start in 1866. In this endeavour, too, they were supported by the British, who gave orders to have all government forms printed there which proved to be quite profitable; they participated in shares and later personally came to see the functioning of the second indigenous press, the Utkal Printing Company. Following in the footsteps of one of the most influential people of the Oriya Movement, Gaurishankar Ray, who brought out the journal *Utkala Dīpikā*[24] from his Cuttack Printing Company, Fakirmohan started with the publication of the journals *Bālasore sambāda vāhikā* for critical exchange and *Bodhadāyinī* for literary

---

[23] Types in Oriya were available only in Calcutta from one manufacturer who, however, could not read Oriya. Another problem was to find composers and trained staff to operate the machine. The first futile attempts produced only ink-blotted paper sheets, and Fakirmohan in a face-saving attempt consoled the disappointed crowd that these blots would turn into characters overnight (Fakirmohan, 50).

[24] *Utkal Dīpikā* was launched as a weekly journal in the midst of the famine on 4 August 1866 by Gaurishankar Ray, patronized by Commissioner Ravenshaw and subscribed by a large number of Rajas. The Cuttack Printing Company was founded by Gaurishankar Ray, Bichitranandan Das and others. Gaurishankar continued to edit the journal until his death in 1917, and the journal, the most important and long-lasting in Orissa, survived until 1936 (Patra and Devi 1983, 173). Cuttack was an important intellectual centre and around 1894, the Cuttack Debating Society was established by Madhusudan Rao as an activity of the Cuttack Training School; it was transformed into the larger body of the *Utkal Sāhitya Samāj* in 1903.

contributions. But there was a lack of contributors, he himself being busy all day with teaching and running the press.[25]

With the gradual establishment of an infrastructure consisting of teaching equipment, press, journals and literary societies,[26] the language agitation caught on. After the decision to prescribe the vernacular instead of Persian had been implemented, a concerted campaign had been going on from outside Orissa to force the Government to abolish Oriya in their schools and to replace it by Bengali.[27] The movement originated in a letter of 14 January 1841, addressed by the Board of Revenue to the Commissioner of the Orissa Division. Naturally, people from outside who had till then occupied almost all posts under the British in Orissa were apprehensive that they would lose their jobs and influence. Fakirmohan's autobiography is extensively concerned with the influence the Bengali section was gaining in Orissa. Kantichandra Bhattacharya, a Bengali Pandit at the Government School at Balasore, is projected by Fakirmohan as his prime opponent in public discussions or committee meetings concerning the language issue. Bhattacharya's booklet, denying the independent status of Oriya and declaring it a mere dialect of the Bengali, sparked off an

---

[25] The circulation of this journal was limited, as Fakirmohan remarks that there were some fifty journal customers, around ten of them paying subscription, and maybe twenty actually reading it (Fakirmohan, 53). It became, however, the most influential journal after *Utkal Dīpikā*, followed in 1889 by the *Sambalpur Hitaiṣiṇī*, one of the few journals not appearing from Balasore, Cuttack, Puri or Berhampur, the main intellectual centres. *Utkal Sāhitya* was founded in 1897 (Patra and Devi 1983, 174).

[26] Another early, informal circle of intellectuals is described to have met at a pond in Balasore every evening, one member being Madhusudana Das, then Third Master at the government school, before he left for Calcutta (Fakirmohan, 32).

[27] In a circular dated 30 May 1837, the Government had directed the use of Persian in offices to be discontinued and to be replaced by the local language, while English continued as before. Anyone who was unable to speak the local language would be debarred from holding an appointment under the British government (G. Mohanty 1978, 11).

agitated debate.[28] It was sent to the School Inspector R. L. Martin at the headquarters at Medinipur, who soon after ordered only Bengali and Sanskrit to be taught at the Government School of Balasore. As Fakirmohan narrates, a certain apathy prevailed among the few educated Oriya Babus, who needed to be awakened to the fact that there was a 'Bengali conspiracy' behind this government order. *Utkala Dīpikā* and *Bālasore sambāda vāhi̊kā* became the major vehicles for the agitation, convincing the people that their sons' career options were at stake if Bengali was to be taught at schools in Orissa schools. Fakirmohan had a petition signed by some 500 people, which was handed over to Collector Beames. Beames forwarded the petition with a favourable comment to Commissioner Ravenshaw. And Ravenshaw, 'the eternal friend of Utkal',[29] convinced the government to give orders, that Bengali was to be banned completely from schools in Orissa, and even more schools were to be founded to teach Oriya.

---

[28] *Uḍiyā svatantra bhāṣā nahe* (Calcutta 1870). Beames' linguistic statement on the independent status of Oriya opens with a reference to this book, describing it as 'a little work, profoundly destitute of philological arguments.... The local excitement on the subject has led me to look into the question more closely' (Beames 1870, 192). Rajendralal Mitra in his reply takes up the defence of Bhattacharya and tries to prove that Oriya indeed was a mere dialect of the Calcutta Bengali, the amount of deviations demonstrated by Beames to be found in a comparable degree in the 'dialect' spoken at Dacca. In his reply Mitra refers to the critical remarks he had made at the Cuttack Debating Club in 1868, where he had pointed out 'the injury that was being inflicted on the Uriya race by their attachment to a provincial patois, which they wished to exalt into a distinct language'. Mitra declares not without pride Bhattacharya's book to be a result of these remarks, as they had incited 'a very warm discussion' (Beames, Mitra 1870, 201).

[29] It should be mentioned here that in spite of frequently showering praise on Ravenshaw, Fakirmohan takes quite a critical stand on the latter's handling of the famine (Fakirmohan, 39). Even amongst the British his autocratic reign raised some criticism: 'Thomas Edward Ravenshaw, the commissioner, was a little king in Orissa. He had his salute of eleven guns, his guards and elephants.... I had no great respect for his abilities, nor had anyone else, but he had much experience and knew his Orissa and his Oriyas thoroughly. They loved him as much as they are capable of loving a European. His very slowness and muddling, hesitating ways commended himself to the sluggish Oriya mind' (Beames 1984, 221).

The sudden favourable attention of the British towards Orissa and Oriya must be seen in the context of the famine of 1865/6, which was caused by insufficient rainfall in 1865, shortage of food grain in stores, lack of foresight on the part of the government and apathy of the landlords. Especially the lack of communication led to the catastrophic dimensions that could have been avoided with a timely assessment. When during a reshuffling in the Civil Department Ravenshaw joined as Commissioner in July 1865, he relied on the reassuring reports of his predecessors and subordinates as there was no local information media whatsoever, and failed to invoke the timely intervention of the Board of Revenue at Calcutta. He even failed to inform the Lt. Governor of the situation during the latter's visit to Orissa in February 1866, and when finally rice was ordered from Burma, it could not leave Calcutta as the rains had set in. The situation became irretrievable and the Famine Commission set up in 1867 reported a death toll of ten million lives. The eclatant deficiencies in the administration of Orissa relying largely on Bengali intermediaries caused serious concern in the British Parliament. Northcote, Secretary of State for India in British Parliament, proposed fundamental changes in the administration of Bengal favouring the formation of separate commissionerships for Assam and Orissa. Although his recommendations were only partly implemented, his report was to open new vistas for Oriya nationalism, as the Government started taking interest in the development of a largely neglected area.[30]

The agitation to abolish Oriya came to an end when a circular dated 8 November 1869 was issued by the Government of Bengal, prescribing the use of Oriya in all schools in the Orissa Division, but the pro-Bengali agitation continued through the press and from every conceivable platform. A strong blow to the privileges of the Bengalis occupying posts in Orissa was dealt by the concerted policy to reach the rural areas in Bengal, launched by Lt. Governor Campbell in 1872, concentrating on a large scale development of indigenous primary education at low costs. Its aim was to no longer promote the education of a select few who would rush for a limited

---

[30] Mohanty 1982, 18-9.

number of white collar jobs, but the training of the local population according to their specific needs. Special allotments were made primarily for the foundation or development of village schools and their local staff, rather than for the expenditure on highly trained masters from the cities. Primary education was to be imparted only in the vernacular. Equally important was his revision of scholarship schemes, granting scholarships to 'deserving' boys already at the primary level. Fakirmohan describes a meeting organized by Lt. Governor Campbell, where 'all important people of Balasore'[31] had been invited to discuss the Governor's plans of reducing governmental funding of higher education in English. Whereas Fakirmohan supported the programme of the British, since it was the first chance to receive official support for the spreading of primary education which he himself advocated so strongly, the Bengalis, prominently represented by his archrival Kantichandra Bhattacharya, were vehemently opposing it, since they had been the main beneficiaries of the higher education schemes and scholarships offered by the British so far.[32]

So, in the early days of the language movement, Fakirmohan saw his engagement towards a recognition of Oriya considerably strengthened by British policies, but later in life, due to his own partly disillusioning working experiences under the British and under the influence of early nationalist tendencies, his distance towards the revered principles of British administration grew. Towards the English language, too, he kept an ambivalent attitude, being well aware that it enabled an elite to acquire advancement in government services, while at the same time it impoverished the national literature by diverting linguistic energies away from the cultivation of the mother tongue. Western education, in his view, was impeding national progress by impeding the access to scientific and technical knowledge of agricultural and artisan classes as well

31 As the narrator was part of it! The Bengalis formed the majority during this meeting, since most of the Oriyas were 'tired of public meetings' that were held mostly to invite donations and raise funds. (Fakirmohan, 58).

32 Patra and Devi 1983, 162. The unpopular effects of Campbell's programmes on the Bengalis described by Fakirmohan is also mentioned by Beames: 'His general policy was intensely distasteful to the natives on whose most cherished prejudices he tramped ruthlessly' (Beames 1984, 201-2).

as of the womenfolk on whom the education of children ultimately depended. He therefore claimed that a genuine progress was only possible if Oriya was to become the language of education and administration.

2. Educating a New Generation: Godavarish Mishra

Godavarish Mishra (1886-1956) had designed his autobiography to cover a time span of roughly fifty years of Orissa's political history, starting with his birth in 1886 up to the independent statehood of Orissa in 1936, followed by a second section covering the developments thereafter. He, however, could not complete the autobiography due to political campaigning, illness and finally his death in 1956. The text reaches only till the year 1927, although in several contexts it also refers to later events.[33] His chronologically organized memories start with elaborate thoughts of what and how to write[34] and then turn to family and early childhood events. Nearly all developments in his life as well as the accompanying political details can be seen subordinated to the dominant topic of education, be it his own through school and college, his teaching activities in the Satyavadi School or his campaigning for Oriya-schools in Singhbhum. His career might be typical for that of an educationist of the nineteenth century, where all personal interests, literary activities and political ambitions appear dedicated to the cause of learning and teaching and lastly, training a new generation in the service of the nation.

---

[33] Out of the 45 chapters of the first part only 34 were completed. The second part envisaged 40 more chapters up to the year 1951. Only the first three quarters were revised by the author, the remainder was dictated to Jagannath Mahapatra, a teacher at Banapura High School (Godavarish, 1-3). All of it was written around 1951, five years before the death of Godavarish.

[34] In his quest for truth he was certainly influenced by Gandhi's autobiography. Godavarish's major concerns as an author evolve as creating a text that is true, comprehensive, worthy, useful and an encouragement to the poor (Godavarish, 1-10).

His involvement with the Satyavadi School, founded on 12 August 1909 by Pandit Gopabandhu Das,[35] thus figures as the realization of a whole set of new principles concerning education, religion and patriotic fervour to which this generation was exposed. Inspired by the approaches of the Brahmo and Arya Samaj with their combination of indigenous knowledge and progressive Western science, a profound knowledge of one's own cultural traditions parallel to studies of Western sciences and English was encouraged as well. At the same time, group activities such as physical exercise, theatre plays, construction work, carpentry, agriculture, and, more importantly, social engagement during emergencies, were meant to create a strong discipline and social consciousness on the campus. 'Oriyaness' was promoted by observing Oriya festivities, preparing traditional dishes, serving the pilgrims during the *ratha-yātrā* at Puri or taking the students out to historical sites as Konarak, Bhubaneswar or Khandagiri. Oriya literature and educational concerns were promoted in two weeklies, *Satyabādi* and *Samāj*.[36] An ambiguity can certainly be observed in the way English culture and knowledge were adopted, be it through subjects, teaching methods or translations on the one hand, and the way the school unobtrusively or outspokenly fostered anti-British sentiments on the other hand. Although the Satyavadians strived for the necessary

---

[35] Gopabandhu Das (1877-1928) and his close associates Neelkantha Das (1884-1967), Acharya Harihara Das (1878-1971), Godavarish Mishra (1886-1956) and Krupasindhu Mishra (1897-1926) are still revered in Orissa as '*Pañca Śākhā*' in the line with the *Pañcasakhā* of Sri Caitanya. All of them were Brahmins, hailing from the vicinity of Puri. Krupasindhu was the nephew of Neelkantha, Harihara was his relative. Even other distant relatives of theirs were in the Satyavadi staff. Gopabandhu had a B.A., Neelkantha, Godavarish and Krupasindhu M.A.s, Harihara an F.A. (Godavarish, 131). Many other brilliant and devoted teachers were there, like Ramachandra Rath, a Brahmin who had worked as a coolie to complete his education. He was later in charge of the 'Asram' at Karua close by, the school Gopabandhu had set up for all the scheduled caste boys (Mohanty 1982, 90).

[36] Gopabandhu and the staff of Satyavadi had earlier contributed regularly to the weekly *Āśā*, but after a short while at Satyavadi, they published their own weeklies from Sakhi Gopal near Satyavadi. Radhanath Rath was in charge of the press, Neelkantha managed the weekly *Satyabādī*. However only *Samāj* expanded and survived even after Gopabandhu's death (Godavarish, 129).

recognition within the prevailing educational system that would enable their students to appear for the school final examinations,[37] their ultimate objective was to generate manpower for the independence of the country. As we read in Godavarish's autobiography, he was already in close contact with secret anti-British circles at Calcutta during his student's days, the path of militant resistance being paved for them; but he, like many other patriots who were reluctant or unfit to join, were later absorbed by Gandhi's teaching of non-violence and non-cooperation. A close community of teachers and students united in the spirit of reformist religious principles and patriotic self-sacrifice made the school, situated close to Puri, a model institution and a sought after place to get admission to, though its caste-denying principles incensed the local Brahmin community to the extent that it was suspected of having torched the school once.[38]

---

[37] As no government support was accepted, the funding remained a problem, and largely relied on donations by feudatory chiefs. The UUC (Utkal Union Conference, *Utkal Sammilanī*) also campaigned for public aid. The initial plan proposed that teachers would render their services free for three years, would then earn money (elsewhere) and contribute one-fifth to the community. Recognition, applied for in 1914, came hesitantly, as the authorities suspected the school to be the breeding ground of anti-national sentiments. It was also briefly considered to attach the school to Shantiniketan. When recognition was finally granted by the Calcutta University, it came with the unwanted boon of governmental financial support of Rs. 75 monthly with the outspoken intention to keep control of the activities there (ibid., 126). The school remained affiliated to the Calcutta University until 1917, after the establishment of Patna University in 1918 the school came under its control (Patra and Devi 1983, 199).

[38] In the chapter *Vanavidyālaya* (Godavarish, 124f) Godavarish narrates how one of the first thatched houses on the campus caught fire, and the Brahmin community was suspected to have caused the fire because it was upset by Neelkantha's advertising the shaving of the beard in an article with strong reformist views in Biswanath Kar's *Utkal Sāhitya.* Classes thereafter were held in the open under Bakula trees, a fact that caused a lot of attention and attracted visitors such as health scientists from England to study the impact of fresh air on the students. Later on the model of open-air schools was propagated as exemplary, and the government came to set up one open-air school (*muktavāyūskūl*) in every district (ibid., 129).

As a writer, Godavarish produced a considerable number of poems, plays and prose writings, but, as it was the general atmosphere within the Satyavadi group, literature was not only the expression of personal genius, but served larger aims such as recreating the glories of ancient Orissa in order to instil a sense of pride in the young generation. Godavarish's two famous plays on historic kings, *Puruṣottama Deva* and *Mukunda Deva*, which were staged first in the Satyavadi School and later all over Orissa with great success, as well as his historical ballads based on legends of Orissa, contributed to this stock of entertaining, yet instructional literature explicitly conceived in the context of building a national consciousness. In fact, the Satyavadians (Satyavadis) were deeply concerned with a reshaping of the image Oriya literature had gained till date, as they were prominently involved in a literary debate revolving around the 'decadent' influences of the Caytanya-Bhakti tradition that had invaded the allegedly pristine purity of Oriya culture from Bengal. The debate that started in the 1890s, was spearheaded by Neelkantha Das but also supported by articles of Gopabandhu Das and others,[39] targeting mainly the works of the utmost revered and influential Oriya author (of Bengali origin) Radhanath Ray (1848-1908), whose preoccupation with depicting physical passion in mythological settings was linked to a writing tradition revolving around the excessive erotic imagery of the Radha-Krishna cult that allegedly had flourished in Oriya literature since Caytanya's times.

[39] Biswanath Kar, initially an admirer of Radhanath, commented in *Utkal Sāhitya* (June 1901): 'The bounds of good taste, of propriety even are exceeded.... What earthly good such scenes achieve for society?' (Boulton 1993, 511). In *Utkal Dīpikā* (3 October 189) Gaurishankar Ray called Radhanath's prose as 'too filthy to read, loathsome, degrading and vulgar'. Even Radhanath's friend Madhusudana Rao was outraged by his defaming historic kings and disparaging the character of women. Other charges concerned Radhanath's plagiarism of Greek and Sanskrit themes and the defective structure of his poems (G. Mohanty 1978, 59). The debate was largely carried on in the journals *Bijulī* supporting Radhanath, and *Indradhanuṣ* criticizing him. In fact Gopabandhu, when studying in 4th standard, had ridiculed Radhanath in a poem published in *Indradhanuṣ*, whereupon Radhanath as Inspector terminated the boy's scholarship and nearly drove him out of school, as Neelkantha remembers (Boulton 1993, 509).

Although Neelkantha Das or Godavarish in principle followed Radhanath's literary example of centring texts around Oriya scenery, legends or history, they sought to present their topics in the spirit of patriotism, keeping an eye on a flawless moral instruction for the youth. Further, Neelkantha Das strongly opposed Radhanath's favouring of Bengali idioms, which had to his mind been imposed onto the Oriya language by Ray's influential works and school textbooks. The Satyavadi School thus rose to figure as a cultural force that challenged the prevailing standards in education, religion and literary tastes.

The degree of public interest in matters of educational or cultural concerns witnessed during the days of the Satyavadi School[40] has to be seen against the background of the reluctance towards the educational system initially shown in Orissa. It might have needed this first generation of Oriyas who had completed the whole circle of Western education to develop a system that was able to combine Western and indigenous ideals and outlooks.

The role of a cultural centre that the Satyabadi School was able to assume reflected also on the broadened base of educated people and a network of journals that enabled interaction between the members of an emerging articulate middle class. Only in the latter half of the nineteenth century did Oriyas begin to be introduced to Western education in larger numbers. Godavarish's narration of his progress in education, from his school days at Puri, his B.A. studies in Cuttack, his scholarship at the Law College along with M.A. studies in Calcutta and later again Teacher's Training at Calcutta, has to be seen against the background of educational history of Orissa, to acclaim the individual standards achieved by the generation born around the 1860s. And the great popularity the School gained over the years speaks itself for the sudden awareness matters of education had gained at the beginning of the twentieth century. Godavarish himself, in his autobiography, thus speaks proudly for his generation which, in his narration,

---

[40] Visitors included dignitaries as the Bihar-Orissa Governor Sir Edward Gait or Sir Ashutosh Mukherjee. – Fakirmohan, too, visited Satyavadi one year before his death, living there for a few days with the community, and was deeply impressed by the dedication to patriotic causes (Mansinha 1976, 83).

appears to have made the quantum leap towards a brighter future on the basis of values of enlightenment and progress.

As compared to Bengal, the development of Western education in the Orissa province initially failed to gain momentum.[41] The people mostly reacted with apathy not only to the English schools but also to the 'Hardinge[42] schools' promoting the vernacular, and new approaches were necessary to develop a network of primary schools[43] until Commissioner Ravenshaw could report in 1874 that the government had brought 832 *pāṭhaśālās* under its umbrella.

The need to locally supervise and co-ordinate this expanding net of educational institutions was met with the appointment of the

---

[41] After the decision by Bentinck's government to introduce the English language in education, the first English school was opened 1835 in Puri with a teacher from Calcutta and 25 pupils. By 1838/9 their number had increased to 75. Instruction was also imparted in Sanskrit. Because of the conservative attitude of the inhabitants and the non-availability of local teachers, the education committee was not in favour of continuing with the experiment. Commissioner Ricketts in turn advocated immediate support of the committee for opening a school in Cuttack. Since the existing missionary English Charity School at Cuttack faced financial trouble, it was taken over by the government and the Puri school was closed. Thus by 1841, only one English school existed in Orissa, which from 1851 was called Cuttack Zilla School, to be joined in 1853 by two more Zilla (District) Schools at Puri and Balasore (Patra and Devi 1983, 158).

[42] Sir Henry Hardinge, Governor General of India 1844-7. Grandfather of Lord Hardinge of Penhurst, Viceroy from 1910 to 1916.

[43] Commissioners A.J M. Mills and his successor Gouldsbury proposed the abolition of fees, supply of books and better job prospects in government services. Even after the Wood's Despatch in 1854, which distinctly laid out plans for the establishments of universities, education departments and a promotion of grants-in-aid for schools, Orissa education suffered from the distance to the headquarters at Calcutta and the resulting communication gap. The most urgent needs, therefore, as formulated by Cockburn in 1856, appeared to be the training of local teachers and the placement of local Inspectors of School. Further, he proposed the development of the existing net of village *pāṭhaśālās*, with the aim of eventually bringing them under the control of the government. The Cuttack Normal School as a first training school for teachers functioned from 1869, training teachers in two sections. Campbell's efforts of 1872 were referred to earlier (Patra and Devi 1983, 160).

first Joint Inspector of Schools for Orissa in 1873/4, a post Radhanath Ray held for long years.[44] Further, the reorganization of the distribution scheme of funds proved to be an enormous incentive for students to get involved, parents and teachers alike: Instead of granting stipends to the local teachers, a 'payment by results' was introduced in 1877. Simultaneously, centres for public examination were installed to establish a fixed standard of examination.

Higher education in Orissa started with the opening of collegiate classes in the Cuttack Zilla School with six students in 1868, to prepare them for the F.A. (First Arts) examination at Calcutta University. As in commerce, transport or communication, in the field of educational promotion, too, the great famine of 1866 was a turning point, as it suddenly invited large scale British enterprise. After the fulfilment of Ravenshaw's appeal for local donations in support of the government, the Cuttack College opened in 1876 with 19 B.A. students in different classes. After five years of experiment[45] the College was placed on a permanent basis in 1881, partly enabled by generous local contributions such as a

---

[44] Radhanath Ray was promoted in 1892 to be the first acting Inspector of Schools. This way, the first graduates of the newly developing middle class were instructed largely under the supervision of Radhanatha. His position as the head of the Education Department of Orissa for nearly 31 years with thousands of scholars, teachers and officers working under him enabled an unprecedented influence on the quality of teaching and the refinement of literary taste, which was largely shaped according to the textbooks and *kāvya* he himself had written. Most of them were printed by the famous De's Press at Balasore belonging to his friend Rājā Baikunthnath De (who earlier had also supported Fakirmohan's press). Since Radhanath had a big say in the approval of textbooks, all his subordinates naturally favoured the ones written by him. This resulted in open charges accusing him of nepotism and favouritism in 1890 (Mohanty 1978, 22).

[45] For the first two years, no student of the Cuttack College could pass the B.A. examination. In 1880 only one student succeeded in doing so in third division, and the college was closed for one day to celebrate the success. The first Oriya graduate was Madhusudana Das, however, from L.M.S. College in Calcutta in 1870. He was also the first Oriya to get M.A (1873) and B.L. degrees (1878) (Patra and Devi 1983, 167). For more details and figures concerning the beginnings of collegiate education in Orissa cf. also Patel 1999, 345-55.

donation of the Rājā of Mayurbhanj, who also had the College renamed Ravenshaw College. In 1878 F.A. classes were opened in the Zilla School at Berhampore, which was handed over to private hands in 1888 and given the name Khallikote College in 1893 after its financial mentor, the Rājā of Khallikote. Although certain restrictions in the funding of primary education were introduced by the Education Commission under W.W. Hunter in 1882, the last decades of the nineteenth century saw a steady growth of education in Orissa in all directions. With the introduction of the Local Self-Government Act in Orissa, the district boards assumed the management of middle and primary schools from 1887 in Cuttack, Puri and Balasore. When around 1919 the need for an independent Orissa University was formulated, the institutions that were proposed to be incorporated as a nucleus consisted of as many as 39 High Schools and 4 colleges.[46]

This way, academic careers like Godavarish's were not only the result of British efforts, but were also made possible by an increasing involvement of the Oriya aristocracy in patronizing educational institutions. Reformist concepts introduced by Rammohun Roy and the Arya Samaj had created a public awareness of educational progress and progress through education; this was transported into action by a growing local network of teachers and administrators working in the field. Education, and higher education in particular, had become the prerequisite for all posts in the British administrative system, but was also propagated from within by influential Oriya educationists such as the founder of the Sanskrit College at Puri, Harihara Das.[47] Education was considered to be the first step on the way to social reforms and the most effective means of 'catching up' with the civilized world. The thorough internalization of the doctrine of education can be traced for

[46] As at that time urgent demands for amalgamation were voiced, the areas included here were Political Orissa, Feudatory States of Orissa, Oriya Tracts of Ganjam and Jeypore Agency, Central Provinces, Singhbhum District and Midnapore District (Two Bachelors 1996, 167).

[47] Harihara Das died in 1872. He is said to have influenced Gopabandhu with his ideas on new approaches of education. He was the coach of Collector Beames, teaching him Sanskrit and Oriya, himself learning Greek and English from him.

example in a certain obsession with academic degrees in Godavarish's autobiography, as he not only mentions his own joy upon receiving the B.A. or M.A., but often refers to other people's standards and achievements, the foreign system of qualification having completely replaced all earlier grades of professional or educational refinement. Considering Godavarish's extremely poor family background, the decision to forego a promising career[48] in favour of the financially rather modest prospects at Satyavadi has to be acclaimed in that connection, too.

One of the main impediments in sending children to school was the belief that education invariably meant the loss of traditional values, and Godavarish's memories could serve as an example that this conviction was not altogether wrong. Apart from various contexts where he reflects critically on the change education had brought about in his life or, for that matter, for the whole country, a whole chapter is dedicated to the 'decline of faith and religion' in his life, a fact he also ascribes to the influence of the 'English language'. Whereas he still admits an at least ambivalent stand towards certain values he inherited from his Brahmin home and gradually lost in the process, such as faith in deities, devotion and humility when observing fasts and other religious family rituals, etc., he comes down heavily on the deeply rooted superstition of his community that had instilled in the timid child a nearly unsurpassable fear of an omnipresent army of malicious ghosts and demons, or of unnatural happenings and inauspicious signs. He narrates how he, after passing upper-primary, had to walk for one-and-a-half miles to the middle school at Bhimapur, and his first walks alone in the dark or close to the crematorium grounds or other haunted places proved to be true tests for his courage and rational thinking.[49] The fight against the 'eight-legged object' of dark beliefs

48 Gopabandhu always played a vital role in keeping him on the track of sacrifice. When once, still during his student's days, Godavarish got the offer to undergo training in England with the prospect of taking over a deaf-and-dumb school in Calcutta on his return, Gopabandhu reminded him of the tasks waiting for him at home in Orissa (Godavarish, 114).

49 Once he had to walk from the Railway station at night to his uncle's place, because the telegram of his arrival had not reached there, and deciphered the

in society, he concludes, therefore, had to be the actual challenge of the reformist, aiming much beyond a 'shallow enlightenment', but demanding instead a thorough reform of behaviour. In another chapter, he narrates how he burned his horoscope while attending the second class in High School, yet at the same time he lists a number of critical events in his life where he certainly felt 'destiny' at work. A later event in life shows him already as a convinced iconoclast when he, as a teacher at Satyavadi, openly destroyed a *shivliṅg* that had formed on an ants hill, declared by the local priests to be a miracle directly stemming from *patāl* and soon attracting large crowds of devotees. Of course this invited the considerable wrath of the villagers and priests alike who had started to live comfortably off the heaps of *prasād* offered to them.

A vital role in the whole Western educational set-up was played by the institution of hostels, a fact that is widely reflected in Godavarish's autobiography and which is, if at all, only fleetingly referred to in historical accounts of education. In fact, this might be quoted as one of the most striking examples of how memories of seemingly trivial things such as food, company, teaching and learning routines, exposure to political activities, etc., are able to recreate a whole cultural micro-cosmos that was shared by and up to the present day appeals to a large community of readers. It is amazing to see how much of the formative experiences of the boy are connected with or directly attributed to his staying in the hostel community. Experiences of cooking together or sleeping in one room,[50] or going out for picnics taking *pān* for the first time (and falling unconscious because probably *bhāṁg* was mixed with it) surely meant a drastic alternative to the secluded family life at

---

'ghosts' on his way one by one as bats, clay pots, wet moss, etc. On his arrival, all the elders gathered and discussed the future of this boy who certainly must have come under the influence of evil spirits now.

[50] He hints at an early experience with homosexuality when, while cooking, one boy tried to come close to him with 'evil intentions', whom he however rejected. He mentions that hostel rules (therefore?) allowed a room occupancy either alone, or with three and more boys in one room, one of them being a monitor (ibid., 29).

home. For the village child,[51] the process of getting familiar with places and people in big town Puri also provided a great deal of self-assertion. After his school-days at Puri were over, Godavarish joined B.A. classes at Ravenshaw College, Cuttack, again living at a hostel there. As in Puri, the slightly elder Neelkantha was his close associate and helped him to cope with the new situation and to conceal his poverty. Godavarish remembers the way the fees that had to be paid to the cook, the kind of food provided within that budget and the tricks he invented to circumvent the morning and evening meals that had to be paid for separately. His memory shows the deep imprint that the financial matter had left on his mind. In order to alleviate his financial despair, he soon looked for a possibility to work as a house tutor, and was hired by the English teacher of the college for his son after he excelled in a drama recital as Shakespeare's 'Caesar'.[52]

The most important aspect of hostel life, however, started for Godavarish around 1909 with the participation in the *Taruṇ Utkal Saṅgh* ('Young Utkal Association'), which had been formed as a students' association of Cuttack College.[53] From the beginning however, the government's suspicious eyes monitored activities, since known 'hard-liners' like Gopabandhu Das, Brajasundar Das or Biswanath Kar were closely associated with it. Secret meetings were, therefore, held in the backyard of Brajasundar's house with

---

[51] In a later context of comparing the difference between his native place Banapura, 'a region of tigers and bears', and Calcutta, he describes his village Banapura of his childhood as a remote and neglected spot with an impoverished population fighting against the very real dangers of the jungle. Even so it had a minor school. Later a middle school was founded by Godavarish, competing even later with another middle-school (ibid., 100).

[52] The student Godavarish tutored in English managed to do very well, but still stood second to his rival co-student, Subhas Chandra Bose, the later famous Netaji, who was also a 'product' of this college.

[53] It was founded, soon after the Utkal Conference, by Gopabandhu Das in July 1904, mainly to undertake social service, especially relief work in times of natural calamities. Gopabandhu's founding of the Satyavadi School is directly related to the excessive relief work rendered by this voluntary organization, as it was then that he felt the need to educate a dedicated generation of young men to serve their motherland, and not the needs of the government.

the recital of Oriya and Bangla revolutionary poems, and other meetings for physical exercise and discussion near Gopabandhu's residence. During the entrance examination in 1909, around two hundred students from all over Orissa came to Cuttack and an impressive welcome function involving many prominent leaders of the city was organized by the *Taruṇ Utkal Saṅgh*. Whereas this organization was a public outfit, another one existed that met secretly at night time, headed by Gopabandhu. Neelkantha and Godavarish used to participate in these meetings[54] and Gopabandhu with his magnetic influence 'paved the way' of these boys by telling them stories about the French Revolution and the independence struggle of Italy. When Khudiram Bose was hanged, the college observed a fast. As the government was closing in on the activities of the students and their leaders, the great Oriya patron Madhusudana Das,[55] who had become worried about the developments, personally questioned the students behind locked doors. Godavarish reveals that college authorities even tried to cover up the student activities, but eventually all were punished. At this point of his narration, Godavarish underlines once more how important the atmosphere of critical exchange and discussion he experienced during his hostel life has been not only for his own

---

[54] Even then, they were observed by police intelligence. In the process of finding excuses for their night-outs, when confronted by the authorities, they developed the art of *Chanakya Niti* as they called it, a shrewdness of pretending, denying and lying in spite of evidence.

[55] He is often referred to as *kulavruddha* ('the eldest of the clan'), in respect of his merits as 'the only guardian of the Oriya race'. This event however reflects 'Madhu Babu's' growing dissent with Gopabandhu's radical approach, especially concerning the attitude towards the British regime, which Madhusudana's generation still respected as the benefactors of Orissa. A liberal man of public spirit, he had entered the Bengal Legislative Council in 1896 as the first elected representative of Orissa. He was the natural choice of the British to fill up the post of the Minister of Local Self-Government in January 1921 after the province of Bihar and Orissa had been formed (Patra and Devi 1983, 211). His acceptance of salaried ministership was, however, bitterly criticized by the *swarajists*.

development, but for the future development of his whole generation, encouraging open dissent with elders and prominent people.

This exposure to influential political activities was even intensified when Godavarish came to stay in the famous hostel 'House number nine' at Calcutta. The fact that this hostel, a rather unsuitable and awkwardly constructed house, was rented by the government especially for Oriya law students on scholarship, made the fellow Bengali students despise their Oriya colleagues as 'sons-in-law of the government'. In many other respects this chapter provides interesting details regarding the way the considerable Oriya community in Calcutta hid its identity before the process of self-assertion slowly caught on.[56] According to Godavarish, the hostel played a central role therein as it was 'a centre for the planning and imagination of the twentieth century national character of Orissa'.[57] Many 'bright students'[58] were sent to this house every year and later on occupied high posts in the administration[59] or worked as lecturers. As the Oriya student's community was divided on the issue of identity, and some preferred to converse in Bangla,

---

[56] According to Godavarish, around 1910 over a lakh of Oriya workers lived in Calcutta, most of them reluctant to disclose their identity and rather speaking in broken Bangla. They were called by the derogative nickname of 'Uḍe', a word that came to be used for 'fool' in the general sense. Similarly, Oriya characters served as the classical simpletons in theatre. Still, nearly one-tenth of the population was Oriya, most of whom worked as cooks and servants in nearly every household, this way forming an intimate part of the city's social structure. The few educated and wealthy permanent residents had switched to Bangla or even changed their surnames, whereas, as Godavarish points out, generations of Bengalis living in Orissa had naturally retained their language (Godavarish, 108).

[57] Godavarish, 107.

[58] Including the narrator!

[59] As one of the profusely employed similes of his flowery speech, Godavarish compares this hostel to a wheat mill where in different degrees of refinement, *āṭā*, *maidā*, *ravā* or husk is churned out, like Bichitranandan Das becoming Advocate General, Ramesh Chandra Mishra District Judge, Laxmidhar Mohanty Member of Public Service Commission, etc. He rates himself modestly as husk, having nothing but his autobiography to contribute (ibid., 107).

the members of this hostel made it a point to publicly tease them in Oriya and to sport the pink turban Madhusudana Das had introduced as the symbol of Oriyas when he inaugurated the Utkal Union Conference (UUC) in 1903.[60] A large function was organized by the students after the formation of the independent province of Bihar and Orissa on the occasion of the return of the Maharaja of Mayurbhanj from his world trip, where Madhusudana was the Chairman and for the first time in Calcutta, the entire proceedings were held in Oriya. Many reformist activities had been initiated in this house, too. Some of the students founded a *Hindu Samāj*[61] with the resolution to remove caste divides while eating, promote inter-cast marriage, enhance the status of women and promote revolutionary acts like shaving the beard, which was a taboo in Oriya's Brahmin community.

As Godavarish came with the fourth batch of Oriya law students to Calcutta[62] he faced little resistance in getting into the social and political circles there. 'Shashi Uncle',[63] whom he knew from the revolutionary circles at Puri and Cuttack, introduced him

---

[60] The first sitting of the Utkal Union Conference (UUC) was held at Cuttack under the presidentship of the Rājā of Mayurbhanj on 20 December 1903. Madhusudana Das was the Secretary. During the following year, 381 branches were organized and the Young Utkal Association included into the Conference. In the second session of 1904, presided over by the Rājā of Dharakote and chaired by the Rājā of Keonjhar, one point on the agenda was 'thanking Lord Curzon for his proposal to unite the Oriya speaking tracts' (Two Bachelors 1996, 250-1).

[61] Members were Neelkantha and Godavarish, Bichitranandan Das, Neelambar Mohanty, Bipin Bihari Roy, Chintamani Samantrai and Shashibhushan Chatterjee among others (Godavarish, 111).

[62] Every year six students with B.A. degrees from Orissa were supported by the law scholarship, along with a provision to study M.A. By the time Godavarish joined, the group had already decided to set up an educational institution at Satyavadi with the view of getting trained in a variety of subjects, Neelkantha took M.A. admission in philosophy, Krupasindhu Mishra in history and Godavarish in economics. Gopabandhu, working as the government lawyer of Mayurbhanj at Baripada, supported Godavarish financially, as Godavarish's studying for his M.A. was part of his future work plan (ibid., 100).

[63] Shashibhusana Ray Chaudhuri, who was connected with underground terrorist activities in Bengal.

again to clandestine meetings in secret places where he found out that, beyond inflammatory speeches or recruiting workforce in educational institutions, a third strategy of armed resistance had formed. Members of this group, 'a generation of teachers dedicated to that task', secretly possessed guns and knew how to fabricate bombs.[64] As Godavarish was, however, not pulling well with one of the leaders, Manindranath Seth, Shashi Uncle decided that he should serve his motherland in a different way and become an educationist. He was excluded from the very inner circle, and in retrospect recalls how many of these fighters were later exposed to cruel torture in jail, some of them went mad or died in attacks, others changed over to a professional life or joined the non-violence movement.

The last chapters of Godavarish's autobiography deal with the gradual erosion and decline of the Satyavadi School, which set in partly due to mismanagement, partly due to personal quarrels within the staff, especially between Neelkantha and Godavarish. Since Gopabandhu was absent for longer periods, a system of rotating headmastership was adopted. Godavarish was made headmaster but was too soft to enforce the financial obligations of the members. Acharya Harihara as his successor was even less successful in re-disciplining the slackening attitude of teachers and students. Finally in 1919, Godavarish was sent to Singhbhum to lead the Oriya movement there.[65] He was briefly introduced by Gopabandhu into his new surrounding at Chakradharpur, and in spite of having yet to

---

[64] Ibid., 102.

[65] Neelkantha went first to his village, then to teach at the Calcutta University. Thereafter he was sent by Gopabandhu to Sambalpur to propagate the Oriya movement, but was called back to teach at Satyavadi which in the meanwhile had become a national school. Krupasindhu in turn was asked to take charge of the school at Bahagoda in Singhbhum to push the non-cooperation cause there. 'At home' in Satyavadi, Acharya Harihara was directed to devote his time to this cause, too. After Gandhi's visit in 1921, many students joined the movement, leaving Satyavadi more a centre of the non-cooperation movement than a centre for higher studies. After the death of Krupasindhu and Gopabandhu (in 1926 and 1928 respectively), the school continued to function and exists until the present day, but without its former distinctive mark (Mohanty 1982, 92-3).

pick up Hindi, settled quickly at his new work place and started with the founding of schools and teaching the Oriya community there.[66] The main reason for the decline of the Satyavadi School after 1919, therefore, seems to have been the withdrawal of the founder's dedicated spirit from the project, as he was increasingly involved with his Congress party work.[67] The cause of independent Orissa, especially the amalgamation of the Oriya speaking tracts, was still on Gopabandhu's agenda, but he considered the liberation of his country from the British rule now of prime importance. This change in attitude caused a major rift between the younger generation and the older stalwarts of the UUC. who were still clinging to the belief that only by loyalty to the government their aspirations could be fulfilled and who considered the association with the national Congress as a virtual death-blow for the cause of an independent Orissa. Both groupings however, the moderates and the nationalists, continued to operate from the platform of the UUC.[68] The visit of Gandhi to Orissa in 1921 finally opened a new chapter, which is reflected in the following autobiographical source.

---

[66] The Oriya initiative in Singhbhum concentrated on the founding of schools for the Oriya population in order to consolidate its status in the outlying areas. In Chakradharpur, the 'old village' around the palace of the King of Podahat, was mainly inhabited by Oriyas. Godavarish founded a high school (funded by a businessmen of Mathura and even ' the Whites') and several primary schools. Gopabandhu raised Rs. 12.000 for Singhbhum by his 'one-paise-contribution' scheme. As a result, the Oriya speaking population increased from 1,24,593 in 1911, to 1,40,821 in 1921 and to 1,71,887 in the 1931 Census (Godavarish, 141-4). In 1920/1, however, Gopabandhu wanted Godavarish to give up the schools and join the non-cooperation movement, but Godavarish, not as mesmerized as his mentor by Gandhi's promise of 'independence after one year', convinced him to convert them into national schools as a basis for the movement (ibid., 146).

[67] Gopabandhu went to attend the Lucknow session of the Congress in 1916, and soon after decided to join Congress (Mohanty 1982, 99).

[68] The Chakradharpur session of the UUC (30 December 1920–1 January 1921) proved to be a turning point. Gopabandhu and Jagabandhu Singh, coming directly from the Nagpur Congress session, managed to convince the UUC members to accept the aspirations and objectives of the Congress. Their trump card was the adoption of the linguistic principle of the Congress. Brajasundar Das, Biswanath Kar and others objected to the move, Madushudan Das did not

3. Towards National Integration: Gopabandhu Das

Gopabandhu Das' text has the outer form of a long end-rhyming poem of thirty pages, the text-flow not divided into stanzas but into six uneven sections.[69] The first person narrator is without doubt the voice of the author. The first three sections, well in the style of a public speech,[70] call for attention, addressing and connecting with the 'audience', by referring to the author's mental worries after four months in prison[71] 'as a warrior in the spiritual war', and awakening memories of common experiences during times of calamities and

---

take part. The Utkal Provincial Congress committee was formed in 1921, Gopabandhu being its first President. Gradually, eight District Committees were formed, with leaders as H. K. Mahtab for Balasore, Krupasindhu Mishra and Jagabandhu for Puri, Neelkantha Das for Sambalpur, Godavarish for Singhbhum, a.o (Patra and Devi 1983, 223). Thereby almost the complete Satyavadi staff was absorbed.

[69] The first three sections cover one page each, section four covers three, section five eight pages, section six fifteen pages. Each sections starts and ends with inverted commas, indicating direct speech. The first three sections open with direct appeals to 'Countrymen, friends and dear ones', 'Oh the people of Utkal, my brothers and sisters', and 'Oh my brothers and sisters of Utkal', the opening lines of the following sections serve as joining links to the narrative string of the train journey ('In India, Utkal is the most sacred place', 'Now the soldiers of administration take me away', 'Now the train has reached Jenapura').

[70] Gopabandhu, although handicapped by an organic speech defect, was famous for his moving speeches that untiringly drew the attention of the authorities to the miserable condition of the people, not only as a member of the Bihar-Orissa Legislative Council to which he was elected in 1916 (Patra and Devi 1983, 203). While campaigning for the Oriya cause, his presence used to attract large crowds and 'like the streams of summertime, his speech used to penetrate through all the small or big cracks' (Godavarish, 141). The skill of delivering convincing speeches is to be regarded especially important in view of largely illiterate audiences that had to be reached in far flung rural areas, where thc whole educated middle-class set-up of printed publications had a very limited impact. In the context of the present poem, it might be interesting to note that during Gandhi's visit, Gopabandhu himself used to translate the public speeches of Gandhi into Oriya (Patra and Devi 1983, 224).

[71] He was in Hazaribagh Jail from 24 January 1923 to 26 June 1924. *Bandirā Ātmakathā* was published during his imprisonment in his journal *Samāj*.

disaster.[72] In fact this poem can be seen as a continuation of the speeches Gopabandhu had delivered during his extensive campaigning, in order to keep up the excitement and hope during his imprisonment.[73] From the fourth chapter onwards, the narrative frame of the train journey is introduced, which has a dramatic effect as it takes the author out of Orissa to Hazaribagh Jail as a political prisoner. Landscapes, towns and rivers pass by, evoking memories of the population there and elsewhere, and of the various man-made or natural disasters that had struck them. But the journey functions only as a loose frame to assemble thoughts, memories, messages, statements and appeals. Lines analysing the social decay that had destroyed the original village organization are interspersed by lofty paragraphs imploring the beauty and uniqueness of Utkal within India. Outspoken political imperatives employing the full manual of Gandhian teaching are succeeded by his plea to join him on the path of martyrdom and sacrifice. Substantial sections are shaped in the form of prayers or invocations of Lord Jagannātha, other Oriya deities or rivers, or refer to the teachings of holy scriptures. Philosophical passages reflect on the fate of humanity, on the union of mankind beyond religious borders and on final salvation from sin and disaster.

The term '*ātmā*' that figures in the title of this poem hints at the prominent position of the author's self which indeed dominates the narrative perspective. Although the dominant concern of the

---

[72] Gopabandhu organized numerous relief operations such as during the flood of 1918 which was followed by a terrible famine in 1919/20. Satyavadi workers and teachers were involved in the relief work, which also attracted Gandhi's attention. Amritlal Thakkar ('Thakkar Bapa'), a member of the Servants of India Society, was sent to Orissa by Gandhi, and, in cooperation with Gopabandhu, opened a number of relief centres in remote areas. Soon after the famine, another flood occurred in 1920 in coastal Orissa (Patra and Devi 1983, 204).

[73] Godavarish mentions that his charismatic influence had suffered even before his imprisonment, due to a general lull in the political activities of the Congress after the imprisonment of Gandhi and other important leaders, and he was mentally preparing to go to jail. Godavarish had to desert the Singhbhum campaign finally for want of financial support, and returned to his native place (Godavarish, 162).

poem is with the misery of the people and their way out of it, the patronizing tone makes it appear as though it was *his* misery and *his* worry, reflecting the rhetoric of a seasoned leader. *His* people must be eagerly awaiting *his* message. *He* is anxious to comfort them as they must be desperate about *his* fate. They must be lost without *his* advice. They will give up hope and fall into despair, so it is *his* duty to send a sign of encouragement from jail. He pleads with them to keep up the spirit of non-cooperation for *him*, as this will bring relief to *him* when he thinks about the condition of *his* land. The sacrifice of *his* life will serve its fight for freedom. The people are *his* children and it is *his* struggle.[74] The intimate relation Gopabandhu in fact had with the population of Orissa as one of the most dedicated workers in the service of its betterment is revitalized in this poem, where his personal memory evokes a huge potential of collective memory, transforming it into a national memory and creating an unbreakable bond of togetherness between *him* and *them*.

The collective memory is appealed to by the use of many aspects and shades. The gruesome experience of disasters like flood, fire or famine, often enough one causing the other, is evoked when the train stops at Jenapur and Bhadrakh. Gopabandhu had come to Jenapur two years before and witnessed a terrible flood. A long painful description of the scenes he had witnessed then follows, with people and cattle dying of hunger as the immediate result of the flood. Other memories are immediately associated when images of floods he had seen all over Orissa, 'from the shores of Chilika Lake to the Subarnarekha River',[75] are recalled in great

---

[74] Only two examples shall be quoted here, the first are the opening lines: 'Country men, friends and dear ones / are you frightened of my imprisonment? / It was known beforehand / why are you sorrowful now?' And on pages 11/12: 'If the condition of my country pains my mind / Where do I get consolation? / What courage will I bear to wipe out the tears? / Oh the people of Utkal, my kith and kin, / If I am worthy of your affection / I appeal to you with folded hands / … / Keep up your mind for the non-cooperation / spend your life achieving *svarāj* / that will console me in my exile.'

[75] As one can observe, all locations mentioned in the poem are restricted to coastal Orissa.

detail like deserted villages, sand-covered fields and emaciated villagers on the verge of death.[76] When the train gives the signal to leave Jenapur station and passes Jenapur bridge, he longs to say farewell to the residents and prays to the rivers Brahmani and Kharaswrata to spare the population of Jajpur and Kendrapara so dear to him. He tells the residents that he recently got the news in prison of yet another disaster that had struck their town in the form of a massive fire causing unprecedented havoc. Apart from these disasters, widespread suffering due to misrule is remembered when the train next halts at Bhadrakh. The freedom struggle against the British 'Bahadur' found a strong base here with the workers of Bhadrakh vowing in large numbers to join Gandhi, who had visited this place to address a large gathering of Hindus and Muslims.[77] From Bhadrakh, his memories take him to close-by Kanika, where the population had to endure the terrors of the king's subordinates quelling a powerful revolt against him. This part covers nearly four pages, where memories of the subjects' exposure to a terror regime are mixed with his own feelings of remorse that he was not able to personally comfort them, although he had visited the king earlier.[78]

---

[76] Ibid., 16.

[77] Ibid., 21.

[78] The events referred to here played a significant role in the *svarāj*-struggle as they were closely connected to Gopandhu's term in jail. Furthermore, it showed the Congress-supporters and the UUC as clear opponents. The King of Kanika, Rajendra Narayan Bhanja Deo, one of the most prominent supporters of the Oriya movement, leader of the UUC and member of both the central and provincial Legislative Council, faced in his own estate serious disturbances that arose in protest against undue taxation by his subordinate officials. Congress leaders like Dr. Atal Behari Acharya were informed about it and visited the place, they were however assured by the king that the situation would improve. The *rājā* in fact favoured the introduction of *charkha* and *panchayat* rule, but remained critical towards the political impact of the non-cooperation movement. When the situation further deteriorated, people refused to pay revenue to the king. In April 1922, the *rājā* resorted to the help of the Cuttack police contingent, resulting in the death of some people, large scale arrests and strong repressive measures against the tenants. The government tried to declare the episode as a part of the non-cooperation movement, forbidding leaders like Gopabandhu to interfere. The violation of that rule led to his arrest. When the case was brought up in August 1922 in the Legislative Council by the Congress,

This reference to local events is the last one in the poem, the memory of it lingering after the departure of the train from Bhadrakh and the Salandi rivers.

The Congress campaign for non-cooperation offers another basis for identification, as at the time of publication, several events referred to in the text were very fresh in the minds of the Oriya population.[79] Considering the successful entrapment of both jargon and spirit, the poem could indeed serve as the manifesto of this campaign. With a sudden rise in the production of patriotic poems, the entering of political matter into the sacred realms of poetry could be observed all over India at that time. Here, too, the analysis of the decline of society at the village level is presented in lyrical lines on money-lenders, landlords and the financial ruin of the villagers through their involvement in endless litigations. Lack of clothes, medical care and food had turned the villages virtually into crematorium sites. The loss of traditional culture, reinvented in Gopabandhu's poem with his icons of a functioning rural society such as *Bhāgabata-Purāṇa* reading, cows, ponds and temples, is lamentable; instead the population is 'caught in the trap of the magic of administration' as he complains.[80] In concise imperatives the essentials of the teaching are repeated,[81] and the future vision of ideal village life is centred around the invincible strongholds of the spinning wheel[82] and the *panchayat*. It is noteworthy that Gandhi is

---

McPherson declared it as 'the most extraordinary case' but justified the *rājā's* action (Patra and Devi 1983, 230).

[79] Gandhi's first visit to the province in the last week of March 1921 provided a boost to the non-cooperation movement. Addressing large gatherings at Cuttack, Bhadrakh, Satyabadi, Puri and Berhampur in just six days, he was deeply moved by the condition of the people. Gandhi knew of Gopabandhu from the relief work done during the famine of 1917, which the former supported with means collected from all over India (ibid., 223-224).

[80] Gopabandhu, 10/11.

[81] 'Adopt the path of *svarāj* / Give up the refined foreign cloth / wear indigenous cloth and refine your body / Don't involve your mind in litigation / Re-establish the tradition of *panchayats* / all of you together in a group, obey them /' etc. (ibid., 13).

[82] In the fight against foreign cloth, Gopabandhu himself initiated the programme in August 1921 at Puri, when a huge pile of cloth was burnt publicly. A fire

the only person that is referred to several times by name (or by his popular title of Mahatma) in this poem. Although he is described as languishing in prison, the reader is repeatedly assured that his struggle will not be in vain.[83] His visit to Utkal with his wife is recalled twice, and his depressing statement made when he was confronted with the incredible suffering is directly quoted within the poem.[84] A variety of speech situations such as questions, appeals, promises, messages, reassurance, consolations etc., are employed to impart the spirit of renunciation, purity and self-sacrifice. Thereby, the fierce tone of agitation is frequently transported to higher spheres of spirituality, achieving a peculiar fusion of politics with religion.[85]

Perhaps the strongest link between the author and his 'audience' is created by these references to the spiritual Self of Orissa. Compared to the outspoken statements of the reformist Godavarish, the only critical statements here are concerned with the enmity between different religions, but at the same time an universal brotherhood of Muslims, Christians and Hindus, across all borders, is also evoked. Although all children born to Mother India are called upon to re-unite, the abundant religious references rest

sacrifice for the same purpose was celebrated as *yajñā* at Cuttack. In September 1921, Gopabandhu convinced the large community of Oriyas in Calcutta working in the shops of cloth merchants, to go on strike. Gandhi addressed them one week later encouraging them to adopt the *carkhā*. A great stir was initiated by Gandhi when he saw that foreign cloth was used and offered at the Jagannātha temple. In *Samāj* of 18 June 1921, Gopabandhu advocated the return to the old practice of temple rituals, and the chief priest later issued an appeal demanding only *svadeśī*-products for worship (Patra and Devi 1983, 226-7).

83 Gopabandhu, 12.

84 Ibid., 17.

85 Only a few lines will serve as an example: 'In India, Utkal is a sacred place of highest virtue / but in the almanac of India it had no name / bravery, literature, wealth and moral strength / the name of Utkal was at the bottom. / In the national assembly of India / Utkal has no independent seat / For that reason Jagannātha / the epitome of mercy / looked with merciful attention. / The holy river of non-cooperation (*asahyoga*) / started flowing in the breast of Utkal / Gandhi, as Bhagirathi empowered by good deeds / brought to Utkal the *Jahnvi* (Ganga) /' etc. (ibid., 5).

nearly exclusively on the spiritual, mythological and historical background of Hindus.[86] In the context of the above mentioned fire catastrophe (which was obviously arson), the misery it brought about is described as a 'touchstone invented by God', for whoever is not burnt, will be rendered even purer, to keep up the fire of truth inside. And as Duryodhana, who had set fire to the lacquer house in the *Mahābhārata*, was defeated eventually, the present incendiary will reap the punishment for his deeds, too, and no Brahma, Hari or Mahādev will be able to prevent it.[87] The principles of the teachings of the *Gita* are invoked to instil patience and confidence in the downtrodden, that the pendulum will eventually swing to the other end. As already mentioned, prayers and invocations to rivers and goddesses as Bhadrakhi are interspersed, as is one to Lord Ganesha,[88] but above all it is Lord Jagannātha and the temple of Puri that spread their sheltering umbrella over the children of Orissa. The poem ends with an appeal to all the gods of Utkal at their daily assembly at *Nīlācal*, to keep an eye on Utkal, to let the conch of *svarāj* be blown at the *siṅghdvāra*, the gate to the Puri temple. The rule of the people will then be established by God and blessed by all the saints. Unity, equality and peace will prevail in the world.

Against the background of Gopabandhu's gradual dissociation from the UUC's pre-occupation of establishing an independent province, it is remarkable how firmly he still tightens the cultural bonds between the *Utkalvāsī,* without however inciting them in the least to fight for their regional independence. Instead, he tries to convince them to join their brothers and sisters in the national struggle for independence against the common enemy represented by the exploitative, imperialistic ruling force. This way, the text reflects the wide range of changes in the perceptions and goals the

---

[86] One exception is the 'borderline case' of Emperor Akbar, who is praised for his vision of equality (ibid., 29). Another is a reference to King Herod, whose infanticide and animosity towards Lord Jesus is compared to the wicked Kamsa (ibid., 20).

[87] Ibid., 19.

[88] He prays to the remover of obstacles as he starts a 'new' life now in jail (ibid., 14).

struggle for an independent Oriya identity had undergone from its beginnings in the mid-nineteenth century.

At the political level, a transition from a 'sub-national' movement to a national one can be stated. But as we have seen, the change also refers to a shift of generations, from the parochial and largely apolitical attitude of the UUC to an explicitly political youth movement enthusiastically joining the all India non-cooperation campaign. The transition is also visible in the emergence of a new class consciousness, as the UUC mainly consisted of 'feudatory chiefs, dressed up for the occasion, and government servants holding virtually closed-door meetings',[89] whereas Gopabandhu's initiative was designed to develop into a democratic mass movement. Further, the unshakeable belief in progressive values, law and order and the blessings of British administration so credulously defended by Fakirmohan is largely shattered in view of the still persisting humiliating dependency on an alien government's fickle politics. Not participation or recognition, but only self-rule became the demand of the hour. What was initially hailed as a means to gain enlightenment and liberation, now figured as the epitome of alien oppression. This is perhaps most evident in the 'sacred' field of education, which was earlier considered to be the panacea to cure all evils of society, but slowly came to be recognized as the most intimate agency of domination. In turn, national schools were set up to function as political platforms, and food, shelter and clothing were propagated as being much more of immediate need for the masses.[90] The role of literature, too, developed along similar lines to function as a tool in the process of national awakening. The influence of the anglicized Brahmo-enlightenment of the urban intelligentsia could be seen waning against a deferential reappraisal of the spiritual devotion of the rural population. Finally, the inner-Indian sibling rivalry in the race for a

---

89 Gopabandhu's opinion as expressed in his paper *Satyabādī*, Nov-Dec 1921 (Mohanty 1982, 104).

90 Gopabandhu in a speech to move a resolution towards famine-relief, in the Legislative Council, 1920: 'What would education or sanitation mean to a people, that has no food to eat, no clothes to wear and even hut to live in' (Patra and Devi 1983, 203).

better position within the colonial system, so prominent in Fakirmohan's world view still, was discarded in favour of a united struggle against the system as such. Thus, a long process of emancipation within an established system of power, values and ideas reached a stage where demands for a complete cultural reorientation were formulated, aiming at the reconstruction of a Self, and of a popular memory allegedly lost under the colonial regime.

References

Assmann, J. 1999. *Das kulturelle Gedächtnis. Schrift, Erinnerung und politische Identität in frühen Hochkulturen*, München: Beck.

Bhattacharya, D. and Jagannath Chakravorty. 1976. 'Biographical Literature in Bengali', in G. Sontheimer (ed.), *Biography and Autobiography in Modern South Asian Regional Literatures. South Asian Digest of Regional Writing, Vol.5*, Heidelberg: South Asia Institute, 18-29.

Beames, J. 1870. 'On the Relation of the Uṛiyā Language to the other Modern Aryan Languages', Remarks on the Above by Rajendralal Mitra, in *Proceedings of the Asiatic Society of Bengal*, January-December 1870, Calcutta: C.B. Lewis, Baptist Mission Press, 192-216.

Beames, J. 1984. *Memoirs of a Bengal Civilian*, New Delhi: Manohar Publishers.

Boulton, J.V. 1993. *Phakirmohan Senapati: His Life and Prose Fiction*, Bhubaneshwar: Orissa Sahitya Akademi.

Das, Gopabandhu n. d. ([1]1924). *Bandira Ātmakathā*, Cuttack: Gopabandhu Sahitya Mandir.

Gandhi, M.K. 1982 ([1]1929). *An Autobiography or The Story of My Experiments with Truth*, Harmondsworth: Penguin Books.

Kaviraj, S. 1995. *The Unhappy Consciousness. Bankim Chandra Chattopadhyay and the Formation of Nationalist Discourse in India*, Delhi: Oxford University Press.

Mansinha, M. 1962. *History of Oriya Literature*, New Delhi: Sahitya Akademi.

Mansinha, M. 1976. *Fakirmohan Senapati*, New Delhi: Sahitya Akademi.

Misra, Godavarish. 1996 ([1]1958). *Arddha Śatābdīrā Oṛiśā o tahire mo sthān*, Cuttack: Granthamandir.

Mohanty, G. 1967. *Utkaḷmaṇi*, Cuttack.

Mohanty, G. 1978. *Radhanath Ray*, New Delhi: Sahitya Akademi.

Mohanty, J.M. 1996. *Madhusudan Rao*, New Delhi: Sahitya Akademi.

Mohanty, N. 1982. *Oriya Nationalism: Quest for a United Orissa. 1866-1936*, New Delhi: Manohar Publishers.

Patel, A.K. 1999. 'Collegiate Education in Orissa during the Nineteenth Century', in S. Pradhan (ed.), *Orissan History, Culture and Archaeology*. Reconstructing Indian History and Culture, No. 16, New Delhi: D.K. Publishers, 345-55.

Pati, M. 1994. *Gourishankar Ray*, New Delhi: Sahitya Akademi.

Patra, K.M. and Bandita Devi. 1983. *An Advanced History of Orissa (Modern Period)*, New Delhi: Kalyan Publishers.

Pradhan, S. (ed.). 1999. *Orissan History, Culture and Archaeology*. Reconstructing Indian History and Culture, No. 16, New Delhi: D.K. Publishers.

Sarkar, T. 1999. *Words to Win. The Making of Amar Jiban: A Modern Autobiography*, New Delhi: Kali for Women.

Senapati, Fakirmohan. 1993. *Ātmajīvancarita*, New Delhi: National Book Trust.

Swain, A. 1999. 'British Impact on Orissa in the Nineteenth Century', in S. Pradhan (ed.), *Orissan History, Culture and Archaeology.* Reconstructing Indian History and Culture, No. 16, New Delhi: D.K. Publishers, 299-314.

Two Bachelors of Arts. 1996. ([1]1919) *The Oriya Movement. Being a Demand for a United Orissa*, Bhubaneswar: Pentacle Printers.

15

Tribal Society of Highland Orissa, Highland Burma, and Elsewhere

Georg Pfeffer

In the social anthropology of Africa the concept of the tribe is met with scepticism. Defined substantially, it has failed to be a useful analytical tool. In India the anthropological category is generally confused with the administrative term. While the elite of the discipline ignores the state-defined Scheduled Tribes, provincial authors are not equipped for universal comparison or theory. Similarly Western approaches, like that of our Orissa Research Programme, remain trapped in their own cultural logic, currently the post-modern trend. Within this context, Leach's classic text on highland Burma is introduced as a contrast. His model of the societal whole in flux can be paralleled in highland Orissa where the indigenous people are not small remainders of some earlier stage of humanity but a large, resistant societal complex characterized by its multivalent social structure and exemplifying the Lévi-Straussian 'cold' type.

Tribes

About a quarter of the Orissan population officially belongs to the Scheduled Tribes of India. The structure of this tribal society is the subject of our[1] current research in and on the 'remote area'. Accordingly, the following article intends to position such an endeavour within the world-wide debate on the category of the tribe and within the history of anthropological research in tribal India. A particular text on the political systems of highland Burma may, by

---

[1] I refer to currently seven Berlin anthropologists involved in a subproject of the Orissa Research Programme.

comparison, show the proximity of the two tribal orders, unnoticed so far, just as the demise[2] of the Burmese is contrasted with the ongoing Orissan structure.

Functionalism in Africa

Tribe used to be the key term of the discipline; anthropological literature dealt with tribes. Its usefulness as an analytical tool has, however, been questioned long since, just as its empirical existence is uncertain. 'The tribal groups that still remain around the edges of expanding civilization are the small remainders of this primary state of living',[3] Redfield pointed out more than half a century ago, while at about the same time, *Notes & Queries in Anthropology* defined the tribe in traditional style 'as a politically or socially coherent or autonomous group occupying or claiming a particular territory'.[4]

Following the social change of the 1950s, Gluckman discussed an artificial survival of the tribe, since 'tribalism persists in the rural areas because of Government support'.[5] In the same vein, Edel, writing on East Africa, was 'hard pressed to find a definition for the tribe as such which would fit all the peoples of Uganda'.[6] She could even demonstrate the shallow historical depth of a number of so-called tribes. Similarly, Uchendu pointed out that 'the word "tribe" as applied to many West African societies lacks a precise meaning'[7] and Southall, contemplating on 'the illusion of the tribe',[8] went on to discard the term altogether. Such disillusionment continued over the subsequent decades. For Kuper 'primitive society' was an 'invention' of the early anthropologists,[9]

---

[2] Leach 1954, viii.

[3] Redfield 1947, 300.

[4] Royal Anthropological Institute 1951, 66.

[5] Gluckman 1960, 55 and 68.

[6] Edel 1965, 367.

[7] Uchendu 1970, 56.

[8] Southall 1970, 28.

[9] Kuper 1988.

and Ranger, writing on South Africa, points to the negative designs of 'Indirect Rule ethnography' which 'privileged the 'tribe' and 'tribal religion'.[10]

Thus, in an initial retrospect the tendency is clear. The tribe, i.e. the unit of research among anthropologists of the first generations in the functionalist school, became a discarded category when the African colonies gained independence in the 1960s and political correctness disallowed the cognisance of non-modern structures. While the Middle-Eastern tribes continue to flourish in numerous academic disciplines, the substantial entity named *tribe* in Africa south of the Sahara is now no more, since its autonomy and homogeneity – if they ever existed – are known to have vanished.

Evolutionist Formations

In a seminal presentation of 1966, Fried[11] dismissed the various functionalist notions of the tribe as well as those of his friends and fellow evolutionists Sahlins[12] and Service[13] in no uncertain terms: 'I do not believe that there is a theoretical need for a tribal stage in the evolution of political organization. Such a stage reveals nothing.'[14] Even till today Fried's followers[15] conceive the 'tribal zone' as secondary, or as an historical outcome of state expansion.

Evolutionist discussions on the tribe had, of course, commenced with Morgan's work in North America. This author had pointed out that 'each tribe was individualized by name, by a separate dialect, by a supreme government, and by the possession of a territory which it defended as its own'.[16] In contrast to the nation, Morgan's tribe arises under 'gentile institutions, being composed of several gentes, developed from two or more, all the members of

---

[10] Ranger 1993, 69.

[11] Fried 1966, 527-40.

[12] Sahlins 1961, 322-45.

[13] Service 1962.

[14] Fried 1966, 539.

[15] Cf. for example Ferguson and Whitehead 1992.

[16] Morgan 1878.

which are intermingled by marriage'.[17] In modern terminology, we would speak of a multivalent structure combining the politico-economic, the religious, as well as the kinship system. Morgan's heirs have retained and transformed this idea. Striking back against Fried, Sahlins, however, departs from the realm of substances since he is defining organizational principles: 'The tribal structure is generalized; in this lies its primitivity. It lacks an independent economic sector or a separate religious organization, let alone a special political mechanism.'[18]

The unified kin-based structure of the tribe goes together with the tribal level of integration within a 'general evolution'[19] of forms. The latter should not be confused with historical sequences. In contrast to band society, the bigger size of the tribe implies a relatively complicated organizational structure. Such a size may or may not[20] have been the result of the domestication of plants and animals since the 'Neolithic revolution'.[21] The generalized structure, in any case, implies the absence of the security of peace provided by the state, just as it implies generalized peace-keeping efforts. Since today states nominally cover the entire globe, Sahlins' tribal level of integration can no longer be observed in the formal sense; but then the monopoly of state power is a relative matter[22] in many countries such as India. Innumerable regions are in fact controlled by powers unaccounted for by the state. Empirical research will be unable to bypass these powers.

The design of the tribal formation is a model of concentric generalized sectors of relative kinship and relative loyalty ranging from the household at the core to the tribe at the periphery beyond which commonalties disappear; 'this sectoral plan is a moral plan of

---

[17] Ibid., 103.

[18] Sahlins 1968, 15

[19] Sahlins and Service 1960, 12-44

[20] Sahlins 1968, 3.

[21] Cf. Childe 1951.

[22] The situation in Afghanistan is significant, since tribal Amirs (later self-styled 'kings') and presidents failed to establish state power beyond the immediate access of their troops in most of the eighteenth, nineteenth and twentieth centuries.

the tribal universe....The concentric social fields are so many steps of diminishing oneness, thus so many moral distinctions in "the way it's done".'[23] Other authors, not usually counted among the evolutionists, are similarly aware of these differences and see '*our own modern culture and society as one particular form of humanity*'.[24] The systems of governing ideas, not certain substantial criteria, are relevant for this sociological classification of Dumont. He mentions 'non-modern societies'[25] in this context, but does not compare them with 'traditional' ones, just as he ignores the empirical Scheduled Tribes of India.

The Context: Tribal Research in Orissa

Global

India was the most important British colony and people classed as 'forest tribes' confronted and astounded the British conquerors since the middle of the eighteenth century. But, until independence, all of the founders of British social anthropology have avoided India.[26] Then 'caste' became the standard subject, whereas 'tribe' continued to be ignored. Certain conjectures may lead us to the reasons for this omission. They point to the Census of India.

The ethnographic results of this decennial administrative stock-taking by the colonial power were presented in numerous volumes on the 'tribes and castes' of the subcontinent[27] compiled by administrative all-rounders. Nobody, not even the brightest members of the new anthropological discipline in Britain, could ever hope to obtain the amount of local knowledge at the command of these Anglo-Indian amateur ethnographers, born and stationed in a district, conversant in the local languages, and eager to overcome

---

[23] Sahlins 1968, 19.

[24] Dumont 1986, 205-6. Emphasis in original.

[25] Ibid., 215.

[26] Rivers 1906 seems to be the only exception.

[27] The climax was perhaps Risley 1915.

the boredom of the civil lines. Perhaps these handicaps prompted professionals to avoid India and instead turn to Africa or Oceania.

After Independence caste and peasantry were the subject of ambitious and often enlightening anthropological debates. Most notably M.N. Srinivas and his students represented the particular brand of Indian sociology, just as the students of D.N. Majumdar[28] belonged to this elite. To divide the post-colonial anthropological discourse by the passports of the leading figures would be a mistake, however. The 'sociology of India' was a global affair. The proponents, often involved in theoretical controversies, moved in the same space, i.e. Delhi, Paris and the major Anglo-Saxon universities, while debating hierarchy and stratification, transaction and meaning, or the Asiatic Mode of Production.

Tribes were left out.[29] Leafing through the volumes of *Contributions to Indian Sociology* (Old and New Series) since 1957, i.e. the platform of the anthropological elite, only a handful of articles are concerned with tribal issues, touching 'development', 'environmentalism' and the like. Keeping in view that at least one hundred million[30] people belong to the tribal society in middle India alone, this lacuna points to a social fact. Westerners, Delhiites, or the outstanding 'Green Card Holders' of the discipline, in spite of their impressive anthropological knowledge and intellectual versatility, seemed to lack access to tribal India. The 'primitives' did not qualify for their sociology, or the very existence of the tribal category was ignored. The elite of the profession was unable or unwilling to approach themes and places denounced as

---

[28] The focal ancestor of this lineage, however, was the author of *The Affairs of the Tribe* 1950

[29] One of the internationally outstanding Indian colleagues has only recently displayed his excellent knowledge of administrative issues as well as his ignorance of the tribal social structure in the following article: Brteille 1998, 187-91.

[30] In 1991 the Census of India counted 67, 758, 388 people or 8.08 per cent of the total Indian population as belonging to the administrative category Scheduled Tribe (Tribal Studies Committee 1999, 5). Inclusion or exclusion had been the result of arbitrary administrative acts. The indigenous classification does not divorce the Scheduled Castes and Other Backward Classes of the hills, numbering at least twice as many individuals.

'obscurantist' not so long ago.[31] Appadurai's 'significance of *place*[32] in the construction of anthropological theory' is evident and so is his point against the 'arbitrary hegemony of one region or regions and civilizations in the making of anthropological theory',[33] even though he may not have thought of inner-Indian distances in his context.

Local

India trains more anthropologists than any other country in the world. Any number of them have published on tribes, but their work is unavailable on the global market. Some of these contributions find few readers in spite of their high quality,[34] others, such as Jha's *Introduction to Indian Anthropology* (1995), are best-sellers. Candidates appearing in the annual examinations for the Indian administrative services need them, since anthropology is a compulsory paper, carrying 500 marks, for those who will later call the shots in the districts and ministries. These examinations lean upon Census ethnography of the 1930s, when racial and other explanations of the more modest type flourished. They keep alive the colonial myths. For example, the 'Tribal Studies Committee'[35] of the highest Indian research institution, the Indian Council of Social Science Research, in 1999 proclaims that the 'dominant racial type among the STs … is proto-australoid' and adds many comparable findings.[36]

Provincial anthropologists of India – not the internationalist elite in Delhi – continue as specialists of tribal society in the pre-independence style. Some have adopted more sophisticated methods

---

[31] Since the rise of the Hindu nationalist forces the standard attributes of the so-called progressives have become less conspicuous.

[32] Emphasis in original.

[33] Appadurai 1986, 356 and 361.

[34] For example Danda1991.

[35] Tribal Studies Committee 1999, 5.

[36] Though no source is mentioned, these considerations must be taken from Guha 1944, 10-1. A Census Commissioner in the 1920s, he had presented the climax of Anglo-Indian racist theories.

of quantitative social research and some are involved in welfare work. I have seen their efforts when it came to fighting tribal alcoholism and providing forest homes with asbestos roofs. As is the case with the distributors of global 'development aid', their wealth of professed goodwill is usually matched by their poverty in cultural understanding.

Until the mid-1950s, a small number of humanitarian amateur ethnographers[37] had been responsible for a large number of tribal monographs. Today the same total is published by numerous authors. From these predecessors, the post-colonial specialists have retained the value of descriptive exactness. Thus in a very short article on 'bond-friendship',[38] for example, an author is eager to enlist the names of each of the twelve villages he had visited as well as those of the various descent groups. Though the value-ideas responsible for 'bond-friendship' are highly indicative of the tribal cultural logic as such, they remain untouched while other authors, if at all, refer to the subject in passing only, stressing issues of 'backwardness' instead.

Specialists of other disciplines are similarly unaware of the tribal heritage. When, for example, in 1999 I circulated an article on certain significant issues of Bondo ideology,[39] I was not understood, and colleagues thought I had landed a most inappropriate joke.

The Current Project

Nobody will be surprised if research proposals of the late 1990s are formulated in the post-modern fashion emphasizing the transaction of meaning, or action as such. Situations are attended to. Then actors come out with their subjective and contradictory convictions and involve themselves in multifarious negotiations, to be studied

[37] S.C. Roy, V. Elwin, and Chr. von Fürer-Haimendorf supplied much of tribal ethnography.

[38] Mohanty 1973/4, 137-40.

[39] Bondo tradition demands that women shave their skulls, wear nothing but a skirt about 25 cm long, and marry violent men who are their juniors by about five years. Cf. Pfeffer 1997, 183-208.

by equally subjective ethnographers. The latter may select or discard situations, as long as they present their choice in attractive prose. Culture is supposed to be written by anthropologists[40] and made or unmade by conflicting activities, 'agency'[41] being the direct negation of Durkheimian sociology.[42] Adversaries of the founding father of social sciences had similarly argued that categories were man-made and that 'the individual is the artisan of this construction'.[43]

Our[44] current Orissa Research Programme is designed in this manner. We proclaim to study smaller, local and peripheral units such as tribal societies. Our basic research proposal is demanding a re-examination of the latter's' epistemological status. It questions whether tribes are really closed, internally and externally demarcated units with exclusive and permanent membership defined by birth or initiation. It rather envisages overlapping, interpenetrating, and competing social constructs liable to change in the course of actors' switching codes from one situation to the next. Thus the proposal is in doubt about the utility of concepts like *the* Kond[45] tribals, or *the* Paik,[46] or *the* Oriya.[47] Porous boundaries between these categories are presupposed.[48]

---

[40] Cf. Clifford and Marcus 1986.

[41] Cf. Archer 1996.

[42] To my knowledge, the first important post-modern critique of Durkheimian anthropology was published by Rosaldo 1980, 13/4.

[43] Durkheim 1915, 13.

[44] Numerous specialists of the region of several universities have joined in the interdisciplinary research programme on 'Contested Centres' in Orissa.

[45] On the Schedules of the Orissa Government, the Kondh or Kond are the major Scheduled Tribe in the province, numbering about one million people.

[46] *Paik* is a title, members of all non-Brahmin castes – except *Scheduled Castes* – liked to adopt when they had migrated into the forested hills in the service of some petty king.

[47] The term 'Oriya' may be applied to all residents of Orissa, or to the indigenous in contrast to immigrants (and their descendants) of the province, or to immigrants in the hills in contrast to the indigenous of the tribal areas.

[48] This paragraph is an English summary of our 'Basic Research Proposal' translated by myself.

The current research in tribal Orissa, in other words, is supposed to be directed by the situationalism and subjectivism of the post-modern trend. Basically variable and fairly constant supra-individual patterns of meaning, endowed with an obligatory character, are viewed with suspicion. Durkheim's social fact is out.[49] Any analytical frame of reference comprising social categories is flatly rejected. Meaning is supposed to be discovered in aspects of action and negotiation. In fact, a man may or may not be making culture when selling a cabbage, standing on his head, or running off with his neighbour's wife. There being no dearth of such situations, it is the ethnographer's privilege to ennoble the performance for further scholarly attention or to forget it. S/he is not bound by a specific scope of social anthropology.

The issue is, of course, not entirely new. Firth[50] opposed the world of action, an irregular but empirical 'social organization', with the regular but non-empirical relational model or 'social structure'. Geertz has called the events, the momentary operations, 'the unique actualization of a general phenomenon, a contingent realization of the cultural pattern'.[51] But whereas the subjectivism and situationalism of the current trend devalue any overall cultural framework, past fashions – be they mentalist or materialist – have proposed the opposite, i.e. a universal operational mode of the human mind or of the political economy. Former trends used to present 'neat little box-like arrangements of non-contradictory categories and unproblematic behaviours',[52] but more recently, the preference is 'to sediment structural relations out of pragmatic actions, rather than determining the actions *a priori* from the relations'.[53] The 'difference between the prescriptive and performative structures parallels the Lévi-Straussian contrast of

---

[49] Cf. Layton 1997, 185.

[50] Firth 1951.

[51] Geertz 1961,153-4.

[52] Sahlins 1985, 27.

[53] Ibid., 9.

mechanical and statistical models',[54] and the priority of the event indicates the professional fashion for some years, even though the tide – as always – is likely to turn.

The Text: Leach on Highland Burma

Regarding the epistemological status of the tribe, a well-known text, addressing the relationship between cultural model and ambitions in action, has discarded the essentialist category tribe long ago. Leach's classic on *Political Systems of Highland Burma* of 1954 may also have initiated the above mentioned functionalist critique. Being a milestone in anthropological theory, most beginners must have been confronted with it, but I am unaware of any reference to it in publications on India.[55] The reasons for this omission have been pointed out above: the international elite of Indianists is unconcerned with tribal society and provincial specialists avoid either comparison or theory.

Leach had dealt with the social structure of people in the hinterland of Burma. Others used to call them tribal in contrast to the dominant peasant population of the plains. His analytical procedure was later summarized by his student Kuper as follows: 'the anthropologist builds up a model.... But this is an idealization of limited value. To get back to the historical reality one must look at the interplay of personal interests.'[56] Thus, the early Leach retained the individualism of his teacher Malinowski, but added a model of the whole as the arena for individual strategies. As if anticipating the post-modern critique, he made no bones about the fact that the model was of his own making.

The tribal whole of the highland was certainly not fitting the substantialist definition of the *Notes & Queries* type (see above). A number of different languages were common among those mountain people Leach called Kachin, so he initially dispatched the linguistic

---

[54] Ibid., xi.

[55] For political reasons, the Indian states bordering the Burmese frontier have been out of bounds for foreign anthropologists for a long time.

[56] Kuper 1983, 156.

fallacy once and for all. In the same vein he wrote: 'the concept "tribe" is of quite negative utility from the viewpoint of social analysis'.[57]

The Kachin Hills were inhabited by a large number of different but interacting tribal communities and, according to Leach, the whole set, not a substantial part, had to be taken into account, if the social system was to be understood. It could then be represented as an equilibrium model, but the latter would contain contradictory elements causing instability. Leach insisted that this weakness could become fully intelligible by the exposition of 'polar types'.[58] Structural change was conceived as 'shifts in the focus of political power within a given system'.[59] For the people themselves, their ritual models contained a symbolic ambiguity that permitted the shifts. 'The structural model of the anthropologist and the rituals of the people are therefore both idealized abstractions, attempts to pose an as if fictional but comprehensible order upon the flux of social life.'[60] For Leach such a 'persistent structured set' always serves the people 'to interpret … the empirical social phenomena'.[61] The three Kachin categories of political order emphasized either an egalitarian kinship model (*gumlao*) or petty autocratic kingship favoured by the Shan neighbours of the Kachin. The intermediary unstable form was called *gumsa*. These were points of reference for observers, while reality knew many variations and shifts in between.

Political activity, responsible for such shifts and contradictions, related to the rules of kinship and marriage. The local lines, assigned patrilineally, were ranked according to the law of ultimogeniture and according to the status of 'givers' and 'takers' of brides, the latter always being inferior to the former. 'As the process of lineage fission proceeds there comes a point at which a choice has to be made between the primacy of the principle of rank

---

[57] Leach 1954, 45 and xv.

[58] Ibid., 9

[59] Ibid.

[60] Kuper 1983, 157.

[61] Leach 1954, xiii.

or the principle of kinship.'[62] The weakness of the *gumsa* system is that the successful chief is tempted to repudiate links of kinship with his followers and to treat them as if they were bond slaves (*mayam*). 'It is this situation which, from the *gumlao* point of view, is held to justify revolt.'[63] The *gumlao* stage, on the other hand, is endangered by the fission of the local lineages, 'elder brothers' moving away, or by the growing tendency of 'givers' of brides to exploit their status and quietly reintroduce the *gumsa* pattern, because these 'givers' have the right to demand ritual donations,[64] economic services and political loyalty.

In conclusion the Kachin may be conceived as a vast assemblage of interacting local groups – among them artisans – who produce by shifting and terrace cultivation, who speak numerous languages and who follow petty kings, or senior kinsmen, unless they revolt against them in favour of fraternal equality. Individuals, aspiring or condemning chiefly status, switch codes and manipulate situations according to their subjective interests; but they do so within a systematic cultural frame of reference. This frame is designed by Leach according to the indigenous model of verbal categories. The author is not interested in action as such but rather in manipulations allowed by the system. Meaning is transacted and negotiated through performances and according to subjective criteria. Codes are being switched from one situation to the next, but situationalism and subjectivism are valid within a certain cultural logic only. The latter may contain internal contradictions leading to its final break-up, but they too exist beyond the particular action.

[62] Leach 1954, 203

[63] Ibid.

[64] Thighs of sacrificial animals.

Tribal Orissa Compared

The society of highland Orissa, by comparison, offers many similarities to that of the Leach text, particularly with regard to cultivation. It is also quite different, however. Any thought of economic or ecological determinism will thus be out of place.
Initially, it seems, certain crucial terminological issues must be untangled: tribe is a standard bureaucratic category in India. A Scheduled Tribe or ST is qualified as such by the decision of the Indian president alone according to Article 342 and the Fifth Schedule of the constitution.[65] By the same nondescript criteria the entire rest of the indigenous population of western Orissa is classed into Scheduled Castes (SC), usually petty hawkers and artisans, as well as Other Backward Classes (OBC). The latter may be ritually superior to the ST, the former inferior, but both SC and OBC share a common culture with the ST as opposed to the caste culture of the plains.[66] If, in the following, I use the expression 'tribal society', I refer to the entire indigenous population of highland Orissa, irrespective of these administrative pigeon-holes, as opposed to those representatives of caste society who have immigrated from the plains within the last 200 years, or those who inhabit most of India. My use of the term 'tribe' will not denote any substantial unit, but a category of reference alone. In the same manner an individual may refer to her or his tribe as 'Sora' without implying that about half a million Sora have ever united for any sort of joint endeavour. In fact 'the burden of culture is carried in small, local, autonomous groups while higher levels of organization develop little coherence, poor definition, and minimum function'.[67]

Authors have never, so far, pointed out the highly artificial character of the bureaucratic classification. On the contrary, debates on the tribes of the constitutional schedules and those on the

---

[65] Tribal Studies Committee 1999, 5.

[66] In highland Orissa the type of hierarchical culture differs from the Hindu hierarchy of the plains in many ways, e.g. by the lack of specialization and the absence of a royal or a Brahmin category.

[67] Sahlins 1968, 20.

empirical order of tribal society are regularly confused. The results of such an indifference are evident. Legal terminology cuts through tribal society in an arbitrary manner with the effect that many ST find themselves as a minority in their own homeland. The sheer size of tribal society, a weighty political issue, can also be minimized in official statistics referring to – apparently – hundreds of different little societies.

The tribal order of Orissa – like that of Burma – is not egalitarian. Landless hawkers and artisans always and everywhere offer services to landholders of superior status, even if the latter are as poor as the former. Among the landholders, some have specialized callings as cattle-keepers, kitchen-gardeners and potters; or they have been known as the local militia of the former petty kings. No two groups are of the same status; no single group contains an egalitarian internal order. Hierarchy is all-pervasive. All segments of tribal society – like those of Burma – share an ideological frame of reference, an indigenous model, pointing to an order of descent-groups and the give and take of brides. If we follow Leach, observed performance is to be seen in the light of this framework of the whole. A man may sell a cabbage, stand on his head, or run away with his neighbour's wife, but he will do so by virtue of his belonging to a particular global society.

The transformation of the economy in Orissa has been the cause of many social changes over the last decades. The north-western districts of Sundargarh and Sambalpur[68] have been covered with huge hydro-electric projects and giant industries of steel, cement, aluminium and paper, or those which are big, ugly and polluting, so that the forest has given way and mass immigration has changed the demographic ratio at the cost of the indigenous people. The Kharia or Oraon industrial workers have, however, retained their totemic clans, their marriage rules, their respective dances, and their techniques of communicating with the deceased. Though, along with the forest, they may have been forced to abandon their sacred groves, they have not become urban individuals simply guided by an all-Indian political economy.

---

[68] All district names refer to the pre-1995 administrative boundaries.

Outside of these industrial districts, conversions to Christianity have made very little impact in tribal Orissa, if we leave aside two or three blocks[69] of the Phulbani and Ganjam districts. In the course of development work, however, roads have been cut through the hills, introducing trucks to ferry the timber. These developments have often brought in their wake incidents of the truck drivers molesting the local women, as well as a plethora of petty traders and scribes to advertize the roadside comforts and the civilizational achievements of the culture of the plains.

In spite of these changes, anthropologists could still retain Leach's method and construct a model of a unified society of highland Orissa, following the indigenous fluctuating model and indicating the leeway for ambition in action. Such a model would take into account the multitude of tribal and provincial languages, the presence or absence of youth dormitories, megaliths and sacred groves, of spectacular feasts of merit and of the annual spring hunt even if in many regions, after deforestation, game has been reduced to rats and squirrels. So far, anthropologists have failed to construct such a model.

Beyond the north-western industrial zone, tribal society of Orissa covers a vast area by adjoining clusters of some 80-100 villages each. The latter are interlinked by ritual and affinal ties without clear-cut geographical or cultural boundaries. Each patch of this kind may contain a single tribe as a whole, e.g. the Didaye, or people who give themselves a particular name – e.g. Kuttia Kondh – without bothering about the fact that some strangers in a cluster further on give themselves the same name – e.g. Kuttia Kondh. The northern districts of Mayurbhanj and Keonjhar and the southern districts of Phulbani, Kalahandi, Ganjam and Koraput contain such an endless patchwork of village-clusters wherever the plains give way to the hills.

In many tribes most inhabitants of a village belong to a single[70] dominant exogamous patrilineal descent category,

---

[69] A block is a small administrative unit below the level of the subdivision.

[70] Among the Koya I found up to four of these categories represented in a single – large – village. In this case the number is likely to be of structural significance –

designated in the totemic style. A limited number of such clans, frequently two, four, eight, nine, or twelve, offer an indigenous formal framework for each tribe[71] and, not infrequently, some of these widespread exogamous unilineal descent categories are linked by fraternal concepts, prohibiting mutual intermarriage. All are interrelated – or enriched with meaningful significance – by the particular tribal myth. These myths show marked 'family resemblances'[72] in all tribes. Mythical ranking of clans is ubiquitous. In contrast to the Kachin ultimogeniture, relative seniority is permanently privileged. The Santhal at the northern corner and the Koya at the southern tip of Orissa share such an hierarchical idea of clan-seniority, as well as totemic titles such as 'tortoise' and elaborate motives of their myths. Other tribes within a sub-cultural complex[73] may even share *all* clan designations. In such cases members of different tribes may meet as members of the same clan in an 'Australian' style.

Clanship of central India is unique. Ethnographers, going by the textbook criteria of patriliny, have produced partial or problematic results on account of the particular combinations and interpenetrations the concept has been exposed to in the region. For whereas each village is usually dominated by members of a single exogamous totemic category, it furthermore unites at least two – if not four – 'local lines'[74] also recruited by patrilineal descent. All landholders of a village are assigned to any of the local lines named according to either sacred or secular leadership. The sacred is the senior of the two. Within a single tribe, all these local lines are designated by the same set of names, but it should be remembered that a local line named 'A' may entertain affinal ties to another local

---

and not the result of recent migrations – but we will have to wait for an ethnography of these people, numbering more than 500, 000 in Orissa alone.

71 As defined above, a tribe may be of the ST, SC or OBC administrative category.

72 The concept is taken from Wittgenstein 1958, 31.

73 As such one could classify from north to south: Bhumia/Santhal; Bhuiyan/ Juang; Kharia/Munda/Oraon; Kondh; Sora; Koraput (i.e. some twenty different tribes) and Gondide.

74 This term is adopted from Leach 1961, 57.

line named 'A', as long as the latter is of a different clan and settled in another village. Thus, the limited number of totemic descent categories (clans) is embodied at the village level by two or four local lines practically executing ties of diachronic affinity and intra- or inter-village agnatic obligations. Within a particular region the names applied to these local lines, e.g. *pahan* and *munda* in the north-west, are omnipresent. By this wide proliferation of very few designations, ethnographers could be trapped and confuse their character as local groups with exogamous categories, or the units of reference – not of action – represented by the clans.

In contrast to the 'African' model[75] of unilineal descent, the middle Indian one operates without pedigrees or segmentation. At the highest organizational level, a tribe is bound by a permanent order of relative seniority to another – a fraternal – tribe, just as – at the next lower level – its exogamous clans or fraternal clan-clusters are interrelated by marriage ties, and at yet a further level down its local lines of a village are mutually opposed by the same status concept of seniority. Many tribes, e.g. Kharia or Gadaba, also happen to be bifurcated at the highest level into a senior and a junior half, while others, e.g. the Bhuiyan of Keonjhar, as such act as seniors in opposition to their particular junior 'siblings' (e.g. the Juang) in the usual style. Similarly some clans and local lines may again be subdivided into senior and junior units.

Outsiders face problems when conceiving the system as a whole, because the three levels – tribe, clan, and local line – do not imply inclusive units. Ignoring the Western taxonomic bent of dividing classes separately into exclusive subclasses, the middle Indian system may assign a certain clan as a sub-unit to numerous tribes, just as any name of a local line reappears within all clans of the tribe, or even a number of tribes. Each one of the three structural levels juxtaposes its classes *irrespective of* the oppositions at the other two levels. For this reason the system can never collapse. Tribal society, in spite of all onslaughts, is able to survive. If the population of one locality or region is displaced or destroyed by a catastrophe, if different tribes or tribal halves allow intermarriage, if

---

[75] The 'African' model has been described at length in Evans-Pritchard 1940.

mutually fraternal clans become mutually affinal ones and vice versa, or if, as observed, the Parenga tribe practically merges with the Gadaba tribe, these events are in no way contradictory or detrimental to the relational pattern of the system as a whole.

The tribal order of highland Orissa comes close to the ideal type of a 'cold' society, because the 'internal environment borders on the zero of historical temperature'.[76] This is the conceptual difference to the 'hot' caste society of the plains. But then the concept of the Parisian master could be modified. The Orissan tribal society is not 'distinguished by the limited number of their people'.[77] On the contrary the very size of the middle Indian tribal population, like that of highland Burma, has been a major factor at work for the preservation of next to 'zero of historical temperature'. Tribal society is a small-*scale* order organized by *face-to-face* relationships. It lasted in Orissa, because – in a marked contrast to the situation in Siberia or America – it was *not* a small island in an ocean of change and energy.

While the ideas of patrilineal descent in Burma and Orissa are not entirely dissimilar, the marriage-rules make all the difference. It should be self-understood, however, that the people of both highlands – like those of most non-Western cultures – view affinal obligations as a matter of individual agency as well as the major value of the whole. Individual love marriages are widespread within the tribal network of preferential affinal ties maintained by the local line. Affinity includes religious, political, economic and even military aspects. Along with the omnipresent ritual feasts of merit,[78] marriage links are responsible for the 'external policy' of a village within the above mentioned cluster. In many cases I have found the rule of highland New Guinea, i.e. the saying 'we marry the people we fight".[79] For the Kachin, the bride-givers,[80] when facing the

---

[76] Lrvi-Strauss 1973, 29.

[77] Ibid.

[78] Cf. Pfeffer 2001.

[79] Cf. Meggitt 1977, 42.

[80] The jargon term 'wife-givers' is avoided due to the derogatory meaning it would carry in India.

bride-takers, are privileged in many domains. In highland Orissa, too, such hypogamous tendencies are evident.[81] The difference lies in the preferential 'oscillation' of brides. Whereas the Kachin are bound by the rules of asymmetric exchange, so that givers can never become takers, the symmetry of the middle Indian model makes those privileged as givers on one occasion appear in the complementary role on the next. Thus, honours can be distributed unequally on a single wedding, but the omnipresent existence of permanent affinal partners, mutually giving and taking brides, disallows any structural inequality of the Kachin type. A local line has one or more permanent *somodhi* (lit.: 'exchange partners') in other villages, who will give and take the young women of and for its members. The politico-economic power of a Kachin chief, amassed through his clever manipulations as a bride-giver, is thus out of reach for a Munda, Sora, or Koya of Orissa. From the egocentric perspective each local line views the own tribal cluster as the overall opposition of agnates and affines and never as takers, agnates and givers in the Kachin style. While Kachin takers tend to revolt and Kachin givers tend to exploit their privileges, no such manipulations are on the cards for Orissan tribesmen. The Burmese model is one of constant modifications. As such it was unlikely to survive the impact of outside forces, i.e. globally organized drug-dealers or interventions from India and China. Highland Orissa has witnessed no such problems and remains unchanged.

Can we speak of tribal anarchy or tribal states in pre-colonial times? Such juxtaposition appears to be rather insignificant. Like the Bhuiyan and Juang of Keonjhar[82] tribal landholders everywhere used to offer token gifts to the petty monarch of some jungle fort on a ritual occasion. The monarchs would settle immigrant Brahmins near their courts and non-tribal officials further away, but this became easy only with the spread of the *pax britannica* since the mid-nineteenth century. The petty administrators would in turn offer land to non-local tribesmen in lieu of the sporadic extraction of levies from local tribes. Such a system, however, would collapse

[81] In contrast to the values of hypergamy in the plains.

[82] Cf. McDougal 1963, 7.

frequently. Those claiming to represent the petty kingdom were rarely in a position to enforce the claim, and those formally representing subjects did not depend upon the benefits of the state. Tribal life, i.e. conflict and peace, provisioning and worship, can be maintained irrespective of governmental affairs.[83] Frequently, the Rājā was said to be of 'tribal origin',[84] but any proof of this romantic hypothesis has always been lacking, just as so-called 'hill chiefs'[85] had immigrated from the plains decades or centuries earlier.

Tribal values do not favour the man who exposes himself as a leader of sorts. Any kind of boasting is illegitimate, as is the hoarding of goods or the introduction of outsider-ruffians. Verbal orders among tribesmen are not just unheeded, they are simply unheard of. Where feuds are carried out to this day, as among certain Kondh,[86] they are not organized campaigns for submission. Those who would fight would marry one another in the preferred symmetric fashion.

Outlook

If the issue of tribal identity is to be studied, one could, of course, resort to Merton's classic 'theory of reference groups'[87] which, half a century ago, was supposed to be applicable in Manhattan, Manipur, or anywhere else on the globe. We could then study how a man would call himself an 'Oriya', a 'peasant', a 'Hindu', a 'tribal', a 'local', an 'elder' or a 'tiger', switching the code according to the situation at hand, just as he would frequently disclose himself as 'Kuttia' or a certain type of Kondh. The contingency, however, would have its limits. The same man would never see himself as a 'Bengali', an 'agricultural labourer', a 'Muslim', a 'Paik', a

83 Today misery and starvation may be observed only in those tribal villages where development agencies have been operating.

84 Cf., for example, Roy 1912, 75-82.

85 Cf. Bailey 1957, 178f.

86 Cf. Nayak 1989.

87 Merton 1957, 279-440.

'Baniya', a 'Cuttacki', a 'priest', or a 'tortoise' and he would not think of calling himself a 'Dangria', or another type of Kondh.

Such an observation of universal code-switching would help little in the efforts to conceive the epistemological status of the tribe. The Orissan tribal culture, however, offers more specific solutions. Highlanders, like the natives of the American Prairie and many others, have avoided the standard Western taxonomy and resorted to 'polythetic classification'.[88] Thus, a man may belong to the tiger clan at the subordinate level and to the Kondh *or* the Rona tribe at the superordinate one. A Kuttia may belong to the local *majhi* line at the inferior level of local lines and yet be a part of *either* the *saraka* or the *gundsika* clan. Furthermore, the large tribe of the Santhal has much in common, e.g. the foundation myth, with the large tribe of the Munda and yet the mythical charter of the latter places them somewhat closer to the Kharia and Oraon. As tribal people, all would oppose the *diku*[89] from the plains, being aware of the basic differences in the order of values, but then they would also conceive relative differences of status between each other. The 'senior' Kisan would be too proud to marry the 'junior' Oraon, the other half of the Khurukh tribe. Everybody may join in the tribal dance, but not everybody is prescribed to play the tribal music.

The lesson from Leach is to avoid the substantialism of the *Notes & Queries* type of definition. Tribes of Orissa are frequently *not* 'politically or socially coherent' just as they are *not* always occupying or claiming a particular territory. Some may have done so in the past, but some may have intermingled within various ethnic patchworks over millennia, just as they have forever been exposed to the armies of the plains. 'People without history'[90] will not be found among them. Contrary to European traditions, past Hindu conquerors never had a policy to convert or exterminate the indigenous tribes.

---

[88] Cf. Needham 1975, 349-69

[89] A derogatory term for immigrants.

[90] Cf. Wolf 1982.

The state of flux is limited, however. Leach adopts a situationalist stance only when he studies groups exploiting the leeway of the system. Thus, in Orissa ethnographers might observe how a Kondh astrologer and healer – taking advantage of the ferocious reputation of his tribe – is called by neighbouring Joria. A modern Gadaba may kill his father to inherit the recently privatized landholding[91] and – by doing so – correspond to the traditional antagonism of adjacent generations. Situations or subjectivities of this kind are tuned to culture or the general structure of ideas. The tribal model, combining given seniority and given affinity, is *not* created or negotiated by certain performances, just as it is *not* the result of some intended action. 'People organize their projects and give significance to their objects from the existing understandings of their cultural order'.[92] This implies, of course, that contingent circumstances of action need not conform to the significance assigned to them. As a result 'the cultural order is an historical object'.[93]

Only years of fieldwork may disclose an intricate model of the sort suggested by Leach. In a 'cold' society, such an outline must conceive the general rules and meanings as articulated within the framework of kinship and affinity. Kinship morality is not a situational affair, not the arbitrary idea of our own society. Tribes are not substantially demarcated units. Villages and households, their most substantial representatives, will be lacking a particular political, economic, or religious domain. Their multivalent order appears to be natural – immune to the teachings of missionaries, the interventions of marauding mercenaries, or the efforts of progressive administrators. Whether in Burma or Orissa, each 'natural' system displays basic differences when compared to another. Anthropology, as long as it has not become 'diluted',[94]

---

[91] Several cases of patricide were observed among the Gadaba and hushed up by the respective village communities

[92] Sahlins 1985, vii

[93] Ibid.

[94] Lṛvi-Strauss 1973, 26.

compares these intricate differences and commonalties to understand *anthropos*.

Like Redfield fifty years ago, but for no good reason at all, the present trend tends to conceive tribal societies as small remainders of some primary state of living, minute pockets in their terminal condition. The misconception, avoided by Leach, is that small-*scale* societies are numerically insignificant and historically obsolete. Recent attempts to grasp the vast variety of their internal cultural rationalities and their structural transformations are few and meagre. The *others* are not supposed to exist any more, and their food had always been indigestible. Political correctness disallows 'exoticism' of sorts and advocates the cultural bear's hug.

References

Appadurai, Arjun. 1986. 'Theory in Anthropology: Centre and Periphery', in *Comparative Studies in Society and History* 28, 356-61.

Archer, Margaret S. 1996. *Culture and Agency,* Cambridge: Cambridge University Press.

Bailey, F.G. 1957. *Caste and the Economic Frontier,* Manchester, Manchester University Press.

Béteille, André. 1998. 'The Idea of Indigenous People', in *Current Anthropology* 39 (2), 187-91.

Boas, Franz. 1914. *Rasse und Kultur,* Leipzig: Veith & Co.

Childe, V. Gordon. 1951. *Social Evolution,* London: Watts.

Clifford, James and George E. Marcus (eds.). 1986. *Writing Culture: The Poetics and Politics of Ethnography,* Berkeley: The University of California Press.

Danda, Ajit K. 1991. *Ethnicity in India: Tribal Studies of India Series T 144,* New Delhi: Inter-India Publications.

Dumont, Louis. 1986. *Essays on Individualism,* Chicago: The University of Chicago Press.

Durkheim, Emile. 1915. *The Elementary Forms of Religious Life,* London: Allen & Unwin.

Edel, May M. 1965. 'African Tribalism', in *Political Science Quarterly* 80/3, 357-72.

Evans-Pritchard, E.E. 1940. *The Nuer,* London: Oxford University Press.

Ferguson, R. Brian and Neil L. Whitehead (eds.). 1992. *War in the Tribal Zone: Expanding States and Indigenous Warfare*, Santa Fe: School of American Research Press.

Firth, Raymond. 1951. *Elements of Social Organisation,* London: Tavistock.

Fried, Morton H. 1966. 'On the Concepts of "Tribe" and "Tribal Society"', in *Transactions of the New York Academy of Science*, Ser. 2, vol. 28, 527-40.

Geertz, Clifford. 1961. *The Social History of an Indonesian Town*, Cambridge: MIT Press.

Gluckman, Max. 1960. 'Tribalism in Modern British Central Africa', in *Cahiers D'études africaines* 1, 55-70.

Guha, B.S. 1944. *Racial Elements in the Population,* Bombay: Oxford University Press.

Gutkind, Peter W. (ed.). 1970. *The Passing of Tribal Man in Africa,* Leiden: Brill.

Jha, Makhan. 1995. *An Introduction to Indian Anthropology,* Delhi: Vikas.

Kuper, Adam. 1983. *Anthropology and Anthropologists: The Modern British School,* London: Routledge & Kegan Paul.

Kuper, Adam. 1988. *The Invention of Primitive Society: Transformations of an Illusion,* London: Routledge.

Layton, Robert. 1997. *An Introduction to Theory in Anthropology,* Cambridge: Cambridge University Press.

Leach, E.R. 1954. *Political Systems of Highland Burma: A Study of Kachin Social Structure*, London: Athlone.

Leach, E.R. 1961 (rpt. 1979). *Rethinking Anthropology,* London: Athlone.

Lévi-Strauss, Claude. 1973. *Structural Anthropology 2,* Harmondsworth: Penguin.

Majumdar, Dhirendra Nath. 1950. *The Affairs of the Tribe: A Study of Tribal Dynamics,* Lucknow: Universal Publ.

McDougal, Charles. 1963. *The Social Structure of the Hill Juang,* unpublished thesis, Albuquerque: University of New Mexico.

Meggitt, Mervin. 1977. *Blood Is Their Argument: Warfare Among the Mae Enga Tribesmen of the New Guinea Highlands*, Palo Alto: Mayfield.

Merton, Robert. 1957. *Social Theory and Social Structure,* Glencoe: The Free Press.

Mohanty, Uma C. 1973/4. 'Bond-Friendship Among the Gadaba', in *Man in Society* 1, 130-55.

Morgan, Lewis Henry. 1878. *Ancient Society,* New York: H. Holt.

Nayak, P.K. 1989. *Blood, Women and Territory: An Analysis of Clan Feuds of Dongra Konds,* New Delhi: Reliance.

Needham, Rodney. 1975. 'Polythetic Classification', in *Man* (n.s.) 10, 349-69.

Pfeffer, Georg. 1997. 'Die Haardebatte: Gender, Glatzen und Gewalt der Bondo', in *Zeitschrift für Ethnologie* 122, 183-208.

Pfeffer, Georg. 2001. 'A Ritual of Revival Among the Gadaba of Koraput', in Burkhard Schnepel and Hermann Kulke (eds.): *Jagannath Revisited: Studying Society, Religion and the State in Orissa,* Delhi: Manohar, 123-48.

Ranger, Terence. 1993. 'The Local and the Global in Southern African Religious History', in Robert W. Hefner (ed.): *Conversion to Christianity*, Berkeley: University of California Press, 65-98.

Redfield, Robert. 1947. 'Folk Society', in *American Journal of Sociology* 52, 293-308.

Risley, Herbert. 1915. *The People of India,* Calcutta: Government Printing.

Rivers, W.H.R. 1906. *The Todas*, London: Macmillan and Co.

Rosaldo, Renato. 1980. *Ilongot Headhunting 1883-1974: A Study in Society and History,* Stanford: Stanford University Press.

Roy, Sarat Chandra. 1912. *The Mundas and their Country.* Calcutta: Government Printing.

Royal Anthropological Institute. 1951: *Notes & Queries in Anthropology,* London: Routledge & Kegan Paul.

Sahlins, Marshall D. 1961. 'Segmentary Lineage: an Organization of Predatory Expansion' in *American Anthropologist* 63, 322-45.

Sahlins, Marshall D. 1968. *Tribesmen*, Englewood Cliffs.

Sahlins, Marshall D. 1985. *Islands of History,* London: Tavistock.

Sahlins, Marshall D. and Elman R. Service (eds.). 1960. *Evolution & Culture,* Ann Arbor: The University of Michigan Press.

Service, Elman. 1962. *Primitive Social Organization*, New York: Random House.

Southall, Aidan W. 1970. 'The Illusion of the Tribe', in Peter W. Gutkind (ed.): *The Passing of Tribal Man in Africa,* Leiden: Brill, 28-50.

Tribal Studies Committee, Indian Council of Social Sciences Research 1999. *Draft Executive Report*. New Delhi: Ministry of Human Resource Development.

Uchendu, Victor C. 1970. 'The Passing of Tribal Man: a West African Experience', in Peter W. Gutkind (ed.): *The Passing of Tribal Man in Africa*, Leiden: Brill, 51-65.

Wittgenstein, Ludwig. 1958. *Philosophical Investigations*, Oxford: Blackwell.

Wolf, Eric R. 1982. *Europe and the People Without History*, Berkeley: University of California Press.

16

Indology and the Cultural Turn

Axel Michaels

In memory of G.D. Sontheimer

1. Introduction

Both classical and modern Indology are basically concerned with the study of texts. They are philological disciplines, i.e. they focus on the written texts of others, have first and foremost to do with editing and translating texts before it comes to an analysis of their contents. This philological work is by no means a subsidiary or minor task. Some Indologists, often the better ones, spend their whole academic life 'just' editing a few texts. In doing so, they throw up a great number of time-consuming grammatical, etymological and factual questions the resolution of which implies further studies. Only if great care is applied are such texts reliable sources for those who cannot read them without translations. After all, philology is slow reading. Any philological subject has enough work constituting and preparing texts for a wider public. This is especially true for Indology where a majority of texts – not only the rare ones, but also the most famous (e.g. English translations of the Ṛgveda or Mahābhārata) – have not yet been satisfactorily edited or translated.

However, Indology (especially in Germany) was and increasingly is confronted with two accusations from practitioners of other disciplines: Indology focuses too much on written texts; Indology lacks a theoretical understanding of the texts.

I wish to discuss these two points not for apologetical reasons but because Indology, like any philological discipline, is linked with a number of other subjects to which it not only contributes but from which it also benefits. I shall first discuss these two points, then summarize the so-called 'cultural turn' and, finally, try to draw some programmatic conclusions for a new understanding of Indology in a changing academic setting.

2. Indology and its Texts

Indology, it is true, focuses on written texts, thus leaving aside a large number of other texts that also contribute to an understanding of a certain culture. The reason for such an approach is historically understandable. It has, I believe, to do with the concept of religious tradition in Christianity. It is the holy and written word that has attracted attention in the European study of cultures. New subjects such as Indology could justify themselves in the canon of academic fields and institutions, especially the faculties, only by demonstrating that non-Christian cultures were also based on scriptures. In a way, the Veda was just a context or a kind of *textus absconditus*, a text that surprisingly survived through living contexts despite the fact that it was greatly ignored by the masses as J. Heesterman aptly remarked.[1] This focus on scripture and the criticism of idolatry, idols and visualizations discriminated against not only cultures that did not have any written texts but also the oral and folk traditions within book religions as well as all those social groups which were generally illiterate, i.e. women or subaltern groups. It was the book religions that were recognized as superior.

The focus on written sources in book religions was so extensive that for a long time scholars in the West could not adequately recognize another peculiarity of Indian, especially Vedic, culture, i.e. the fact that scripture was based on a great mnemotechnical capacity for the transmission of texts or, in other words, that scripture was ideally not a written text. The attitude towards written texts or books in its narrow sense culminates perhaps best in the famous Latin dictum of an Indian pandit:

---

[1] Heesterman 1998, 208.

vedam est quidquid ad religionem pertinet, vedam non sunt libri.[2]

or, if you prefer a similar statement in Sanskrit:

pustakapratyayādhītaṃ nādhītaṃ gurusaṃnidhau /
bhrājate na sabhāmadhe jāragarbha iva striyāḥ //
Nārada in Parāśaramādhavīya[3]

All this has been brilliantly studied and described by Harry Falk in his bibliographical overview 'Die Schrift im alten Indien'[4] and Oskar von Hinüber 'Der Beginn der Schrift und frühen Schriftlichkeit in Indien.'[5]

However, even if one understands why written texts constituted the major attraction for the beginnings of the study of Indian culture, it does not mean that one should continue with such an approach. This brings me to the normative aspect of the critical argument that Indology is almost exclusively concerned with scripture and written texts.

It is true that the preference for written sources neglects to a great extent other forms of texts understood in a broader semiotic sense. By this I mean all forms of non-verbal signals and communication, e.g. visual and acoustic signs, gestures, actions, behaviour, etc., in short: contexts. Even if there should be some division of labour in academic work, even if the non-verbal aspect of communication should remain the work for sociologists, anthropologists, psychologists, art historians, etc., even if written texts remain the most important sources not only for Indology but for any historical study in cultures, it would be misleading to assume that

---

[2] Quoted after Zachariae 1921, 160.

[3] Quoted after Kane 1974, 348.

[4] Falk, 1993.

[5] v. Hinüber, 1990.

texts, written or not,[6] can be understood, i.e. translated, without their contextualization. After all, reading a culture is translating its contexts into texts.

However, a written text or book often originates in special contexts – for several reasons which can be summarized as follows:[7] It is by the book that knowledge can be easily kept, preserved and transported to other regions and, thereby, has the greatest impact on culture among the media. The holy book creates a common point of reference and, thus, a centre for religious communities.

The book separates texts from its subjective, regional, emotive contexts and, thus, from its creators as well as from its historical limitations. The book is, in principle, available to everybody, it is not necessarily related to a personal and intimate relationship between author and recipient. The book, therefore, makes the reader or listener independent from author and reader, preacher and priest even if in many religions the forms of reading, writing and listening have been restricted or ritualized. The principle of *sola scriptura,* according to which just the reader of the Bible is responsible for its proper understanding, and not anybody who is placed between him and the text, is basically part of the medium itself. You can yourself find out what the scripture means which also implies what Jack Goody called the 'individualizing tendency' of books.[8] Moreover, the book is a durable collective expression of the memory of cultures and a constant source of popularization and canonization.[9] In short, written texts or books mean cultural memory but also a culturally independent point of reference, the possibility of diversification and, because of these many advantages, the medium of the written text, especially the book or, more specifically, even the printed book, was and still is the most important source for the study of cultures. If one looks at how religions and cultures are spread and mixed by the new medium of the internet, this power of written texts is again confirmed. In short, with regard to religion, written texts and their exegesis establish not only

---

[6] Cf. Graham 1987, Coward 1988.

[7] Michaels 1996, 114f.

[8] Goody/Watt/Gough 1991, 28.

[9] Assmann/Assmann/Hardmeier 1983; Assmann ^{2}1997.

'sacred persistence' as defined by Jonathan Z. Smith in his seminal article,[10] but also cultural persistence. They remain the best source for any historically orientated study on cultures, and as long as the texts are not properly presented, far-reaching conclusions are extremely preliminary. However, as I will try to demonstrate shortly, all analysis of written texts is preliminary, for there is no Archimedean point of view on them.

However, the written text or book is not an entity that is free from contexts. As mentioned before, it is only constituted by writing, reading and translation. This process implies intentions of persons involved: the author, the reader, the translator. The meaning of a text is negotiated between these three. Philology, thus, is not only slow reading but also part of a communicative context in which it cannot claim any superiority.

3. Indology and its Theoretical Deficiency

Let me now turn to the second criticism levelled against Indology as a discipline: its theoretical deficiency. This argument has also been used within Indological circles, e.g. F. Staal's criticism of J. Gonda on Mantras or rituals ('very little insight').

It is true that Indology has rarely initiated theoretical debates on general social or cultural problems. It has been in the forefront of mostly social scientists, anthropologists and historians who have raised important issues on the basis of material from South Asia, e.g. H. Hubert on sacrifice, M. Mauss on the gift, P. Dumézil on myth, L. Dumont on hierarchy and purity, M. Weber on asceticism, B. Stein on little kingdoms, R. Schechner on performance, C. Humphrey and J. Laidlaw on ritual – to mention just the most influential theories.

I can only think of two general or interdisciplinary debates during the past decades which were initiated by Indologists, namely the meaninglessness problem of rituals by F. Staal and the theory of inclusivism by P. Hacker. To be sure, Indologists have contributed to many other interdisciplinary debates – e.g. the origin of script, the myth-and-ritual debate, the authority of the canon, the tradition of

---

[10] Smith 1982, ch. 3, 36-52.

hermeneutics,[11] etc. – moreover some specific debates were dominated by Indological material, e.g. the Indo-Aryan invasion debate, the date of the Buddha, the origin and development of Indo-European languages, but all those debates have not had any impact beyond the limited circle of specialists.

It is perhaps significant in this regard that F. Staal's theory on the meaninglessness of ritual was not at all discussed by Indologists. I know only of a single Indological review[12] of his monumental study of the *agnicayana* ritual, though this pioneering combination of textual studies with field work was not only jointly carried out by a number of Indologists (R. N. Dandekar, J. Heesterman, A. Parpola, etc.) but also received great attention in the anthropological scene and the media. Moreover, F. Staal presented this theory on the meaninglessness of the ritual – debatable and questionable as it is – on several occasions in Europe, e.g. as a fellow of the Wissenschaftskolleg in Berlin. However, the response was nil, the Indological answer was silence. This is all the more pitiful, the closer one studies the material presented by Staal and his colleagues. I would even argue that this theory would have been better received by non-Indologists if, for once, Indologists had examined his often superficial or wrong references, quick conclusions and lack of philological precision.

To give just one example: In his famous article 'The meaninglessness of ritual', Staal often refers to textual material from India (and not only to the song of birds). He argues that even the *mīmāṃsakas* developed such a theory referring indirectly and without quotation of the original (namely, Jaiminīya's *Mīmāṃsasūtra* 4.2.27: *yajati codanādravyadevatākriyaṃ samudāye kṛtārthatvāt*; see also 4.4.34) to the common Śrauta definition of sacrifice (*yāga*) as constituted by *dravya* (material, substance), *devatā* (deity) and *tyāga* (abandonment). In order to strengthen his argument he reads *tyāga* as 'renunciation of the fruits of the ritual acts', i.e. the abandonment of any interest in reward or motive in the ritual.[13] And he comes to the

---

[11] Timm 1992.

[12] Mylius 1986.

[13] Staal 1979, 6.

conclusion: 'What the Mīmāṃsā in fact ended up teaching is that rituals have to be performed for their own sake.'[14] However, in this context the term *tyāga* means that the sacrificer offers (and thereby abandons) substances to deities. P.V. Kane paraphrases it correctly: '*yāga* means abandonment of *dravya* intending [!] it for a deity'.[15] In a *homa*, for instance, the sacrificer pours ghee into the fire and thus abandons it. This Mīmāṃsā definition of sacrifice does not imply that the sacrificer has no motives in the ritual or that he is not interested in rewards. It now becomes apparent that Staal misuses this passage for his argument that 'ritual has no meaning, goal or aim'.[16] However, Staal will hardly find any textual reference in Sanskrit literature – beyond the general *Bhagavadgītā*-like propagation of disattachement – that advocates the meaninglessness of ritual. After all, these texts have been written by theologians and ritualists who are not interested in declaring the meaninglessness of what they are doing. Finally, Staal suggests that rituals and sacrifices are identical. But then, what about the other terms that can be translated as 'ritual': *iṣṭi*, *karman*, *kriyā*, *homa*, *saṃskāra*, etc.? The very fact that there is no single term for ritual in Sanskrit is to be considered in any general theory on Indian or Hindu rituals.

All this criticism does not mean that Staal's basic argument, i.e. the meaninglessness of rituals,[17] is not worth discussing, but it means that his theoretical and methodological approach is dissatisfactory. To understand a complex phenomenon such as ritual it needs both a comprehensive study of the textual and non-textual material and a participation in the theoretical debates.

My plea for an intensified engagement on the part of Indology in theoretical debates is backed by a trend in humanities that is linked by the term 'cultural turn'. What does it mean? What are the implications of this trend? Or is it just a fashion that Indologists who are allegedly concerned with more durable material can ignore?

---

[14] Ibid., 1979, 7.

[15] Kane 1974/II.2, 983, cf. also Jha 1942, 359ff.

[16] Staal 1979, 8.

[17] Cp. Humprey/Laidlaw 1994; Michaels 1999, 2000 and forthcoming

Linguistic turn, performative turn, cultural turn, and – most recently – pictorial turn – one gets dizzy with so many turns and seems to lose one's orientation.

4. Indology and the Cultural Turn

The most significant turn in the post-modern approach to texts is the concern for the anthropology of texts. This means an interdisciplinarity that cares not only for the words and letters but also for the context of the texts, i.e. its agents, users, readers, etc. The study of texts thus becomes a study of social structures that generated the texts, a study of the application of texts (e.g. in rituals), a study of the performance and reception of texts, and a study of their historical conditions. To be sure, all this has been considered in previous Indological research, but within the cultural turn such an approach becomes a theoretical (and, at times, even political) programme.

Culture, then, is claimed to be an entity that encompasses everything that is made by human beings. It is not another realm beside others such as politics, religion or law. It is the cover term for the study of all arte- and mentefacts. In Germany it was mainly Ernst Cassirer who developed a modern semiotic theory. Culture is defined as an assembly of complex and dynamic signs which show social material and mental dimensions. Each cultural object or sign presupposes a class of users, belongs to a group of signs (texts, pictures, gestures, etc.) and is generated by mental codes,[18] but none of these symbolic forms is beyond history and can thus be established as an a-historical entity. What is most important in this theory, which must be regarded as one of the earliest concepts of the cultural turn, is that it deconstructs any form of essentialism. The advantage of this turn is that all forms of essentialism and dogmatism are avoided, that a naive empiricism is not applied, and that arguments of Orientalism can no longer be easily formulated. Given the great amount of works in which the soul or frame of India seems to be discovered by authors, given the holistic errors which have been presented so often and

[18] Böhme et al. 2000, 68.

which had been often unveiled as more or less racist arguments, this cultural turn was justified. It helped to concentrate on the agents, and by doing so a number of new and fascinating topics were raised: the gender aspect, the subaltern perspective, the everyday life, the performative and transformative part in texts. All this furthered the understanding that culture is more than high culture, and it was due to such a turn in the humanities that Indology questioned the relationship between little and great traditions and stressed the importance of regional studies and vernacular languages. New terms as McKim Marriott's parochialization, S. Sinha's Rajputization or H. Kulke's kshatriyaization are expressions of this turn. R. Inden rightly criticized in his book *Imagining India* the open and hidden colonial and/or orientalistic, essentializing background of many of these studies.[19]

Another outcome of this turn was that texts were no longer understood as monolithic documents but as having been produced by particular interests and conflicts. This means that when reading texts one must also consider those who are not within the text. Texts are often produced as arguments against differing positions – this is especially true for ritual and philosophical texts – and thus reflect a more or less hidden reality. Texts are written not only as a passive storage of information but also for reasons of power, influence, honour, prestige, etc.

One important outcome of the cultural turn in the humanities has been the stress on a collaboration of philologists and anthropologists. Such arguments had been brought up several times earlier. The Indologist Sylvain Lévi, for example, did pioneering work on Nepal considering the anthropological aspects of texts, or the contexts of text, to such an extent that A. Höfer wrote an article on him with the significant subtitle: 'What we anthropologists owe to Sylvain Lévi'. His conclusions are worth quoting because they underpin the necessity of cooperation between these two academic fields in certain regards.

---

[19] Inden 1990.

> Lévi is generally considered as an Indologist. In reality, he saw himself as an historian. Although a philologist by training and acquainted with an amazing number of languages,[20] the documents of the past were, for him, not ends in themselves, but sources of information to be decoded with the suspicion of the historian. As Renou aptly states, Lévi developed a particular sensitivity for meanings hidden 'beneath the word' (*un sens profond des réalitées sous les mots*).[21] In fact, Lévi extended his quest for meaning into the realms of what we now call ideology, ethnotheory and contextual analysis. […] he kept a close watch on the social functions of his sources. What fascinated him was the intricate relationship between the author and the public, rather than the mere literary value of a source, the process which produced a source, rather than the product, the source itself.[22]

Such recognition of the work by the other side is rarely stressed by Indologists who often do not deny the importance of field-work but generally do not appreciate its results. One exception is M. Witzel who wrote in a long review article of Robert Levy's impressive book *Mesocosm: Hinduism and the Organization of a Traditional Newar City in Nepal*:

> *Mesoscosm* successfully combines a well-informed textual and historical background, with anthropological observation and […] insightful analysis. […] This book […] presents Hinduism as it operates on the ground, from private beliefs to the city-wide Tantric religion, from private rituals to the public festivals of a whole realm, from individual sacred space in private houses to the sacred geography of the town of Bhaktapur and surrounding areas. It thus has intrinsic value not only for

[20] Cf. Renou 1936, 57.
[21] Ibid., 1936, 8-9.
[22] Höfer 1979, 176.

understanding local Newar Hinduism but also for the wider study and understanding of Hinduism in general.[23]

The reason for a combination of Indology and Anthropology is, of course, the link between tradition and modernity in South Asia – a point that has led to a number of seminal articles: M. Singer's 'Text and Context in the Study of Contemporary Hinduism';[24] L. Dumont's and D. Pocock's 'For a sociology of India';[25] St. Tambiah, 'At the confluence of anthropology, history, and Indology'.[26] However, only within the new trend (and the cheaper and facilitated possibilities for research in South Asia) a considerable and coordinated number of studies were possible: the village studies in the fifties,[27] the first Orissa Research Programme in the sixties and seventies, the Agnicayana Project, he Nepal Research Programme in the eighties, etc.

Indology has participated in these projects and has quite often been its driving force. However, old prejudices between anthropology and Indology have remained. Anthropologists generally still believe that Indologists are primarily concerned with diacritics, and Indologists still believe that the study of contemporary phenomena are popularizations and vulgarizations, deviations and corruptions of the ancient traditions.[28]

However, Dumont and Pocock argue that 'The first condition for a sound development of a sociology of India is found in the establishment of the proper relation between it and classical Indology,'[29] and St. Tambiah adds history to it: 'In due course I found that there was something lacking in this credo: a sociology of India (and of South-East Asia) must establish a relation between three terms, the third being history.'[30] Tambiah even claims that 'today

[23] Witzel 1997, 501.

[24] Cf. Singer, 1972.

[25] Cf. Dumont and Pocock, 1957.

[26] Cf. Tambiah, 1987.

[27] Cf. Kolenda 1978.

[28] Cf. Tambiah 1987, 188.

[29] Dumont and Pocock 1957, 7.

[30] Tambiah 1987, 188.

virtually no South or South-East Asian anthropologist can afford not to engage with Indology and history even if his or her work is focused on the study of contemporary phenomena'.[31] If Indologists had adopted a similar approach, many discussions could be easier, but generally speaking Indologists do not read the theoretical works of anthropologists. The results are often the naive application of theories, the use of everyday arguments and articulations of prejudices.

Let me be a bit more precise on this point by coming back to the unparalleled richness and variety of material on Hindu rituals. There are (a) the Vedic and post-Vedic literature on still practised sacrifices (*yajña, iṣṭi, homa*), rites of passage (*saṃskāra*) and optional rituals (*vrata,* etc.); (b) performative rituals such as dance, theatre and musical performances which are partly based on a rich Sanskrit literature; (c) theoretical works on exegesis of rituals as well as texts on the aesthetics of performances developed, for instance, as a special theory of aesthetical moods (*rasa*).

All the textual material has been compiled by – among many others[32] A. Hillebrandt (1897), P.V. Kane (1968ff.), R.B. Pandey (1969) or J. Gonda (1980). There have also been impressive examples of work on rituals which combine textual studies with field-work, e.g. Gonda (1980), Tachikawa (1993), Einoo (1993) or Witzel (1986, 1987) on Vedic rituals; Bühnemann (1988), Einoo (1996) and Tachikawa (1996) on the *pūjā*; several studies on initiation (see Michaels 1998: 85-114 for further references); and Knipe (1976), Evison (1989) or Müller (1992) on death rituals. Moreover, there are many other Indological works on rituals. Yet, almost none of these studies deal with or even refer to the general discussion on rituals! If at all, one mostly finds V. Turner mentioned. Other authors such as Durkheim, Malinowski, Douglas, Goffman or Schechner (not to speak of modern scholars such as Bell, Humphrey/Laidlaw, Rappaport, etc.)

---

[31] Ibid.

[32] Cf. the comprehensive online-bibliography on ritual studies of the Department of Classical Indology at the South Asia Institute: http://www.sai.uni-heidelberg.de /IND/index→Materialien→Ritual Bibliographien.

are virtually non-existent in Indological literature on rituals. Staal, Heesterman and B.K. Smith remain the only exceptions as far as I can oversee it.
However, it was a great – in my view the greatest – insight of the cultural turn in the humanities that there is no way without theory, in other words, that any work of culture is already theoretical by definition. Clifford Geertz, being the most famous proponent of this argument, demonstrated that culture had to be studied as texts and by creating texts. Culture can only be construed, and it is the anthropologist (or Indologist) who does this job. As a consequence the interpretatory work of the researcher and author became more and more important. Culture became itself a text, or there was no culture any more without text. Culture was written, not discovered. *Writing Culture* by James Clifford[33] was a significant title of a student of Geertz.

An important outcome of this cultural turn is to be seen in the attitude towards the 'victims' of theories. It is not any longer asked how a culture is or was, but how it is or was seen by others or within itself. In other words, any form of empiricism is rejected, each statement on culture has to consider the producers. Writing about culture does not mean searching for truth but for opinions. The outcome is a bunch of interpretations, a polyvalent and polyvocal representation of culture seen as a heterogeneous and divergent mixture of everything that is produced by men.

However, the result of this open and almost unlimited concept of culture was not only the new bottom-to-top perspective with all the advantages mentioned earlier, but also an inflationary mess of new topics. Thus, a major representative of the cultural turn who just co-published a substantial book on cultural studies (Kulturwissenschaften) is currently involved in the following work: review of a dissertation on the cultural history of the skin, review of a habilitation thesis on the scientific community of the CERN in Geneva and another on rapidity in the work of R. Musil and W. Benjamin, reading papers on construction sites, cellars and closed spaces, cultural consequences of the internet, the Goldhagen debate,

[33] Clifford 1986.

cultural theory on borders, 'the rhetoric of cultural discourse: Jews and Germans in the Epoch of Emancipation', on Heinrich Zimmer (brother-in-law of Hugo von Hoffmannsthal), preparing lectures and articles on fetishism and idol (on Goethe), literature and ecology, cultural studies, carrier pigeons and the future of bureaucracy.[34]

Hartmut Böhme, the tortured professor I am referring to, complains himself about the new complex and bewildering situation in cultural studies and the diffusion of topics that has been constantly pointed out by critics of the cultural turn:

> Die Kulturwissenschaften lassen sich nicht auf bestimmte Objektbereiche, Theorien oder Methoden festlegen. In der Vieldeutigkeit liegt aber auch eine Gefahr: Wer glaubt, in ihrem Namen die Eigenlogik und das Forschungsniveau des jeweiligen Fachs ignorieren zu können, dessen Generalismus wird sich als Dilettantismus erweisen. 'Ku Wi' wäre dann das Label einer Unterhaltungsdisziplin, die auf methodische Genauigkeit, exakte Kenntnisse und kritische Reflexionsformen verzichtet, die dafür aber ein Sammelsurium des jeweils Modischen und der jeweils Modischen präsentiert – 'Hip-Hop bei den Hopis' oder 'Genesis und Gender bei Demokrit und Derrida'.[35]

However, this scepticism regarding the cultural turn in the humanities is not totally justified. The history of humanities has proved that studies which transgressed the at times narrow frames of the disciplines developed most fascinating and vividly discussed theories. I will mention only a few[36]: studies on cultural history, world history (Universalgeschichte), Freud's cultural studies, the theory of symbolic forms (Cassirer, Warburg), the French studies on mentality or the German Völkerpsychologie. Many of these theories became obsolete a few decades after they were published, but most of them have stimulated further studies and opened up new fields of research. Thus,

---

[34] Böhme/Matussek/Müller 2000.

[35] Bollenbeck 1997, 262.

[36] Following Böhme et al. 2000, ch. II.

without the studies on the history of mentality, the periodization of history according to nothing but political criteria would probably have continued, without Freud, the irrational behaviour and non-linguistic impacts on culture could not have been discovered, and without the theory of symbolic forms the importance of a semiotic understanding of cultures would have been more difficult, etc.

5. Prospective Conclusions

Given the chaotic and partly superficial situation in many modern cultural studies, I propose that Indology does not simply mimic the trend but also its best theoretical implications. These I characterize as broadening the concept of texts, the contextualization of texts, and the textualization of texts. Let me clarify these points.

Firstly, a broadened concept of what constitutes a text is, I think, unavoidable in Indology. As a matter of fact, it is already applied to a great extent even though the study of many texts is left to anthropologists. Let me briefly summarize which new forms of texts should, in my opinion, be incorporated in the corpus of Indological text material besides the given corpus of Sanskrit, Pāli and Prakrit texts, historical material (inscriptions, chronicles, records) or texts in vernacular languages:

1. Oral literature (see below) should be recorded, transcribed and edited.
2. Grey literature, school books: pamphlets and small booklets of various institutions should be systematically collected. (A major project collecting school books from South Asia has been started at the South Asia Institute, Heidelberg).
3. Internet sources: links to various Hindu, Jain, Sikh or Buddhist organizations and communities have been installed on Indological homepages. However, a systematic study of these sources has, to my knowledge, not yet been undertaken.
4. Texts communicated by mass media such as journals, comics, television and video recordings, etc.
5. Modern Indian research texts and their reception of the great traditions: in India more and more texts are produced – by

scholars and journalists – which are in the West generally not accepted as genuine Indian texts because they reflect Indian culture through the filter of Western education. However, it must be recognized – as it is already done with regard to the Islam – that the monopolism on how ancient texts should be methodologically studied and understood is not justified. Thus, scholars like W. Cantwell Smith, Annemarie Schimmel, Seyyed Hossein Nasr or Mohammed Arkoun are, as J. Waardenburg argues, not detached authors and yet scholars. The same holds true, for instance, for S. Radhakrishnan or R. Panikkar.

6. Visual sources such as paintings, posters, material objects of the culture: these products should be studied since they are, as was shown, for instance, by Aby Warburg, important codes of cultural expressions which are generally ignored by art historians. Such visualizations are important representations or 'texts' of cultural sentiments and fantasies. Recent trends such as the anthropology of films or the journal *Visible Religion* are first steps, and F. Staal's film on the Agnicayana should not remain the only Indological exception.
7. Maps: a fascinating, reluctantly studied material are geographical and religious maps which are expressions of spatial concepts. Cultural and mental mapping has become a recognized method for the study of cultural memories. (The first project on religious maps and cartography in India, focussing on Varanasi, has been recently started by the South Asia Institute.)

Secondly, texts have undoubtedly to be studied in their contexts in order to better understand their meanings *and* functions. For Indology this means that a number of textual genres must include fieldwork studies on texts. This holds especially true for performative texts (*nāṭyaśāstra,* some epics) and ritual texts. However, the study of texts in their contexts often means their study in their philological context since for most historical texts fieldwork is not possible any more. The best that can be done in studying and analysing texts is – as I argued before – minute philological work on details, for every wider conclusion depends on a precise meaning of words and syntax. This specific linguistic turn is the best contextualization of texts. And this remedy also helps anthropologists against the fluidity of results and against too many turns. The linguistic turn also results in the use of the term 'culture' always in its plural form and not in singular (or there is no singular of culture except as a theoretical, de-contextualized concept), as there are only many languages and not a single concept of language.

It is obvious that beside the linguistic turn other forms of contextualization of texts which have been mentioned should be considered as far as possible. This concerns the communicators of texts (Brahmins, mendicants, story tellers, scholars, pandits), the patrons of texts (kings, institutions such as *maṭhas*, etc.), the presentation of texts in performances, the negotiations of texts (e.g. debates, *śāstrārthas*, etc.), the locality of texts (city, village, neighbourhood, etc.), the community of texts (family, clan, caste, working group, specialists, etc.), the economy of texts (production costs, printing, manuscript distribution, etc.).

All this symbolic and semiotic material contributes to a transformation of cultures. With its simplicity, easy distribution of information and principal openness, it often offers solutions, and as such it creates a sharp contrast to the elaborate, often exclusive material of the high traditions and their closed pool of information on the one hand, and the localized, basically orally transmitted texts on the other. To be sure, the texts produced by the mass media also mean a great trivialization of cultures, but the study of them can teach how cultures are transformed and encoded, how social or religious symbols work, how texts are separated from their religious and social contexts, how standardization influences the form and even content of texts. Given the process of globalization, Indology should not refuse the study of such texts but try to understand them and thus contribute to actual debates.

The most important outcome in the study of this modern material could, however, be a theoretical turn. It is no longer the stasis of texts that matters, the often disappointing search for a single, unique text written by a single author at a certain historical time. I do not mean by this that such a research is in vain, but I do reject the hidden implications that often go together with any reconstruction of an Ur-text. These are, as was mentioned by St. Tambiah, the conclusions that the past is either seen as sanction or destiny.[37] The past (or the Ur-text) is either legitimating the present or it is unfolding a future in a 'linear pattern'. Quite often the search for an Ur-text which is not corrupted by history or by many authors and users is regarded as more valuable than those texts which are transmitted. In this case the scholar is not only creating a new, previously non-existing text but also valuing different forms of cultures. Thus, in India, the author of a text is often less important than the text which, then, even becomes de-sacralized by its reconstruction by a human author.

To be sure, if texts are studied, the historical stratification of texts remains a most important tool to understand them, and the above mentioned philological work on details often leads to only this form of contextualization. But the argument that historical truth or authorship are more precise or even better forms of knowledge is itself a culturally biased Western argument which cannot be drawn from the studied material. I therefore agree with R. Adriaensen, H.T. Bakker and H. Isaacson that – despite several attacks on the so-called 'Textgeschichtliche Schule' – philological research based on manuscripts counts a lot,[38] but I do not agree with their implicit argument that philology counts much more than general methodological observations and structural analysis when it comes to a proper understanding of written texts.

Thirdly, I consider the textualization of texts as a major task for a new Indology. By this I mean the fact that Indology is not only a recipient of texts but also a creator of (primary) texts. By this, of course, I do not mean the increasingly torturing number of publications which must be regarded as secondary since they draw all their conclusions from primary texts. As I have argued above, Indology also produces primary sources. This is to be regarded as a normative act, for most of these texts did not exist before an Indologist reconstructed them from manuscript material or tape recordings. The criterion of a critical edition is not unbiased but unavoidable for scientific research, although many such so-called

[37] Tambiah 1987, 194.

[38] Adriaensen, Bakker and Isaacson 1998, 17.

critical editions are simply based on a more or less uncritical selection of just a few manuscripts. In general, the number of available manuscripts on certain texts is mostly too vast for a critical edition that deserves this specification by a single person. And for various reasons, it is only rarely that a collective group of Indologists work on such a venture. However, if there are desiderata regarding Indological material it is the preparing of critical editions and translations of basic texts, the collection of data on the contextualization of texts. A form of Indology that considers critical editions as its only task may not only be seriously endangered in the future of academic structural changes, but does not understand how culture works, either.

Another increasingly relevant form of textualizing texts are oral texts. Recording such texts becomes more and more important because the continuity of oral transmission is heavily endangered. However, the textualization of oral texts is also a shift in the form of the texts. Oral texts have their special elements and styles such as repetitions, rhymes, meters, formulas, redundancy and parallelism. Written texts do sometimes keep these oral techniques of memory, but they are sooner or later replaced by other, visual forms of reducing complexity such as titles and subtitles, graphical and numeric structures, punctuation, etc.

6. Summary

To sum up, Indology can and should not avoid the cultural turn in the humanities, but it should concentrate on its basic and most important features, i.e. the languages and literatures of South Asia. Thus, Indology should basically remain a philological discipline, but it should also broaden its concepts of the textual core and its theoretical understanding by three means:

It should, first of all, open up to an intensified study of the contexts of texts by accepting fieldwork as a legitimate, adequate and proper (and not just supplementary) method for an appropriate analysis of the contents, functions and productions of texts. This form of Indology, which I call Ethno-Indology, is at the confluence not only of anthropology and history, but also at the history of religions (Religionswissenschaft). Also, Indology should continue to 'create' (primary) texts, especially through preparing critical editions and translations as well as preserving oral texts that are threatened with destruction. Finally, Indology should participate more in the debates about the theory of cultures which are especially intensive in the social sciences.

If, then, Indology becomes a bit more bare-footed both orally and socially it might help to avoid further criticism that Indology is predominantly concerned with useless, other-worldly or ancient topics which do not contribute to an understanding of the modern problems of people in South Asia *and* the West.

References

Adriaensen, R., H.T. Bakker and H. Isaacson. 1998. *The Skandapurāṇa, Vol. I: Adhyāyas 1-25. Critically edited with Prolegomena and English Synopsis,* Groningen: Egbert Forsten.

Assmann, Aleida and Jan, and Chr. Hardmeier (eds.). 1983. *Schrift und Gedächtnis. Archäologie der Literarischen Kommunikation I*, München: Wilhelm Fink.

Assmann, Jan. 1997. *Das Kulturelle Gedächtnis. Schrift, Erinnerung und Politische Identität in Frühen Hochkulturen*, München: C.H. Beck.

Böhme, Hartmut, Peter Matussek and Lothar Müller. 2000. *Orientierung Kulturwissenschaft: Was sie kann, was sie will,* Reinbek: Rowohlt.

Bollenbeck, Georg. 1997. 'Die Kulturwissenschaften - mehr als ein modisches Label?', in *Merkur* 2, 259-65.

Bühnemann, Gudrun. 1988. *Pūjā. A Study in Smārta Ritual*, Wien: Institut für Indologie der Universität Wien.

Clifford, James. (ed.) 1986. *Writing Culture,* Berkeley: University of California Press.

Coburn, Thomas. B. 1984. ' "Scripture" in India: Towards a Typology of the Word in Hindu Life', in *Journal of the American Academy of Religion*, vol. 52, 435-59.

Coward, Harold. 1988. *Sacred Word and Sacred Text: Scripture in World Religions*, Maryknoll, New York: Orbis Books.

Einoo, Shingom. 1993. 'Changes in Hindu Ritual: With a Focus on the Morning Service', in *Senri Ethnological Studies* 36, 197-237.

Einoo, Shingom. 1996. 'The Formation of the Pūjā Ceremony', in *Studien zur Indologie und Iranistik* 20 [= Festschrift P. Thieme], 73-87.

Evison, Gillian. 1989. *Indian Death Rituals: The Enactment of Ambivalence,* Oxford University, [unpubl. dissertation].

Dumont, Louis and D. Pocock. 1957, 'For a Sociology of India', in *Contributions to Indian Sociology* 1, 7-22.

Falk, Harry. 1993. *Die Schrift im Alten Indien,* Tübingen: Gunter Narr Verlag (ScriptOralia; 56).

Fouquet-Plümacher, Doris. 1976. 'Buch/Buchwesen III', *Theologische Realenzyklopädie*, 272-90.

Goody, Jack. 1987. 'Oral Composition and Oral Transmission: The Case of the Vedas', in Jack Goody, *The Interface between the Written and the Oral*, Cambridge, 110-22.

Goody, Jack and Ian Watt. 1968. 'The Consequences of Literacy', in J. Goody (ed.), *Literacy in Traditional Society*, Cambridge, 27-68.

Goody, Jack; Ian Watt and Kathleen Gough. 1991. *Entstehung und Folgen der Schriftkultur*, Frankfurt am Main: Suhrkamp.

Gonda, Jan. 1980. *Vedic Ritual. The Non-Solemn Rite,* Leiden, Köln: Brill.

Graham, William A. 1987. *Beyond the Written Word. Oral Aspects of Scripture in the History of Religion,* Cambridge: Cambridge University Press.

Heesterman, Jan. 1998. 'Review of L. L. Patton (ed.) *Authority, Anxiety and Canon: Essays in Vedic Interpretation*', in *History of Religion* 38, 205-9.

Hillebrandt, Alfred. 1897. *Ritualliteratur*, Straßburg: Karl J. Trübner.

Hinüber, Oskar von. 1990. *Der Beginn der Schrift und frühe Schriftlichkeit in Indien*, Mainz (Abh. d. Geistes- und Sozialwiss. Kl./Akad. d. Wiss. u. d. Lit.; Jh. 1989, Nr. 11).

Höfer, András. 1979. 'On Re-reading *Le Nepal*: What we Social Scientists Owe to Sylvain Levi', in *Kailash* 7, 175-90.

Humphrey, Caroline und James Laidlaw. 1994. *The Archetypal Actions of Ritual. A Theory of Ritual Illustrated by the Jain Rite of Worship*, Oxford: Clarendon Press.

Inden, Ronald. 1990. *Imagining India*, Oxford: Basil Blackwell.

Jha, Ganganatha 1942. *Pūrva-Mīmāṃsā and its Sources,* Varanasi: Banaras Hindu University.

Kane, Pandurang Vaman. 1974. *History of Dharmaśāstra*, vol. II, Poona: Bhandarkar Oriental Research Institute.

Knipe, David M. 1976. ''*Sapiṇḍikāraṇa*: The Hindu Rite of Entry into Heaven', in F. E. Reynolds and E. H. Waugh (eds.), *Religious Encounters with Death: Insights from the History and Anthropology of Religions,* University Park: Pennsylvania State University Press, 111-24.

Kolenda, Pauline M. 1978 (rpt. 1985): *Caste in Contemporary India: Beyond Organic Solidarity*, Prospects Heights, Ill.: Waveland Press.

Levering, Miriam. 1989. *Rethinking Scripture: Essays from a Comparative Perspective,* Albany: State University of New York Press.

Michaels, Axel. 1996. 'Das Buch als Fundament von Religionen', in P. Rusterholz and R. Moser (eds.), *Die Bedeutung des Buches*, Bern, Stuttgart, Wien: Haupt, 111-142.

Michaels, Axel 1998. *Der Hinduismus. Geschichte und Gegenwart*, München: C.H. Beck.

Michaels, Axel. 1999. '*«Le rituel pour le rituel?» oder* Wie Sinnlos sind Rituale?', in Corinna Carduff and Joanna Pfaff-Czarnecka (eds.), *Rituale heute*, Berlin: Reimer Verlag, 23-48.

Michaels, Axel. 2000. 'Ex opere operato: Zur Intentionalität Promissorischer Akte in Ritualen', in K.-P. Köpping and U. Rao (eds.), *Im Rausch des Rituals. Gestaltung und Transformation der Wirklichkeit in Körperlicher Performanz,* Münster: Lit-Verlag, 104-23.

Michaels, Axel. forthcoming. 'Saṃkalpa: the Beginning of a Ritual', in Joerg Gengnagel, Ute Huesken and Srialata Raman Mueller (eds.), *Ritual in South Asia: Text and Context*, Würzburg: Ergon.

Müller, Klaus-Werner. 1992. *Das Brahmanische Totenritual nach der Antyeṣṭipaddhati des Nārāyaṇabhaṭṭa*, Stuttgart: Franz Steiner.

Mylius, Klaus. 1986. Review of F. Staal's *Agni* (Berkeley 1983), in *Orientalische Literaturzeitung* 81(5), 496-501.

O'Flaherty, Wendy Doniger (ed.). 1979. *The Critical Study of Sacred Texts*, Berkeley: The Gradual Theological Union.

Pandey, Raj Bali. 1969. *Hindu Saṃskāras: Socio-Religious Study of the Hindu Sacraments*, Delhi: Motilal Banarsidass.

Renou, Loouis. 1936. 'Sylvain Lévi et son oevre scientifique', in *Journal Asiatique* 228, 1-59.

Schechner, Richard. 1990. *Theater-Anthropologie: Spiel und Ritual im Kulturvergleich*, Reinbek: Rowohlt.

Singer, Milton. 1972. 'Text and Context in the Study of Contemporary Hinduism', in idem, *When a Great Tradition Modernizes: Text and Context in the Study of Hinduism*, New York, Washington, London: Praeger Publishers, 33-54.

Smith, Jonathan Z. 1982. *Imagining Religion: From Babylon to Jonestown*, Chicago: University of Chicago Press.

Staal, Frits. 1979. 'The Meaninglessness of Ritual', in *Numen* 26, 2-22.

Staal, Frits. 1983. *Agni. The Vedic Ritual of the Fire Altar*, 2 vols., Berkeley: University of California Press.

Tachikawa, Musashi. 1983. 'A Hindu Worship Service in Sixteen Steps, Shoḍaṣa-Upacāra-Pūjā', in *Bulletin of the National Museum of Ethnology* 8, 104-86.

Tachikawa, Musashi. 1993. '*Homa* in Vedic Ritual: The Structure of the Darśapūrṇamāsa', in *Senri Ethnological Studies* 36, 239-67.

Tambiah, Stanley. 1987. 'At the Confluence of Anthropology, History, and Indology', in *Contributions to Indian Sociology* (n.s.) 21, 187-216.

Timm, Jeffrey R. (ed.) 1992. *Texts and Contexts: Traditional Hermeneutics in South Asia*, Albany: State University of New York Press.

Witzel, Michael. 1987. 'The Coronation Rituals of Nepal - with Special Reference to the Coronation of King Birendra', in N. Gutschow and A. Michaels (eds.), *Heritage of the Kathmandu Valley*, Sankt Augustin: VGH Wissenschaftsverlag, 415-68.

Witzel, Michael. 1997. 'Macrocosm, Mesocosm, and Microcosm: The Persistent Nature of "Hindu" Beliefs and Symbolic Forms', in *International Journal of Hindu Studies* 1, 501-39.

Zachariae, Theodor. 1921. Rezension von W. Caland, *De Ontdekkingsgeschiedenis van den Veda*, in *Göttingische Gelehrte Anzeigen*, Bd. 183.

Index